THREE WHEELERS
A-Z

by
Chris Rees

Quiller
Print

First published 2013 by Quiller Print

Printed and bound by CPI Group (UK) Ltd,
Croydon CR0 4YY

ISBN 978-0-9926651-0-4

www.quillerprint.co.uk

Quiller
Print

THREE WHEELERS
A-Z

The definitive encyclopaedia of three-wheeled vehicles from 1940 to date

by
Chris Rees

Cover images

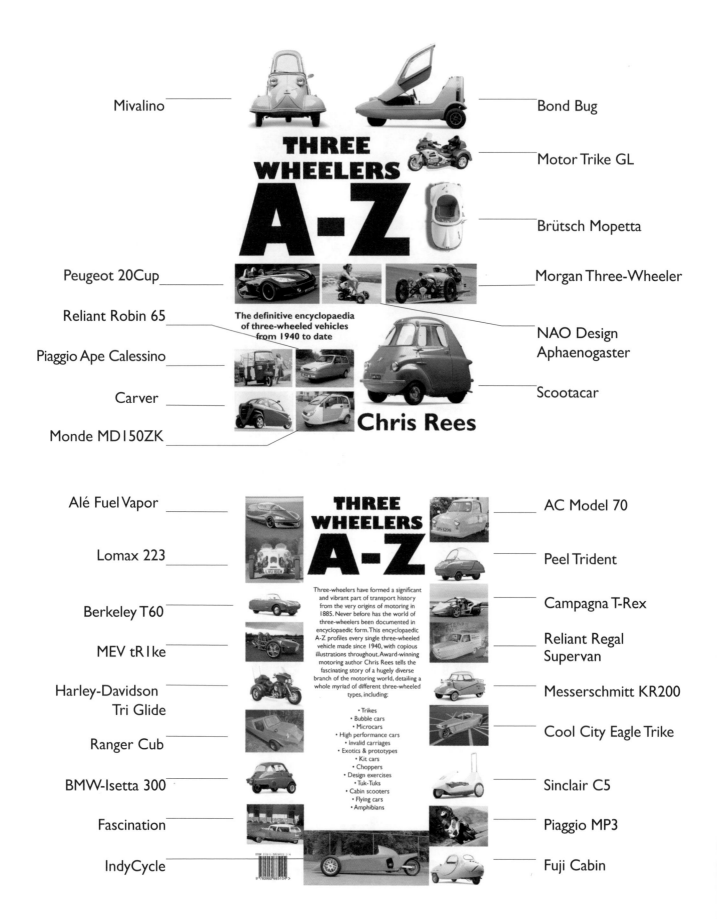

Mivalino

Bond Bug

Motor Trike GL

THREE WHEELERS A-Z

Brütsch Mopetta

Peugeot 20Cup

Morgan Three-Wheeler

Reliant Robin 65

The definitive encyclopaedia of three-wheeled vehicles from 1940 to date

NAO Design Aphaenogaster

Piaggio Ape Calessino

Carver

Scootacar

Monde MD150ZK

Chris Rees

Alé Fuel Vapor

THREE WHEELERS A-Z

AC Model 70

Lomax 223

Peel Trident

Three-wheelers have formed a significant and vibrant part of transport history from the very origins of motoring in 1885. Never before has the world of three-wheelers been documented in encyclopaedic form. This encyclopaedic A-Z profiles every single three-wheeled vehicle made since 1940, with copious illustrations throughout. Award-winning motoring author Chris Rees tells the fascinating story of a hugely diverse branch of the motoring world, detailing a whole myriad of different three-wheeled types, including:

Berkeley T60

Campagna T-Rex

MEV tR1ke

Reliant Regal Supervan

Harley-Davidson Tri Glide

Messerschmitt KR200

• Trikes
• Bubble cars
• Microcars
• High performance cars
• Invalid carriages
• Exotics & prototypes
• Kit cars
• Choppers
• Design exercises
• Tuk-Tuks
• Cabin scooters
• Flying cars
• Amphibians

Ranger Cub

Cool City Eagle Trike

BMW-Isetta 300

Sinclair C5

Fascination

Piaggio MP3

IndyCycle

Fuji Cabin

AUTHOR'S NOTE

The moment that did it for me is as clear today as was all those decades ago. As a kid, I saw a car parked outside our house which really fired my imagination: a bright tangerine object with a shape wedgier than a slice of red Leicester cheese – and one wheel short of the full four-square. It was a Bond Bug, a machine I found intoxicatingly fascinating; so much so that I promised myself that I would, one day, own one. In fact a Bug became my very first car as soon as I had passed my driving test.

Sighting of a Bond Bug as a kid was what started it all off

That was the start of a life-long relationship with three-wheelers. My next vehicle with only three tyres was a Lomax 223, which I built from a kit while working as a writer for Which Kit? magazine. The fact that someone as mechanically inept as me could turn a Citroën 2CV into a Morganesque fun car was a revelation, as was the car itself. Dynamically, it was completely different to the

Chris Rees built this Lomax 223 from a kit in 1987

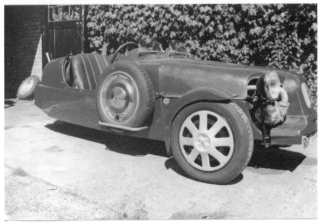

single-front-wheel Bug, and thankfully had far less of the Bug's alarming tendency to lift a wheel at the first sight of a corner. I even used the Lomax as my sole transport for 18 months through sun, snow and ice. Subsequently I explored the outer reaches of the three-wheeled world by remodelling a Citroën 2CV with a single back wheel, a move that proved wayward in the extreme.

I've been lucky enough to drive dozens of three-wheelers in my day job as a motoring journalist, from the sublime (Grinnall Scorpion III) to the ridiculous (AC invalid carriage). And like countless thousands

Rees's very odd converted 2CV behaved in a wayward manner

of people, I've had experience of Bangkok tuk tuks, know several chopper trike-owning friends, and constantly hear from enthusiasts who lust after a Morgan Three-Wheeler.

Three-wheelers continue to play a rich role in the periphery of the motoring world's vision, as rarefied exotica in the supercar scene; as an established branch of motorcycledom; and as genuinely revolutionary economy transport for millions of people in developing nations. In fact, it's perfectly true to say that today, three-wheelers have never been more popular. They deserve an encyclopaedic reference work – and I sincerely hope that the volume you're holding meets this need.

Chris Rees
Berkshire, 2013

THREE WHEELERS A-Z

INTRODUCTION

Cornish engineer Richard Trevithick built this sizeable steamer

There is a very good reason why the photographer's tripod has three legs. Three is the smallest number required to create a stable self-supporting structure. Exactly the the same is true of cars. With the exception of gyroscopically assisted two-wheelers, and possibly wheel-less hovercars, three wheels is all that's required for a stable 'footprint' that won't fall over.

Armed with this fact, you may be surprised that the world is not populated with three-wheeled vehicles. Instead the people of the planet are, by and large, transported by four-wheeled cars and two-wheeled motorbikes. Three-wheelers have almost always occupied a shadowy corner in the territory of transportation.

Yet a large proportion of the population have, at some time, had some experience of three-wheelers. That may be in the back of a tuk-tuk taxi in Thailand, or perhaps attending a show where bubble cars provide the focus of everyone's attention, or even having a biker as a neighbour who owns a trike.

It is the aim of this book to bring the spotlight on to a much ignored part of the motoring world, yet a highly significant one. The book you hold in your hands is a comprehensive review of every single three-wheeler produced since 1940.

Early years: rise and fall

In the beginning, man invented something that does not exist in nature: the wheel. From the time he began rolling bluestone megaliths over logs, through yoking his oxen to Bronze Age wagons, to some unknown point in history when he did a Fred Flintstone and created a wheeled device powered by his own legs, the wheel gave him the ability to move around far more freely. In all the cases mentioned so far, however, the number of wheels would have been two or four. Never three.

With the age of steam came an ability to travel using an on-board motor. Arguably the first ever self-propelled vehicle (other than railway engines) was a three-wheeler: French military engineer Nicholas Cugnot built a cumbersome steam-powered machine as early as 1769, and it had a single front wheel. But with an immense boiler slung out in front, it was wildly uncontrollable and, having crashed his car into a wall, the inventor was jailed

Cugnot's steam wagon was probably the world's first self-propelled 'car'

by the authorities. Not an auspicious beginning.

In Cornwall, first William Murdock (1786) and then Richard Trevithick built and tested steam-powered three-wheeled carriages on the roads, but steam power was ultimately better suited to the railways, and self-propelled cars remained a dream for a full century.

The very first internal combustion car was also a three-wheeler. Karl Benz's pioneering prototype chugged off its blocks in 1885, and bizarrely, during its first drive, it suffered the same fate as Cugnot's steam carriage by driving into a wall. But the Benz's rosier destiny was already written: it would become the first car ever to enter producLion.

Three wheels were adopted by Benz as the simplest and lightest way to become mobile. By the time the production version (known as the Benz Patent-Motorwagen) arrived in 1888, self-propelled vehicles had already been banned in Benz's home region, so selling his cars proved rather difficult!

Benz staunchly followed the three-wheeler format while others, notably arch-rival Gottlieb Daimler, switched to four. But while the trike offered advantages in power-to-weight ratio, the typically rutted roads of the day made their use less comfortable than four-wheelers, and Benz himself switched to four wheels in 1894.

Another early experimenter was Count de Dion in France. His first vehicle, a steam-powered three-wheeler built in 1883, formed the basis of the pioneering de Dion tricycles produced between 1896 and 1902. These were much copied, notably by Humber in Britain.

Leon Bollée coined the term voiturette in 1895 for his three-wheeler with tandem seating for two. In its day, it was the fastest road car around, and inspired the design of

1896 Pennington was fancifully claimed to set nine people

Karl Benz naturally opted for the simplicity of the three-wheeled format for his first internal combustion car of 1885

many other machines but even Bollée realised the limits of its potential and had turned to larger four-wheelers by 1903.

In Britain, things took a little longer to get off the ground, largely because of the infamous Road Locomotives and Highways Act, which limited the top speed of self-propelled machines to 4mph and required a man to walk in front of the machine with a red flag to warn of its impending arrival. Probably the first ever British road car was – surprise, surprise – a three-wheeler called the Butler Petrol Cycle. Patented by Edward Butler in 1887 and completed in around 1890, it had two steering front wheels.

The infamous Act was not repealed until 1896, after which there was a flurry of British activity. Three of the very first British cars, all trikes, arrived in that year: the Knight, the

Pennington and the Wolseley.

The Knight was almost certainly the first true British car, and very much inspired by the Benz. Edward Pennington's Torpedo Autocar was really nothing more than two bicycles joined together with a motor attached. The Wolseley was

The French 'La Va Bon Train' was a typical early pioneer

Leon Bollée's two-seater powered tricycle was something of a hotshot for its day – the turn of the 20th century

Based on the Autocarrier, the AC Sociable founded the AC dynasty in 1910 and brought affordability to the masses

the first design of Herbert Austin and therefore much more significant, even though production did not start until 1899, and then with four wheels.

Other famous British firms whose first forays were trikes included Singer, Humber, Riley and Lagonda. In an age dominated by large, expensive cars, a range of vehicles derived from the Autocarrier, a commercial tricycle, came to achieve notable popularity. The AC Sociable (the first car to wear the AC badge) sold for a bargain £100, and ushered in an era of affordable three-wheeled transport. Most machines of this era were very crude and basic, slotting in just above motorbike-and-sidecar combinations.

However, one name stood out: Morgan. Founded by HFS Morgan, who had bought an Eagle Tandem trike in the early 1900s, founded a true motoring dynasty in Malvern, Worcestershire. His first commercial effort of 1910 was a very simple single-seater three-wheeler with tiller steering, using patented sliding pillar suspension. Power came from a V-twin engine mounted up front – a format that Morgan would follow for several decades. It had the distinction of being cheap and reliable, and really struck a chord with buyers. When Morgans started winning races, more sporting models were produced, starting with the Grand Prix of 1914. In the other direction, a Family four-seater was also offered from 1915. By 1919 production was running at 50 units per week. The long-tailed Aero model of 1920 became an absolute icon, offering tremendous speed for very little outlay, while the Super Sports of 1928 with its rounded rump and a claimed top speed of 80mph represents the Morgan that everyone pictures when asked to recall what a Morgan looks like.

Like many three-wheelers, Morgans were fantastic value:

as little as £80 at one point, while cruder machines such as the JMB, Coventry-Victor, Scott Sociable and Harper were even cheaper. But by 1922, they had a new force to contend with: the Austin Seven, which almost overnight rendered most three-wheelers obsolete. Only the lower annual horsepower tax levied on three-wheelers kept the genre alive.

There was always fierce controversy about three-wheelers.

Two Morgan contemporaries: the Coventry-Victor (top) and BSA

There was correspondence in the motoring magazines about the "beastly" tricycles, which held up faster cars and were often regarded as unsafe. Three-wheelers were banned from racing against four-wheelers in the 1920s on the grounds that they were dangerous. In the case of the Morgans, the real reason was probably that they were doing rather too well, a fact proven by a Morgan's emphatic win against Rileys, Austins and Amilcars after the ban was lifted in 1928.

Three-wheelers also found some favour abroad, although in smaller numbers because the same tax advantages were rarely duplicated. In France, there were Morgan rivals such as the D'Yrsan and Sandford. In Germany, trikes like the Phanombil, Magnet and Tourist enjoyed some success by offering cheap transport during an economic depression. By

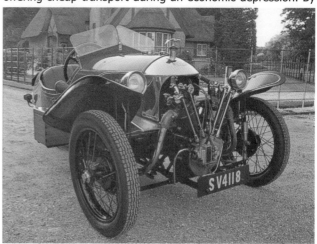

Morgans were the quintessential pre-war three-wheelers, from the 1912 Runabout (above) to the racer (below left); Cyclecar magazine celebrated HFS Morgan's exploits in 1912

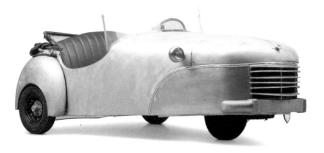

The hyper-frugal Bond Minicar of the early 1950s was the perfect means of transport in an economy ravaged by war

Japan took to the three-wheeled format with gusto, but passenger cars – such as the Daihatsu Bee above – were rarer

contrast, Americans avoided three-wheelers like the plague.

Even further abroad, in Japan took to three-wheelers in a big way. Two current Japanese giants began with tripeds: Mazda with its motorcycle-derived trucks from 1931, and Daihatsu from 1930.

In Britain, the three-wheeler craze had effectively died by the mid-1930s. The economy models were having an impossible time competing with the new strain of mass-produced 'proper' small cars. Even sporting three-wheelers like Morgan and BSA stood little chance against a new breed of cheap sports cars, such as the MG M-Type Midget. The final nail in the coffin was the announcement in 1936 that Road Fund Tax would be abolished on all cars, effectively ending the edge on running costs traditionally enjoyed by three-wheelers. Just before the announcement, both Morgan and BSA introduced four-wheelers and that was basically the end of it. Only Morgan was making three-wheelers by the time of the outbreak of World War II.

Post-war boom

After the war, too, the sole manufacturer of three-wheelers in Britain was Morgan, and that was on a very limited scale. Morgan was not joined by any other three-wheeler manufacturers in Britain until Bond in 1949, and that was a very different type of three-wheeler – an economy car along

the lines of the microcars popping up all over continental Europe at that time.

The scope of this book is three-wheelers from 1940 onwards, and the story since then has again been one of vacillating fortunes. But the immediate period following World War II marked a real boom period for three-wheelers, which were ideally suited to the austerity years. The microcar boom of the 1950s – typified by bubble cars – was probably the single most successful period in history for the three-wheeled layout: perhaps as many as half-a-million three-wheelers were sold in one decade.

The rise of the bubble car was almost single-handedly responsible for decimating the popularity of motorbike-and-sidecar combinations as family transport during the 1950s. Despite their crudity, microcars offered much more comfort than a motorbike, as well as complete weather protection, all for similar running costs. In the UK, tax and licensing concessions granted to lightweight three-wheelers put them on level ground with motorbikes.

The rich variety of cars which ensued included some brilliant designs like the Messerschmitt and Berkeley, as well as iconic creations like the Isetta and Heinkel. The Isetta of 1953 was the original 'bubble car', which spawned a whole gamut of spheroids. Most continental bubbles were in fact four-wheelers with very narrow-set rear tracks, but manufacturers were quick to exploit legal loopholes in other countries by offering three-wheeled versions.

The Suez oil crisis of 1956 provided another push, but as the crisis eased, and affluence steadily rose, three-wheelers

The bubble car boom of the 1950s kept the world motoring when times were tough. The era was typified by the Heinkel (below left) and even Cary Grant got in on the act in an Isetta (below right) but micro-bubbles had all but burst by the early 1960s

The Reliant Robin – affectionately known as the 'plastic pig' – kept three-wheeled family motoring going as late as 2002

became increasingly stigmatised. Brilliant new small cars like the Austin/Morris Mini of 1959 persuaded most to switch to four-wheel motoring and by about 1966, the microcar was effectively dead.

Only Bond and Reliant continued the flame in Britain, succeeding in filling a niche for family three-wheelers long abandoned by others. Indeed, Reliant continued to produce the Robin – at once celebrated and notorious – right into the 21st century.

Economy three-wheelers had a small comeback in France during the 1970s, thanks to a law that said that anyone over 14 could drive a speed-restricted moped-engined vehicle without the need for a driving licence or registration plate. A whole generation of strange devices sprang up, their 50cc single-cylinder engines buzzing headily to a government-restricted top speed of 45km/h (27mph). But four-wheeled machines inevitably prevailed, and the last French three-wheeler, the Cedre, left production in 1987. It was the same in Italy, although some three-wheeled machines survived into the 21st century.

If that looked like the end for micro three-wheelers, in fact the genre began to flourish once again in the new millennium. Inspired by public interest in reducing carbon dioxide emissions, and the upsurge in electric vehicle development, the possibilities offered by three-wheelers once again came to the fore. Lightweight trikes such as the City-El, Twike and Corbin Sparrow achieved some success in both Europe and the USA, and many more like the Aptera looked set to take the genre on into the future. In China, meanwhile, a whole new industry formed around small, economical three-

America's Aptera was one of a new generation of 'green' three-wheeled vehicles that flourished in the 2000s

Tuk tuks provided economical transport in many countries across the world, including Thailand as pictured here

wheeled vehicles, which even achieved some export success, such as, for instance, the ZAP Xebra in the USA.

Why three wheels?

Why do people build and buy cars with three wheels? There are appropriately three principal explanations: economy, legality and weight.

Three for economy

Economic reasons explained why many of the earliest cars were three-wheelers. It was simply cheaper to make a vehicle with three wheels than four. With fewer parts, less complexity and less to replace if it went wrong, it was the ideal arrangement. In difficult economic times – such as the early 1930s and the ration-ravaged post-war period – three-wheelers gave impecunious owners a first step on to the ladder of family transport.

In developing nations, three-wheelers consistently provided – and indeed continue to provide, in Asian and African markets – a means to own a car without the cost of a four-wheeler. And hyper-economy three-wheelers that aim to eke out every litre of fuel remain a significant part of the motoring scene right across the globe.

The three-wheeled loophole

On the second reason – legality – everyone loves a loophole. In many countries, three-wheelers are afforded special status in the eyes of the law.

In Britain, for example (but equally in many other countries), three-wheelers have always enjoyed a special position. As long as their weight is below a certain level, they are treated as motorcycle-and-sidecar combinations, so it's legal to drive a three-wheeler with only a motorcycle driving licence, you pay the same road duty as a motorcycle and can even drive unaccompanied on a provisional licence. Bikers with new families happily moved on to Bonds and Reliants without having to pass a new driving test, or shell

Laws favourable to microcars brought a revival in France in the 1970s

out the extra tax a fourth wheel brought.

In the USA, three-wheelers are legally treated as motorbikes. In France, 14-year olds could drive lightweight low-powered cars on the road – the so-called 'voiturettes sans permis'. In the early days of the genre in the 1970s, it was in three-wheelers that a young generation gained their first motoring experience, and an older population was kept mobile.

In Japan, three-wheeled taxis could charge customers lower fares by law, so became popular in economically hard times following WW2. Even into the 1970s and 1980s, Japanese moped riders could happily move up to safer machines in the form of 'cabin scooters' that were weatherproof, sheltering them from incoming typhoons.

Lightening the load

Light weight is the final major reason why designers choose three wheels. Losing a wheel and its suspension saves vital kilos, which has big advantages for performance and efficiency. This is why there have been so many sports designs with three wheels – and why, even where the law does not give three-wheelers a tax edge, you can still find three-wheelers being made and purchased.

Three-wheelers can also be much more manoeuvrable than four-wheeled machinery. Designs such as the Bond Minicar allowed the single front wheel to spin around through 180 degrees, and therefore the car to be able to turn around within its own length.

Three for fun

Most of the three-wheeled designs in the pages of this book are about fun. Fun combines the advantages of light weight, legal loopholes and often low prices to make a great slice of carefree motoring enjoyment. For example, the fun car explosion that happened in the 1960s, that bursting bonanza of beach buggies, also included three-wheelers.

In 1970, a 17-year old buying his first-ever car could steer well clear of motoring boredom and opt for a cool slice of tangerine psychedelia called a Bond Bug. The author did the same in the 1980s – my first car was a Bug.

But the fun didn't end in the 1970s. A generation of easy riders took things a little easier by adding a third wheel to

Motor magazine in the UK asked if three-wheelers might be making a comeback when it tested the Triking in 1982

their choppers, creating trikes with Beetle four-pot engines in the back. Then as the market got more sophisticated, Harley-Davidson owners added rear axles to their soft-tails – up to and including some with air suspension. Many motorbike brands took the logical step and dabbled in trikes too – from Moto Guzzi and Lambretta, right up to Harley-Davidson itself.

The boom in kit cars from the 1970s onwards also saw great interest revive in cars with three wheels. In the USA, machines like the Quincy-Lynn and Tri-Vator fired the public imagination, while the UK became a real hot bed of activity following Triking's decision to reproduce the spirit and style of the pre-war Morgan. A deluge of kit-form three-wheelers followed, including JZR, BRA and Lomax.

No car epitomises the contribution three-wheelers made to the 1970s fun car boom more than the Bond Bug

Tilting pioneer: George Wallis's ill-fated Ariel 3 of 1970

Also firmly in the fun category are tilting three-wheelers. Although the idea of cars that lean into corners like motorbikes originated as far back as the 1950s, it took until the 1970s for the idea to reach the market. Japanese giant Honda launched the tilting Stream and Gyro, using a patent from British inventor George Lesley Wallis, and has never looked back. Another variety of tilter arrived when Dutch genius Chris van den Brink brought to market the remarkable Carver, which really did combine the worlds of enclosed cars and leaning motorcycles.

The three-wheeled format has also been a happy hunting ground for major car brands and the world's most prestigious design houses wanting to capture the public imagination with radically different ideas. The list of names in this book is truly revealing, including such brands as BMW, Mercedes-Benz, Honda, Toyota, Ford and General Motors.

Three for performance

High performance is not an alien concept in the world of three-wheelers. Morgan was probably the first company really to exploit the advantages of light weight that a three-wheeled design can offer. Witnessing a Morgan Supersport in race trim lapping a circuit every bit as quickly as a supercar – and that's no exaggeration – is all the convincing most people need that three-wheelers have no conceptual handicap to travelling at very high speeds.

Others followed – like the Phantom, Badsey Bullet and Fire Aero. Two Canadian designs, however, eptiomise the move towards the enthusiast audience. The superbike-powered Campagna T-Rex looked great and out-performed contemporary Ferraris. And the BRP Can-Am Spyder, marketed by one of the world's largest corporations, offered the thrill of a superbike with the comfort and added safety of two front wheels.

There's one more piece of evidence not to reject three-wheelers because 'they're not capable of going quickly'. At least one outright world land speed record holder has had three wheels: Craig Breedlove's Spirit of America, which was the world's fastest car in 1964, exceeding 526mph.

Craig Breedlove achieved a world land speed record in the three-wheeled Spirit of America in 1964 – over 526mph

Three for commuting

The modern commuter now has another option open to him, and it has three wheels. A whole generation has discovered how much less intimidating a form of transport a three-wheeled scooter can be than a moped or scooter. Thank the Piaggio MP3 (below) for that. Although Piaggio was not the

Piaggio MP3 (above) brought tilting trike technology to the scooter market. Canada gave birth to two iconic high-performance three-wheelers in the 21st century: the sit-on BRP Can-Am Spyder (below left) and the semi-enclosed Campagna T-Rex (right)

first company to put two wheels on the front of a scooter, it was the first to popularise the idea, and now every major city in the world has three-wheeled Piaggios swaying in and out of traffic – and many other pretenders in its wake.

Three for disability

One final footnote in the three-wheeler story is the long association of the three-wheeler with disabled drivers. This genre really came about as a result of the two world wars, when injured veterans needed transportation, and the three-wheeled option provided it in straitened economic times. In the UK, this situation continued until the 1970s, when at last it was decided that disabled people should no longer be forced to put up with inferior and antiquated designs that were potentially lethally dangerous.

So-called invalid carriages like this AC Model 70 were axed in the UK in 1978 and subsequently removed from public roads

Formats: 1F2R or 2F1R?

There are essentially two formats of three-wheeler, which I have described in this book as 1F2R (one front wheel, two rear wheels) and 2F1R (two fronts, one rear). These layouts are known by other names, too. The 1F2R set-up is often called a 'delta' layout, while the 2F1R is often dubbed a 'reverse' or 'tadpole' layout.

There are rare cases of other formats, for instance where one of the three wheels is placed at neither the front nor rear of the car, but somewhere in the middle (usually a development of a motorcycle and side car combination), and at least one case of a gyroscopic three-wheeler with all three wheels in one line, front to rear.

Each of the two main formats has its adherents. Neither format has achieved pre-eminence, as proven by the fact that the proportion of designs using each layout detailed in this book is about even. However, the 2F1R layout is clearly favoured in the fun car market, while the 1F2R is much more often selected among economy vehicles.

Stability is a major concern with three-wheelers. Any three-wheeler design forms a triangle between the centre points of each wheel. Where you put the weight is crucial to the design's stability. The greater the proportion of weight over the single wheel, the more unstable is the vehicle. Conversely, place as much of the weight between the paired wheels and you have greater stability.

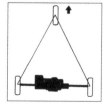 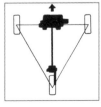

1F2R 'tadpole' design (left) contrasts with the more stable 2F1R 'delta' layout (right)

1F2R layouts like the Chinese Wanhoo remain popular in developing markets as cheap and economical transport

2F1R layouts are generally seen as more stable. The single rear wheel simply holds the rear end up, although many sports trikes (such as the Grinnall Scorpion III, Campagna T-Rex and BRP Can-Am Spyder) take their power to the rear end. Alternatively, front-wheel drive trikes (like the Lomax or Mini-based kit cars) often drive very much like their four-wheeled cousins. 2F1R layouts brake more controllably and are less likely to roll over in extreme manoeuvres.

In contrast, hard braking or rapid directional changes are more likely to upset the balance of a 1F2R car, as weight is thrown sideways against thin air. It can be very easy to lift a rear wheel or, if you've really stepped in it, topple right over. One way to make a 1F2R design more stable is to engineer in an ability to lean into corners like motorbikes, and many designs have adopted this route over the years.

The re-invented Morgan Three-Wheeler of the 21st century has true sports car dynamics that only a 2F1R layout can offer

What's in and what's out

The book you are holding is a comprehensive encyclopaedia of every three-wheeler since 1940. For the purposes of this book, that means roadgoing vehicles designed to carry passengers rather than goods, which were actually produced or intended to be commericalised.

Four-wheelers are always excluded, even when they appear to be three-wheelers. So the narrow-gauge four-wheeled Iso Isetta bubble car doesn't count, for example. The only exceptions are four-wheelers that could be driven on three wheels by design (such as the Fascination), or where two tyres are attached to a single wheel hub (such as the T3 Motion GT3) – rarities both.

The Iso Isetta with its narrow-track pair of rear wheels is excluded

Commercial vehicles are excluded – this is a Trojan Estate Van, based on the Heinkel passenger-carrying bubble car

Since this book is restricted to roadgoing vehicles, ATVs (All Terrain Vehicles) and racing cars are out, as are pure off-road trikes, because they're not generally intended for road use.

As this book is about cars, vehicles designed exclusively for commercial use have been excluded, except where such designs were also marketed as passenger vehicles. However, I have elected to include military three-wheelers because there are so few of them.

Part of the definition of a car is that it should have its own autonomous power source. Therefore human-powered three-wheelers such as velomobiles, recumbent trikes and any vehicle whose principal power source is human legs are also not allowed in. There is a grey area in the form of dual-power trikes which have pedals and an additional power source (such as a small engine or electric motor) on board. The general rule is that, if the trike is principally human-powered, it's not included. However, many French microcars of the 1970s included pedals inside the cabin in addition to an engine but the pedals were intended for emergency use only, so I have included these cars.

Mobility scooters – at least, those not designed to be used on the road – are also out. However, so-called invalid carriages, which form an important part of three-wheeler lore, are most certainly in the book, except where they were designed to be powered only by the driver's own limbs.

Only production vehicles are included, which means the car should have been offered for sale to the public, or at least there has to be evidence of a credible intention to market the vehicle. I've made an exception in the case of concept cars and prototypes from known companies or design houses.

One-offs are too numerous to include but ones by major companies like BMW are in

Also not included are any projects where there is no evidence that any cars were actually built, so 3D renderings and the like are out. While I would love to have included one-offs, the sheer number of them has sadly made it impractical to include them.

Key to information bars

Every vehicle listed has an information bar at the beginning. Four pieces of information are presented: the country or countries of origin, the dates between which the model appeared and/or was on sale, the format of the three-wheeled layout and the number of units built in total.

Country ID codes

The international country ID abbreviation system – as seen on the rumps of cars across the world – is used to identify the country of origin for every three-wheeler in this book. Below is a complete list of all the countries which have made three-wheelers and which appear in this encylopaedia.

A	Austria
AUS	Australia
B	Belgium
BD	Bangladesh
BDA	Bermuda
BG	Bulgaria
BR	Brazil
C	Cuba
CDN	Canada
CH	Switzerland
CL	Sri Lanka
CN	China
CO	Colombia
CZ	Czech Republic
D	Germany
DDR	East Germany
DK	Denmark
E	Spain
ET	Egypt
F	France
FIN	Finland
GB	Great Britain
GBM	Isle of Man
GR	Greece
H	Hungary
HKC	Hong Kong China
I	Italy
IND	India
IR	Iran
IRE	Ireland
J	Japan
MA	Morocco
MEX	Mexico
N	Norway
NGR	Nigeria
NL	Netherlands
NZ	New Zealand
P	Portugal
PK	Pakistan
PE	Peru
PL	Poland
RA	Argentina
RC	Republic of China (Taiwan)
RCH	Chile
RI	Indonesia
ROK	Republic of Korea
ROU	Uruguay
RP	Philippines
RSM	Republic of San Marino
RUS	Russia
S	Sweden
T	Thailand
TN	Tunisia
USA	United States of America
VN	Vietnam
YV	Venezuela
ZA	South Africa

Note: the symbol ⇨ in the text indicates that the car being referred to can be found elsewhere in this A-Z encyclopaedia.

Acknowledgements

No book is ever produced in isolation. I extend my heart-felt thanks to all the people who have helped along the way, and especially to the following people who have kindly dedicated time and resources to the project, in no particular order: Liz Jeyasingham, Jeremy Renals, Julie Cooper, Steve Hole and all at TKC magazine, Ian Stent and all at Complete Kit Cars, Peter Filby, Ian Hyne, Charles Morgan, Jean Hammond and all at the Register of Unusual Microcars, Mike Shepherd, Francesco Maurizi, Malcolm Wood, Harold Pace, Richard Heseltine, Paul Negyesi, Barry Stimson, Erik van Ingen Schenau, Arunas Racelis, Vaidas Gerikas, Mr Scharoo, Brian Snelson, André Ritzinger, mosquito-triad.com, Newspress, The Science Museum, RM Auctions and the Dezer Collection.

Thanks also go to the many manufacturers of three-wheelers who have kindly provided images for use in this book. I must also praise the community at www.autopuzzles.com, the world's most knowledgable collection of motoring enthusiasts, full stop, which cannot be recommended highly enough as a fount of wisdom for future research.

A note about photographs

I am firmly of the view that, in an encyclopaedia, a picture – however grainy or small – is always better than no picture at all. The nature of the subject matter in this book means that in many cases there are simply no high-quality images of many older and rarer cars in existence, but I have always attempted to use the best images available.

And so... 1,122 three-wheelers

The thing that really draws all three-wheelers together is that they offer something different, something outside the normal frames of reference for conventional motor cars. One glance through the pages of this book should convince you of that.

Trikes have remained a consistent part of the motoring scene from day one. But there is more to it than that. Far from being the oft-quoted 'missing link' between motorbike and car, three-wheelers can in fact be said to be the true fathers of modern motoring.

Three-wheeling is today a truly global phenomenon. From India with its motorised rickshaws and China with its super-economy cars; from modern microcars to concept cars created by the big styling houses of Europe; from supertrikes to commuter trikes: three-wheelers are today enjoying a boom such as has not been seen since the 1950s.

So enjoy the ride. Whether you think three-wheelers are one wheel shy of the full four-square, or one wheel beyond preventing the whole show falling over, trikes are endlessly fascinating and intriguing. From AB1 to Zzipper, I hope you will appreciate the full breadth and variety of three-wheelers in this book, from 1940 to the current day – all 1,122 of them.

Grinnall Scorpion III ▲

Morgan Super Sports ▲

▲ Bond Minicar MkB

▲ Sbarro UMA2

◄ Lehman Renegade

▼ ZAP Xebra Xero

15

THREE WHEELERS

A-Z

333

AAA

AC Model 70 ▲

AF Grand Prix ▲

Alé Fuel Vapor ▲

Allard Clipper ▲

Attica ▲

▼ Avolette

Aptera ▼

3-E Minicar / XEP-100
USA • 1969-1970s • 1F2R • No built: n/a

3-E Vehicles of San Diego, California offered a three-wheeler called the Minicar in kit form. An unusual doorless car of rigidly square appearance, it had no weather protection, a single headlamp and a Perspex windscreen. 3-E followed this up with a more aerodynamic electric model called the XEP-100 but this did not enter production.

3-Rod
D • 2006 • 1F2R • No built: Probably 1

The 3-Rod fell into the sidecar-based three-wheeler category. Martin Scheufler was behind the car, which was designed by Scala Design and engineered by sidecar company Mobec. A carbon-fibre sandwich body overlayed a chassis with independent suspension. Features included drive-by-wire handlebars, foot clutch and electronic gears with reverse.

■■□■

3VG
USA • 1983 • 2F1R • No built: 7

Mother Earth News magazine published articles on a series of prototypes that it built featuring tilting technology. It was called 3VG because of its triple-variable geometry system: it would lean into corners by means of mechanical, hydraulic and electronic components. A multi-tube steel chassis incorporated a single rear swinging arm, while the power came from a two-cylinder, horizontally opposed Onan industrial engine (730cc and 16bhp) driving through a continuously variable automatic transmission. The aircraft-style body was in glassfibre, and the two tandem occupants entered via a sliding canopy. A plans set was due to be published but never made it to press.

ABC Trimini / Tricar
GB • 1968-1973 • 2F1R • No built: Approx 25

The Auto Body Craft (ABC) Tricar was probably the first-ever road-going Mini-based trike (Owen Greenwood had raced a Mini-powered trike in the early 1960s, but it was not a road car). The West Midlands firm was run by Bill Powell and Ken Heather, and Powell's 16-year old son Trevor was the reason for building the Tricar (initially referred to as the Trimini).

The whole front end of the Mini was retained, but the rear half was chopped away, except for the floorpan. This was stiffened and a frame was welded in to accept half of a Mini rear subframe. A glassfibre open two-seater body was bonded on top, and a soft-top was optional.

ABC would convert your Mini into a Tricar for £400. At 450lb (205kg) less than a Mini, performance was strong. Later Tricars (as pictured) had all-glassfibre bodywork whose front end swung forwards for access to the engine.

AC All-Weather Tricycle
GB • 1950-1952 • 1F2R • No built: n/a

AC Cars remains one of the longest-established of all British car firms, and is easily best known for its high-powered sports like the Cobra. Yet its first foray into car making was a three-wheeler: the 1908 Auto Carrier Sociable. AC never lost its microcar roots, and after WW2 became involved in the production of invalid carriages with rather more weather protection than the norm.

The All-Weather Tricycle had a rear-mounted single-cylinder BSA 249cc engine in a tubular backbone chassis. The steel-and-aluminium bodywork featured a double-folding door on one side only to ease access, and had space in the rear of the car to fit a folded wheelchair. Only one survivor was known at the time of writing.

AC Petite

GB • 1952-1957 • 1F2R • No built: Approx 4000

The Petite was an earnest attempt to make a comfortable economy car with three wheels. Compared to most microcars, it was indeed more comfortable and civilised, although hardly pretty, charismatic or fun to drive. A squarish two-to-three-seater with steel-and-aluminium bodywork, it almost looked like a four-wheeler but it had a single front wheel that was smaller than the rears. Initially a single-cylinder 346cc Villiers engine sat in the tail, and a 50mph (80km/h) top speed was claimed. The MkII version of 1955 had a slightly larger (353cc) Villiers engine and the same size wheels all round. A "temporary" halt in production in October 1957 was announced by AC, but it never in fact restarted.

Go anywhere on your Farm or Estate with the **AC** 'PETITE'

60-70 m.p.g.
Tax £5
Ins. £7.10.0
Running cost under 1¼d. a mile ALL IN!
Price £255 plus £53.13.9. P.T.

Ask your local agent, or write:
A. C. CARS LTD., THAMES DITTON, SURREY

AC Acedes

GB • 1957-1972 • 1F2R • No built: 15,337

AC returned to disabled vehicle manufacture in 1957 with the Acedes, which despite appearances was not related to the Petite. A Villiers Mk9E 197cc engine was fitted initially (replaced by the Mk11E in 1961), and a 72V electric version was also launched in 1958 (2182 of these were built in total). Both convertible and hard-top models were offered, each with metal bodywork, and such 'luxuries' as proper glass windows and a sliding seat were added over time.

AC Acedes Mk14/Mk15

GB • 1967-1971 • 1F2R • No built: 5928

The new Mk14 Acedes of 1967 switched to glassfibre bodywork featuring a 'Drop-Open' door which pivoted outwards before sliding forwards to allow entry. The Mk15 version received improved suspension.

AC Model 70

GB • 1971-1978 • 1F2R • No built: Several thousand

Of all the so-called invalid carriages, the AC Model 70 is the most archetypal. Also produced by Invacar ⇨, the 70 was however an AC design through and through. It was improved in many ways, notably in the power department, as a 493cc Steyr-Puch flat-twin engine was now fitted. The Salisbury variable belt transmission was also much easier to use, and tiller bar, handlebar or conventional wheel steering could be ordered. The government axed the Model 70 in 1978 amid safety concerns, and in 2003 made it illegal to drive the cars on UK roads, crushing all but a handful of vehicles.

AC Prototype

GB • c1972 • 1F2R • No built: n/a

AC built several three-wheeled prototypes in the early 1970s as a kind of modern AC Petite. These were glassfibre-bodied four-seaters with a rear-mounted Steyr Puch two-cylinder 493cc engine, but the new car never came to market.

AC Donington

GB • 1982 • 2F1R • No built: Probably 1

The obscure AC Donington turned up at a kit car show at Santa Pod in 1982, where a notice in its windscreen advised showgoers that if they wanted a replica, it would cost them around £2000. This Mini-based trike with curvaceous aluminium bodywork was professionally finished, with swoopy wings, a Mini windscreen, instruments and tail-lights, extremely narrow tail and indented rectangular headlamps. Nothing more was heard of the Donington, so it seems likely that it remained a one-off.

ACAM Nica
I • 1983-1989 • 1F2R • No built: n/a

ACAM (Azienda Costruzioni Auto Mini) was based in Catania on the island of Sicily, and produced its Nica microcar in both three- and four-wheeled forms. Both were enclosed glassfibre-bodied two-seaters, but while the three-wheeler version was a monobox design, the four-wheeler had a two-box style. Piaggio Ape engines were fitted, in various sizes including 50cc, 125cc and 218cc. Independent suspension with hydraulic dampers was fitted. Incidentally, 'Nica' is Sicilian dialect meaning small.

ACAM Galassia
I • 1987-1989 • 1F2R • No built: n/a

In 1987, ACAM updated its three-wheeled offering with a more rounded style called the Galassia (Italian for 'galaxy').

This was powered by a rear-mounted 50cc moped engine, and had a single front headlamp and the option of a convertible rear roof section in its plastic bodywork. The whole ACAM operation had bitten the dust by 1989.

Acoma Mini-Comtesse
F • 1975-1978 • 1F2R • No built: Several thousand

Acoma was an Angers-based enterprise making the Mini-Comtesse, one of the crudest of the new breed of French microcars. The 1975 debut of the Mini-Comtesse made it one of the trailblazers, allowing Acoma to account for 30% of the entire French microcar market within just a few years. The car itself was an exercise in idiosyncrasy. Not only did its single-seater polyester bodywork look decidedly odd, it also boasted the exotic feature of a folding gullwing door on one side. Acoma also made a slightly wider version with two conventional doors, sold under the name Willam Cyclo 49 (yellow car pictured above).

Placing the 50cc Motobécane engine in the front of the car, where the single wheel sat, did not help its cornering ability. Indeed Acoma fitted the car with extra stabiliser wheels as a precaution. The magazine L'Auto-Journal tested

one in 1976 and concluded that it was so unstable that the authorities ought to do something about it. They didn't; however, Acoma did. In 1978, it turned the Mini-Comtesse into a four-wheeler and so ended one of the crudest three-wheelers of the time. The whole Acoma project had been derailed by 1984.

ADB E-Trike
RP • 2011-date • 1F2R • No built: n/a

The Philippines is a country noted not only for its colourful modes of transport, but also its pollution. The Asian Development Bank (ADB) and the Philippine Department of Energy joined together to create a new 'clean' electric taxi called the E-Trike. A pilot of 20 units was released in Mandaluyong City and full production had started by the end of 2012. Lithium ion batteries were used.

Addis P3
NGR • 1987 • 1F2R • No built: n/a

A Nigerian firm called Addis made this crude three-wheeler whose boxy four-door bodywork was made of plastic and palm fibre. It was powered by a Yamaha motorbike engine, good for 62mpg and 34mph (55km/h).

ADI
D • 1950-1954 • 1F2R • No built: n/a

The ADI was built by Fahrzeugbau Arthur Diebler of Berlin. The company started making simple three-wheeled delivery vehicles whose 120cc Ilo powerplant was placed above the front single wheel, driving it by chain. Most were used by the Berlin postal service, but in 1950, ADI produced a passenger model: an open-topped doorless two-seater. The single-cylinder two-stroke Ilo engine allowed a top speed of 30mph (50km/h). After 1954 ADI reverted to making mopeds and three-wheeled commercial vehicles.

Adiva AD3
I/J • 2010-date • 2F1R • No built: n/a

Designed in Italy but made in Osaka, Japan, the Adiva AD3 tilting trike was aimed at the Piaggio MP3 market, but had the novelty of a retractable roof. Power came from a single-cylinder four-valve 300cc engine with a remarkable

29.5bhp, and there were disc brakes on all three wheels. Production was scheduled to begin in 2013, while there was also a cargo-carrying model called the Moose.

Aeon Elite
RC • 2011-date • 2F1R • No built: n/a

Launched at the 2011 Taiwan motorbike show was this take on the three-wheeled scooter format from Aeon, a company better known for its motorbikes and ATVs. The three-wheeled Elite had a 313cc engine, and was marketed as the Quadro 3D ⇨ in Europe.

Aériane Scoot
B • 1994 • 1F2R • No built: Approx 12

Aériane was a microlight aircraft manufacturer from Belgium, but it also dabbled in electric trikes. The Scoot had two batteries, allowing it a range of 31 miles (45km) but a meagre top speed of 6mph (10km/h). It

was intended to be made available to the public for rent, but in the end only around 12 were ever made.

Aero 3S
CDN • 2006-date • 2F1R • No built: n/a

The Aero 3S was essentially a Campagna T-Rex ⇨ made rather more aerodynamic thanks to the addition of opening doors, rudimentary side windows and an array of phantasmagorical spoilers.

Aérocarene 700
F • 1947-1948 • 2F1R • No built: 1

This aircraft-inspired machine featured highly unusual light alloy bodywork with very unconventional entry for passengers: the whole front of the body slid forwards to allow access

to the two seats, which were afforded protection from the elements by Plexiglass panels. A two-cylinder two-stroke engine of 684cc transmitted its 23bhp of power to the single rear wheel via a Cotal four-speed electromagnetic gearbox. The front suspension was independent, and the rear was coil-sprung. The Aérocarene's creators, engineers called Desbenoit and Bodu, said the car weighed 280kg, reached 75mph (120km/h) and averaged 70mpg (4l/100km). A planned production run of 30 cars never materialised, however.

Aerocomet
GB • 1980s • 2F1R • No built: 1

This Mini-based car was very much in the mould of the AF Grand Prix ⇨. Some 20 Aerocomets were built, but only the prototype had three wheels; the rest were four-wheeled.

Aero Merlin MG3
GB • 2007-date • 2F1R • No built: Approx 50 (to 2013)

Aero Cycle Cars of Ditchling, Sussex took over production of the BRA CX3 ⇨ in 2002. In 2007, it developed a new version called the MG3, swapping the previous Honda CX500 engine for Moto Guzzi V-twin power (850cc, 950cc or 1100cc units from the Moto Guzzi Spada, G5, Le Mans or California motorcycles). Aero also made the 2CV-based BRA CV3 ⇨.

Aeronova / Aerauto
I • 1946-1949/1949-1953 • 1F2R • No built: n/a

Carrozzeria Colli was founded in Milan in 1931. It was most famous for its Alfa Romeo coachwork, but it also built a series of aircraft engineer Luigi Pellarini's extraordinary flying cars. There is conflicting information about the exact format of the Aeronova, but its main feature was a pair of wings that folded upwards and backwards to travel on the road. Power came from either a Gilera single-cylinder or a Lycoming four-cylinder engine. As well as a single-seater, two- and three-seater versions followed. Then in 1949 came the Aerauto PL5C, powered by a Continental C85 engine. Pellarini emigrated to Australia where he designed the Transavia Air-Truk crop-sprayer, which famously appeared in the film, Mad Max 3.

Aero Trike Roadster
USA/CN • 2007-date • 2F1R • No built: n/a

The Aero Trike Roadster (or ATR) was a kit designed by Maurice Bourne of Marquez, Texas, who had previously designed the Texas Rocket ⇨. It could transform almost any motorbike into a two-seater 'reverse' trike. A sliding rear section covered the back end of the motorbike, simply bolting into place in the tubular steel chassis, which housed MacPherson strut front suspension. The complete kit, including glassfibre bodywork, cost $5000, but a simple chassis was $4000; the parts were actually manufactured in China and shipped to Texas.

AeroVisions California Commuter
USA • 1980-date • 2F1R • No built: n/a

Having been involved with daredevil Evel Knievel's motorbike stunts, partners Doug Malewicki, Richard Long and Gary Cerveny set up a company called AeroVisions Inc in Irvine, California to make a highly economical single-seater three-wheeler. The California Commuter was based around a Honda 85cc power train, and returned a claimed average of 155mpg, while being capable of a top speed of 82mph. At one stage Malewicki held two Guinness World Records: 157.192mpg at 55mph (petrol) and 156.53mpg at 56.3mph (diesel).

The car's Buck Rogers-style appearance was claimed to be aerodynamically efficient. After the open-roof prototype, it was planned to sell a fully-enclosed version with a flip-up canopy but this never materialised. In 2013 it was still possible to buy plans to build your own California Commuter. Doug Malewicki also built the C2C ⇨.

AF Spider / AB1
GB • 1969-1972 • 2F1R • No built: 8

Alexander 'Sandy' Fraser was a fervent Morgan three-wheeler fanatic who, with Colin Crabbe, built a small Mini-based trike with the name AB1. The marine ply monocoque body/chassis was mated to a Mini front subframe, while a special steel subframe with a single Mini trailing arm supported the pointed tail – although without the Mini's rubber cone, a coil/spring damper doing the work. The tail was in aluminium on the prototype, but later cars had glassfibre tails. The vintage flavour was evoked by an exposed Mini engine and headlamps squatting on waist-high running boards. Antique Automobiles Ltd of Baston, Peterborough offered AB1 body/chassis kits from £275.

Fraser built a second car, the AF Spider, differing in detail from the AB1 and offered as a rather more up-market kit from 1971 at a price of £699. A handle was provided on the rump with which the Spider could be swung into tight parking spaces. Any Mini engine could be used in the 430kg (950lb) frame of the Spider.

Motor magazine tested one with a tuned 1275S engine, clocking a top speed of 96mph and 0-60mph in just 8.7secs. It won the magazine's coveted award as the Most Fun Car of the decade 1966-1976, the testers adding: "It looks like a wooden wardrobe laid on its back. It is supremely responsive and swervable." Autocar called it "the most stable and delightful three-wheeler we have ever driven." Of the eight Spiders built, one was shipped to Australia as the Baston Spyder.

AF Grand Prix
GB • 1973-1980 • 2F1R • No built: 5

AF was wound up in 1972, but from his workshops in Marlborough, Sandy Fraser went on to build a development model called the AF Grand Prix. This was basically of the

same style and layout as the Spider but was distinguished by its cycle-type front wings and rounded rear bodywork. The last of a total of five eamples of the AF Grand Prix was built in 1980, while there was also a solitary four-wheeler (also made in 1980). Under the aegis of Lion Omnibuses, Fraser later made a Scammell Scarab three-wheeled truck replica based on a Reliant chassis.

Ahmed Automobile Safari
PK • 2000s-date • 1F2R • No built: n/a

Ahmed Automobile Co made the Safari range of rickshaws for the Pakistani market, which were entirely typical of the genre.

Aircar
USA • 1994 • 1F2R • No built: 1

The brainchild of Texas-based Kenneth Wernicke, the Aircar was a novel take on the flying car theme. Its wingspan was a mere 10ft (2600mm) – enough, said the designer, to provide lift to get the 24ft (6600mm) long, 2800lb car off the ground. Indeed, he likened his car's aerodynamics to those of a paper aeroplane. The prototype used a 180bhp Mazda rotary engine and featured controls that could be used for both road and air, with a propeller at the front providing forward thrust. Despite plans to sell production Aircars for $100,000, the project never, so to speak, got off the ground.

Airscoot
USA • 1947 • 2F1R • No built: n/a

Certainly one of the smallest cars ever built, the ingenious Airscoot was designed to transport pilots to and from airports, the idea being that you could fold it up and stow it on board. It measured just 934mm (37in) long, 508mm (20in) tall and weighed 33kg (72lb), yet could carry 204kg (450lb). Top speed was 25mph and it could do 60mpg. The Airscoot was made by Aircraft Products of Wichita, Kansas.

AISA
E • 1954-1955 • 2F1R • No built: 2

AISA (Actividades Industriales SA) was based in Cervera, and run by Martí Martí. Two three-wheeler passenger vehicle prototypes were made. The first one (1954, pic right), resembled the Fuldamobil in

layout: a very compact enclosed three-wheeler. AISA was an early company working with plastic bodywork. The two-seater had a Hispano-Villers 197cc single-cylinder two-stroke engine mounted in the rear, plus a three-speed gearbox. Weighing only 220kg, a top speed of 50mph was claimed. The second prototype (1955) had a squarer shape and a roll-top canvas roof. The operation then morphed into Jurka ⇨.

Alé
CDN • 2006 • 2F1R • No built: 1

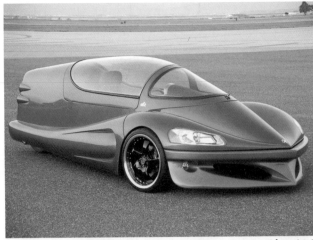

Significant publicity was gained by the unique Alé, which pioneered the concept of 'fuel vapour' power, whereby the engine ran on vapours rather than liquid petrol. In practice this meant an air/fuel ratio of 20:1 rather than the normal 14.7:1. The reason was to boost overall range (the company behind it, Fuel Vapor Technologies, claimed over 900 miles, based on 92mpg).

A 180bhp Honda 1.5-litre turbo engine drove the front wheels, enabling 0-60mph in 5.0 seconds. Fully adjustable suspension used a Honda CRX front end and a single rear swing arm, while the steering box came from a Porsche 911!

The aerodynamic glassfibre body seated two in tandem, but it was quite big at 4420mm (174in) long and weighed 635kg (1400lb). The car's creator, George Parker, planned to put it into production in British Columbia, Canada, but investment had not been forthcoming as of the time of writing.

Alesin ALX110ZK
RC • 2010s • 1F2R • No built: n/a

This Chinese trike seems to have been marketed under various brand names, including Alesin, Tianxi and Jialong. It weighed 310kg and could be powered by engines from 50cc to 200cc.

Aleu Bambi
E • 1954-1956 • 2F1R • No built: n/a

Manufacturas Mécanicas Aleu of Esparraguera, Barcelona was best known for its motorbikes, but it also made three-wheelers. The Aleu Bambi was a very small roofless, doorless three-wheeler weighing only 145kg (320lb). The rear-mounted 200cc Nito single-cylinder two-stroke engine drove the single rear wheel, and a top speed of 45mph was quoted. After a showing at the 1954 Feria de Muestras in Barcelona, not much more was heard of the Bambi, although Aleu did make a rickshaw called the Cachorro (Puppy) with a two-stroke engine of 125cc or 200cc and a cargo tricycle called the M-125. Aleu was absorbed by a metals company called Monfort in 1956.

Allard Clipper
GB • 1953-1955 • 1F2R • No built: Approx 20

Alongside AC, Reliant and Bond, Allard was one of the few firms engaged in the peculiarly English practice of making microcars and sports GT cars both at the same time. The Clipper was an almost wilfully odd and desperately crude device. This was one of the first cars in Britain ever fitted with a glassfibre body (made by Hordern-Richmond). Designed by David Gottlieb (who later created the Powerdrive ⇨), the Clipper looked like a pair of eggs given a styling job by Chevrolet. On at least one example, there was even an antiquated dickey seat in the rear 'boot'.

The Clipper was a light car at just 672lb (305kg). The engine was a 346cc Villiers 8bhp unit mounted in the rear and driving only one of the rear wheels, but cooling problems and a driveshaft weakness made it woefully unreliable. Ultimately, it was a failed project.

All Cars Charly / Snuggy
I • 1974-1985 • 1F2R • No built: Several thousand

The Charly was initially created by a firm called Autozodiaco in 1974. An amusing and genially shaped three-wheeler, it used a plastic two-seater body composed entirely of straight lines. Typical of Italian city cars, it used a Minarelli 49cc engine.

Production of the Charly transferred to a new Bologna-based enterprise called All Cars in 1978. The model now used a 50cc Morini 4.5bhp engine. All Cars eventually renamed the car, with considerable brilliance, the Snuggy. A new

convertible version (complete with a spare wheel on the back) was also introduced with the yet more inspired name of Snuggy Tobrouk. Later versions switched to Motobécane 50cc engines, or could even be had with a rorty 250cc unit. The Charly was sold in Germany as the City Boy.

Allied

PK • 2008-date • 1F2R • No built: n/a

New Allied Motors built the Allied brand of autorickshaws for the Pakistani market. Its largely conventional passenger-carrying designs were powered by 200cc four-stroke engines.

Allied Industries International

USA • 1970s • n/a • No built: n/a

This prolific kit car maker based in Fremont, Nebraska essayed just one three-wheeler model: a kit car of its own design in the 1970s.

Alpha Z 103

J • 1980s • 1F2R • No built: n/a

This was a very small enclosed glassfibre-bodied three-wheeler with a single headlamp, handlebar steering and simple moped mechanics. The same manufacturer also made a larger four-wheeler model called the Alpha Z 104.

Alsport Tri-Sport

USA • 1970s • 1F2R • No built: n/a

Alsport's Tri-Sport range of off-road ATV-style three-wheelers is outside the scope of this book but, from 1974, it added a road-going model called the SL (Street Legal) which had cycle wings, engine cowling and full lighting. It could be ordered with a 230cc or 340cc engine.

Alta

GR • 1968-1977 • 2F1R • No built: n/a

After the Attica ⇨ – a Greek licence-built version of the Fuldamobil S-7 – ended in financial disaster, Alta picked up the pieces and modified the design. Notably there was more angular rear bodywork, more generous 2+2 seating and a 198cc Sachs engine with 10bhp. The Alta became one of the stalwarts of the Greek motor industry but, even in that protectionist market, its attractions steadily faded. Alta also made an open three-wheeler version, and built the A700 BMW 700-engined three-wheeled truck up until 1982.

Altona Condor

B • 1946 • 2F1R • No built: 1

Altona Motors of Antwerp made three-wheeled vans from 1938 onwards and also showed an open-topped two-seater in 1946 called the Condor, powered by an 800cc engine, but it remained a sole prototype.

A&M

D • 1986-date • 1F2R • No built: n/a

Based in Herbertingen in Germany, Markus Rothmund's A&M brand offered chopper trikes in a wide variety of styles with rear-mounted engines from VW Beetle up to Porsche. Model names included Rico, Cesare, Renegade, Colani and Tri Star.

AMC

GB • 1950s • 2F1R • No built: n/a

The parent company of the Matchless and AJS motorbike brands, Associated Motor Cycles (AMC), made a three-wheeler with a cabin for passengers in front of the driver.

American Chariot

USA • 2000-date • 1F2R • No built: n/a

Described as a "versatile, manoeuvrable and practical personal transportation vehicle," the American Chariot was a tiny single-person vehicle – not a single-seater, as the driver simply stood on a platform and controlled it via handlebars. Powered by an electric motor, a top speed of 20mph and a range of 15 miles were claimed.

American Thunder Tryke
USA • 1990s • 1F2R • No built: n/a

When this thunderous Gothic chariot first emerged in 1992, it was quite unique in the marketplace. The powerplant was a small-block Chevrolet engine (4.3 to 6.0 litres), with a power output of up to 345bhp. Performance was epic: one Thunder Tryke was timed from 0-60mph in 3.3 seconds. Because of the long (54in/1370mm) chopper front forks, manoeuvring the tandem two-seater was something of a challenge. Built in Santa Fe, New Mexico, a basic chassis kit cost $4500, while complete vehicles were priced from $24,400.

American Trike
USA • 1997-date • 1F2R • No built: n/a

This conversion kit was designed to fit any bike. Standard or custom-made swinging arm designs made of aluminium were offered, with adjustable coilover suspension or air dampers, plus an anti-roll bar. Prices started at $6500. Options included different styles of rear wings up to full glassfibre rear ends with an opening bootlid.

AMES Trio
I • c2001-c2006 • 1F2R • No built: n/a

AMES was based in Pegognaga, in Mantua, Italy, whose Trio was a very small microcar that strongly recalled the BMA Brio ⇨. This two-seater electric car was classed as a moped for licensing purposes, and indeed was almost as basic as a moped.

Ammar K-SL
PK • 1990-date • 1F2R • No built: n/a

The Ammar Motor Company was a Karachi-based manufacturer of three-wheelers which achieved some fame by exporting its cars to the USA, where they were sold as the Wildfire WF250-C ⇨. In Pakistan, the K-SL range was offered in various body types, including enclosed and open-topped passenger cars, as well as pick-up trucks. They were powered by a single-cylinder four-stroke water-cooled engine driving through a five-speed gearbox.

Anderson Dynamics RKTSHP
USA • 2011-date • 1F2R • No built: n/a

The model name of Carey Anderson's RKTSHP might look like a mouthful but it signified 'Rocket Ship'. This was a two-seater trike designed for high performance, using a front-wheel drivetrain relocated to the back of the vehicle in a tubular space frame chassis to create a mid-engined layout. The donor powerplant was a Toyota Camry 2.4-litre four-cylinder or 3.5-litre V6. The RKTSHP was quite long at 139in (3530mm) but weighed only 498kg (1095lb). A patented front suspension system based on equal-length control arms was claimed to enhance handling. Classified as a motorcycle, kits and turnkey cars were both offered, priced at $15,000 and $32,000 respectively.

Andy's Modern Microcars
GB • 2000s-date • 2F1R • No built: n/a

This UK operation offered replica bodyshells and fully-built recreations of numerous microcar three-wheelers, including the Peel P50 (12 built), Peel Trident (28 built), BMW Isetta, Messerschmitt, Brütsch Mopetta, Scootacar Mk1 and Bamby (all ⇨).

Antilope
NL • 1952 • 1F2R • No built: Probably 1

The Antilope was built in Hiversum in the Netherlands. A 60cc Ilo engine drive the single front wheel, and two people could sit in the doorless open bodywork, which was realised in sparkling aluminium. If the Antilope had reached production – which it did not – it would have sold for between 1200 and 1400 florins.

API 175
IND • 1955-2002 • 1F2R • No built: Many thousands

Automobile Products of India became India's first scooter manufacturer when it started assembling Lambrettas in 1955. After Scooter India Ltd purchased the defunct factory from Innocenti in 1972, scooters were sold as the MAC and Lamby. API also made the 175 rickshaw, based on the Lambro trike and fitted with a 175cc 'FLI' engine under the driver's seat. The API had the advantage of being taller, more spacious and more powerful than its main rivals.

Apollo Mopsen
S • 1958 • 2F1R • No built: Probably 1

M. Berlin & Co of Värnamo in Sweden made this moped-based trike. The Mopsen ('pug') was designed by Valentin Heurlin, weighed under 75kg and its top speed was just 19mph (30km/h). Despite a plan to market it at 1400 florins, that never happened.

Aprilia Los Angeles
I • 2002 • 2F1R • No built: Probably 1

Years ahead of the Piaggio MP3 ⇨, Italian motorbike maker Aprilia proved itself to be a real trailblazer with this prototype. Aprilia said the Los Angeles perfectly combined scooter and car strengths, notably improving wind protection and safety versus ordinary scooters. The two front wheels featured tilting independent suspension, interconnected via a rocker. Other sophisticated elements included ABS brakes, sat nav and a radio intercom.

Aptera
USA • 2006-date • 2F1R • No built: n/a

Accelerated Composites of Carlsbad, California achieved widespread media coverage with its unusual Aptera. This was a two-seater with an extra central child seat, bodied in glassfibre and claimed to have "the lowest drag coefficient of any production car."

The initial Aptera 1h (above) was claimed to average 330mpg from its hybrid powertrain, consisting of a 12bhp diesel engine and a 25bhp electric motor. However, concerns over emissions led the company to pursue pure electric power. The all-electric 1e offered a 120-mile (193km) range and had solar-powered climate control. Weight was just 385kg (850lb), so a 0-60mph time of 11 seconds was expected, plus a top speed of 95mph, in the hybrid model. Power was transmitted to the front wheels.

Despite an aim to sell the Aptera for under $20,000, no cars had been delivered by 2009, when an updated 2e model (above) was presented. This had larger doors and a faster 0-60mph time of less than 10 seconds. One Aptera achieved 206mpg in US government tests. However, investors did not feel the three-wheeler offered enough sales potential, and a larger four-wheel saloon was developed. Even so, the company went bust in 2011. By 2013, the project had been revived by ZAP ⇨, which planned to farm construction of the chassis out to Zhejiang Jonway in China.

Arcimoto Alpha
USA • 2008 • 2F1R • No built: 1

Inspired by the BugE ⇨, Oregon-based Mark Frohnmayer built a single-seater electric runabout prototype called the Alpha. He said it had "a little bit too much of the 'I'm going to die' feeling" to drive and offered no weather protection, so it was shelved.

Arcimoto Pulse
USA • 2009-2011 • 2F1R • No built: 2 prototypes

The Pulse was a much more serious effort: a tandem two-seater with enclosed and quite mature bodywork, a steel space frame chassis and front-wheel drive. You could have a range of 40, 80 miles or 160 miles, depending on the battery pack selected. With eight 12V batteries and a 65bhp DC motor, a maximum speed of 65mph (105km/h) was quoted.

Arcimoto SRK
USA • 2011-date • 2F1R • No built: 14 (to 2013)

The SRK was so-named after someone said it drove like a shark. Its maker said it was a mix of "an electric motorcycle and an aerodynamic jeep on steroids." The SRK had more power (89bhp) and could be bought in any of four interchangeable body designs: base (no upper body covering), LT (fabric bodywork), Deliverator (single-seater light commercial) and Pulse (hard bodywork). A pilot run of 40 cars was announced, priced at $41,000 each, with a full production run due to begin in 2013 for around half that price.

Ardex
F • 1934-1950 • 2F1R & 1F2R • No built: n/a

The ultra-economy three-wheeled Ardex from Nanterre, France, was first launched in 1934. The company made its first four-wheeler in 1937 and mostly concentrated on quadrupeds after this date. However, during WW2, Ardex made three-wheeled electric cars with crudely formed metal bodywork and a 2F1R layout. Then in 1950 it displayed a three-wheeled prototype with a 1F2R configuration and narrow bodywork seating two in tandem.

Argson

GB • 1922-1954 • 1F2R • No built: Approx 8000

Argson Engineering started off making hand-propelled disabled vehicles, but made its first petrol-powered model in 1922 (using a 174cc Villiers engine). Following WW2 it marketed the Victory until 1953. Electric models  were offered from 1923 until 1954, latterly as the De Luxe with better seating. Harper ⇨ took the company over in 1954.

Ariel 3

GB • 1970-1973 • 1F2R • No built: Approx 2500

In 1966 George Lesley Wallis built a series of 75cc-engined prototypes of a tilting three-wheeled moped in an effort to make it safer than a two-wheeler. His efforts attracted the attention of motorcycle maker BSA, which bought the rights to Wallis's idea. BSA reportedly spent £2 million developing the Ariel 3. The production vehicle used a 49cc Anker two-stroke engine with 1.7bhp, and its leaning mechanism was controlled by torsion bars. Its top speed was sluggish at 30mph, but it was claimed to achieve 125mpg. BSA planned to make 8000 units a month priced at £95 apiece but its market success fell well short of that.

Armec Citi Mobil

CH • c2004-c2009 • 1F2R • No built: Probably 1

This 'cabin scooter' prototype from a Swiss sidecar maker was only 900mm wide and 2250mm long. Like the Carver ⇨, the front half tilted as it went round bends, the rear section remaining upright. The driver used conventional foot pedals and a continuously variable  automatic transmission mated to a 600cc four-cylinder engine (electric, diesel and hybrid options were also mooted), and a top speed of 100mph (160km/h) was claimed. The 'gullwing' type door could be made to open up for targa-style driving. Finance was still being sought for a production run in 2009.

Arola

F • 1976-1982 • 1F2R • No built: Several thousand

One of the most successful of all French microcars was the Arola. First presented in 1976, it was the brainchild of Daniel Manon and had a very simple polyester-and-glassfibre-bodied design. Its single-cylinder air-cooled two-stroke 47cc Sachs engine, mated to a two-speed automatic gearbox, produced only 3bhp. That was not even powerful enough to propel the 242lb (110kg) car to the permitted top speed of 45km/h (27mph) – it puffed its last at 25mph. A soupier Type 12 version had a Motobécane 50cc engine with a reverse gear.

Still, its single-seater bodywork looked cute, especially with detachable funky transparent Plexiglass doors fitted. Underneath sat a tubular steel frame with coil suspension both front and rear, plus cable brakes. The Arola was certainly cheap at 7880 Francs in 1978, which partly explains why it sold in its thousands. With a pick-up tray on the back, it was also sold as a commercial vehicle dubbed the Super Pratique (or SP). Arola also started making four-wheelers in 1979 but the whole enterprise had gone bust by 1983. A new operation called Aixam picked up the pieces and still makes four-wheeled microcars to this day.

Asaka Puchi

J • 1980s • 2F1R • No built: n/a

This was one of many very small plastic-bodied moped-powered three-wheelers offered in Japan in the 1980s.

ASMC Electrike

RP • 2010-date • 1F2R • No built: n/a

ASMC (Applied Systems Manufacturing Corp) was founded in 1986 and made its first car, the Electrike, in 2010. This four-seater had a steel chassis and a glassfibre body but its 3kW motor allowed it a maximum speed of a mere 25mph (40km/h), and a range of 40km.

Atlas Mishuk

BD • c1989-date • 1F2R • No built: n/a

Most rickshaws in Bangladesh were imported, but Atlas designed and built its own rickshaw called the Mishuk, a name derived from a local deer. Distinctive features included spoked wheels and green livery, while there was more passenger space than in many other rickshaws. Its four-stroke engine helped in a country blighted by air pollution.

ATS Azuma

F • 2009 • 2F1R • No built: n/a

French company ATS Design built this smartly styled two-seater trike, which was electric-powered and cleverly used Renault Clio II doors and wheels.

Attica

GR • 1964-1967 • 2F1R • No built: Approx 100

A company called Vioplastic in Piraeus, run by Georgios Dimitriadis, obtained a licence to build the Fuldamobil ⇨ in Greece in 1964. Renamed the Attica, the three-wheeler used a 198cc Heinkel single-cylinder engine and could reach

a top speed of 60mph (97km/h). In 1966, it was joined by an open-topped Cabrioletta version, as well as a beach model that had no doors or windscreen. The project transferred to Alta ⇨ in 1968.

Atul Gem Paxx & Shakti

IND • 1970s-date • 1F2R • No built: Approx 150,000

Atul Auto Ltd started making rickshaws (locally called 'chhakada') in the region of Saurashtra in the 1970s. The first examples were crude conversions using a motorcycle front end, but quickly Atul became one of the larger three-wheeler manufacturers in India. Petrol engines were soon joined by diesel, CNG and LPG alternatives. At the time of writing, the range consisted of three- and six-passenger rickshaws in three model ranges: Gem Paxx, Shakti and Shakti Smart. The latter was powered by an 8bhp four-stroke single-cylinder 395cc engine, but the others came with a 435cc unit developing 7.5bhp; CNG and LPG versions had 275cc engines.

Auranthetic Charger

USA/IRE • 1974 • 1F2R • No built: n/a

American corporation Auranthetic created this electric-powered trike with a two-speed transmission. A range of 50 miles at speeds up to 30mph was claimed. There

were plans to assemble the machines in the Irish Republic and sell them for £300 but these came to nothing.

Autocykl

CZ • 1948 • 1F2R • No built: 1

The Autocykl was the brainchild of watchmaker Rostislav Dyna. It was a narrow (800mm wide) tandem two-seater that, remarkably for the time, could lean into corners. A BSA 500cc 12bhp single-cylinder engine drove the rear wheels by chain at up to 50mph (80km/h).

Autoette

USA • 1947-1970s • 1F2R • No built: n/a

The Autoette Electric Car Co of Long Beach, California was founded by Royce Seevers in 1947. The batteries were made especially by Trojan for the car, and the motor was initially a converted Dodge starter motor (later a unit designed specifically for Autoette). Various models were made, from golf buggies to trucks, but the CruiseAbout (pictured above) was the closest thing to a road car that Autoette made. Two- and four-seater versions, as well as open-topped and closed models, were built up to the 1970s.

Automirage 3

I • 1976-1987 • 2F1R • No built: n/a

Automirage was one of Italy's biggest beach buggy manufacturers in the 1970s, but it soon abandoned buggies in favour of microcars. The Mirage 3 was an angular glassfibre-bodied three-wheeler with a 50cc Morini engine sited in the rear, driving the single rear wheel by chain through a three-speed gearbox. It was officially described as a '1+1' seater.

SENZA PATENTE

Automirage S3R
I • 1982-1987 • 1F2R • No built: n/a

A larger body with side-by-side seats clothed Automirage's new S3R (which was also sold in four-wheeled form as the S4R). The Bologna-based company offered the S3R with either a BCB 125cc single-cylinder or 251cc two-cylinder engine, plus automatic transmission.

Automite
USA • 2002-date • 2F1R • No built: n/a

The Automite (by Masterworks of Long Green, Maryland) was a fully-enclosed single-seater microcar with uncompromisingly flat body panels. It was designed to be built at home from plans for as little as $300, but kits were also available. Engines between 4.5bhp and 10bhp were possible, with a top speed of up to 55mph. It measured only 68in (1727mm) long and weighed a mere 75kg (165lb).

Autostudi A-Trix
I • 2002/2007 • 1F2R • No built: n/a

Turin-based design company Autostudi's first A-Trix of 2002 (pic right) was a single-seat, semi-enclosed trike prototype, built on a scooter chassis and powered either by a petrol engine (50cc to

125cc) or electricity. A completely different A-Trix was presented in 2007 (pic left): a stand-on skate-like three-wheeler, initially powered by a battery mounted in the front forks, but later modified to run on hydrogen. Steering was effected by the driver simply leaning into bends.

AVG
USA • 2000s • 1F2R • No built: n/a

AVG Engineering of California offered plans sets for the P-40 Nitro Express and P-40 Tiger Trike chopper trikes, both of which used a Volkswagen rear-mounted engine.

Avolette
F • 1955-1958 • 2F1R • No built: n/a

The Avolette was one of many cars whose origins lay with Brütsch ⇨ – in this case the Brütsch Zwerg. The design was modified significantly by the French licencee, Air Tourist. The Avolette was a glassfibre two-seater whose open-topped body was moulded in two parts; a flop-forward hardtop was optional. In its T-shaped tubular backbone chassis, a 175cc Ydral single-cylinder air-cooled engine was fitted (other options spanned Sachs, Maico and Lambretta, from 125cc to 250cc), with chain drive to the single rear wheel. The makers claimed a top speed of up to 62mph (100km/h) and fuel economy of 94mpg.

From 1957, the glassfibre bodywork was completely redesigned with far less rounded lines (pictured below), when engines of either 125cc or 150cc were being fitted. However, by this stage, the life-cycle of the Avolette was virtually spent, and survivors of either generation are very few.

Axis V2
GB • 2007 • 2F1R • No built: n/a

The Axis V2 was a conversion kit designed to turn a Yamaha V-Max motorbike into a three-wheeler. It was marketed by Breakin Bikes of Newcastle-upon-Tyne, and the all-in price was £16,000 in 2007.

THREE WHEELERS A-Z

BBB

BMW C1 ▲

Berkeley T60 ▲

Bond Minicar MkC ▲

▼ BRP Can-Am Spyder

Bond Bug ▲

▼ Brütsch Mopetta

Badsey Bullet
ZA/USA • 1981-c1998 • 2F1R • No built: Approx 8

When South African Bill Badsey created the Bullet in 1981, he boldly claimed his extraordinary three-wheeler was capable of reaching 200mph (in reality, probably more like 150mph). The chassis housed what was essentially the rear end of a

Suzuki motorcycle, although the engine – either a GSX1100 or 1300cc six-cylinder – was sited up front, between the passengers' knees, driving the single rear wheel. Another feature was inboard coilspring dampers. The wedge-shape glassfibre body featured a flop-forward canopy with gas struts for entry. Unusually, the two passengers had separate cockpits, which made the Bullet rather wide by trike standards.

The Bullet was set to be imported to the UK from 1982 by The Unique Vehicle and Accessory Co of Berkshire, either in kit form (at £4500) or complete (at £6000), but it's believed that no cars ever made it to the UK. Badsey emigrated from South Africa to the USA in 1983 to set up Bill Badsey Racing USA in Ventura,

California. Engine choices now encompassed Yamaha Venture V4, Suzuki GSX and 1.2-litre turbocharged engines with up to 200bhp, with a hefty price tag of $16,900.

Badsey Fun Machine
USA • 1984-1990s • 2F1R • No built: n/a

Bill Badsey's second three-wheeler was based on a ladder chassis with outriggers, using a 552cc Yamaha Vision motorbike engine mounted just behind the front axle, powering the single rear wheel via a shaft drive. The driver sat astride the engine, and steered via a pair of handlebars to a car steering rack. Front suspension was by lower track control arms, upper rocking arms and coil/spring damper units plus an anti-roll bar, while at the rear a Yamaha Venture swinging arm was used with double coil/spring dampers. You even had the luxury of an electric reverse gear. With its one-piece glassfibre body, the Fun Machine weighed just 381kg. Prices in the USA started at $5995 but few were sold, leaving Badsey to go on to make electric go-peds and boats.

Bajaj Autorickshaw
IND/RI • 1959-date • 1F2R • No built: 100s of thousands

Bajaj can trace its origins back to 1945, and it began importing Piaggio three-wheelers into India as early as 1948. It won a licence to build Piaggios locally (in Pune) in 1959 and became the pre-eminent Indian scooter brand. Its main three-wheeled output was miniature trucks and rickshaws, and it also produced the Tempo ⇨ from 1958 right up until 2000. Bajaj trikes were powered by numerous fuel sources: two- and four-stroke petrol, electric, CNG, LPG and diesel engines were all offered. Model designations include DV, FE, RE and Mega Max. From 2004 the Bajaj was also assembled in Indonesia, while it was built in Nigeria too. At the time of writing, Bajaj still makes the Autorickshaw three-wheeler virtually unaltered and is claimed to be the world's largest rickshaw manufacturer. See also Force ⇨.

Bajaj PTV
IND • 1988 • 1F2R • No built: 25

Two decades before Tata launched its Nano people's car, Bajaj Auto had very much the same idea with the Private Transport Vehicle (PTV), intended to sell for 25,000 rupees (under £1000 at the time). A 150cc scooter engine and four-speed gearbox enabled a top speed of 50mph (80km/h). Some 25 prototypes were built; early ones were four-seaters but later ones had two seats and a shorter wheelbase, all with enclosed bodywork. After appearing at the 1988 Delhi Automotive Fair, sadly this proto-Nano never made full production.

Bamby
UK • 1983-1985 • 2F1R • No built: Approx 50

Hull-based Alan Evans was a microcar enthusiast who loved his Peel P50 ⇨ so much that he made a modern equivalent: the Bamby. Like the Peel, it was a single-seater glassfibre-bodied three-wheeler with a 49cc engine. It had front hydraulic discs brakes and three-speed automatic transmission, weighed a mere 107kg and was claimed to do 100mpg. Design changes

through its lifetime included a switch from a single gullwing door to a conventionally hinged door, twin headlamps in place of the original single 'cyclops' lamp and a conventional steering wheel instead of the initial handlebar. The engine was progressively upgraded from a 49cc Minarelli to Yamaha, then Suzuki moped units.

Targeted at 16-year olds and housewives, the Bamby was too expensive (at £1,597) to make much impact. An initial production rate of 20 units per month proved over-optimistic and the Bamby died after only a year or so. However, in 2011 Alan Evans reformed Bamby Cars and started producing an updated replica of the Peel P50 called the Bamby P50.

B&Z Electra King
USA • 1961-c1981 • 1F2R • No built: Several hundred

One of the most successful and long-lived electric cars ever made was the Electra King made by B&Z Electric Car Co of Long Beach, California. This boxy glassfibre-bodied microcar was built virtually unchanged for around 20 years. Both three-wheeled and four-wheeled models were built, the trike having a single front wheel. A series-wound DC electric motor fed around one horsepower to one of the rear wheels via a chain and a three-speed transmission. This would provide a top speed of 18mph and a range of 45 miles. More powerful (2bhp and 3.5bhp) versions were added from around 1972, and in its most potent guise (!) its top speed rose to 36mph. There was a choice of tiller or steering wheel, and foot or hand controls. A variety of bodywork was made over the years, the most popular being a two-seater with a fixed rood, but there was a four-seater with a Surrey-type roof and a rear-facing back seat.

BaoYa
CN/HKC • 2006-date • 1F2R • No built: n/a

Shandong BaoYa Vehicle Co was a joint venture of two companies from Hong Kong and China. As well as light commercials, ATVs and electric cars, it made scooter-based trikes and rickshaws. Power sources included single-cylinder four-stroke units of either 149cc (6.2bhp) or 198cc (14bhp), mated to manual or CVT gearboxes, or electric power.

Baron

UK • 2011-2013 • 1F2R • No built: n/a

Baron Trikes of Yeovil, Somerset made full-bodied Honda Goldwing-based trikes, but also open-back trikes on many types of motorbike. Trikes cost from £7000, and each one was said to be unique.

Barrett Minor

UK • 1956-1959 • 1F2R • No built: very few

Bristol-based W&F Barrett Ltd started making invalid tricycles in around 1948 with tiller-steered vehicles powered by 250cc Villiers single-cylinder engine. Its best-known products, commissioned by the Ministry of Health, were for special use. The 'Model 41' was intended for 'patients up to 20 stone living in hilly districts'. The 'Model 58' Minor, launched in 1956, was intended for "small persons with a short arm reach" and the car measured only 38in (96cm) wide, and 96in (244cm) long. It was powered by a 197cc Villiers Mk9E engine mounted in the rear. The enclosed bodywork was in glassfibre and featured a rear-hinged door and single front headlamp.

Barrett Midget

UK • 1959-1968 • 1F2R • No built: n/a

Years before MG grabbed the name, Barrett produced its own Midget. A politically incorrect name by modern mores, the 'Model 60' Midget was a special-use invalid car designed for people up to 4ft 6in (137cm) tall. Its glassfibre bodywork (always in green) was slightly enlarged over the Minor and had a front-hinged door, two headlamps and a convertible roof. All production was bought by the Ministry of Health, but the Midget was axed in 1968 when the authorities declared that smaller drivers should use the Tippen Delta ⇨.

Basson's Star

USA • 1956 • 1F2R • No built: very few

Basson's Industries of the Bronx, New York was behind this car, which was styled by Gil d'Andrea. The unusual open-topped two-piece glassfibre body was quite compact at 125in (3180mm) long and had a sizeable luggage area in the rear. Weighing 400lb (181kg), it used a small Ilo single-cylinder two-stroke engine and was claimed to average 80mpg.

Features included independent rear suspension, hydraulic brakes and a steering wheel that was described as "airplane-type". Even priced at just $999, it found very few buyers. Basson's was also involved with the Martin Stationette ⇨ and the Tri-Car Suburbanette ⇨.

Belcar

CH • 1955-1956 • 2F1R • No built: very few

This was a licence-built version of the Brütsch 200 Spatz ⇨. It swapped the original 191cc Sachs engine for a 197cc single-cylinder Victoria unit (good for 53mph) and its headlamps were repositioned, but it kept the original layout of a monocoque glassfibre shell. Since this was judged dangerous in a German court, production of the Belcar ceased very quickly. The Belcar was also marketed as the Sprint.

Berkeley T60

UK • 1959-1960 • 2F1R • No built: Approx 1750

Lawrie Bond's remarkable Berkeley T60, the three-wheeled version of his micro-sports car, effectively became a kind of Morgan for the 1960s. In 1955, Bond had approached Charles Panter of Berkeley Coachworks, the caravan maker and glassfibre pioneer, with his idea for a new micro sports car. The result was a tiny (10ft 2in) four-wheeler weighing just 280kg (620lb). It took until 1959 for a three-wheeled version to appear. Panter modified the rear end of the four-wheeled Berkeley B65 to create the T60, which became an instant smash hit, offering genuine sports car-like ability and handsome lines. With its 328cc Excelsior front-mounted engine, a top speed of 60mph (96km/h) was possible, and it offered a sharpness of handling that was unheard of by the standards of contemporary three-wheelers.

A four-seater version was made from 1960 under the name T60-4. Squeezing four passengers into such a tiny space was a challenge and the performance with four up was severely curtailed. Probably only 40 four-seaters were ever sold, but the standard-issue T60 notched up around 1750 sales in just over a year – a remarkable total. The whole Berkeley marque died in late 1960 when its main caravan business slumped dramatically.

Berkeley Bandini
UK • 1991-2002 • 2F1R • No built: 7

A Berkeley enthusiast called Andy Argyle started offering replacement chassis, panels and bodyshells for Berkeley cars in the 1990s. By 1993, his Berkeley Cars operation had entered full production with complete T60 body/chassis kits, but unlike the original Berkeley, had a tubular steel spaceframe chassis designed to accept a Mini front subframe. Any A-series engine, from 848cc up to 1275cc Metro Turbo, could be used, or alternatively engines such as motorbike units or Citroën 2CV. The only external difference from the 1960 T60 was wider wheel arches, although options included head fairings, a blanked-off passenger's seat, a hardtop and alternative nose designs.

BET 125
GR • 1965 • 1F2R • No built: 1

BET was a mercifully pithy acronym of Biothechnia Ellinikon Trikyklon (literally Greek Three-Wheeler Manufacturer). Founded in Athens by Petros Konstantinou, its main business was light three-wheeled commercial vehicles but it created its own economy passenger car in 1965. The BET 125 seated five people and was powered by a BMW 125cc motorbike engine.

BET 500
GR • 1973-1975 • 1F2R • No built: 15

BET's second passenger three-wheeler arrived in 1973, with slightly more success. The BET 500 used a rear-mounted Fiat 500 engine and its metal five-seater bodywork was more resolved.

BGW Tri-Rod
USA • 1970s • 1F2R • No built: n/a

BGW Industries of Mansfield, Ohio mostly made off-road 'dirt' trikes but also offered street-legal models such as the Tri-Rod.

Bichibi
E • 1957 • 2F1R • No built: 1

Bichibi was the phonetic extraction of BCB, the initials of this car's creators: Bultó, Carreras and Biolino. Made in Monresa, Spain, it never reached intended production but the prototype remains in existence.

Binzhou Pride
CN • 2008 • 2F1R • No built: Probably 1

Binzhou is a city in the Chinese province of Shandong, where a company called Binzhou Pride Automobile created

a number of unusual car projects, including one little-known three-wheeler: a very narrow tandem two-seater powered by a small petrol engine. It seems unlikely that a production run began, as the whole Binzhou Pride brand expired in 2008.

Biotrike
US • 2008-date • 2F1R • No built: n/a

Unusually, the Biotrike was a plug-in hybrid designed to run on biodiesel. Its powerplant sat in the tail, driving a single rear wheel. It used a steel tubular rollcage for safety and featured an aerodynamic body shape with a single door. Prices in 2012 started at $24,000. There were several models: the B3X2 two-seater, B3X4 four-seater, and B3XH for handicapped drivers. Biotrike was based in Ridgeland, South Carolina.

Blackjack Avion
UK • 1996-2004 • 2F1R • No built: Approx 69

Celebrated specialist car designer Richard Oakes was behind this exceptionally good-looking three-wheeler. Undoubtedly inspired by pre-war racing Morgans, the two-seater Avion was based on Citroën 2CV mechanicals. However, unlike most 2CV-based cars, it did not use Citroën's chassis, but its own chassis into which the 2CV powertrain was fitted. The front suspension was by vertically mounted dampers, while the rear end had a single swinging arm with a coil spring/damper unit. The open-topped doorless bodywork was in plastic over subframes and featured a moulded-in windscreen. Oakes formed Blackjack Cars at his base in Helston, Cornwall, and offered both fully-built and kit-form cars, at which he was modestly successful.

Blackjack Zero/Guzzi
UK • 2004-date • 2F1R • No built: Approx 30 (to end 2012)

The Zero was a much finessed update from Richard Oakes. As the 2CV-powered Avion was hardly a quick machine, it moved on to four-cylinder power, namely the VW Beetle engine, still slung out front, driving the front wheels. The brakes and front suspension were modified VW Golf GTi. As before, a steel chassis was clothed in a glassfibre body, and weight was 450kg (992lb). In 2008, a new derivative was introduced using the Moto Guzzi 1100 V-Twin engine, still driving the front wheels through a VW Beetle gearbox. Sometimes referred to as the Blackjack Guzzi, it weighed less than the Beetle-engined Zero. Kits cost from £4112 initially, but in time Oakes moved on to sell complete cars only.

Blohm & Voss
D • 1944-1946 • 2F1R • No built: 1

Blohm & Voss was a shipbuilding company that also made aircraft in Nazi Germany. It planned to make cars, too, and asked its engineer Gerd Grebs (who later built the Staunau microcar) to design a small enclosed car with two seats, two front wheels, a single rear wheel and small rear-mounted engine. The project was halted in 1946, but shipbuilding continued – which it does to this day.

Blue Energy Jack
I • 2001-2004 • 2F1R • No built: Approx 1500

The Jack from Blue Energy started life as a concept scooter from Italjet. Designed by Massimo Tartarini and Massimo Zaniboni, it was powered by a 590W electric motor. It was strictly for local commuting, as its top speed was just 16mph (25km/h) and its range was only 16 miles (25km). Like the Italjet Scooop ⇨, the Jack was designed to lean as you steered. Examples were sold in Italy, Japan and the Netherlands, priced from around £1100.

BMA Amica
I • 1971-1980 • 1F2R • No built: Several hundred

One of the earliest Italian microcars, the BMA Amica was first seen in 1971. Produced in Alfonsine, Ravenna, it sported engines from 50cc up to 223cc. Its plastic bodywork featured gullwing doors, no less.

BMA Brio
I • 1978-1986 • 1F2R • No built: Approx 2000

Symmetrical shapes which minimise tooling costs are a recurring part of minimalist motoring history, but few cars have been quite as bizarrely symmetrical as the BMA Brio. Smaller than the Amica, this was quite the most surreal microcar offering from Italy. The Brio's polyester resin bodywork resembled a wedge of sculptured gorgonzola turned on its edge. A fully convertible version was also available. Technically, the Brio recalled the bare-boned days of cyclecars and represented the absolute minimum in transportation. Its tiny 47cc Sachs engine sat in the tail, driving the rear right wheel only. This putt-putted the Brio to a distinctly un-brio-like top speed of just 23mph (37km/h).

BMA Nuova Amica
I • 1980-1994 • 1F2R • No built: Several hundred

BMA's Nuova Amica of 1980 had rather more normal-looking bodywork than the original Amica and could be purchased with either three or four wheels. A choice of 50cc, 125cc or 250cc petrol engines and a 360cc diesel were offered, with BMA remaining active into the 1990s.

BMW C1
D • 1991 • 1F2R • No built: 1

Although BMW's 1991 C1 prototype was never made a runner, BMW said that it was to be powered by an air-cooled flat-twin engine of 800-1000cc developing up to 68bhp for a top speed of 125mph. Steering was by handlebars and the C1's body tilted by up to 45 degrees, so bikers would feel at home. But there were also such car-like refinements as a five-speed gearbox with reverse, a removable hard top and foot-operated brakes. The C1 name was later used for BMW's enclosed two-wheeled scooter, while the whole BMW trike concept was revived with the CLEVER three-wheeler ⇨ in 2006.

BMW SIMPLE
D • 2008 • 1F2R • No built: 1

BMW's final three-wheeled prototype, the SIMPLE, was an acronym of Sustainable and Innovative Mobility Product for Low Energy consumption – phew! Its enclosed bodywork resembled something out of Star Wars, but inside it was claimed to have as much seat space as a BMW 3 Series coupe. A drag coefficient of 0.18 was claimed, with a weight of only 450kg (992lb). The small internal combustion engine and electric motor were claimed to power the beast to 124mph, with 0-62mph coming up in under 10 seconds, while it could average 118mpg. Like the C1, it was designed to lean into corners. After being shown at the BMW Museum in Munich, the SIMPLE was quietly retired.

Bode MC-369
CN • 2012-date • 2F1R • No built: n/a

Zhejiang Bode Industrial Co specialised mostly in making dirt bikes and ATVs, claiming to produce no less than 1500 units every single day. Of several three-wheeler products it offered, easily its most interesting was the MC-369, an exo-skeletal sports trike, apparently identical to the Kaxa KXA-R22 ⇨ and Trike Factory 1it ⇨.

Bonallack Minnow
GB • 1951-1952 • 2F1R • No built: Very few

Produced by a commercial body builder called Bonallack & Sons in East London, the Minnow was a very small economy car. Its box-section alloy chassis box was braced with crossmembers and the front suspension was independent by coil springs while a pivoted alloy subframe carried a single coil-sprung wheel at the rear. The Excelsior Talisman 250cc two-cylinder two-stroke engine was rear-mounted. The simple open bodywork was made of aluminium sheet and featured a single headlamp. At £468 including tax, it was too expensive and too crude to make any impact.

BOND

Alongside Egon Brütsch, Lawrie Bond was one of the most prolific post-war microcar designers. The marque to which he have his name was one of the very first new British post-war car ventures. Just after the end of WW2, in 1948, Bond had developed an extremely basic three-wheeled prototype. He approached Sharp's Commercials of Preston, Lancashire, which agreed to make the tiny car under the Bond name.

In terms of conception was ideal for the period, offering buyers the chance to step on to the first rung of the car ownership ladder. The Bond Minicar went on to become the most successful British microcar of the time.

Bond also designed, or had a hand in, many other cars of the 1950s and 1960s, notably the Berkeley and Coronet which were both marketed in three-wheeled form.

As the market for micro cars stumbled, Bond switched its attentions to a fun car, the Bond Bug, which proved that the three-wheeled format chimed with the surge in interest in buggies and the like.

Bond was taken over in 1969 by its greatest rival, Reliant of Tamworth, and from that moment on the writing was on the wall for one of Britain's most prolific car marques.

Bond Minicar
GB • 1948-1951 • 1F2R • No built: 1973

When the Bond Minicar was launched in 1949, it was the only British-made three-wheeler other than the Morgan. The aluminium-bodied Minicar had an ultra-basic specification, including cable-and-bobbin steering, a Perspex windscreen, no doors, no front braking and rear suspension that consisted only of the tyres. A 122cc single-cylinder two-stroke Villiers engine with 6bhp sat immediately behind the single front wheel, driving it by chain through a three-speed gearbox. The early Bond was intended as a runabout but, such was the success of the model, many people wanted to use their Minicars as all-purpose transport. To oblige them, Bond also

offered a larger 197cc Villiers engined De Luxe version with 8bhp. This model was retrospectively known as the Minicar Mark A, and licensed production also took place in Denmark (as the Erla-Bond) between 1950 and 1952.

Bond Minicar Mark B
GB • 1951-1952 • 1F2R • No built: 1414

An improved and lightly restyled Bond model, the Minicar Mark B, arrived in 1951 with the luxury of rear suspension (although it still had no dampers). Like the Mark A, most production cars were two-seaters, although vans, Minitrucks, Minivans and Family Safety Saloons (based on the van but with 2+2 seating – pictured below right) were also offered. All Mark Bs had 197cc Villiers engines, giving them great fuel economy, if rather anaemic performance.

Bond Minicar Mark C/D
GB • 1952-1956/1956-1958 • 1F2R • No built: 6399/3761

A door appeared for the first time on the 1952 Bond Mark C, albeit on the passenger's side only. There was also now braking on the front wheel as well as the rears, and improved suspension. The new Bond's shaped front wings made it look like

a much larger car, and now allowed a curious manoeuvre to be performed: the front wheel and engine could turn through 180 degrees, permitting

the Bond to turn within its own length. By 1955, Bond was making 100 cars per month. The Mark D of 1956 (below) shared the C's body but added 12 volt electrics. The Mark D was exported to the USA as the Sharp's Bearcub.

Bond Minicar Mark E/F/G
GB • 1957-1958/1958-1961/1961-1966 • 1F2R • No built: Approx 1189/6493/3253

The Mark E of 1957 marked a complete design overhaul for the Minicar. It featured a proper chassis for the first time (as opposed to mere stressed bodywork with added strengthening crossmembers, as used on the earlier models), and the Bond was now strong enough to be fitted with full-size doors on both sides of the car. The bodywork sported a slab-sided full-width profile and squarer lines, and had a longer wheelbase. As the weight had increased, Villiers was approached in 1958 to supply a bigger engine. Reboring the existing unit to 246cc

provided an extra 4bhp and a 25% increase in performance. Cars fitted with this engine were known as the Mark F; a four-speed gearbox was now standard and the top speed was a heady 55mph. In 1961, the Mark G (or 250 G) added a few more refinements: a hardtop with a reverse-angle rear window, larger (10in rather than 8in) wheels, hydraulic brakes, independent rear suspension and wind-up windows. Much of the bodywork was now made in glassfibre. An estate version (which Bond claimed to be "the world's first three-wheeled estate car") arrived shortly after – as pictured below.

There were also Ranger van and open-topped Tourer versions. From 1963, a two-cylinder Villiers 4T engine option was added (still with only 250cc).

The Bond Minicar had been probably the most popular British microcar of its era, but sales of what was a very basic car declined drastically in the 1960s. A total of just under 25,000 Minicars of all types had been built by the time production finally ended in 1966.

Bond 875
GB • 1965-1970 • 1F2R • No built: 3441

Since 1963, Bond had been making a Triumph Herald-based sports car called the Equipe. The experience gained in making

its glassfibre body was put to use in the Minicar's 'replacement', the 875 of 1965 – a very different car. The engine now switched to the rear of the car – and Bond turned to Rootes in the form of a detuned (34bhp) Hillman Imp Van 875cc unit. That

gave the new Bond pretty impressive figures of 80mph (128km/h) and 50mpg. The interior was quite crudely finished, though, and the car was expensive, while the press posed questions over the 875's stability at high speeds. A mild MkII facelift in 1968 (pictured above) brought a fake front grille and better cabin trim, but the death knell for the 875 was the takeover of Bond by arch-rival Reliant in 1969.

Bond Bug
UK • 1970-1973 • 1F2R • No built: 2269

No car epitomises the 'Tangerine Dream' swoon of the early 1970s more than the Bond Bug. The head of Ogle Design, Czech-born Tom Karen, had long wanted to do a completely original three-wheeler fun car based on a Reliant chassis. Karen had worked with Reliant since 1963 and had frequently suggested such a machine to the Tamworth car maker. When Reliant bought Bond in 1969, Karen finally got his chance.

The Bond Bug was a bold design that cleverly combined the economies of three-wheeled motoring with a sporting, youthful image. Using a modified and shortened version of the forthcoming Reliant Robin chassis as its basis, the rest of the mechanical package came from the then-current Reliant Regal.

The Bug's most striking feature was its one-piece canopy which tilted forwards on a gas strut to allow entry; removable sidescreens provided ventilation and there was a rudimentary heater. There were only two seats (simple cushions placed over moulded-in hollows) and a small amount of luggage space accessed via a wooden bootlid in the sharply cut-off tail. The passengers sat in a reclined position with the engine effectively between them. To get at the engine, a cover had to be taken off from within the cockpit: probably the only car where changing the plugs requires you to keep the door open!

The wedge-shaped body was available in any colour you liked, as long as it was bright tangerine. The use of aircraft-type black decals, indicating the required fuel octane rating and instructions for opening the canopy, was a revolutionary touch of which Karen was proud.

The Bug was publically launched in June 1970 as "The fun car of the seventies". At the press launch party in May 1970 at Woburn Abbey, one over-enthusiastic journalist called Stuart Marshall managed to roll a Bug right over, which set the tone for future encounters with owners. Handling was not as wayward as it might have been thanks to four rear trailing arms, an anti-roll bar and a Panhard rod.

Initially it was intended to sell the Bug in three versions: the 700, 700E and 700ES. In the event, the base 700 never entered production: only one prototype was ever built. The 700E used a 29bhp version of Reliant's 701cc Regal/ Rebel engine, while the ES used a high-compression version with 31bhp, sufficient to power it to a top speed of 77mph. In addition, the ES came with better trim, rim embellishers and a spare wheel. The price was £579 for the E and £629 for the ES – more than a contemporary Mini. Autocar magazine predicted that the Bug might become "the Ford Mustang of its class" but that didn't happen. Perhaps it was the price, or the sheer impracticality of a car with only two seats and virtually no luggage space. Whatever the reason, the Bug never did quite catch. Early Bugs were built at Bond's old Preston factory, but following Reliant's decision to close the works in 1970, production transferred to Tamworth. At that stage, about 350 had been made.

From October 1973, Bugs received the bigger 748cc engine and the models became known as the 750E and 750ES. Faced with dramatically declining sales for a car which had always cost Reliant a lot to make, production came to a close in May 1974 as Reliant concentrated on production of the new Robin. Around 2270 Bugs had been made. It took a long time to sell the existing stock, the very last cars being registered in 1975. That marked the end of the line for the Bond brand after 25 years. However, the Bug was later revived as the SP Spi-Tri ⇨ in the USA, and by WMC ⇨ in the UK.

Bond Bug Sprint
UK • 1995 • 1F2R • No built: 1

In 1995, Reliant's new owner, Avonex, planned to relaunch the Bond Bug in updated form. It got the original designer Tom Karen to modify the shape with circular front and rear lamps and a new rear end with extended wheelarches. However, the financial problems of Avonex scuppered the project before its intended launch in April 1996.

Boom
D • 1990-date • 1F2R • No built: Approx 10,000 (to 2013)

Over the course of more than 20 years in production, Boom Trikes of Sontheim in Germany produced a bewildering variety of models, most of which were on the classic rear-engined chopper theme. The first was the Highway, followed in 1993 by the Chopper and Family, then in 1995 the Low Rider, in 2002 the Fighter, 2004 the Fun, 2005 the Muscle-Trike, 2007 the V2, 2008 the Power-Fighter X11 Ultimate (with 200bhp) and X12, and 2010 the Mustang and ultra-high-powered Hayabusa (claimed to do 186mph/300km/h). The usual power source was a VW Beetle engine, but alternatives included Ford and Peugeot four-cylinder units, with optional automatic transmission. From 2009, Boom also offered the Moto-Trike, a front-engined American-style chopper trike conversion based on bikes such as the Harley-Davidson, Honda Shadow 750 and Suzuki Intruder 1800. Another departure was the Boom Scooter-Trike (pictured right) based on a 49cc scooter. Boom was claiming a 50% share of all trikes sales in Europe in 2007.

Borgman Dwerg
NL • 1952 • 1F2R • No built: n/a

Vaguely reminiscent of a Bond Minicar to look at, the Borgman Dwerg ('dwarf') was made by a company based in Utrecht. Powered by a front-mounted 150cc Ilo two-stroke engine, this was economy motoring at its most frugal, but even so there were very few takers.

Boselli Libellula
I • 1952 • 2F1R • No built: Very few

The Boselli brothers founded FB-Mondial, a motorcycle company based in Milan that was active from 1948 to 1979. Their sole three-wheeler project was the Libellula ('dragonfly'), based on the Austrian Libelle ⇨ and powered by a 6bhp 160cc Mondial two-stroke single-cylinder engine that could take the 170kg car to a top speed of 43mph (70km/h).

Bosmal
PL • c1992 • 1F2R • No built: n/a

Bosmal was a major design and engineering company based in Bielsko-Biala, Poland. It presented this glassfibre-bodied open three-seater trike using a 652cc Fiat 126p as its mechanical basis.

Boss Hoss
USA • 1990-date • 1F2R • No built: n/a

Boss Hoss Cycles was established in Dyersburg, Tennessee in 1990 and made its name building Chevrolet V8-powered motorcycles and trikes, the latter sold under the BHC-9 label, and both Corvette LS-engined and ZZ4-powered models were offered. Easily the most charismatically styled models in its range had classic car style rear ends grafted on, such as 1957 Chevrolet and 1963 Corvette Sting Ray.

Bouffort City-Car
F • 1952 • 2F1R • No built: Probably 1

Having previously built the JB ⇨, aeronautical engineer Victor Bouffort went on to create a whole series of prototypes, none of which ever came to production, despite his best intentions. Two designs were three-wheeled. The first was an extremely small three-wheeler of ovoid appearance, with a rear-mounted Sachs engine and a single front headlamp.

Bouffort Enville
F • 1961 • 2F1R • No built: 1

Victor Bouffort's next three-wheeled effort was the Enville single-seater microcar which, like Bouffort's other city cars, had a Sachs engine. Extremely short, it featured a canopy that hinged forwards for entry.

Bowen Tricar
GB • 1957 • 1F2R • No built: Probably 1

Very little is known about this British-made three-wheeler which was powered by a rear-mounted 225cc engine.

BPG Uno III
CDN • 2011-date • 1F2R • No built: n/a

BPG Werks made the extraordinary DTV Shredder all-terrain machine, but its entry in this book is another equally unusual product. The Uno III was described as "the world's first transformer". In extended mode, it had three wheels, the rear pair sitting very close together to boost traction and stability. The front wheel had retractable forks, which at low speeds could bend up inside the bodywork to transform the Uno III into a type of unicycle, kept upright by gyroscopes and motion sensors. The all-electric machine was unveiled at the 2011 Consumer Electronics Show in Las Vegas, where a production run was announced.

BRA CX3 & MG3
UK • 1992-2007 • 2F1R • No built: Approx 130

John Berry and Peter Ibbotson were AC Cobra replica pioneers who also both owned Morgan trikes, which inspired their CX3 Super Sports (based on the Honda CX motorbike). The main body tub was in glassfibre, with the rest of the bodywork in aluminium or sheet steel. Distinguishing features included a barrel-tail and a centre-hinged aluminium bonnet. Kits retailed at £2200 in 1992. From 1996, the CX3 passed to BRA Engineering of Holywell, Wales (from 1998 renamed BRA Motor Works), which added 4in to the cockpit. A further variant was the BRA MG3, a Moto Guzzi-powered model, of which five were sold before the project passed to Aero Cycle Cars ⇨, which also took over production of the CX3 in 2007. There was also a Honda Pan European-engined variant.

BRA CV3
UK • 1998-2011 • 2F1R • No built: Approx 460

The CV3 was a new model by the Welsh owners of BRA, James Mather and David Wiles. Designed as a budget model around a modified Citroën 2CV chassis, it was powered by the 2CV's two-cylinder air-cooled 602cc engine.

BRA MR3
UK • 1999-2000 • 2F1R • No built: 2

This Metro-based variant of the CV3 actually started life as a 1994 one-off called the Mini Plug but was productionised by BRA. With its rather graceless front-end styling, it was not popular – only two were ever made.

Brissonet Soucoupe Roulante
F • 1953 • 2F1R • No built: Probably 1

Having brought the Speed scooter to market, Ets Brissonet (based in Neuilly) branched out into microcars with the Soucoupe Roulante ('rolling saucer') at the 1953 Paris Salon. A tiny doorless open-topped car weighing only 150kg, it was powered by a 200cc two-stroke engine with a three-speed gearbox.

Brogan
USA • 1946-1951 • 1F2R & 2F1R • No built: Approx 30

Beer pump manufacturer Frank Brogan set up B&B Specialty Co in Rossmoyne, Ohio to make a three-wheeler named after himself (some early models were sold under the name B&B Three Wheel). His first car was an extremely small (88in long) roadster with a single front wheel. A small Onan two-cylinder air-cooled 10bhp engine was rear-mounted, mated to a clutchless transmission. Both two- and four-seater versions were offered, the latter with the name Broganette. Light delivery three-wheelers were also made, as well as a three-wheeled sit-on two-passenger scooter. A later Brogan design had a single rear wheel.

Brooke 135
UK • 1994 • 2F1R • No built: 1

Toby Sutton's Brooke featured a central driving position and a head fairing that evoked a 1950s racer. The 135 tag referred to the number of seats (1), wheels (3) and the fact that the car was based on a Renault 5. After a showing at the 1994 Stoneleigh Kit Car Show, a four-wheeled version called the 245 was productionised, and the 135 remained unique.

Brookland Swallow
UK • 1993 • 2F1R • No built: 1

This peculiar beast was designed and built by kit car journalist Iain Ayre. The idea was to create a 1960s-style trike based on Mini parts, including Mini doors and, bizarrely, Volvo P1800 rear wings. The chassis was frankly oversized, and the four-passenger bodywork was too heavy to benefit from motorbike classification in the UK. The Brookland Motor Company therefore produced no more Swallows.

Brooklands 500
UK • 1997 • 2F1R • No built: Probably 1

Lloyd Pennington of Heyes Cycle Cars in Chorley, Lancashire built the Morgan-inspired Brooklands 500, which used Honda CX or Pan European power in a steel tube chassis with double wishbone front suspension.

BRP Can-Am Spyder
CDN • 2007-date • 2F1R • No built: Approx 30,000 (to 2013)

There are a handful of iconic three-wheelers that really set a precedent of huge significance: the Morgan, Isetta and Reliant to name but a few. The Can-Am Spyder can lay a strong claim to joining this elite. It was the brainchild of Bombardier, a major Canadian company behind such brands as Ski-Doo and Evinrude.

The Spyder in fact started life as a snowmobile concept that morphed into a road-going production trike. Bombardier Recreational Products (or BRP) created a whole language of its own for the Can-Am Spyder, which it described as "at the outer fringe of reality" and as having "the Y-Factor" (curiously, a phrased it trademarked). The 'Y' was a reference to the Surrounding Spar Technology (SST) chassis, which consisted of a steel beam encompassing the engine.

That engine was a Rotax 998cc V-twin DOHC water-cooled unit with 106bhp. Drive was by belt via a five-speed gearbox created specifically for the Spyder, with a mechanical reverse gear. A semi-automatic sequential gearbox was optional. ECUs monitored wheel slippage, bringing into action the stability and traction control systems, while other sophisticated elements included power steering and ABS. Dry weight was a mere

316kg (697lb), so performance was excellent.

The Spyder was a starkly open two-seater whose practicality was boosted by a 44-litre front storage box, and there was even an optional trailer. Prices started at $16,499 in the USA, and some 12,500 Spyders were sold in the first two years on the Valcourt, Québec assembly line, with the very first going to Jay Leno.

As well as the regular RS model, an RT version was added in 2010, with an electrically adjustable windscreen, touring seating and extra storage. An ST version (half-way between the RS and RT) was a good compromise of sportiness and comfort. Higher-spec versions with custom trim and different 15in wheels followed: the RS-S (which had Fox dampers) and the RT-S (with footboards and rear air suspension). A Hybrid petrol-electric version debuted at the 2011 Geneva Motor Show (pictured above) but this was still under development at the time of writing.

Brudeli 654L Leanster
N • 2007-date • 2F1R • No built: n/a

The Leanster was designed by Geir Brudeli of Hokksund, Norway. As its name suggested, it could lean into corners (at an angle of up to 45 degrees), and was born to be used as much on gravel surfaces as on-road. It was based on a KTM 690 Supermoto, with its 655cc, 63bhp single-cylinder engine, and weighing only 238kg, it could achieve a top speed of 106mph (170km/h). Prices started at 19,500 euros (around £17,000).

Brütsch 200 Spatz
D • 1954-1956 • 2F1R • No built: Approx 5

Egon Brütsch was one of the most prolific microcar designers of his day, but ultimately had little commercial success. His first three-wheeler project was the 200 Spatz ('sparrow'), a smoothly shaped three-seater roadster. A 191cc Sachs 10bhp single-cylinder engine sat in the tail. It had no chassis, relying solely on the strength of the plastic shell, and Brütsch seriously over-estimated its strength. The Spatz proved to be so weak that it cracked all too easily, leading a German judge to rule that the car should be banned. This Spatz later re-emerged as a much-modified four-wheeler, and was built in Switzerland as the Belcar ⇨ and in the Netherlands as the Hostaco Bambino ⇨.

Brütsch Zwerg
D • 1955-1957 • 2F1R • No built: 16

Zwerg means 'dwarf' in German, and this was a truly dwarf-sized car, measuring just 2200mm long in single-seater form and weighing a mere 98kg. It was made in both

one- and two-seater forms, the former with a 74cc DKW 3bhp single-cylinder engine, the latter with a variety of larger one-cylinder engines (191cc Sachs, 197cc or 247cc Victoria and 247cc Maico). In France this model was also made under the name Avolette ⇨.

Brütsch Mopetta
D • 1956-1958 • 1F2R • No built: 14

If the Zwerg was small, the Mopetta was positively Lilliputian – indeed, many have called it the world's smallest car, as it measured only 67in (1700mm) long, 34.7in (880mm) wide and 39in (1000mm) tall. With lightweight glassfibre bodywork, it also weighed just 134lb (61kg). Its 49cc Sachs engine sat exposed beside the left rear wheels and had to be kick-started. It developed a mere 2.3bhp, enough to give it an unhurried top speed of 27mph (45km/h). In appearance it resembled an egg in the process of hatching its one and only passenger.

The original publicity preposterously stated that the Mopetta could float in water. Georg von Opel (late of Opel) hoped to produce the car in series as the Opelit, but the project came to nought because the German authorities objected to its roadworthiness. Most Mopettas in fact were exported to the UK. Only 14 were ever made, but continuing fascination with the Mopetta has led to many replicas being made.

Brütsch Rollera
D • 1956-1958 • 1F2R • No built: 8

A slightly larger sister model to the Mopetta was the Rollera, which was 2100mm long and 1000mm wide, and tipped the scales at 85kg. It also had a larger engine: a 98cc Sachs one-pot motor developing 5.2bhp, enough for a top speed of 50mph (80km/h). Licensed production in France also took place.

Brütsch Bussard
D • 1956-1958 • 2F1R • No built: 11

The Bussard ('buzzard') very much resembled the original Spatz of 1954, although by now Brütsch had deigned to give it a steel tube chassis. It used the familiar 191cc Fichtel & Sachs 10bhp single-cylinder engine. Despite weighing 265kg, a top speed of 59mph (95km/h) was claimed.

BSA Ladybird
GB • 1959-1960 • 2F1R • No built: 2

Motorbike maker BSA famously made three-wheelers before the war (from 1929 until 1936), rivalling the Morgan but featuring front-wheel drive. BSA considered returning to car manufacture in 1959 with the Ladybird. Two prototypes were built, the first with a rounded tail and the second with a squarer tail and a removable hardtop. The extremely compact open two-seater bodywork was hand-formed using a single sheet of steel, and a Triumph Tigress 250cc vertical twin engine sat in the tail. Plans were afoot to sell the Ladybird for £285, but production was not approved. BSA later made the Ariel 3 ⇨.

Bubble Bike
CN • 2009-date • 1F2R • No built: n/a

This curious Jetsons-style machine could seat two people under a transparent canopy that flipped back for entry. It was tiny at 2000mm long and 1100mm wide, and its 600W electric motor provided a top speed of 28mph (45km/h). In 2013, it sold in China for the equivalent of £700.

Buchanan Tryker
USA • 1983-1987 • 2F1R • No built: Very few

From Carpentaria, California, Buchanan Auotmotive Technology offered the Tryker, a front-wheel drive device with an exposed motorbike engine up front (either two- or four-cylinder Yamaha) driving through

a modified Honda Accord front-drive unit in a box-section steel chassis. The classically-styled doorless roadster bodywork was realised in aluminium, and kits cost from $5250.

Buckland B3
GB • 1985-1999/2011-date • 2F1R • No built: 33 (to 2013)

Dick Buckland's B3 has been widely acknowledged as one of the best three-wheelers ever made. A Morgan trike owner, Buckland decided that he could improve on the old Mog. His Buckland B3 used a strong steel backbone chassis in which was housed a Ford Kent engine. The prototype used a 1300cc unit tuned to 95bhp, transmitting that power to the single rear wheel through an Escort gearbox and a specially-made propshaft and torque tube to a Reliant crown and pinion and

thence to a sprocket and chain. Production versions had front suspension by double wishbones, with a swinging arm and coil/spring damping at the rear.

Perhaps the B3's most unusual feature was its glassfibre bodywork: the entire main body tub hinged upwards just aft of the engine to reveal the rear suspension, while the one-piece bonnet hinged forwards to allow access to the engine and luggage area. The total weight of the B3 was 880lb (399kg), and it achieved a top speed of 130mph. The handling was widely praised in press reports.

Only 12 kits were built at workshops in Llanwern, Wales before a production pause in 1999, but the Buckland B3 eventually returned to the market in 2011 in Series 2 guise via Penguin Speed Shop, still based in Wales.

Budget Trikes
GB • 1969-date • 1F2R • No built: n/a

Lincolnshire-based Alan Cayliss made trikes from 1969, using Ford Sierra or Reliant Robin rear-end parts.

BugE
US • 2007-date • 2F1R • No built: n/a

Mark Murphy was behind BlueSky Design of Creswell, Oregon, which was involved with the NEVCO Gizmo ⇨. The later BugE was an even simpler car than the Gizmo, and was described by Murphy as "a Model T for the 21st century." Using a steel chassis and glassfibre body seating a single passenger, it measured 236cm (93in) long and weighed only 159kg (350lb). It was powered by a 48-volt DC motor with 17bhp, and its claimed range was 30 miles at a speed of 30mph, with a top speed of 50mph. The BugE was launched in kit form in 2012, priced at $3850, with the power unit costing an extra $1412.

Bullex JB1KWZK
CN • c2008-date • 1F2R • No built: n/a

Jinan Bullex Vehicle Co of Shandong made this fairly originally styled rickshaw-style vehicle with electric power courtesy of a 1kW motor and 48V lead-acid batteries. It could seat three people and reach a top speed of 21mph (35km/h).

Bullex JB150ZK
CN • c2008-date • 1F2R • No built: n/a

This enclosed trike could seat three people (including driver) in a 2710mm body. Power came from a 150cc single-cylinder engine.

Bullex JB250ZK / JB580ZK
CN • c2008-date • 1F2R • No built: n/a

Bullex's largest model could seat four and measured 3140mm long. To pull the greater weight (545kg), a 250cc engine with 16bhp was used and a top speed of 34mph (55km/h) was possible. A 5kW electric version was also offered as the JB5KWZK-1, and a larger-engined two-cylinder model was sold under the name JB580ZK-7.

Bünger
DK • 1947-1949 • 2F1R • No built: Probably 1

Engineer Borge Bünger from Odense, Denmark created a three-wheeled 'people's car' with the help of a coachbuilding company. The front end looked conventional, with a sloping coupe rear over the single rear wheel. A front-mounted 600cc Ilo two-cylinder 19bhp engine was fitted and a top speed of 56mph was claimed. Three people could be fitted in the rather cramped interior. No production run ensued.

ByBy
IND • 2012-date • 1F2R • No built: n/a

The ByBy was a very basic open rickshaw powered by an 850W 48V electric motor. Its metal bodywork made use of the front forks of a motorbike, and its roof was an unsophisticated concoction of canvas and tassels.

BykaTryka SK8
GB • 2006 • 1F2R • No built: n/a

No less prestigious an event than the 2006 British International Motor Show witnessed the launch of the BykaTryka SK8 'concept' three-wheeler. It used a Piaggio trike as its basis, keeping the 49cc engine and four-speed gearbox so that it could be driven as a moped by 16-year-olds in the UK. A larger version with a 218cc engine was also mooted but it's not known if this ever materialised.

THREE WHEELERS A-Z

Corbin Sparrow ▲

Campagna T-Rex ▲

Carver ▲

City-El ▲

▼ Cool City Eagle

C2C
USA • 2002 • 2F1R • No built: n/a

In 2002, Doug Malewicki – who had previously designed the AeroVisions California Commuter ⇨ – built the C2C (Coast to Coast) which was designed to traverse the USA from west to east on a single tank of fuel. Its two-seat tandem

enclosed bodywork was very aerodynamic, helping it achieve 125mph and 100mph. Six cars were planned to be built.

California Sidecar
USA • 1990s-date • 1F2R • No built: n/a

Ironically, California Sidecar (or CSC) was based not in California but in Arrington, Virginia, making a wide range of trike conversion kits. Its Harley-Davidson range encompassed the Daytona, Cobra, Custom and Volusia, the latter claiming to be inspired by Formula 1 technology (thanks to its vertically stabilised opposing rocker mono damper suspension). Honda-based trikes included the Viper, Sport, Cobra and Valkyrie; for Kawasaki there was the Kruze; for Victory the Ventura; and for Yamaha the Vantage.

Calleja
E • 1999 • 1F2R • No built: n/a

This was a motorbike-based tilting trike prototype by Carlos Calleja Vidal of Granada in Spain, but it was not made in series.

Campagna T-Rex
CDN • 1995-date • 2F1R • No built: Several hundred

The fact that high-performance three-wheelers became popular in the 1990s is perhaps almost entirely down to one of the most extreme trikes ever built: the Campagna T-Rex. Its striking design has been widely copied throughout the world. Campagna Motorsport was established by Daniel Campagna, the ex-mechanic of Formula 1 driver Gilles Villeneuve, who set up a factory in Plessisville, Quebec.

The T-Rex's dramatic glassfibre-and-carbon bodywork was designed by ex-Callaway stylist Paul Deutschman. It could seat two side-by-side, with practicality boosted by optional removable lockers (like motorcycle panniers) and an optional windscreen.

The T-Rex was a mid-engined trike using a steel tube chassis. The front suspension was by unequal opposed

triangular arms, and the rear swinging arm featured two dampers. Cross-drilled brake discs and four-piston front callipers made sure it stopped with gusto.

In its original form, the T-Rex was powered by a 1.1-litre four-cylinder motorcycle engine developing 155bhp, driving through a five-speed sequential gearbox. A mechanical reverse gear was also fitted, and the single rear wheel was driven by chain. A top speed of 130mph and 0-60mph in 4.3

seconds were claimed. Autocar said of the handling: "The short wheelbase and a surfeit of power over traction means you'll have to be quick and accurate with the opposite lock to avoid a spin."

The later 14R version used a Kawasaki 1352cc engine with 197bhp and six-speed gearbox, good for 144mph (230km/h) and 0-60mph in 3.9 seconds. An even more extreme 14RR track-orientated version weighed only 472kg (1040lb). A new model in 2013 was the T-Rex 16S (pictured above) with a 1.6-litre six-cylinder BMW bike engine rated at 160bhp. In 2011, Campagna also assumed production of the V13R trike from Cirbin ⇨.

Caprera Algol
I • 1969 • 1F2R • No built: 1

The Turin coachbuilder, Caprera, was active between 1959 and 1971, mostly building upgraded Fiats. Easily its strangest creation was the Algol, presented at the 1969 Turin Motor Show. This enclosed single-seater electric-powered trike was envisaged as a coin-operated taxi of the future. Needless to say, the future arrived with a notable absence of Algols.

Carter Model E/F/G
GB • 1936-1955 • 1F2R • No built: n/a

Carter was a pioneer of the invalid carriage industry, producing its first version, the Model A, in 1915, a tiller-steered electric trike which was basic in the extreme. The Model E and F had open bodywork and 24V and 36V batteries respectively, while the Model G offered weather protection for the driver's legs and a nearside door.

Carver
NL • 1997-2009 • 1F2R • No built: Approx 200

The idea of tilting three-wheelers has been a persistent one over several decades, but the Carver was one of very few designs that actually made production. Dutchman Chris van den Brink formed a company called Brink Dynamics, whose initial brief was to make an eco-friendly commuter vehicle, blending the comfort of a car with the agility of a motorcycle. The first prototype was completed in 1997, but there was a feeling that greater commercial success would come if the car was a leisure vehicle rather than a city car, so in 1998 the project changed direction.

A new company, Vandenbrink BV, was formed in Rotterdam in 1999, and the new Carver debuted at the Frankfurt Motor Show that year. However it would take until 2002 for the car to go on sale, priced at around £35,000. It even passed its EU homologation test.

Its steel chassis incorporated a single front arm with hydraulic damping and a MacPherson rear system with rear-wheel steering. The engine sat in its own 'pod' the rear: this was a Daihatsu turbocharged 659cc four-cylinder engine developing 64bhp, or an ECU upgrade was offered to boost power to 85bhp. As the car weighed only 620kg (1367lb), a top speed of 115mph (185km/h) was quoted, together with a 0-62mph (0-100km/h) acceleration time of 8.2 seconds.

The transmission was a five-speed manual with reverse gear. The single front wheel was larger than the rear wheels (17in versus 15in), and all wheels had ventilated disc brakes.

The Carver was just 1300mm (52in) wide and had an enclosed cockpit with tandem seating for two, accessed by a single door. The front section could lean into bends like a motorbike thanks to the hydraulic Dynamic Vehicle Control (DVC) system. At low speeds, the Carver remained almost upright but at higher speeds it could tilt up to 45 degrees, and could switch from hard left to hard right in under one second. Steering was by a conventional car steering wheel, and it was claimed to corner at the speed of a Porsche.

The company became Carver Europe from 2006, and the car was henceforth known simply as the Carver One. However the company went bust in 2009 having sold around 200 cars in all. The ideas that formed the Carver didn't end there though, as the tilting technology had been licensed to a US company called Persu ⇨ which hoped to launch its own tilting three-wheeler. Vandenbrink was also involved with the Phiaro ⇨, while the PAL-V ⇨ was an autogyro developed from the Carver.

Casalini Sulky

I • 1969-1987 • 1F2R • No built: Approx 20,000

Piacenza-based Giovanni Casalini founded his eponymous company in 1939, and made his name producing mopeds and three-wheeled trucks. In 1969 Casalini presented the surreally-named Sulky. This was a very basic two-seater

powered by a 50cc or 60cc engine. Unusually for the microcar class, it had steel rather than plastic bodywork, which was all straight lines, mounted on a tubular steel chassis.

As the model developed, it got two headlamps instead of one and the option of four wheels from 1980. Through the 1980s, Casalini was making as many as 1000 cars a year, helped by strong demand through the French importer (Willam). But, like most Italian micros, developments were too few to make it competitive with French micros and, by 1987, the three-wheeled Sulky was definitely looking down-in-the-dumps, so Casalini pulled the plug on it, but it continues to make four-wheeled microcars to this day.

Casarva

GB • 2005-date • 1F2R • No built: n/a

Peterborough-based Casarva Custom Conversions offered complete and kit-form trikes based on the Honda Valkyrie and Suzuki Intruder. A BMW E39 5 Series rear end was utilised.

CC Trikes

USA • 2000s-date • 1F2R • No built: n/a

Texas-based CC Trikes was run by Craig Whitford, who offered a Cadillac Northstar V8-powered trike called the Trizilla, which was claimed to be the lightest V8 trike on the market at

532kg (1174lb). A further model used a Volkswagen engine. All CC trikes featured glassfibre bodywork of an unusual and original style designed to appeal to the custom biker market.

CDM Triune

GB • 1983 • 2F1R • No built: Probably 1

In 1983 CDM showed a prototype of a car that could be transformed from a three-wheeler (called the Triune) into a four-wheeler (Pharos), but it was never productionised.

Cedre

F • 1974-1987 • 1F2R • No built: n/a

Virtually unique among French microcar makers, Toulouse-based Francois Guerbet's Cedre brand stuck with the three-wheel format to the bitter end, rather than switching to four wheels as almost all rivals did. Not only was the Cedre one of the first French 'sans permis' three-wheelers, it was also the last to leave production.

The first prototype, called the Soubrette, appeared in 1974. The Midinette appeared the following year, although production did not actually begin until 1979. This single-seater was little more than a shed on wheels with all-flat panels and sliding Perspex doors. Suspension was no more sophisticated than rubber blocks. The Cedre was unusual in being offered only with electric power, at a time when virtually all rivals had petrol or diesel power. Its 1200W motor could take it about 35 miles at a top speed of 31mph. Cedre finally accepted that demand for its cars was running flat in 1987.

CEL

IND • 1995-date • 1F2R • No built: n/a

As its name suggested, Continental Engines Ltd was an Indian manufacturer of engines, formed in 1987. CEL also had designs on the three-wheeler market with a range of cargo and passenger models. Rear-mounted engines were fitted, derived from VM

of Italy, and a top speed of 37mph (60km/h) was quoted.

Celimo

CN • 1995-date • 1F2R • No built: n/a

Celimo Vehicle Manufacturing of Jiangsu in China made basic electric rickshaw trikes like the QLM-JW600K and QLM-JW800K, which had 600W and 800W motors respectively.

Centaurus 400

BR • 1956 • 1F2R • No built: Very few

The Centaurus was the brainchild of two Brazilians, Renato Heinzelmann and Kleber de Araújo. It was a basic trike with a single-cylinder two-stroke air-cooled 400cc engine developing 12bhp above the front wheel, which it drove. A six-speed gearbox used an automatic clutch. Weighing 900kg, the makers claimed a top speed of 50mph (80km/h).

Ceres

USA • 1983 • 1F2R • No built: 10

A company called Creative Cars Corporation of Rockford, Illinois, conceived the Ceres. This was an original and for the most part well-designed glassfibre-bodied coupé whose aerodynamic coefficient of drag was claimed to be just 0.18. It was powered

by a rear-mounted Daihatsu Charade 993cc three-cylinder engine with 55bhp, good enough for a 90mph top speed, helped by a weight of 669kg (1475lb). The cabin seated three and had such luxuries as air conditioning, walnut dashboard, cassette player and leather seats. Despite advertising the car for $13, 875, only 10 prototypes were constructed because of the investment required to productionise it.

Cestar
CN • 2000-date • 1F2R • No built: n/a

The Shandong Cestar Electric Vehicle Co offered two three-wheeled models: the Sunset (apparently aimed at people at the end of their lives) and the Felstar. Both were electric-powered enclosed four-door cars.

C-Fee
T • 1999-date • 1F2R • No built: n/a

C-Fee (Clean Fuel Energy Enterprise) made one of Thailand's many tuk-tuk designs. Among its unique features were an electric motor, glassfibre-and-teak bodywork and larger-than-average passenger space thanks to a 3000mm overall  length. The 5.5bhp 48V electric drive system allowed a range of up to 50 miles (80km) and a top speed of 25mph (40km/h).

Chair-E-Yacht
USA • c1974-c1977 • 1F2R • No built: n/a

This device offered by a company from Shoshoni, Wyoming, allowed wheelchair users to drive at speeds of up to 15mph by mounting a three-wheeled frame with a petrol motor attached to the front wheel.

Champion
USA • 2000-date • 1F2R • No built: n/a

At the time of writing, Champion Trikes offered no less than 17 different 1F2R trike conversions for motorbikes. It started out making conversion kits for the Honda Gold Wing  GL1800 but branched out with Harley-Davidsons (Dyna, FL, Sportster and Softail), Honda VTX, Kawasaki Vulcan and Yamaha Road Star. Either a solid rear axle or fully independent suspension could be specified. Most models featured a large boot and extra over-wheel storage.

Chaowei
CN • 2000s-date • 1F2R • No built: n/a

 Chaowei Power was a company based in Zhejiang province in China, whose speciality was making electric tricycles of an exceedingly basic nature. The F and G models came with motors ranging from 500W to 2000W in power, while a Solar Electric model with 350W to 1500W was also offered.

Chapeaux
F • 1940-1941 • 2F1R • No built: 4

Emile Chapeaux made an original three-wheeler during WW2 from his base in Lyons. It was electric-propelled but a lack of raw materials scuppered the project. A plan to return to electric three-wheelers in 1968 also came to nothing.

Charabon
U • 1970s • 2F1R • No built: 1

 This was basically an old Heinkel bubble car modified by the Uruguayan Alfa Romeo concessionaire, albeit with different rear body styling. Production cars were to have had steel-reinforced glassfibre bodywork and a Tecnomoto 13bhp single-cylinder, two-stroke, air-cooled engine, but production never began.

Charbonneaux
F • 1970s • 1F2R • No built: 1

This three-wheeler from the celebrated designer Philippe Charbonneaux was created in collaboration with Compagnons Carrossiers du Devoir. Apparently it was realised only as a 1/1 scale model.

Cheetah
CH • 1992 • 1F2R • No built: 1

The Cheetah has the distinction of being designed by the celebrated eccentric, Luigi Colani, and was commissioned by Martin Kyburz to take part in the 1992 Solar Cup. It had a 30bhp  electric motor, could reach a top speed of 81mph (130km/h), and reputedly cost 80,000DM to develop. Kyburz later developed the DXP, a three-wheeled delivery vehicle used by the Swiss post office.

Cheetah
USA • 2000s-date • 1F2R • No built: n/a

Cheetah Trikes (built by Cheetah Choppers) used V8 engines and automatic transmission in a frame made of aluminium and stainless steel.

Cherban Urban Jet
USA • 2010-date • 1F2R • No built: n/a

Hailing from Newark, Delaware, the Cherban Urban Jet was an electric vehicle designed to top 150mph and reach 60mph in less than 3.5 seconds. Made of carbon-Aramid, it was very strong yet light at 350kg (770lb).

Chinnaraje
T • 2005-date • 1F2R • No built: n/a

This company, headquartered in Chiang Mai, was the leading manufacturer of rickshaws in Thailand. Two sizes

were offered: a standard size (3300mm x 1420mm) and King size (3500mm x 1500mm). Various body styles were available, the taxi versions bearing the model names Smile and Sawasdee. A three-cylinder Daihatsu 659cc engine and transmission were fitted, for a maximum speed of up to 43mph (70km/h). Electric-powered versions were also built.

Chongqing Union
CN • 1999-date • 1F2R • No built: Hundreds of thousands

Located in Chongqing, China, this company made motorcycles, ATVs, and scooters as well as tricycles (principally rickshaws of various styles with 110cc and 125cc engines, or electric power). As of 2012, it claimed to be making 250,000 three-wheelers per year.

Chuangtai
CN • 2010s • 1F2R • No built: n/a

The Chuangtai Motorcycle Co from Zhejiang built a scooter-based trike typical of Chinese mores, powered by a 200cc engine.

Church Pod
GB • 1998 • 2F1R • No built: 5

The Pod was the brainchild of Russell Church, who also made Messerschmitt replicas. A tubular spaceframe picked up Messerschmitt-inspired front suspension and handlebar steering, with most of the rest of the mechanicals coming from the rear half of a scooter, which was simply bolted to the back of the Pod's chassis. The glassfibre bodywork seated one person in a 'pod' up front, accessed by a gullwing door, with pillion passengers possible on the exposed scooter rear end. Any scooter from 50cc to 500cc was suitable as a donor.

Cicostar
F • 1980-1984 • 1F2R • No built: n/a

Made by a company called CICO in Limoges, the Cicostar was a quite smart microcar. Its enclosed glassfibre coupe bodywork seated two and was mounted on a steel chassis with independent front suspension. A single 10-inch front wheel was supplemented by two 8-inch rear wheels mounted on a solid axle. In three-wheeled guise it came with a 47cc Sachs rear-mounted engine (four-wheelers used 50cc Motobécane units), plus automatic transmission, enough to get the 165kg car to a top speed of 25mph (40km/h). A version was marketed as the Primo in Belgium.

CIMEM Girino / Motospyder
I • 1951-1955 • 2F1R • No built: n/a

The Girino was a tiny doorless open three-wheeler built in Milan. A rear-mounted Vespa single-cylinder engine with

4.5bhp and a three-speed gearbox drove the swinging rear wheel. It weighed 200kg and could travel at up to 32mph. Another prototype, the 1955 Motospyder (pictured), used a 125cc engine.

Cimera
E • 1954-1959 • 2F1R • No built: 3

José Bolinches, from Valencia, made his first three-wheeler in 1952: the Boli truck with a wooden box mounted up front. He intended his next vehicle (1954) to be a four-wheeled car, but the authorities didn't grant permission, so his prototype, named Cimera, ended up being a trike. This was a very small open-topped car, shortly followed by another convertible with plastic bodywork by a Valencian company called Samões. A final prototype had elements of the Pegaso sports car to it, but the founder's death in 1959 scuppered all plans of production.

Cimveco Hanma
HKC • 2000s-date • 1F2R • No built: n/a

This Hong Kong-based electric bicycle maker also produced very basic three-wheeled rickshaws with all-metal bodywork.

Cingolani
I • 1952 • 2F1R • No built: Probably 1

Ezio Cingolani of Recanati, Ancona, built this minute but handsome three-wheeled coupé using the mechanicals of a Vespa scooter, complete with its 125cc 3bhp single-cylinder engine and three-speed gearbox. Compact aluminium bodywork – only 2600mm (102in) long – kept weight down to a mere 119kg, giving it exceptional fuel economy and a top speed of 37mph (60km/h). An intended production run apparently never happened.

Cirbin V13R
CDN • 2006-date • 2F1R • No built: n/a

By 2006, Canada already had two major trike makers – Campagna ⇨ and BRP ⇨ – but a third was added when Cirbin Motors displayed the VT-Rod at the 2006 SEMA Show. This morphed into production as the Cirbin V13R. If the T-Rex was the equivalent of a Japanese banzai machine, the V13R was more like an all-American chrome express – indeed,

Cirbin described it as a "neo-retro hot-rod." Just in front of the rear wheel sat a Harley-Davidson Revolution V-Twin 1250cc engine, whose 125bhp drove

the rear wheel by chain via a bespoke sequential five-speed gearbox (plus mechanical reverse gear). Top speed was 122mph, with 0-60mph coming up in 5.6 seconds, helped by the fact that the V13R weighed only 524kg (1156lb). Suspension was by unequal opposed triangular arms with coil over dampers up front, and an adjustable motorbike monodamper at the rear. Rival Campagna ⇨ took over production of this fully open glassfibre-bodied two-seater in 2011, when the entry-level price was $47,999.

CityCar
USA/D • 1965 • 2F1R • No built: n/a

Leopold Garcia of Bernallio, New Mexico, designed the CityCar. Entry to the four-seater cabin was via a bottom-hinged single front door, while power came from a rear-mounted Wisconsin four-cylinder air-cooled engine (top speed: 60mph/97km/h). Production of the $995 runabout was due to start in Germany in 1966, but it's believed this never happened.

CityCom Mini-El / City-El
DK/D • 1987-date • 1F2R • No built: Approx 6000

The meagre Danish motor industry was given a huge fillip by this unlikely electric three-wheeler. CityCom launched its Mini-El with the intention of providing green transportation at low cost (at a time when most other electric cars were vastly expensive). It didn't matter if it was tiny, basic and uncomfortable – running costs were what mattered.

The Mini-El resembled a grown-up Sinclair C5 but it was in fact far better. Its electric propulsion was by a front-mounted 2.5kW or 3.6kW electric motor fed by three 12V batteries, powering the right-hand rear wheel only via a belt. A range of 30 miles and a top speed of 30mph were quoted. Later 'FactFour' models had four batteries, a more powerful 4kW motor and better performance.

An acrylic sandwich tub was topped by hinging upper bodywork, all built over an aluminium-and-steel chassis. Three distinct body styles were offered: enclosed, half-open and fully-open, all with seating for one adult plus a rear-facing child behind. Total weight was 280kg.

The original name of Mini-El had to be changed to City-El after Rover objected to the use of the name Mini. Citycom received a big boost in 1992 when a large batch of cars was used at the Barcelona Olympic Games. Despite this, the company went bankrupt and the tooling was removed, first to Sweden (where no production took place) and then in 1995 to Aub in Germany, where the City-El remains in production at the time of writing.

As well as being sold in the UK by CCSA Zero Emissions Vehicle at around £5500, a diesel-engined version called the Combidrive Mouse was made in Wales, powered by a 265cc oil-burning motor, which set a world record for fuel consumption of 568mpg.

City Mobile Micro
GB • 1980-1987 • 1F2R • No built: n/a

Dr Edmund Jephcott's City Mobile Micro commuter car was one of the earliest tilting three-wheelers ever made. Its narrow (30in/762mm wide) enclosed glassfibre body was designed by Richard Oakes and had one side door only. The patented tilting mechanism was initially mechanically operated by pedals but was later modified to a damped pendulum system because of weight factors. Its maximum tilt angle was 25 degrees, and at the time it was claimed to be more stable than a four-wheeled car. At least two different mid-mounted engines were tried: initially a 75cc, 4bhp scooter engine but later a 350cc snowmobile unit with 12bhp, driving through an automatic gearbox to the rear wheels. Despite some interest from Honda, Jephcott never got a backer to put the car into production.

Claeys-Flandria Mobilcar
B • 1979-1980 • 2F1R • No built: n/a

Belgium's best-known motorcycle company dipped its toe in the microcar market with the short-lived Mobilcar, which was offered as a three-wheeled saloon and a four-wheeled convertible, both with polyester bodywork only 2200mm long. It featured coil spring suspension and a 49cc air-cooled 3bhp engine that could eke it to 25mph (40km/h).

CLEVER
D/GB • 2006-date • 1F2R • No built: 5

The CLEVER (Compact Low Emission VEhicle for uRban transport) was a collaboration between several partners, principally BMW, Berlin's Technical University and the University of Bath, and it had the distinction of receiving funding from the EU. In many ways the CLEVER recalled the Carver ⇨ in that it was a narrow-bodied tilting three-wheeler, but its message was more environmental than sporty.

Measuring a mere 1000mm wide and weighing less than 400kg, the CLEVER was certainly economical. The 17bhp single-cylinder 230cc engine (mated to a CVT transmission) used compressed natural gas as fuel, and some 188mpg

was claimed, along with a top speed of 62mph (100km/h) and 0-62mph in 7.0 seconds. The range wasn't huge, though, at 124 miles (200km).

The driver and passenger sat in tandem in an aluminium space frame 'survival cell'. The first of five prototypes was built in 2006, and BMW hinted that any production version would cost around the $10,000 mark. The leaning system developed for the car was called Direct Tilt Control (DTC), in which hydraulic actuators tilted the cabin; the rear-mounted engine sat in its own non-tilting capsule. It would tilt by up to 45 degrees, but it proved unstable and as of 2013, research was still progressing on the car and its tilt mechanism. Steer-by-wire was also being investigated (the original system was a novel H-shaped swing-arm system).

Cobra Trike
D • 1990s • 1F2R • No built: n/a

In an age when the whole kit car world seemed to be making copies of Lamborghinis, a company called Cobra-Freizeitfahrzeugbau in Bad Oeynhausen made a bizarre chopper trike with a Lamborghini Countach-style rear end.

Cock Cockpit 70
NL • 1970 • 1F2R • No built: Probably 1

Dutch truck maker Cock produced a four-wheeled microcar prototype in 1968 before returning in 1970 with a three-wheeler. A Sachs 50cc two-stroke engine powered the rear wheels via chain, or electric drive was mooted. The Cockpit 70 measured only 2070mm long, and the two seats swivelled to ease access. Cock was later involved with the Witkar ⇨.

Cocotaxi
C • 2000s-date • 1F2R • No built: n/a

Anyone who has been to Havana in Cuba will have seen curious yellow motorised eggs plying the streets. The so-called Cocotaxi was a cheap-to-hire Cuban rickshaw, most often with globular-shaped glassfibre bodywork, mounted over a 75cc two-stroke engined moped transformed into a three-wheeler. There was space behind the driver for two passengers.

Colenta
D • 1985-1986 • 1F2R • No built: n/a

This was an electric three-wheeler built near Frankfurt, Germany by Colenta-Mobil, a company that later made a name for itself in electric vans. It had open, doorless plastic bodywork that could carry either passengers or goods.

Collicar/Colliday
GB • 1960s-1970s • 1F2R • No built: 5

Sutton Coldfield-based Bob Collier built some five microcar prototypes but none ever made production (although the intention was always there). One was a 273cc Briggs & Stratton industrial-engined car with infinitely variable belt gearing, whose only on-board controls were the steering wheel and 'stop' and 'go' pedals; braking came on automatically as the vehicle slowed. Another design used a 350cc Kohler engine which could be swivelled through 360 degrees, in unit with the single front wheel.

Comet
USA • 1946-1948 • 1F2R • No built: n/a

The new *Comet* Convertible

The General Developing Company of Ridgewood, New York offered this very basic open car, which has the distinction of being the first plastic-bodied car ever to be marketed – although whether any were actually built is less certain. The brainchild of an eccentric called Julius Rose, it measured 2895mm (114in) long yet weighed just 77.5kg (171lb). Its rear-mounted 4.5hp air-cooled engine drove the rear wheels at very low speed, but 100mpg was claimed. It was advertised at just $320, but Rose became mired in court cases and the Comet (and a three-wheeled truck, the Marvel) departed, never to return.

Condor-Puch
CH • 1950s • 1F2R • No built: n/a

Condor was a Swiss company based in Courfaivre which made two-wheeled motorcycles and bicycles from 1893 right up until 1995. The Condor-Puch 125cc-engined scooter was also offered in three-wheeled form in the 1950s.

Conquest
GB/USA • 2007-date • 1F2R • No built: n/a

The Conquest (originally launched as the Martin Conquest) was a wheelchair motorcycle for the disabled, created by Alan Martin in the UK as a wheelchair-accessible motorbike conversion for his son. After production in Britain came to an end in 2010, the Conquest migrated to Akron, Ohio, where Mobility Works continued production. Based on a BMW 1170cc motorbike, it could do 0-60mph in 7.6 seconds.

Cool City Eagle
USA • 2004-date • 1F2R • No built: n/a

Cool City, Inc. was formed in 2000 to make a trike called the Eagle Sport Trike, which it launched in 2004. It was powered by a GM 3.4-litre V6 engine mated to a four-speed automatic transmission with overdrive. An Active Roll Control system for the rear suspension was claimed to maintain a level body in corners. Disc brakes on all three wheels kept the braking stable, while the steering was by an 'aircraft-style' oblong steering wheel that housed an electronic display. The open-topped car (with optional roof) could seat two people in tandem. Other models planned but not productionised included the Gladiator and the V8-powered Double Eagle.

Cooper T47
GB • 1958 • n/a • No built: n/a

Very little is known about the celebrated Cooper Car Company's apparently abortive Cooper-Anzani three-wheeled road car project of 1958.

Corbin Sparrow
USA • 1996-2003 • 2F1R • No built: Approx 350

The Corbin Sparrow garnered a lot of publicity as it was one of few electric cars of its time that was widely available commercially. Created by Mike and Tom Corbin who had built up a motorcycle seat business in California, it was a tiny single-passenger commuter vehicle that was classified as a motorcycle in the USA.

A top speed of 75mph and a range of up to 60 miles was claimed, possibly optimistically. Its electric motor put out up to 40bhp and was

fed by some 13 12V batteries, sending its power via cog belt drive. The suspension was a by double wishbone front end and a single rear swinging arm.

In construction, the Sparrow was a glassfibre monocoque formed of two sections glued together with polyurethane foam injected in. Overall weight was 612kg (1350lb), while it measured 2440mm (96in) long and 1320mm (52in) wide. Luxuries included electric windows, CD player and a heater.

The first prototype, dubbed Alpha Sparrow, debuted at the 1996 San Francisco Auto Show, where it was well received, but production by Corbin Motors did not begin until 1999. Despite talk of thousands being built, production difficulties, mechanical issues and financial problems forced Corbin into bankruptcy in 2003 after only 285 Sparrows had flown the nest. Myers Motors ⇨ would later build around 70 more from left-over parts under its own name.

Corbin Merlin
USA • 2001-2003 • 2F1R • No built: 12

Corbin's second model was the 2001 Merlin. Unlike the Sparrow, this was not powered by electricity, but by a petrol engine – a 102bhp Harley-Davidson V-twin driving the front wheels through a Volkswagen four-speed gearbox. Designed as a sporty vehicle rather than a commuter, the front suspension was by coil/over dampers and wisbones up front and a single-sided swinging arm at the rear. Both coupe and roadster versions were developed, the former never reaching production and the latter hardly so – some 12 chassis and associated components were built before Corbin entered bankruptcy, but few customers, if any, received their $23,900 cars.

Corbin Raven
USA • 2007 • 2F1R • No built: Probably 1

In 2007 Mike Corbin came back with a new project that recalled many aspects of the Merlin: the Raven. Like the Merlin, it used a V-twin powerplant, giving it a claimed 150mph and over 100mpg. One big difference over earlier Corbins was the addition of rear-wheel steering (making this a three-wheel-steer car), as well as scissor doors. The less complex construction and planned production in China would have kept the asking price down to less than $12,000, said Corbin, but apparently no production run ensued.

Corda
S • c1985-c2003 • 1F2R • No built: n/a

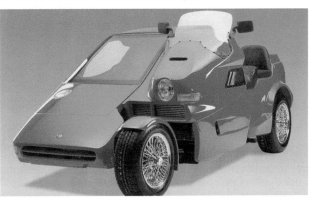

Sidecars don't form part of this book, but Wolfgang Rabe's extraordinary Corda is an exception. That's not just because it looked a bit like a car; nor because so many car parts were used; it's more that all three wheels were driven (by chain and belt). A number were built in the Swedish town of Falkenberg, with high prices (around £20,000), most of which were fitted with a VW turbodiesel engine and automatic transmission, although some used Volvo power. A German company called Blackbull planned to market a 21st century version of the Corda (pic right), but as of the time of writing this appeared to be a plan only, with no cars actually built.

Coronet
GB • 1957-1960 • 2F1R • No built: Approx 250

The Coronet represented an attempt to offer full-size car refinements in a microcar package, and indeed it was immodestly advertised by the manufacturer as "the world's best three-wheeler." An open two-to-three-seater designed

by the prolific David Gottleib, it was manufactured in Denham, Bucks, although production eventually devolved to the coachbuilders, James Whitson & Co of West Drayton, which also made the glassfibre bodywork. The Coronet's chassis employed suspension and steering taken from the Standard 8 saloon, while a 328cc Excelsior two-cylinder 18bhp engine was fitted in front of the single rear wheel, together with a three-speed Albion gearbox with reverse gear, driving the rear wheel. The 368kg (812lb) car boasted a top speed of 57mph (92km/h). Despite its attractive styling, the Coronet enjoyed limited commercial success because of its high price.

Corsair
USA • c1987-date • 1F2R • No built: n/a

John Edwards founded Corsair Trikes, offering a wide variety of fairly original chopper-style designs from his base in Beaumont, California.

Cosmopolitan
D • 1990s • 1F2R • No built: n/a

This was a typical chopper trike from Germany, so naturally it had VW Beetle power. It weighed 500kg when empty.

Covco ZEMF / MicroMax
ROK • 2001 • 1F2R • No built: n/a

Covco was a Korean company that made a range of city vehicles, including three-wheelers. The ZEMF was a microcar seating two in tandem. Its four 12V batteries allowed a range of 35 miles (60km) and a top speed of 45mph (70km/h), and it measured only 990mm

wide and weighed 300kg. The MicroMax was another tandem two-seater trike that was longer but even narrower (950mm wide) – resulting in a claim that it was the world's narrowest enclosed car. A scissor door on one side allowed it to be parked very close to other cars. It was powered by a 255cc engine and had a four-speed gearbox, but its main claim to fame was its ATCS (Active Tilt Control System) that let it lean into corners.

Cozine
USA • 2003 • 2F1R • No built: Probably 1

Ken Cozine from Cozine Design made this motorcycle-engined trike in 2003, but little is known about it.

Creation Customs
GB • 1990s • 1F2R • No built: n/a

This Dorset-based company made typical motorbike-based trikes based on models such as the Yamaha Dragstar.

Creative Engineering Jutta
USA • 1974 • 1F2R • No built: Probably 1

Creative Engineering of Orlando, Florida was all set to put the Jutta into production, until the car's creator, Aaron Fechter, switched careers, becoming an animator for the amusement park industry. Had the two-seater made production at an intended $1500, its 12bhp Tecumseh mower engine would have delivered 90mpg and 55mph, and would have had enclosed glassfibre bodywork, but only a running bare chassis was ever made.

Cricket

USA • 1970s • 2F1R • No built: n/a

The Cricket was made by Fleming MFG of Jackson, Michigan and was a tiny minibike-style three-wheeler powered by a 5bhp Briggs & Stratton engine.

Crosley

USA • 1940-1941 • 1F2R • No built: Very few

Powell Crosley started making simple economy cars in 1939, but as part of the war effort, he built a handful of three-wheeled prototypes. The front end was shared with an abortive Crosley motorcycle, and it used Crosley's air-cooled flat two-cylinder engine.

Crossbow

CDN • 2008-date • 2F1R • No built: n/a

A company called Jesler Enterprises of Peterborough, Ontario was behind the Crossbow. The prototype was powered by a Kawasaki 1100cc engine with 140bhp but other units could be used. Weighing 445kg (980lb), the claimed 0-60mph time with the Kawasaki unit was 4.4 seconds. A tubular steel chassis housed the engine up front, driving the single rear wheel. All the controls were of the standard motorcycle configuration. The original rounded glassfibre bodywork was later modified to a more stripped-down look.

Crossbow

USA • 2012-date • 2F1R • No built: n/a

A website called DIY Den offered a plans set for a trike called the Crossbow. Any road superbike could be used as the basis from 600cc to 1100cc, but the Yamaha R1 was recommended. The engine fitted into the front of a square-tube steel chassis. Innovative 'reverse roll' suspension was claimed to provide very sharp handling, while performance from the 300kg machine was equally sharp.

Cushman

USA • 1936-date • 2F1R & 1F2R • No built: Thousands

The Cushman Motor Works of Lincoln, Nebraska began making three-wheeled light delivery vehicles in 1936, which remained its main stock in trade for many years. Early vehicles were essentially motorbikes with two front wheels. Cushman branched out into the passenger-carrying market with cars like the Personnel and Golfster, available in both petrol and electric-powered versions. As Cushman's designs

progressed, it switched to a single front wheel format, allowing larger engines to be fitted. Cushman also became famous for supplying three-wheelers to US police departments.

Custer Chair

USA • 1916-1960 • 1F2R • No built: n/a

Levitt Lucern Custer had worked with aircraft pioneers, the Wright brothers, and so was fittingly a pioneer of mobility vehicles for wounded soldiers from WWI. The Custer Specialty Company offered disabled cars with both electric and petrol power for 44 years.

THE CUSTER SPECIALTY CO.

Custom Trikes

USA • 1977-date • 1F2R • No built: n/a

Custom Trikes Inc of Phoenix, Arizona was one of the longest-lived chopper trike manufacturers in the world. It started making traditional

choppers powered by VW Beetle engines mounted in the rear, and at the time of writing, its trike range consisted of five models: Scorpion, Stallion, Stinger, Spider and Streak.

Cy-Car TigerCat 3V2

USA • 2012-date • 2F1R • No built: n/a

This exo-skeletal two-seater trike used a Harley-Davidson V-twin engine (or other V-twin) driving through a Toyota pick-up truck gearbox, plus suspension by rubber torsion springs with telescopic dampers all round. The TigerCat 3V2 was earmarked to retail for $35,000 fully built.

Cyclone

CDN • 1997-1998 • 2F1R • No built: 1

The Cyclone was a performance trike created by Eric Bellavance, Bruno Miron and Benoit Ouellette of the School of Industrial Design at the University of Sherbrooke, and

University of Montreal students. It used a snowmobile engine and could do 124mph (200km/h) and 0-62mph in 6.5 seconds.

THREE WHEELERS A-Z

DDD

David ▲

Davis Divan ▲

▼ Dolphin Vortex

DA Mongoose
GB • 1994 • 2F1R • No built: Probably 1

The Mongoose was the brainchild of David Arthur, who ran an engineering firm in Warrington. Its box section spaceframe chassis incorporated front wishbones and a rear double-sided swinging arm. Various mid-mounted motorbike engines, or diesel or electric units, could be fitted, with drive to the rear wheel by shaft, chain or toothed belt. However, only one chassis was ever shown; the intended glassfibre-and-aluminium tandem two-seater body apparently never materialised, and nor did the kit at £2300.

D & A Minikin
GB • 1983-1986 • 2F1R • No built: 17

D & A Vehicles of St Cloud, Minnesota produced this development of the H-M Freeway ⇨. It kept that car's 16bhp 453cc Tecumseh engine and chain drive to the single rear wheel, but had larger bodywork that could seat two rather than just one. The  price was $4490 but the slender attractions of the Minikin hardly justified that cost, and it didn't last long.

DAF
NL • 1942 • 1F2R • No built: 1

Huub van Doorne (who founded DAF with his brother) developed this three-wheeled prototype during the early years of WW2. Nicknamed either the Dafke or Regenjas ('raincoat'), it had a 125cc two-stroke engine and was extremely narrow at just 750mm wide. A production series of 1000 units was planned at a price of 325 florins, but this never happened, and the one and only car made ended up in the hands of a circus clown. It's now on display at the DAF Museum.

Dafeng
CN • 2000s • 1F2R • No built: n/a

This was an electric rickshaw seating three people, with an 800W motor enabling a top speed of 22mph (35km/h).

Daifo

CN • 2000s • 1F2R • No built: n/a

Guangdong Daifo Motorcycle made small scooter-based trikes such as the DF100ZK.

Daihatsu 750

J • Early 1950s • 1F2R • No built: n/a

Daihatsu (under its predecessor title of Hatsudoki Seizo) started building three-wheeled delivery vehicles as early as 1930, and after WW2 it continued offering various body styles, including a rickshaw type. Powered by a 736cc air-cooled single-cylinder side-valve engine with just 14.5bhp, it could seat five passengers. Its three-speed gearbox worked via a shaft drive to the rear axle.

Daihatsu Bee

J • 1951-1952 • 1F2R • No built: Approx 300

Daihatsu's first true passenger car was the Bee, which was based on a commercial vehicle chassis. Power came from a rear-mounted 804cc 'boxer' two-cylinder air-cooled engine. It was quite big at 4080mm long and heavy (960kg) so the top speed was 49mph (78km/h). The enclosed two-door saloon bodywork seated four, and was popular as a taxi, because local laws allowed a cheaper meter rate than four-wheelers.

Daihatsu Midget

J • 1957-1972 • 1F2R • No built: 336,534

STATION WAGON TYPE

"Station wagon" used as a 4-passen

The Midget was primarily a commercial vehicle. However, passenger-carrying bodywork was made for it, albeit marginally. Daihatsu continued to make three-wheeled delivery vehicles as late as 1972, while vehicles based on this design were still being made in Thailand at the time of writing.

Daihatsu Hallo / ES38V

J • 1974-1975 • 1F2R • No built: n/a

After BSA lost faith with George Wallis's Ariel 3 ⇨, he sold a licence to Daihatsu, which developed the Hallo tilting trike based on his ideas. Effectively it was a three-wheeled scooter with the two rear wheels mounted in a subframe, which also contained the 50cc engine. It was pricey at 179,000 yen, however, so was short-lived. An electric version called the ES38V was also offered with two 12V batteries giving a range of 30km at speeds of 30km/h (19mph).

Daihatsu BC-7

J • 1989 • 1F2R • No built: Probably 1

Daihatsu made a whole string of electric prototypes, mostly four-wheelers. Its 1989 effort was the BC-7, a three-wheeled single-seater with an open-sided, roofed glassfibre body measuring only 2000mm long. Its electric motor powered the car to a top speed of 31mph (45km/h).

Dajiang DJ150

CN • 2010s • 1F2R • No built: n/a

Chongqing Dajiang mostly made motorcycles and generators but it also offered an enclosed three-wheeler passenger car. The DJ150 weighed 520kg, so its 150cc engine struggled to deliver a top speed of 43mph (70km/h).

Dale

USA • 1974-1975 • 2F1R • No built: 3

The extraordinary story of the Dale begins with a woman – Elizabeth Carmichael – who was in fact a transgender man who had been born as Jerry Dean Michael. She founded the grandly named Twentieth Century Motor Car Corp in California and proceeded to concoct some outlandish claims for her Dale three-wheeler. Among them was that it used no wiring (only a printed circuit board), that it was "safer to handle than four-wheeled vehicles" and that the "space age" Dale was "the best car ever built."

The spec sheet did look promising. There was to be a purpose-designed two-cylinder two-stroke air-cooled rear-mounted engine producing 40bhp, 70mpg and 85mph. The two-seater self-coloured glassfibre body was said to be so strong that it could withstand sledgehammer blows.

In fact the engine fitted to the only car that ever ran was an 850cc Onan two-cylinder unit normally seen in generators. Carmichael claimed that sales of three million units would be achieved for a car costing $2000 a piece, but in the event only three prototypes were ever made. A planned five-seater version called the Revelle and commercial trike called the Vanagen never materialised. As for Carmichael, she ended up in jail on fraud charges.

Dalong

CN • 2005-date • 1F2R • No built: Hundreds of thousands

Jinan Dalong Vehicle Industry was the new name for the major Chinese company Qingqi ⇨, which by 2009 ranked in the top 15 motorcycle brands for sales in China. Dalong claimed to have over 100 different three-wheeler models on sale in its home territory at the time of writing. Engine sizes available included 50cc, 100cc, 110cc, 125cc, 150cc and above, while the factory boasted a production capacity of up to 500,000 units per year.

Danger Autino

D • 1947-1949 • 2F1R • No built: n/a

This very small car, intended for disabled people, had one very odd feature: its open doorless bodywork hinged forwards to provide access to the single seat. The Autino was powered by a 125cc Ilo engine that sat over the front axle.

Danson

USA • 2005-date • 1F2R • No built: n/a

Danson Trikes produced bolt-on trike kits for larger (400cc-650cc) scooters such as the Suzuki Burgman 400 and 650, Honda Silverwing 600 and Yamaha Majesty 400.

Darmasai

IND • 2010-date • 1F2R • No built: n/a

Darmasai Motors of Chennai, Tamil Nadu made electric autorickshaws with a 3kW motor mounted in a ladder chassis. A top speed of 26mph (42km/h) was claimed for the open-topped rickshaw, which could seat three passengers plus the driver.

D Art Hagane

J • 2008-date • 2F1R • No built: n/a

D Art of Hiromi Seki-city in Japan made a tilting three-wheeler called the Hagane, which used a proprietary D Art two-wheeled front end mated to a Yamaha Majesty scooter with a 250cc 19bhp engine. It could tilt up to 30 degrees, and was stopped by Brembo front brakes. An optional kit for disabled drivers gave it a reverse gear too.

D Art Style

J • 2011-date • 2F1R • No built: n/a

D Art's Style was an original-looking trike powered by electricity. It was minute, weighed only 30kg and seated only one person. It could run for around 20km at speeds 25km/h, and cost the equivalent of $6500.

Daulon

F • 1950 • 2F1R • No built: 1

This cigar-shaped single-seater three-wheeler was created by M. Daulon in collaboration with the coachbuilder Gordia. It was powered by a Villiers 250cc single-cylinder two-stroke engine, later changed to a JAP 350cc.

Daus M6

D • 1956 • 2F1R • No built: n/a

By the 1950s, Otto Daus had retired from Tempo ⇨ but he continued working on amphibious prototypes with Tempo. Several examples were built and assessed by the German army, but not pursued. Only one example survives today.

David

E • 1950-1957 • 1F2R • No built: n/a

David Autos of Barcelona had been making vehicles since 1914, but the first post-war David was an extremely simple three-wheeled microcar with a steel tube frame and independent front suspension by a telescopic fork. The usual bodywork was a basic open style that was designed for the driver to sit centrally with either luggage or two passengers behind, though later designs had more conventional side-by-side seating. Initially a 175cc single-cylinder engine drove the single front wheel by chain but later a 345cc unit was substituted. In this form, in a car weighing only 280kg, it could reach 47mph (75km/h). The David was a popular choice among Spanish economy car buyers.

Davis Divan

USA • 1947-1949 • 1F2R • No built: 17

The story of Gary Davis's extraordinary three-wheeler reads like a work of fiction. It started when he acquired a three-wheeled open-topped prototype called the Kurtis-Thorne Californian ⇨ in 1947 and saw in it a great opportunity to make money. Having founded the Davis Motorcar Co in Van Nuys, California, Davis set about revolutionising the motoring world with a three-wheeler that was presented as an advanced, aircraft-inspired, high-technology car.

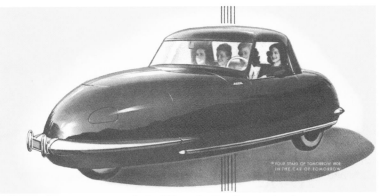

DC Design Rickshaw
IND • n/a • 1F2R • No built: Probably 1

Dilip Chhabria founded an Indian legend when he set up DC Design in Mumbai in 1993. Of the dozens of designs he came up with, only one was a three-wheeler: an updated version of the Indian autorickshaw.

DD
VN/MA • 1949-1950 • 1F2R • No built: 42

Frenchman Marcel Degant had a plan to replace Vietnamese rickshaws, whose passengers were carried ahead of the driver, with a safer vehicle. He hired Louis Descloitre to design a small open three-wheeler powered by a 125cc Jonghi engine, with the driver sitting solo up front using handlebars, and space for two passengers behind. Only six cars were built in Saigon, before Degant decamped for Marrakech in Morocco, where a further 36 cars were made. Financial problems caused in part by Degant's alcoholism ended the project prematurely.

The reality was somewhat different. By three-wheeler standards, the Davis was massive, measuring 185in (4700m) long and weighing 1111kg (2449lb). The first cars were powered by 2.2-litre 46bhp Hercules four-cylinder engines, but later models came with 2.6-litre 57bhp Continental units. Davis claimed a top speed of 116mph and 30mpg, but these claims were rather fanciful – tests indicated 65mph and 28mpg were closer to the mark.

The car was so wide that four people could be seated side-by-side on the single bench seat (Davis's extravagant claims stated five passengers). The bodywork was in aluminium over a steel chassis, and a standard feature was a removable hard top. Pick-up and 'woody' estate body styles were also mooted but never built.

Davis claimed that his car would do sharp U-turns at 55mph, but attempts to do this in fact resulted in the rear driving wheel lifting off the ground and spinning freely (thus indicating a higher speed on the speedometer). Excessive weight over the front wheel and a top-heavy centre of gravity resulted in the car being quite unstable.

The Davis was scheduled to sell at $1400 in 1949 (rather expensive at that time) but production never began, despite Davis selling franchises to the tune of around $1 million. Combined with financial irregularities, Davis ended up in jail and was obliged never to re-enter the car business. Some 17 prototypes had been built by then.

There was an attempt by some ex-franchise holders to revive the project under the aegis of a new operation, the Delta Motor Car Company, which tried to get Reliant in the UK to build the car, but this never got off the ground. Gary Davis apparently hoped to develop another three-wheeler, the Interceptor safety vehicle, in the 1960s.

Davis 494
USA • 1948 • 1F2R • No built: 3

A curious adjunct to the Davis Motorcar story was the creation of a three-wheeled jeep as a potential military vehicle. The Pentagon actually ran tests on the Davis 494 at the Aberdeen Proving Grounds in Maryland, but no more than three examples were built.

Dayang
CN • 2000s-date • 1F2R • No built: n/a

Shandong Dayang Automotive was based in Jining in Shandong Province, making a wide range of electric vehicles. The Dayang SDDY DY-102 E-Bike, for example, was an enclosed electric tricycle that could seat three people. Power came from a 350W electric motor powering the rear wheels, and a range of up to 28 miles (45km) was claimed. The price was very low indeed – the equivalent of $760 in 2012. Dayang also made several rickshaw models with electric power.

Decolon
F • 1957 • 2F1R • No built: n/a

The Decolon grew out of the ashes of the PB ⇨. With its dumpy open glassfibre bodywork, the shape drew on the company's main business, which was making fairings for motorcycles. The Decolon was powered by a two-stroke Ydral air-cooled 5bhp 125cc or 10bhp 175cc engine mounted in the rear, driving the single rear wheel by chain, while a 250cc version was also mooted. However, it was priced too high for an economy car.

DECSA Lisa
RSM • 1982-1987 • 1F2R • No built: n/a

San Marino's first ever car manufacturer, DECSA, made the Lisa which was effectively a restyled FIAM Johnny Panther ⇨. Its two-seater glassfibre body housed a choice of 50cc and 123cc single-cylinder engines or a 250cc twin. Both three- and four-wheeled versions were built. Sales in Germany (where it was called the ATW Microcar Lissy) and in France (under the aegis of Willam) helped production continue until 1987.

Defiant EV3

USA • 2009-date • 1F2R • No built: n/a

Shockwave Motors was the company behind the Defiant EV3 electric car. This was a strange-looking three-seater trike with no doors and an open roof. The production version (still to be launched as of 2013) was to be called the Predator EV3, and included a roof and doors. The makers claimed a top speed of over 75mph, a range of 100 miles and the equivalent of 225mpg, and anticipated a retail price of under $25,000.

Deltamobil

D • 1954-1955 • 2F1R • No built: Approx 20

Looking something like a fairground dodgem car, the Deltamobil hailed from Munich. In the rear end sat an Ilo 197cc engine with 9.5bhp and three-speed gearbox. This enabled the 310kg two-seater to reach 50mph (80km/h), or even faster in later spec with a 250cc engine fitted. The open-topped bodywork was made of aluminium, while the seats were, oddly, made of fabric-covered inflatable rubber.

DEMM

I • 1952-1962 • 1F2R • No built: n/a

DEMM was a contraction of Daldo e Matteucci, a Milanese maker of motorcycles and three-wheeled delivery vehicles with single-cylinder two-stroke engines of between 50cc and 172cc, which drove the rear wheels by shaft through a four-speed gearbox. Some passenger versions of these trikes were also made, two of which are pictured left.

De Vos

NL • 1941 • 2F1R • No built: n/a

Having made racing cars before WW2, AJ de Vos turned to an electric-powered car during the war, which was adapted from a child's pedal car.

DFT

USA • 2000s-date • 1F2R • No built: n/a

The DFT range was made by Doc's Harley-Davidson of Addison, Illinois. The rear end conversion was fully independent, weighed 79kg (175lb) and could be applied to any Harley-Davidson FL, Sportster or Softail from 1985 onwards.

DG Phoenix

GB • 1982-2000 • 1F2R • No built: Approx 420

The very American phenomenon of the chopper trike was an unlikely export to Britain. Wellingborough-based DG Motors was one of the more successful UK operators with its Phoenix. This boasted a simple steel chassis, basic glassfibre bodywork, motorbike front forks and a VW Beetle rear engine. Models with seating for two, three or four passengers were offered in various kit-form stages.

Dibla 7

I • 1968 • 1F2R • No built: n/a

Rosario Di Blasi experimented with folding scooters before showing, at the 1968 Turin Auto Show, the Dibla 7 folding three-wheeler. When folded, it was no bigger than a suitcase (920mm x 390mm x 480mm) and even when opened out it was only 1180mm long. It used a 48cc Zanetti engine, powering the 34kg vehicle to a top speed of 19mph (30km/h). Sadly it never reached production.

Di Blasi R30

I • 2000-date • 1F2R • No built: n/a

After the Dibla 7, a range of folding two-wheelers was made under the Di Blasi name. A folding pedal tricycle, the R32, followed, of which an all-electric version (the R30) was made. Simply pressing a button would fold it up within five seconds.

Diehlmobile

USA • 1961-1964 • 1F2R • No built: n/a

This ultra-basic runaround was designed to be disassembled and carried around in the boot of your regular car. A single-cylinder 3bhp engine was mounted in the rear driving the

rear axle by chain. Its spec included tiller front steering, basic rear mudguards and a removable bench seat that could be used for picnics.

Dingwall

GB • 1922-1953 • 1F2R • No built: n/a

London-based GH Dingwall made its first hand-powered tricycles for disabled people as far back as 1892, and its first motorised example in 1922. The De Luxe model was launched in the 1930s, and this continued after WW2 with its 147cc Villiers engine. Post-war Dingwalls were also made with flat-twin Coventry-Climax engines and, supplementing hand power, a 32cc Berini engine.

Dirigo

USA • 2009 • 2F1R • No built: 1

A group of enthusiasts from Maine built the Dirigo to compete in the 2010 Automotive X Prize competition. It was a well-conceived coupe with side-by-side seating for two, a rear-mounted Daihatsu three-cylinder diesel engine and many components taken from a Kawasaki Mule all-wheel-drive vehicle. Unusually, the body was made of red cedar sheathed in glassfibre at the sides. The team had hoped to attract production interest from the car industry but the Dirigo remained a one-off.

Doddsmobile
CDN • 1947 • 2F1R • No built: 1

The Doddsmobile was presented as an economy three-wheeler, with a small air-cooled engine driving the single rear wheel, open plywood bodywork and automatic transmission. Only one prototype was constructed.

Dohom
CN • 2000s-date • 1F2R • No built: n/a

Dohom (also sold under the Tohon brand) was based in Chongqing, making very typical Chinese trikes. The DH110ZK rickshaw could be powered by petrol or CNG, while the larger DH150ZK had enclosed glassfibre bodywork.

DH150ZK-2
DH110ZK-2

Dolphin
GB • 2000-2006 • 2F1R • No built: 1

The provenance of the Dolphin was impeccable: it was designed by Bob Curl, whose credits included working with Gordon Murray on the Light Car Rocket and with Lord Hesketh's Formula 1 team. The Dolphin was a tandem two-seater weighing only 215kg. Its 200cc two-stroke Piaggio scooter engine and four-speed sequential gearbox (no reverse) enabled a top speed of 65mph and economy of over 90mpg. Curl planned to make Dolphins for around £5000, and was still seeking backers in 2006, but sadly this never happened.

Dolphin Vortex
USA • 1985-date • 2F1R • No built: n/a

Like the Quincy-Lynn ⇨, the Dolphin Vortex – created by Dann Parks in California – was designed to be built from a set

of plans. You had to be determined to want one, because that meant fabricating metal subframes, a triangulated plywood chassis and a spruce-and-glassfibre body. This daunting task did not deter a band of enthusiasts, who usually created their own design of bodywork, often with scissor doors that lifted upwards and forwards for entry.

Under the front end sat Triumph Spitfire double wishbones with coil/spring dampers, disc brakes and an anti-roll bar. Power could come from any one of a number of motorbikes, the prototype having a four-cylinder Kawasaki 750cc unit, whose 82bhp made the 500kg (1100lb) car a rapid machine. Drive to the single rear wheel was by Harley-Davidson toothed belt. Alternatively, you could install an array of eight 12 volt batteries and a 10hp electric motor with belt drive (range 40-80 miles, top speed 60mph). Sets of plans to allow you to build your own Vortex were still available at the time of writing for $90 apiece.

Dongben
CN • 1996-date • 1F2R • No built: n/a

Chongqing Dongben Industry Co made typical tuk-tuk type vehicles with 150cc or 200cc engines that could seat up to five passengers. Dongben products also appeared with alternative branding, including Rightway, Maxi and Fomoto.

Dongcheng
CN • 2000-date • 1F2R • No built: n/a

Suining Dongcheng Car Co made tuk-tuk style three-wheelers with 150cc, 200cc and 250cc engines (SZ150ZK, SZ200ZK and SZ250ZK), as well as battery-powered models. An annual production capacity of 100,000 was quoted.

Dongfang
CN • 2002-date • 2F1R • No built: n/a

Established in 2002 by Xi'an Orient Group in Zhejiang Province, China, Dongfang Lingyun specialised in motorbikes and three-wheelers. Scooter-based 2F1R trikes were offered in 150cc and 300cc sizes. Dongfangs were sold in the USA badged as the Sunny, Roadrunner and Ice Bear.

Dongfeng BM021
CN • 1960s-1970s • 1F2R • No built: n/a

The Dongfeng brand (part of Beijing Auto Works) was synonymous with cargo trikes in China in the 1960s, but it also made passenger-carrying rickshaws as well. Power came from a single-cylinder air-cooled two-stroke 250cc engine with 12hp, driving the rear wheels by chain; there was no reverse gear.

Doran
USA • 1994-date • 2F1R • No built: n/a

Rick Doran formed the Doran Motor Company in Sparks, Nevada to market his three-wheeler. Unusually, it was a front-wheel drive machine using a Subaru L-series (1980-1989) drivetrain. With an 82bhp 1.8-litre engine in place, a 0-60mph time of 8.7 seconds was claimed. With as much as 74 per cent of its 580kg (1280lb) weight over the front wheels, it was claimed to be able to corner at up to 0.8g. A DC electric motor could also be used, still going through a Subaru five-speed manual gearbox, which could reach 80mph and travel for up to 60 miles.

The Doran had a backbone chassis, double wishbone front suspension using Honda Prelude dampers, Subaru steering and a single trailing arm at the back. The idea was that builders would create their own doorless targa-roof bodywork from plans, making a foam structure and then fibreglassing it over. As of 2013, sets of DIY plans were still available.

Doran Chimp
USA • 2000s-date • 1F2R • No built: n/a

The Chimp was described as a "stand-up, rapid response, electric utility vehicle" aimed at "soft security" uses such as warehouses, airports, amusement parks and security patrols. Designed to fit through standard doorways, it measured just

28.5in (724mm) wide and 44in (1118mm) long. The soft plastic body was intended to be pedestrian-friendly – not that its 11mph top speed threatened them much. A 24V 1.3bhp electric motor drove the front wheel, and the cost was $3195.

Dot
GB • c1942-c1958 • 2F1R • No built: n/a

Dot motorcycles were made from 1903 until 1978, but the Salford-based firm also built a three-wheeled vehicle called the Dot Motor Truck during WW2, which was also offered in passenger rickshaw form with a 'cabin' up front housing two passengers. Power came from a 197cc Villiers two-stroke engine driving the rear wheel by chain.

D-Rad-Rikscha
A • 1951 • 1F2R • No built: n/a

This very short-lived Austrian three-wheeled microcar was essentially a motorbike fitted with two rear wheels and basic open bodywork. It had a 12bhp 50cc engine and could seat three people.

Dragonfly
GB • 1994-1995 • 2F1R • No built: Probably 1

Although built as a one-off, Bernard Beirne's Dragonfly was set to become available in kit form for £1500, although it's believed it never did. It recreated almost exactly the form of the Morgan F-Type. Under its steel-skinned plywood body were a steel ladder frame chassis, sliding pillar front suspension, Morris 8 wheels, Honda CX500 rear swinging arm and a Reliant Robin 848cc engine and gearbox, connected via a shaft drive to power the rear wheel.

DRK
GB • 1987-1998 • 2F1R • No built: 59

The DRK was unusual in that almost everything was made by the Ellesmere Port-based concern, with the exception of the mechanicals, which could be Renault 4, 5 or 6, giving a wide span of engine options from 845cc to 1300cc turbo. The body was formed of layers of plywood encased in aluminium, while the metal chassis which accepted Renault front suspension and a Spax coil/over damper for the single rear wheel. To drive, the DRK was remarkably civilised compared to most kit trikes, with a very soft ride. Typically, the customer's mechanicals were fitted by the factory as part of a `hand-made' package, although kits were available for around £2400.

Drolette
CH • 1969-1970 • 1F2R • No built: Probably 1

This was an absolutely tiny single-seater by André Thaon. Shown at the 1969 Geneva Motor Show in Switzerland, this electric trike measured just 69cm wide and was powered by a Bosch 1200W motor to a top speed of 50km/h (30mph). It had a removable roof panel, rotating quarter-circular doors and a handle on the back to help get the car into parking spaces.

DS Malterre
F • 1955-1956 • 2F1R • No built: Very few

Better known for its motorcycles, DS Malterre also essayed a three-wheeler in 1955. This was an attractive two-seater coupe styled by M. Berlemont, with glassfibre bodywork and Plexiglas headlamp cowls. The tubular steel chassis featured 'Evidgum' suspension. The engine was rear-mounted: either a 6bhp 125cc or an 8bhp 175cc engine, from Ydral or Sotecma, and

drove through a three-speed gearbox. Its high price forced it into competition with mass-produced cars and few were sold.

DS Motors Unique
PK • 2004-date • 1F2R • No built: n/a

DS Motors produced the Unique range of motorbikes and three-wheelers, the latter offered with petrol and CNG powerplants of 175cc, 200cc or 250cc sizes. Several body styles were available, including six-seaters and the Lamleta with two longitudinal rear benches.

DTB Panther
GB • 2007-date • 1F2R • No built: Approx 100 (to 2013)

DTB Panther Trikes was sited near Cleckheaton, Yorkshire (where Panther motorcycles had been manufactured), making bike-to-trike conversions for almost any cruiser/tourer bike. Open-back enclosed styles were offered with model names such as Touring, Deluxe, Ultimate and Evolution. Reverse gearing was optional, as were adaptations for disabled riders.

Dunjó
E • 1956 • 2F1R • No built: 3

Arcadio Dunjó was a motorcycle designer based in Santa Perpetua de Moguda who built three Iso 125cc three-wheelers in 1956, each one different to the other.

Dura Isabelita
AR • 1960 • 1F2R • No built: Probably 1

The Isabelita was built by Dura Sociedad en Comandita, based in Cordoba in Argentina, and was an electric-powered three-wheeler. A rear-mounted 50V power pack provided momentum up to a top speed of 30mph (50km/h). The designer of this four-seater was Werne Dura, who claimed to have lots of orders for the Isabelita, but it's believed no production run occurred.

DUV
USA • 1995 • 2F1R • No built: n/a

The DUV (Design Universal Vehicle) was a vehicle built to take a folding wheelchair. Designed by Joe Warren of Walter Dorwen Teague Associates, the two-seater had an aluminium chassis, attractive glassfibre bodywork and scissor doors. A Briggs & Stratton 18bhp V-twin engine provided the power to reach a top speed of 45mph. The DUV was set to sell for $5000 in kit form, or $6000 fully built but it is not known if it ever made production.

Dynamo Junior
USA • 1959 • 1F2R • No built: n/a

This very small electric runabout used tiller steering.

THREE-WHEELERS A-Z

EEE

Epic Torque ▲

▼ Elio

Eagle
RP • 2006-date • 1F2R • No built: n/a

Puerto Princesa was one of the first cities in the Philippines to adopt E-Trikes to replace polluting petrol-powered taxis. DWG Eagle Electric Vehicles supplied its first electric three-wheelers in 2006, and made a variety of rickshaw body styles.

Eagle Express
PK • 2000s-date • 1F2R • No built: n/a

This three-seater rickshaw used a four-stroke CNG-fuelled engine.

Eaglet
GB • 1948 • 1F2R • No built: Approx 7

Electric cars made much more of an impact in continental Europe than in Britain in the post-war period, but the Eaglet was a rare British example. It was produced by Silent Transport Ltd of Woking, Surrey, and was a lightweight three-wheeled coupe with a range of up to 30 miles per charge and a top speed of 30mph. At an expensive £412, it scored little success.

Eccles
GB • c1963-c1971 • 1F2R • No built: n/a

Eccles Enginnering of Redditch, Worcs, made a range of electric three-wheelers called the Workmaster, mostly for commercial use, although leisure use was also mooted. 24V batteries powered the rear wheels via a differential and reduction gear. Up to 20 miles' range and a top speed of 7.5mph were quoted. The bodywork was glassfibre with an aluminium floor, and the cost in 1964 was £355 excluding batteries.

Eco-Exo
GB • 2010-date • 2F1R • No built: Approx 20 (to 2013)

Designed by MEV ⇨ but built by a separate operation run by Stuart and Scott Turner, this tiny (2690mm long) trike drew on the exo-skeletal themes of the Ariel Atom, but with an emphasis on economy rather than performance. It used a Suzuki Burgman scooter as a donor, which meant a choice of engines from 125cc to 650cc, and up to 100mpg was possible. As it was so light, it could reach 100mph with the right engine fitted. The standard car was a tandem two-seater with scooter handlebars, but an Eco-Exo-R model was added in 2012 with a single seat and conventional steering wheel and throttle pedal. Kit prices started at £1995.

Eco-Fueler American Roadster
USA • 2006-date • 1F2R • No built: n/a

The Eco-Fueler Corporation of Oregon designed the American Roadster as a kind of ecological hot rod. Unusually, it was fuelled by compressed natural gas, feeding a rear-mounted in-line three-cylinder engine with 100bhp. Manual or automatic transmission was possible. The company claimed 70mpg, 120mph and 0-60mph in 7.0 seconds. The glassfibre body seated three in a 1+2 format, and was bolted to a tubular steel chassis, all for a purchase price in 2012 of $19,900.

ECO Motor EMC3 Commuter
USA • 2008-2011 • 2F1R • No built: n/a

The ECO Motor Company of Newcastle, Washington state, built the EMC3 as a commuter vehicle. Its 1.0-litre engine resulted in a claimed 60mpg. Among its sophisticated features were airbags, electric windows and air conditioning. The intended price was $13,995, and grand plans were announced to sell up to 200,000 cars a year, with production taking place in China. However, in 2011 the enterprise ended in the courts over financial issues.

EcoSpin Road Raptor
GB • 2012-date • 2F1R • No built: n/a

This electric-powered stand-on vehicle was targeted at the security patrol market. The Raptor was claimed to be the first in its class to be fully homologated for road use in the EU, and sold worldwide to many police forces. Two in-wheel motors of 2kW each were mounted at the rear, giving a top speed of 25mph (40km/h). Depending on the battery pack, a range of up to 56 miles (90km) was possible. It was famously seen being ridden by celebrities such as Stephen Fry and Boris Johnson.

Edith
AUS • 1952-1956 • 2F1R • No built: Approx 10

Gray & Harper Pty of Oakleigh, Victoria conceived this unpretty device, which was claimed to be Australia's first ever microcar. It used a

197cc Villiers two-stroke engine mounted in the tail, driving the single rear wheel by chain via a four-speed gearbox. Using a glassfibre open two-seater body, it weighed only 250kg and could do 40mph and 50mpg. A four-wheeled version succeeded it in 1956, while Edith also supplied chassis for the Tilli Capton ⇨.

EEC Worker's Playtime
GB • 1952-1954 • 2F1R • No built: 1

Worker's Playtime may sound a bizarre title for a car to modern ears, but it was the name of a popular BBC radio show of the 1950s. This eponymous ultra-economy three-wheeler had enclosed aluminium bodywork over a steel frame. Three passengers sat abreast, with entry via an unusual hinged front panel. Power came from a rear-mounted Excelsior 250cc two-cylinder two-stroke engine. Suspension was by torsion bars up front and a rear trailing fork. Only one of an intended run of six prototypes was ever finished by the Electrical Engineering Company, a boatbuilding and electrical firm based in Totnes, Devon, although cars were advertised at £280 plus tax.

E-Eco-Rent
I • 2000 • 1F2R • No built: Probably 1

The E-Eco-Rent was a prototype electric vehicle designed by Studio Lenci and exhibited at the 2000 Fiera di Rimini. The idea was that you would rent the car from a charging station and return it to any other such station, where the battery pack could be swapped within a few minutes. A basic roof and windscreen offered some weather protection, and there was a small boot too. Two versions were suggested: one with front-wheel drive and one with rear drive.

EFM
USA • 2011-date • 2F1R • No built: n/a

It may not have won any awards for beauty, but the trike built by Garry Buzzelli (of Ohio-based EFM Auto Clutch) was one of the quickest ever. At least one example had two Yamaha V-Max engines mounted in the tail, for a combined total of 300bhp. With both engines running (you could stick with one if you preferred), a 0-60mph time of just 2.5 seconds was quoted.

Egan
GB • 1952 • 1F2R • No built: n/a

The Egan was a small and basic open two-seater with a single front headlamp.

Eggasus
USA • 2012-date • 1F2R • No built: n/a

Living up to its name, the Eggasus looked like a rolling dinosaur egg. Measuring only 1778mm (70in) long and 914mm (36in) wide, it weighed a featherweight 136kg (300lb) and could do 25mph, courtesy of an electric motor driving the rear wheels. Launched as a single-seater costing $5,000, a two-passenger model was also due for launch in 2013.

Egy-Tech
ET • 2010-date • 1F2R • No built: n/a

Egy-Tech Engineering was a joint Egyptian/ Chinese project based in Cairo making three-wheeled city cars and rickshaws, said to be the first car manufacturer to use components made only in Egypt. Two main types were sold: the Maestro and the Micro. Both models used the same range of engines, which were made by the Arab Industrialization Authority: 150cc, 175cc, 200cc or 250cc (from 11.7bhp to 15.3bhp). The maximum speed was up to 37mph (60km/h) and local prices started from £17,450.

Electraph 225
F • 1942-1944 • 2F1R • No built: Approx 40

The Electraph 225 was a wartime electric car with smooth coupe bodywork by Brandone. Conceived by a Cannes-based racing driver called Raphael 'Ralph' Bethenod, it was said to have a range of 130 miles at an average speed of 25mph.

Electric Shopper
USA • 1952-1962 • 1F2R • No built: n/a

The succinctly named Electric Shopper was produced by the Electric Car Co of Long Beach, California by ex-employees of Autoette ⇨. It was no coincidence, therefore, that it looked so similar: indeed, Autoette soon forced the company to become its licensee. A three-wheeler with a single front wheel, tiller steering and a 1.5bhp, 24V DC electric motor,

it topped out at 18mph and could travel for up to 35 miles between charges. Both glassfibre and metal bodywork was offered, with a more modern body shape arriving in 1960, which boasted styling inspired by contemporary full-size American cars.

Electrobile
USA • 1951 • 1F2R • No built: n/a

Details of a three-wheeled, two-seater runabout with a DC electric motor appeared in 1951. If the reports were correct, this may have been one of the very first cars with a glassfibre body, but it is uncertain if any cars were actually built by the Chicago-based creators.

Electrociclo
E • 1941-1953 • 1F2R • No built: n/a

Fuel shortages in the Spanish Civil War led to the development of several electric vehicles. Electrociclos, based in Eibar, essayed electric bicycles and tricycles in the 1940s, the latter mostly being delivery vehicles fitted with a 1bhp motor and 24V batteries. A four-door passenger saloon was also presented, with a quoted range of up to 62 miles (100km) and a top speed of 27mph (45km/h), but the company soon switched to manufacturing machine tools.

Elio
USA • 2008-date • 2F2R • No built: n/a

Elio Motors was founded by Paul Elio, who designed an enclosed tandem two-seater three-wheeler. It featured disc brakes all round, a three-cylinder 70bhp engine, front-wheel drive and performance figures of 107mph top speed and 0-60mph in just over 9 seconds. At the time of writing, it was expected to reach the market in 2014 priced at $6800, and was set to be made in the ex-General Motors plant at Shreveport, Louisiana.

Emax EM-200ZK
CN • 1996-date • 1F2R • No built: n/a

The Emax Motorcycle Co was formed in Chongqing in 1996, with a sideline in three-wheelers. The four-seater EM-200ZK was powered by a 197cc single-cylinder engine allowing a top speed of 43mph (60km/h).

EML
NL • 1999-date • 1F2R • No built: n/a

This Dutch sidecar maker began making trikes based on the Honda Goldwing in 1999 with names such as Bermuda and Martinique. Options included an electric reverse gear and 'ExtensoDrive' front forks.

Enzo Custom Cycle
USA • 2012-date • 2F1R • No built: n/a

The Enzo was clearly inspired by the Campagna T-Rex ⇨ but was some 3in taller, 6in longer and 6in wider. From a base near Austin, Texas, kits were offered from $9500, or complete cars from $23,000. Engine options included Honda CBR 1000cc or Suzuki Hayabusa 1300cc, with reverse gear optional.

Epic Torq
USA • 2010-date • 2F1R • No built: n/a

The Torq from Epic Electric Vehicles was a high-performance electric two-seater made in Vivian, Louisiana. Carbon-fibre body panels for the doorless, roofless Torq helped keep the weight down to 770kg (1700lb). The chassis and suspension were designed by Palatov Motorsports, and Epic claimed 1.3g of cornering force and 0-60mph in less than 4.0 seconds. The electric motor had an output of 200bhp and was fed by lithium-ion batteries mounted under the floor, while a single-speed transmission with reverse was used. The Torq had yet to come to market by the time of writing.

EPower EP-308
CN • 2010s • 1F2R • No built: n/a

The EP-308 electric three-wheeler from China had a 5kW DC motor, 48V gel battery, disc brakes, independent suspension and seating for four. A top speed of 40mph (65km/h) and a range of 50 miles (80km) were claimed.

Erad Capucine
F • 1975-c1978 • 1F2R • No built: n/a

Erad (Études et Réalisations du Douaisis) was one of France's longest-lived producers of microcars. Its first model was the Capucine, a plastic-bodied single-seater with a 47cc Sachs engine, made in three- and four-wheeled forms, but the former was short-lived.

E-SaVe E-Taxicle
RP • 2010-date • 1F2R • No built: n/a

E-SaVe Transport Systems was a partner company of Manila Autogas, offering various electric vehicles that seemed to be identical to the Gerweiss ⇨ range, including the E-Taxicle three-wheeled taxi.

ESO T-250
CZ • 1959 • 2F1R • No built: 1

The Czech motorcycle brand ESO, founded by racer Jaroslav Simandl, also produced a prototype microcar called the T-250. Its two-seater coupe bodywork was made of glassfibre and it used many components from a Jawa CZ 250cc motorbike.

Esoro Gaston / E2
CH • 1986/1988 • 2F1R • No built: n/a

Swiss engineering company Esoro made a name for itself in the 1980s and 1990s with a string of electric car prototypes. The Gaston (later developed into the E2, below right) was claimed to the world's most efficient two-seater car, the world's most aerodynamic two-seater (Cd 0.165) and the first electric car with stability control and ABS. It competed in the Tour de Sol, which it won every year from 1988 to 1991.

Espenlaub
D • 1949 • 2F1R • No built: Probably 1

Few three-wheelers can claim to seat nine people, but coachbuilder Gottlob Espenlaub's prototype did. With an aeronautical background, his design was very aerodynamic.

Etricycle
IND • 1991-date • 1F2R • No built: n/a

This Indian rickshaw maker boasted six models: Aashrit C, Aashrit P, Hathi, Raja, Rani and Shera. All were very basic vehicles with electric power.

E-Trike
RP • 2010-date • 1F2R • No built: n/a

The E-Trike was an attempt by the Department of Energy of the Philippines to create a new form of eco-friendly taxi. After a

tendering process, with several designs presented to a judging panel, the eventual winning design was that of Japanese developer Itchiro Hatayama. This was then developed into a running prototype that went on to form the basis of several locally-made E-trikes across the Philippines.

Eurotech Trike
GB • 1991-date • 1F2R • No built: n/a

Eurotech Trikes of St Leonards-on-Sea, Sussex was run by ex-pilot Peter Funnell and could convert almost any motorcycle to a trike, either with independent rear suspension or a live axle. At the top end,  you could order elliptical wishbones, fully adjustable suspension and Protek racing dampers. It also built trike conversions for disabled people.

Eurotech Hammerhead
GB • 2010-date • 2F1R • No built: n/a

Eurotech's Hammerhead was an interesting piece of design: a 2F1R conversion of a Yamaha YZF-R1 superbike, which featured a nose section that strongly recalled a hammerhead shark. The model was eventually developed (as pictured above right) into a kind of Campagna T-Rex ⇨ rival with enclosed bodywork and side-by-side seating for two people. As of 2013, the conversion from motorbike to three-wheeler cost £6000.

Everwell
CN • 2010-date • 1F2R • No built: n/a

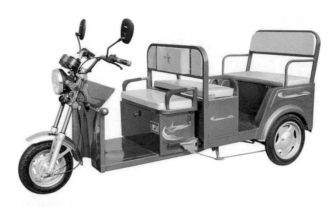

Everwell Industry of Zhongshan in Guangdong province made a variety of electric three-wheelers, from cargo vehicles to rickshaws. At least 11 different passenger models were listed, from the ETP-01 to the ETP-11, all very much targeted at the undemanding Chinese market.

EVette
USA • 2007-date • 1F2R • No built: n/a

Tom Sines built the extraordinary EVette from a base in Okeechobee, Florida. It looked like a three-wheeled Countach (it used a modified Lambo replica shell) with tractor rear wheels (chosen to boost the top speed to 60mph because there  was no stepped transmission). Power came from lead-acid batteries feeding two DC electric motors, and a range of 200 miles was claimed. One peculiar feature was joystick 'drive-by-wire' steering/throttle control, and the car could turn 360 degrees in its own length. The car was also suitable for wheelchair users. As of 2013, Sines was still seeking funding to go further.

EVI EPV/Impello
USA • 1973-1975/2011-date • 1F2R • No built: Approx 5000

Launched in 1973, the PPV hit the oil crisis zeitgeist spot on. Its acronym stood for People Powered Vehicle, as human legs were required to pedal it. The PPV's maker (EVI of Sterling Heights, Michigan)  also offered the EPV (Electric Powered Vehicle) with two 12V batteries on board to provide a range of 45 miles and a top speed of 25mph. One additional benefit was that it had the remarkable ability to be parked on its end (as pictured on the following page). A version was also offered in France with a petrol engine under the name Petit Puce (Little

Flea). In 2011, the human-powered PPV was revived as the Impello with a new steel chassis, seven-speed transmission, disc brakes and optional electric hybrid power.

Excel
PK • 2000s-date • 1F2R • No built: n/a

Excel Industries assembled motorcycles and the XL two-stroke rickshaw in Pakistan.

Exertec Spykster
AUS • 2000s • 2F1R • No built: n/a

Exertec of New South Wales, Australia was formed in 2000 to create a new 'dual joystick' steering system for non-leaning trikes. The Spykster's power came from a Yamaha R1 engine with  chain drive to the single rear wheel, which was mounted on a swinging arm. A power-to-weight ratio of around 370bhp per ton made performance impressive.

ExerTrike Tri-Hybrid Stealth
USA • 2007-date • 2F1R • No built: n/a

American company ExerTrike's main business was making a range of hybrid electric/pedal recumbent trikes, a genre that is outside the scope of this book. However it did attempt something more car-like with  the Tri-Hybrid Stealth. As its name suggested, it had no fewer than three power sources: a diesel engine, an electric motor and pedals (which were used to charge the batteries). The Stealth was also claimed to be the first hybrid trike to offer hand controls and an extending seat designed for disabled drivers. Its creators said the Tri-Hybrid Stealth would do 80mph, or 40mph in electric-only mode, and average 200mpg. It could seat two passengers in its very lightweight, enclosed, rigidly straight-lined bodywork.

Expertise
T • 2003-date • 1F2R • No built: Many thousands

This company, based in Chonburi in Thailand, made several different models of tuk-tuk, including the Sabai, Icon and Wise, with seating for three to ten passengers in either open-sided or fully enclosed body styles. An Expertise was listed by Guinness World Records for completing the longest autorickshaw journey ever made, between Bangkok and Germany – a distance of 23,236 miles (37,410km).

EZS Retriever
NL • 2012-date • 2F1R • No built: n/a

Having made sidecars and trailers for motorbikes since the early 1990s, the firm of EZS (based in Zelhem in the Netherlands) launched a performance-orientated trike in 2012. Called the Retriever, it had double wishbone front suspension with wide 215/40 front tyres. While the very first example was based on the Suzuki B-King, at least one subsequent model used a Honda GL 1800 cruising motorbike as its basis.

THREE WHEELERS A-Z

FFF

Frisky Family Three ▲

Fuji Cabin ▲

Feora ▲

▼ Fuldamobil N-2

FA Dreiradroller/Kabrio-Roller
D • 1949-1955 • 1F2R • No built: Approx 600 / 6

Friedrich Albrecht Fahrzeugbau, based in Berlin, made Ilo-engined disabled three-wheelers from 1949 (pictured above left), of which a rickshaw model was also built (middle left). In 1953 this was followed by the Kabrio-Roller (bottom left), a small (2560mm long) open-topped two-door car for the economy market. Over the single front wheel (and driving it) sat a Sachs 175cc single-cylinder two-stroke engine with 9bhp, enough for a top speed of 37mph (60km/h). A tubular steel chassis supported a car-like steel body but it was too expensive and only six were made.

Faka Motorrikscha
D • 1949-c1952 • 2F1R • No built: n/a

Faka was a contraction of Fahrzeugwerke Kannenberg, a company based in Salzgitter-Bad. It built the Motorrikscha, a basic rickshaw with a self-contained motor/front wheel and a three-person 'trailer' at the rear. The engine was a 118cc Ilo with 3bhp, driving through a two-speed gearbox. Faka concentrated on scooters in the 1950s.

Falcon LX-3
GB • 1986-2002 • 2F1R • No built: Approx 60

Having been involved with the Lomax ⇨, Peter Bird formed Falcon Design in 1984 to launch a Lotus Seven lookalike called the Falcon Sports, based on a Citroen 2CV floorpan. Two years later, he followed this up with a three-wheeled version called the LX-3, which kept the Lotus-like front end but substituted a boat-tail rear end over the single rear wheel. The main body was made of plywood bonded together with glassfibre, with a steel substructure; this tub could be clad in aluminium, vinyl or simply painted. The front wings, nose, tail and bonnet were all made of glassfibre. Unlike the Lomax, the method of obtaining the third rear wheel involved removing both Citroen 2CV rear arms and putting in a new structural beam and suspension arm. Both sides of the Citroen linked-spring suspension were bolted to the beam. The basic kit cost just over £400, or you could use a £10 set of plans. From 1991, a replacement chassis also became available. The LX-3 eventually came to rest with the 2CV Centre in Frome, Somerset.

Farspeed
CN • 2001-date • 1F2R and 2F1R • No built: n/a

The Farspeed Vehicle Industry Co of Ningbo, China mostly made ATVs, scooters and go-karts, but it also offered scooter-based trikes, some of which seem to have been rebranded products from other companies.

The FPM150E-D was a covered scooter with a 150cc single-cylinder four-stroke air-cooled engine; the FPE1000-G was a tiny 2F1R electric scooter; the FEC-N85KD was apparently a rebranded Green Vehicles Triac ⇨; the FPM250E-G was a conventional chopper trike with a 250cc V-twin engine; the FPM200E (pic above) was a three-wheeled scooter with a 200cc four-stroke engine and automatic transmission (with reverse); and the FPA250-1 (pic below) was apparently the same as the Baoma ⇨.

Fascination
USA • 1971-1977 • 1F2R • No built: 3

This book resolutely does not include four-wheelers, but the Fascination is an exception because, although it had a very narrow-set pair of front wheels, the manufacturer claimed that the car could be driven with a blow-out on just one of the front wheels – making it a three-wheeler after all! This was a giant by three-wheeler standards, measuring 5230mm

for entry. A two-cylinder Rotax engine sat beside the single driven rear wheel: initially, this was a 350cc 12bhp unit, but it soon increased to 398cc and 15bhp.

(over 17ft) long – bigger than a Rolls-Royce – although it was claimed to weigh only 815kg (1796lb). Firestone pneumatic air ride suspension was used. Bizarrely, the brochure claimed that the Fascination would "simply roll over and come to rest upon its wheels again should it for some reason be overturned."

Designed by Paul Lewis (who had built the three-wheeled Lewis Airmobile in 1937), its teardrop glassfibre body seated five and had curious all-enveloping bumpers. The doors opened up taking part of the roof and floor with them; none of the windows opened, so air conditioning was standard.

When it was announced in 1971, it was said to have a horizontally-opposed air-cooled engine. There were also plans to power it by steam, an electromagnetic engine running on static electricity, a gas-powered two-cycle engine and a thermonuclear gas plasma engine! In fact, every Fascination made had a prosaic 70bhp Renault 16 four-cylinder engine

and automatic transmission. The Highway Aircraft Corp of Denver (and later of Sydney, Nebraska) was set to make 10,000 per year priced at $7200 each. However, only three cars were ever built, all with Renault power.

FBI
USA • 2000s-date • 1F2R • No built: n/a

Fat Baggers Inc made a range of trike conversions with a solid rear axle and oversized 18in rear wheels. Options included a reverse gear, matching front wheel and passenger back rest.

Felber Autoroller
A • 1950-1954 • 2F1R • No built: Approx 400

The Austrian car industry is hardly world-renowned, but Ernst Marold's Viennese Felber marque was, for a while,

quite successful with the Autoroller. The 1950 prototype (pictured left) had a single headlamp and no doors, but production versions from 1952 (pictured above right) featured a curious canopy which hinged towards the rear

Fend Flitzer
D • 1948-1949 • 2F1R • No built: Approx 30

Fritz Fend was an engineer who worked for Messerschmitt during WW2. With the cessation of aircraft-building following hostilities, he left to apply himself to road transport. He initially designed a string of pedal-powered three-wheelers and vehicles for veterans injured in the war. The first powered road car was the Flitzer of 1948, a desperately crude and tiny (2000mm long) single-seater with the most basic specification imaginable: bicycle wheels and, in the first versions, pedal power. Those unable or unwilling to use their legs could opt for what was one of the smallest engines ever fitted to a motor car: a 38cc single-cylinder Victoria unit with 1bhp – powerful enough to take the 75kg (165lb) car to a heady top speed of 25mph. Unhurried drivers were rewarded by a claimed fuel consumption of 235mpg. Enclosed and convertible versions were offered.

Fend Flitzer II
D • 1949-1951 • 2F1R • No built: 252

Barely more sophisticated, the second-series Flitzer used scooter wheels and its engine grew in size to 98cc (Sachs 2.5bhp), which meant its top speed rose to 38mph (60km/h). The convertible version of this car had a bizarre transparent inflatable ribbed roof. In 1950 came an improved model with

marginally more substantial bodywork that looked even more portentous of the Daleks of Dr Who. This used a more robust 98cc Riedel engine (4.5bhp, 47mph). Fuel consumption was down to a `mere' 100mpg.

Fend/FMR Mokuli Rikscha
D • 1949-1965 • 2F1R • No built: n/a

Fend branched out into delivery trikes with the Lastenroller of 1949, which developed into the Mokuli, a design which remarkably remained in production until 1972. A Rikscha passenger version was sold with seating for two up front in place of the normal load area, while power came from a 125cc engine.

Fend FK150
D • 1952-1953 • 2F1R • No built: Very few

Fend's famous collaboration with Professor Willy Messerschmitt began in January 1952, just after his Fend enterprise had gone bust. Fend had been working on a prototype for a new car, the Fend Kabinenroller (or FK150), and his former employer saw huge potential in it, especially as it used a Plexiglass dome roof that recalled Messerschmitt planes. This early iteration used a 148cc Sachs engine with 6.5bhp. The car received a spurt of development and, by 1953, was relaunched as the Messerschmitt KR175 ⇨.

Fengyi
CN • 2003-date • 1F2R • No built: n/a

The Yongkang Easy Vehicle Co made a range of scooter and motorbike-based trikes under the Fengyi FY brand, with engines ranging from 110cc to 250cc.

Feora
USA • 1981-1984 • 2F1R • No built: n/a

Half fighter plane, half Star Wars out-take, the Feora was built by a Los Angeles mechanic called Chuck Ophorst. Its claimed drag coefficient was just 0.15, achieved by a small frontal area, teardrop shape and an extremely narrow body. The all-glassfibre bodywork sat atop a space frame chassis

and the completed projectile weighed a mere 229kg (505lb). There was seating for two in tandem, accessed by a canopy. With a 22bhp 175cc or 400cc Honda two-cylinder engine installed in the tail, Ophorst claimed a top speed of 92mph and a fuel consumption in excess of 90mpg at a constant 55mph. The wheels were motorbike-derived but the steering was rack-and-pinion and the brakes were discs all round. Ophorst offered built-to-order replicas and plans sets for DIY builders, but not kits.

FIAM Johnny Panther
I • 1978-1982 • 1F2R • No built: n/a

The Johnny Panther was a two-seater microcar built in Rimini. A tubular steel chassis was topped by an angular plastic body some 2380mm long and 1250mm wide. Various engines were fitted, from Sachs or Zündapp engines of 50cc, through 124cc Morini and, from 1981, 272cc units. The  Johnny Panther could be bought with three or four wheels, with all-independent suspension, rear-wheel drive and automatic or manual transmission. In 1982 it was restyled and made by DECSA ⇨.

Fiberfab Scarab
USA • 1975-1979 • 2F1R • No built: n/a

One of America's first kit-form three-wheelers came from the prolific stable of Fiberfab, based in Bridgeville, Pennsylvania, where the idea of the motorbike-based three-wheeler originated. The Scarab STM (Sports Transport Module) was certainly ingenious. Everything but the front forks was taken from a motorbike (almost any model larger than 450cc), including the whole frame, engine and rear wheel, which bolted into a simple twin-rail chassis. The front end was supported by VW Beetle suspension,

and reverse gear was obtained by using a starter motor with a rubber wheel operating on the rear wheel.

The glassfibre body came in three pieces, including a large flop-forward cab/nose section which provided access for two passengers. A surprise up its sleeve was the ability to switch back from three wheels to two: in an operation that took 35 minutes, you could spanner your Scarab back into a motorbike. Kits were sold for $1795, but the Scarab wasn't a huge hit in its day.

Fiberlite Lance
CDN • 1980s • 1F2R • No built: n/a

The Lance from Fiberlite Designs of Alberta, Canada was a decidedly odd-looking beast. Very long by trike standards (4470mm), the two-seater featured a pointy nose with two close-set square headlamps. The Lance was available as an open-topped Roadster, a Coupe with a hardtop that included a flip-up roof section, or (as the Elite) with doors. Either a Chevrolet V6 or small-block V8 engine could be mounted up front, driving the rear axle.

FIM Chihuahua
I • 1974-1980 • 1F2R • No built: n/a

FIM (Fabbrica Italiana Macchine) was based in the province of Salerno and made the amusingly titled Chihuahua. This was a very small glassfibre-bodied three-wheeled car offered in either saloon or convertible body styles, with styling that was as comical as its name. Three engines were offered: a 50cc Morini, a 125cc BCB four-stroke or a 250cc two-stroke; in the latter case a heady top speed of 50mph (80km/h) was quoted.

Fioretti F50 / Hallo
I • 1978-1981 • 1F2R • No built: n/a

The Roman firm of Autofioretti based its glassfibre-bodied Fioretti F50 (also known as the Hallo) on the Piaggio truck, complete with its 50cc air-cooled single-cylinder engine. Its specification featured hydromechanical brakes and a four-speed gearbox. This economy vehicle was optimistically described by the maker as a 'targa-top'.

Fire Aero
USA • 1984-c1990 • 2F1R • No built: Approx 200

Ex-General Motors and Toyota designer David Stollery, who had previously penned the Trihawk ⇨, went on to make the Fire Aero, which was marketed through his company, Industrial Design Research of Laguna Beach, California. In format it was very different to the Trihawk, in that it had a motorcycle engine and running gear bolted as a unit into the rear end, while at the front end were VW Beetle front suspension and Chevrolet steering gear. Stollery's own car had a Honda 750cc engine but a wide variety of bikes could be used, right up to Kawasaki 1300. The glassfibre two-seater bodywork featured a T-top open roof with optional gullwing doors, and the tail section lifted up for access to the engine. It was quite long by trike standards (at 3610mm) but weighed a skimpy 430kg. Kits were sold from $1995. A new outfit called California Alternative Vehicles (CAV), sold turnkey cars from 1988, but Stollery later regained control of the project and in 2010 was reportedly developing a much-modified Fire Aero dubbed the ACX.

Fitt Continental
GB • 1950-1953 • 1F2R • No built: Approx 500

George Fitt Motors of Tankerton, Kent made the Continental invalid tricycle from 1950. This was a very conventional open-topped vehicle for the disabled inspired by the Invacar ⇨. The chassis was built by the Co-op Cycle Works and was fitted with a 197cc Villiers engine, three-speed gearbox and steering/braking by tiller. There was a small scooter-type front wheel and the larger rear wheels had independent suspension by rubber blocks.

FIVES Sciarà

I • 1990s • 2F1R • No built: n/a

Sciarà a Cagli Alburni (SA)

A merciful contraction of Fabbrica Italiana Veicoli Ecologici Speciali, FIVES produced a range of people carriers aimed at the local taxi market. The Sciarà was a five-door MPV-style machine with a tubular steel chassis fitted with polyester-and-glassfibre bodywork that could seat five people in three rows of seats. Motive power came from Lombardini diesel units (either 602cc 15bhp or 903cc 24bhp), or an 899cc unit designed for LPG. Also available was a pick-up version called the Centauro.

FIVES Rondo

I • 1990s • 1F2R • No built: n/a

For the Rondo, FIVES reversed its wheel layout with a single front wheel (taken from a Piaggio) and a rear-mounted engine (a 652cc 23bhp two-cylinder unit which came from the Fiat 126). Larger than the Sciarà (at 3570mm long), it could seat six passengers, the rear four facing each other, suiting its intended role as a taxi. A roofless version was also offered for hot climates. The Rondo weighed 890kg and could reach 46mph (74km/h).

Flycar

F • 2005 • 2F1R • No built: Probably 1

Seen at the Concours Lépine in Paris, this was a flying car prototype that was basically an ultralight aircraft with headlamps and indicators to make it suitable for road use. It could reach just 30mph (50km/h) on tarmac.

FN AS 24

B • 1959-1965 • 1F2R • No built: 460

Military three-wheelers are a rare breed, and Belgian ones unique; the AS 24 was made by Fabrique National d'Armes de Guerre in Herstal, Belgium. It was ultra-compact (only 34in, or 864mm, tall) and lightweight at 170kg (374lb) as

it was designed to be parachuted into action, carrying up to four soldiers. A 244cc FN two-cylinder two-stroke engine and four-speed gearbox powered the rear wheels at up to 31mph (50km/h) with a full load. Although tested by the US military, almost all of 460 built were used by Belgian paratroopers.

FNV Carcará

BR • 2006 • 2F1R • No built: Probably 1

The FNV Carcará was a trike made in Brazil, measuring 3360mm long, and powered by a 1200cc motorcycle engine with a sequential gearbox.

Fomoto

CN • 1996-2010 • 1F2R • No built: n/a

Under the aegis of Chongqing Rightway Industry Corporation, the Fomoto brand made all sorts of cargo and passenger three-wheelers, some bearing Velorex badging, somewhat surprisingly.

Force Minidor / Ultrador

IND • 1996-2010 • 1F2R • No built: Many thousands

Bajaj ⇨ was one of the big names of the Indian autorickshaw industry. As well as three-wheelers, Bajaj made a Mercedes-Benz-based SUV called the Tempo, badged under the Force Motors name. Force launched its own range of autorickshaws called Minidor in 1996 with a 499cc, 9.5bhp engine. The Ultrador, launched in 2002, had the same bodywork but a 72V electric powerplant combined with a 90cc 4.5bhp 'booster' engine. Force withdrew from the tricycle market in 2010 to concentrate on four-wheeled vehicles.

Ford Maxima

USA • 1954 • 1F2R • No built: 1

Designer Alex Tremulis penned the Maxima for Ford in 1954 to commemorate the 50th anniversary of Henry Ford's land speed record attempt. Although only a 3/8-scale model was ever completed, Ford boldly said the Maxima would be powered by a jet engine at speeds up to 500mph. It seems that the Maxima may have inspired Craig Breedlove to build the Spirit of America three-wheeled land speed record car.

Ford Volante

USA • 1961 • 1F2R • No built: 1

Despite Ford claiming that its Volante prototype of 1961 could fly, it was in fact a non-functioning model that very much stayed on terra firma. Ford stated: "The tri-athodyne concept calls for ultra-sophisticated use of the ducted fan principle, employed in a unique manner," which sounds exactly like the pie-in-the-sky that this project was.

Ford Model T2

AUS • 2008 • 2F1R • No built: 1

To celebrate the 100th anniversary of the Model T in 2008, Ford got students at six schools from around the world to come up with "a revolutionary global vehicle for today that shares the Model T's attributes." It had to be simple, lightweight, practical, have a range of 125 miles (200km) and cost less than $7000. Deakin University of Australia's three-wheeled T2 design won the contest. It was designed to use a revolutionary power source: compressed air rotary hub motors. A full-scale model was made, and contemporary reports stated Deakin was building a full-sized working car.

Foton FT175ZK

CN • c2009-date • 1F2R • No built: n/a

Most Chinese cars drew at least some inspiration from already existing designs, and in the case of the Foton FT175ZK, it was clearly the Peugeot 206. Both three- and four-wheeled versions of this four-door economy car were made, powered by a 175cc single-cylinder engine with 12.5bhp. The design evolved in time, and eventually lost its Peugeot-inspired flavour; this later car was also apparently known as the Lovol.

Frankenstein

USA • 1995-date • 1F2R • No built: n/a

Frankenstein Trikes offered not only trike conversions for Harley-Davidsons but also a full rolling chassis for DIY builders.

Free Wheel A250 Scorpion

J • 2000s-date • 2F1R • No built: n/a

Free Wheel imported Rewaco ⇨ trikes and others to Japan, as well as offering its own design, the A250 Scorpion. This featured disc brakes and independent suspension, and was based on 250cc Japanese-built motorbikes.

Frisky Family Three

GB • 1958-1964 • 2F1R • No built: Several hundred

Captain Raymond Flowers went into production with the Friskysport in 1957, which was a four-wheeled microcar with a very narrow-set rear pair of wheels (requiring no differential). This was made by Henry Meadows Ltd of Wolverhampton, which was then producing engines. One year later came a more basic three-wheeled model, the Frisky Family Three.

This was one of the more stylish microcars of its day, with sharp lines realised in glassfibre by the nearby Guy lorry works, plus small doors and the modish addition of embryonic tail fins. There was accommodation for four people (just) in a coupe body style, whose roof was however so low that it connected to passengers' heads perhaps a little too readily. A convertible was also advertised but it seems that no such cars were ever built.

Under the body sat a separate ladder chassis, which was initially advertised with a choice of rear-mounted 197cc Villiers single-cylinder or Excelsior 246cc two-cylinder units. In both cases, the single rear wheel was driven by chain. From 1959, the model was improved with MacPherson strut front suspension in place of rubber, the 197cc engine was standardised and the car became a strict two-seater.

Four-wheeler production ended in 1961, leaving only three-wheelers on the price lists (which by now also gave buyers the choice of building cars from kits). After four changes of premises (production switched to Kent in 1961), Meadows finally abandoned car production in 1964.

Frisky Prince

GB • 1960-1964 • 2F1R • No built: Very few

The larger and more conventional-looking Prince three-wheeler had totally different enclosed bodywork to the Family Three, featuring fuller front-hinged doors and seating for four passengers. The Prince was powered by either a 324cc Villiers or 328cc Excelsior engine. However, Frisky's heyday was over and few, if any, cars were actually sold.

FRS S2
GB • 2011-date • 2F1R • No built: Approx 3 (to 2013)

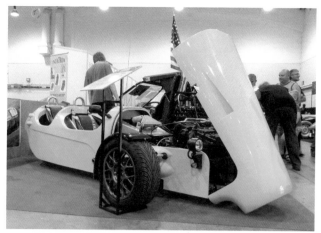

The father-and-son team of Fred and Jason Reeves built the FRS S2 from a base in Bradford, Yorkshire as a roadgoing version of their successful three-wheeled hillclimb racer. The S2 was a roofless, doorless tandem two-seater with an unusually long nose. Its tubular spaceframe chassis housed a 98bhp Suzuki Bandit 1200cc engine driving the front wheels via a Suzuki five-speed sequential gearbox and belt drive. Suspension was by inboard single monodamper up front and a single-sided rear swinging arm.

Fuji Cabin
J • 1957-1958 • 2F1R • No built: Approx 85

The Fuji Cabin built by Fuji Toshuda Motors of Tokyo was one of the most successful of Japan's post-war three-wheeled microcars, although that's not saying much as only 85 were made. It had a 5.5bhp air-cooled single-cylinder 123cc two-stroke engine giving a top speed of 37mph. It looked utterly distinctive with its rounded two-seater coupe glassfibre bodywork and single headlamp.

Fuldamobil
D • 1950-1951 • 2F1R • No built: 74

If the very first Fuldamobil looked like a three-wheeled caravan, it should perhaps come as no surprise, since its builder (Norbert Stevenson) relied heavily on caravan construction techniques. A wooden skeleton had plywood panels fixed on it, either painted or covered in faux leather. A 198cc Zundapp engine sited in the tail powered the prototype, but production cars had a single-cylinder Baker & Polling 248cc engine that developed 8.5bhp, which was bolted directly to the floor.

Coupe and open-topped versions of these early Fuldas were sold, both two-seaters, measuring 2720mm long and weighing 320kg.

Fuldamobil N-1 / N-2
D • 1951-1952/1952-1955 • 2F1R • No built: Approx 320 / 380

The N-1 (pic above) grew in size somewhat (2850mm long) but kept its Baker & Polling engine, which was rather unsatisfactory in terms of reliability. The N-2 of 1952 (pic below) was much improved, with restyled bodywork in unpainted hammered aluminium, which earned it the nickname of 'silver flea'. Coupe and roadster choices remained, but the former was now a 2+2 seater, rather than a strict two-seater. A 9.5bhp Sachs 359cc single-cylinder engine and less overall weight gave it a more useful turn of speed (50mph/80km/h) and average fuel consumption of over 60mpg.

Fuldamobil S-1 / S-2
D • 1953-1955/1954-1955 • 2F1R • No built: Approx 704 / 430

In 1953, Stevenson built a prototype with a new, more rounded aluminium coupe body, incorporating a hinged bootlid, although a wooden frame remained underneath. S-1 production was actually licensed to bus manufacturer Nordwestdeutsche Farzeugbau (NWF), which also offered it under its own name as the NWF 200 (1954-1955). The engine was now the ubiquitous Ilo 197cc single-cylinder, which produced 9.5bhp. This engine was also available in Fulda's own version of the 'S' model, which it named the S-2, but the Sachs 359cc engine was also available. The S-2 sold for a small premium over NWF's version, with which it was concurrently sold.

Fuldamobil S-3 / S-4 / S-6
D • 1955/1955-56/1956-57 • 2F1R • No built: Approx 2/168/123

The S-3 was a 191cc Sachs-engined prototype, the production version of which was called the S-4. This model marked Fulda's shift away from three-wheelers, with a close-set twin rear wheel system similar to the BMW Isetta's; however a version with a single rear wheel remained available to order. With the popular smaller engine fitted, the S-4 sold for considerably less than the outgoing S-2. Its slightly improved successor, the S-6, had a redesigned chassis with revised front suspension.

Fuldamobil S-7
D • 1957-1969 • 2F1R • No built: Approx 700

1957 was a year of revolution for Fuldamobil. The S-7 had much-revised body styling, now realised in glassfibre. That meant lighter weight, and improved performance and economy from the same Sachs 191cc engine. Also new was the chassis which featured close-set twin rear wheels in the German market, but many export markets favoured the three-wheel version. From 1965, the company switched to a 198cc Heinkel two-stroke engine with 10bhp. The Fuldamobil lasted longer than any other German microcar, and was also manufactured in more overseas countries than almost any other car: licensed production took place in Britain with the Nobel 200 ⇨, the Netherlands (Hostaco Bambino ⇨), Sweden (Fram King Fulda), Norway, Chile and Argentina (Bambi – also available as a pick-up), India (Hans Vahaar) and Greece (Attica ⇨ and Alta ⇨).

Fulu FL200/250/600/5000ZK
CN • 2000s-date • 1F2R • No built: n/a

The Fulu brand was part of the Shandong Jindalu Vehicle Co, and three-wheelers were its speciality. At least five different body styles were offered, including enclosed four-door saloons and an open-sided leisure car. The shape of one version was clearly inspired by the Daewoo Matiz. Sold as the FL200ZK and FL250ZK with 197cc and 249cc single-cylinder engines respectively, or as the FL600ZK with a 600cc two-cylinder unit (35bhp), this was slightly more sophisticated than the norm for Chinese cars. An electric version, the FL5000ZK, was also made, powered by a 5kW electric motor, achieving fame in the USA where it was marketed as the ZAP Xebra ⇨.

Fulu FL150ZK / FL17
CN • 2000s-date • 1F2R • No built: n/a

The FL150ZK was a smaller four-door vehicle from Fulu, sometimes referred to as the Lesser Panda, perhaps because the headlamp design had resonances with China's most famous mammal. The driver sat up front steering by handlebars, with two passengers behind. Buyers could choose between 149cc or 175cc single-cylinder engines. The FL17 was a more modern design with the same mechanicals.

Fun E-Cycle Kone
CDN • 2011-date • 2F1R • No built: n/a

Fun E-Cycle, a Quebec-based company, offered several electric three-wheelers including the Kone. This single-seater had a 60V battery and was steered via two joysticks, boasting a top speed of 20mph (32km/h) and a range of 37 miles (60km). In Canada, you needed neither a licence nor a registration plate to drive one.

Fuping
CN • 2000s-date • 1F2R • No built: n/a

Weihai Fuping Motor Tricycles offered a range of three-wheelers with open, semi-enclosed and fully-enclosed bodywork, including the FPD150ZK and FPD200ZK.

FWR
GB • 1959 • 2F1R • No built: Probably 1

This mysterious miniature coupe was registered in March 1959 and produced by a company called FWR Ltd based in Bournemouth, Dorset. It is not known if it ever entered production.

THREE-WHEELERS A-Z

GGG

Ghia Ford Cockpit ▲

General Motors Runabout ▲

▼ Gerweiss

Grinnall Scorpion III ▲

▼ Gordon

G-2
CDN • 2007-date • 2F1R • No built: n/a

One of many trikes inspired by the Campagna T-Rex ⇨, the G-2 also hailed from Canada. In its tubular steel chassis sat one of a number of motorbike engines – and with the 'right' one fitted, the 523kg G-2 could accelerate from 0-60 mph in 3.8 seconds. The glassfibre body could be open or, as the VTR-S, fully enclosed with doors and a different front end. Kit prices started at $19,995. The manufacturer, G-2 Cycles, was bought by Customs Alley in 2012.

Gaia Deltoid

GB • 1994-2002 • 2F1R • No built: 11

Nothing like it . . . .

Gaia Cars described its Deltoid as "a fusion of superbike and supercar" and "Batman meets Stealth bomber." It was certainly striking. A complete motorbike rear end (usually Suzuki, right up to Hayabusa) bolted on to a tubular steel fore-chassis, and you could even convert it back to a motorbike. The glassfibre centre body was bonded on to the chassis, and an aeroplane-style sliding canopy featured on early cars (gullwing doors were later adopted).

Gaici Mini Tre

I • 1990s-date • 1F2R • No built: n/a

Gaici, based in Capena (RM) in Italy, offered the Piaggio Ape-based Mini Tre principally as a small luggage carrier, but its glassfibre bodywork was suitable, said the manufacturer, for summer leisure use by removing the doors, front roof and rear hardtop.

Gaici Cricket 50

I • 1990s-date • 2F1R • No built: n/a

The Cricket 50 used 50cc moped mechanicals and could seat two people under cover, with 80 litres of luggage space and a removable roof for summer motoring. Its glassfibre bodywork was optimistically described as "modern and aerodynamic," in both regular and notchback 'Sport' body styles.

Gaitán Auto-Tri

E • 1953 • 1F2R & 2F1R • No built: Very few

Construcciones Gaitán of Seville, Spain mostly made invalid carriages, but the Auto-Tri was also sold with various dbodywork options such as rickshaws. Notable were two models: a 1F2R open-topped car, and a 2F1R 'bubble' car with a Dr Seuss-style rear fin, whose 125cc motorcycle engine powered the front wheels. All Gaitáns had aluminium bodywork.

Gallati Tri-X

USA • 1982-1983 • 1F2R • No built: n/a

The Tri-X was made by Gallati-Tenold of Rogers, Minnesota. It was a commuter coupe with a steel chassis and a glassfibre body. You could choose from petrol or diesel engines, and kit-form or fully-built cars.

GAP Sherpa

F • 1955 • 1F2R • No built: n/a

GAP stood for Générale Automobile Parisienne, a company which made the three-wheeled Sherpa, powered by a Panhard Dyna engine. The Sherpa was principally a delivery vehicle, but a model that could carry passengers was also offered.

Gashopper

USA • 1980s-date • 2F1R • No built: n/a

An ultra-basic commuter car of a type seen time and again in the USA, the Gashopper emerged from Miami, Florida. Its two-seater glassfibre body (with a roof) kept weight down to 91kg (200lb) and it could reputedly do 100mpg. MotoAmerica was still hoping to productionise, in 2013, an updated Gashopper with a 90cc engine for under $3000.

GBS Bullet

GB • 2008 • 2F1R • No built: Probably 1

This single-seater monocoque sports car was intended to be sold in kit form, although it's doubtful that it ever made it to the market. Engines from 50cc to

1000cc, or even electric power, were all suggested by the manufacturer, with 50cc versions having the distinction of being legally drivable in the UK by 16-year olds.

G-Car Eagle
RP • 2001-2012 • 1F2R • No built: n/a

Founded by Gerry Caroro, G-Car Motors of Quezon City in the Philippines produced this compact four-seater E-trike whose design was apparently inspired by the Philippine eagle. Electric power offered a range of up to 50 miles (80km) and a top speed of up to 50mph (80km/h), while solar panels were an optional extra.

Geely McCar
CN • 2011 • 2F1R • No built: 1

The very oddly-named Geely McCar prototype was a hybrid-powered four-seater hatchback with the novelty of a folding three-wheeled electric scooter built into the rear. When the scooter was docked, it could either extend the all-electric range of the main car, or be charged up on the hoof.

Gef Motors Queen Star
TN • 2010 • 1F2R • No built: n/a

Making its debut at the Salon de l'Auto in Paris in September 2010 was this Tunisian-made solar-powered electric three-wheeler. Perhaps understandably given its comically tortured styling, it is believed that the Queen Star did not make another public appearance.

Geier Rikscha
D • 1950s • 1F2R • No built: n/a

The German firm of Geier was best known for its mopeds, but it also made a range of three-wheelers, including passenger rickshaws with open or weather-protected bodywork, powered by an Ilo 145cc engine.

Gemini
I • 1982-1983 • 1F2R • No built: n/a

This small electric microcar (2040mm/80in long) had one distinctive novelty: its doors cut into the roof and opened on cantilevers towards the front of the car, thus saving space, while they could also be removed for open-air motoring. The Gemini sat three people in a row and delivered its power to the rear wheels using eight 48V batteries and a 6kW motor.

Genata
CN/J/D • 2008-date • 1F2R • No built: n/a

This brand (based in Frankfurt and Japan, but with factories in China) offered scooter-derived trikes with the delightful names of Simple, Space (above left) and Big One (above right). Power was either 200cc petrol or 800W electric.

General Motors Runabout
USA • 1964 • 1F2R • No built: 1

General Motors dabbled in three-wheelers as early as 1964. The Runabout hatchback was designed as a shopping vehicle, so its single front wheel could spin 180 degrees to allow the car to be turned within its own length. Reinforcing the message, two removable shopping trolleys were built into the rear of the car. The cabin could seat two adults and three children, and featured a pad with electronic dials instead of a steering wheel.

General Motors XP511
USA • 1969 • 1F2R • No built: 1

This sporty-looking trike was a concept prototype from GM. It featured a large forward-opening canopy, seating for two and an overall height of just 1015mm (40in). Fitted with an Opel 1100cc engine and a three-speed gearbox, it weighed 590kg (1300lb) and was claimed to reach 80mph (130km/h).

General Motors Lean Machine
USA • 1983 • 1F2R • No built: 2

One of the world's first tilting three-wheelers – and possibly the best known – emerged from the bowels of General Motors. Designed by Frank Winchell, the humorously named Lean Machine tilted into corners, years before the Vandenbrink Carver ⇨. The whole of its front bodywork leaned over, with pedals controlling the movement. The single-seat glassfibre body was very narrow at 910mm (36in) wide and the whole machine weighed just 181kg (400lb). A 38bhp Honda two-cylinder engine sat in a non-tilting rear pod, and could take the car to 80mph (130km/h) and do 0-60mph in 6.8

seconds, while 120mpg was claimed. A CVT automatic gearbox took drive to the solid rear axle. Having made its debut at Disneyland, perhaps fittingly it subsequently made a movie appearance in the 1993 film Demolition Man.

GerWeiss
RP • 2008-2012 • 1F2R • No built: Approx 300

GerWeiss Motors Corporation claimed to offer "the most number of electric vehicle models" of any company in the world. As well as cargo trucks, jeepneys, shuttle buses and boats, it presented a series of electric tricycles that fitted into the Philippine government's e-Trike format. Many of GerWeiss's models seemed to be speculative, but the company did build around 300 vehicles in all. The E-3 was its first effort, built in two- and four-seater forms, with a claimed range of up to 62 miles (100km), which could be boosted with an optional extra battery pack. GerWeiss even contemplated making an amphibious three-wheeled electric car. Its website beame inactive in 2012 but its designs also appeared under the E-Save brand ⇨.

GG Taurus
CH • 2009-date • 2F1R • No built: n/a

Having made waves with its revolutionary high-performance four-wheeled GG Quad, Swiss company Grüter + Gut GmbH added a three-wheeler called the Taurus. It could be fitted with a BMW 1150cc flat-twin engine, or a 1293cc four-cylinder unit with as much as 175bhp. Weighing only 397kg,

the performance was spectacular (top speed was a claimed 137mph/220km/h). Front crossmembers and a rear swinging arm in aluminium were part of a sophisticated specification, which included a reverse gear.

Ghia Lambretta Surrey
I • 1958-1959 • 1F2R • No built: n/a

Italian design house Ghia turned its hand to the Lambretta FDC ⇨ commercial vehicle and morphed it into a rickshaw taxi called the Surrey. Ghia's bodywork allowed for three passengers to be seated on a rear bench, with an optional roof to provide weather protection. The Surrey was powered by the same 150cc two-stroke engine as the Lambretta on which it was based, and was claimed to average fuel economy of 75mpg. The world was not yet ready for rickshaws, however, and only a handful were made, including some sold in the USA for $1300 a piece by the Innocenti Corp of New York (the US distributor for Lambretta).

Ghia Ford Cockpit
I/USA • 1981 • 2F1R • No built: 1

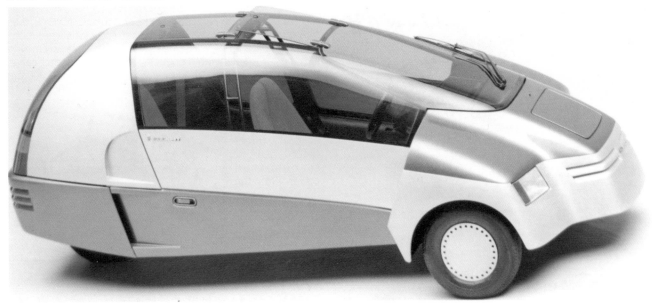

A re-invention of the Messerschmitt KR200 was what many journalists called Ghia's Ford Cockpit when it made its debut at the 1981 Geneva Motor Show. Its narrow body, tandem seating for two and aircraft-style canopy very much

mimicked the Schmitt's layout and even the 12bhp 200cc Piaggio single-cylinder engine sitting in the back was the same size. Measuring only 3290mm (129in) long, the Cockpit was touted as a "freeway commuter" and averaged 75mpg. Sadly, it was destined not to have a production future. The one and only Cockpit ever made was auctioned by Christie's in 2002 for $35,250.

Ghia Selene III
I • 1962 • 1F2R • No built: 1

Turin-based Carrozzeria Sibona & Basano built this amazing prototype for Ghia, based on a design of Virgil Exner. It was meant as a follow-up to the 1960 Ghia Selene II concept car, as a kind of speed record-breaker of the future. It was due to appear at the 1962 Turin Motor Show but was perhaps too radical even by show car standards and was never finished.

Gilbert Patriot
USA • 1974 • 1F2R • No built: n/a

A company in Manhattan Beach, California created this electric

two-seater commuter car. There was an on-board charger so you could plug into any 117V socket, and the car could run for up to 50 miles at a top speed of 50mph (80km/h). The Patriot was to be priced at $2695 but it's not known if a production run ensued.

Gilcolt
GB • 1972 • 1F2R • No built: n/a

A Streathham, London based dealer for Reliant ⇨ by the name of Ricketts was responsible for the Gilcolt. It was conceived as as a sporty car based on the Reliant Regal chassis (rather like the contemporary Bond Bug ⇨). The style of the glassfibre

bodywork was hardly pretty, but the Gilcolt boasted the exotic addition of gullwing doors. Kits were advertised from £250, or complete cars could also be supplied.

Gilera Fuoco
I • 2007-date • 2F1R • No built: n/a

Under the name of Gilera Fuoco 500ie, the Piaggio MP3 ⇨ was marketed with a larger 492cc engine and more aggressive styling. Described as an "urban-offroad style" trike, the Fuoco (Italian for 'fire') was a 'maxi-scooter' with two front wheels. It used the MP3's electro-hydraulic suspension to allow the vehicle to lean. The 40bhp single-cylinder engine, mated to a CVT automatic transmission, permitted an impressive top speed of around 100mph (160km/h).

Gladway

CN • 2005-date • 1F2R • No built: n/a

Various three-wheeled rickshaws were made by Gladway Holding, which was made up of sub-brands such as Shandong Mulan and Jinan Gladway. The company also planned to set up an assembly plant in Hungary. Electric, petrol-powered and hybrid rickshaw-style trikes were made, and models included the ML-TN02, ML-TO1, ML-T02 and the most original style of all, the ML-JT (pictured lower left). The latter's bubble-shaped glassfibre bodywork was just 34.5in (878mm) wide, and its 500W electric motor and 48V batteries allowed a top speed of 31mph (50khm).

GMT Microcab

GB • 2000-2007 • 1F2R • No built: n/a

London-based GMT (Greenheart Millennium Transport) built the Microcab as a hybrid pedal/electric taxi prototype. The first car had a 600W electric motor combined with pedal power, and was very light (125kg) and narrow (1060mm). In 2001, GMT won UK government funding to develop a 750W hydrogen fuel cell hybrid version. Pedal power was dropped in favour of 150W solar panels on the roof, and the top speed of this version was 26mph. GMT then abandoned the three-wheel format, going on to develop a four-wheeled Microcab.

Gnat

GB • 1969-1979 • 1F2R • No built: n/a

The long-standing firm of Aimers McLean, based in Galashiels, Scotland, designed and produced the Gnat as a truly go-anywhere vehicle – as proved by one summiting Ben Nevis. A basic open two-seater with tiller steering, it

was powered by a Briggs & Stratton 400cc four-stroke engine with 10bhp, driving the rear wheels via a three-speed gearbox at speeds up to 25mph (40km/h). It was claimed to be able to climb 45-degree inclines and traverse 30-degree slopes.

Gnom

D • 1949-1950 • 1F2R • No built: 3

IFG (Ingenieurbüro Fahrzeug- und Gerätebau C. M. Gick) was a company based in West Berlin that had successfully produced clip-on engines for bicycles since 1921. In 1949 it briefly moved into the car market with a doorless, roofless two-seater called the Gnom, which measured only 2200mm long and 1000mm wide. An Ilo 123cc air-cooled single-cylinder engine with 5.5bhp sat in the tail, and had to be started by hand. A three-speed gearbox transmitted power to the right-hand rear wheel only, at speeds of up to 37mph (60km/h).

Gommel

D • 1947 • 2F1R • No built: Probably 1

This Hohenheim-based company produced a single-seater cabin scooter just after WW2. Just ahead of the single rear wheel was a 147cc single-cylinder two-stroke engine with 3bhp. No production run apparently ensued.

Gordon

GB • 1954-1958 • 1F2R • No built: Several hundred

Vernon Industries of Bideston, Cheshire was most famous for running the football pools, but its Gordon microcar was the very antithesis of a jackpot winner's transportation. Vernons ⇨ had been making disabled cars since 1952 and used this design as the basis of its Gordon – and it was extremely

crude as a result. For instance, the Villiers 197cc single-cylinder two-stroke engine sat outside the main bodywork in a little 'pouch' of its own, meaning there was only one door to get in by (on the passenger's side). Drive was transmitted to only the offside rear wheel by chain.

Designed by Erling Poppe of Sunbeam motorcycle fame, the steel bodywork was big (134in/3400mm long) and heavy, so the Gordon struggled to reach a top speed of 45mph (72km/h). It was hard to believe Vernon's claim that the Gordon was "Britain's finest three-wheeler family car." Among few selling-points were simplicity, a folding roof and cheap prices (Britain's cheapest car, in fact, at just over £300).

Gordon Trikes
J • 2010s-date • 1F2R • No built: n/a

This Japanese trike maker essentially took a Trike Japan ⇨ trike and made its own dynamically styled rear ends. Top of the range was a Hayabusa 1340 trike with a double-wishbone rear axle; less powerful trikes had a live rear axle. Various models based on Yamaha, Harley-Davidson and Honda were offered.

Greaves Garuda
IND • 1995-1998 • 1F2R • No built: n/a

Greaves was an Indian rickshaw maker which eventually entered into an alliance with Piaggio ⇨ to make Italian-designed rickshaws in 1998.

Green Auto SH8500Z
CN • 2007-date • 2F1R • No built: n/a

Green Auto Industry Co of Wucheng in Shandong Province started making electric cars in around 2007. The SH8500Z was very distinctive, with fish-like glassfibre bodywork over a steel cage frame, looking very narrow but in fact seating two passengers side-by-side. An 8.5kW electric motor provided enough power to reach 75mph (120km/h), with a range of up to 112 miles (180km). This car achieved a lot of publicity because a Californian company called Green Vehicles was all set to sell it – and indeed manufacture it – in the USA as the Triac ⇨, priced at around $25,000. However, the US company closed its operations in 2011.

Green Auto SH5000Z
CN • 2010-date • 2F1R • No built: n/a

A smaller, simpler sister model to the SH8500Z, the SH5000Z had less power (5kW), so its top speed was only 43mph (70km/h) and its range was 100 miles (160km). Measuring only 1540mm wide, its narrow body seated two in tandem; versions with and without doors were marketed.

Green Lite
USA • 2011-date • 2F1R • No built: n/a

Green Lite Motors developed a fully enclosed hybrid leaning three-wheeler. Petrol and electric motors enabled performance of 85mph and 100mpg. A steel roll cage protected the two passengers (seated in tandem). At the time of writing, sales had yet to start at a planned price of $19,500.

GreenTech T1

CN • 2008-date • 2F1R • No built: n/a

Unlike most Chinese electric car companies, GreenTech was outward-looking, employing engineers from the UK, France, Germany and Switzerland, and exhibiting at the Geneva Motor Show. The T1 was original, at least, with a single central front seat for the driver and two seats behind. It weighed 730kg and an 8kW motor drove the single rear wheel via a three-speed automatic transmission, with speeds up to 62mph (100km/h) and a range of 93 miles (150km) quoted.

GreenTech T2

CN • 2010-date • 1F2R • No built: n/a

The T2 was more compact than the T1 at 2505mm long, and was designed mainly for short journeys, especially by the elderly. It also had a three-seater layout, and both three- and four-wheeled versions were offered. Powered by a 1.2kW electric motor, it had a modest top speed of 25mph (40km/h).

Grewe & Schulte S54

D • 1954-1956 • 1F2R • No built: Approx 20

Based in Lünen in Westfalia, Grewe & Schulte started making vehicles for the disabled in 1952. Its curiously styled S54 model used tiny 8in scooter wheels and a front-mounted 197cc Ilo single-cylinder two-stroke engine with 9.5bhp.

G-Rex

CDN • 2007-date • 2F1R • No built: Approx 7

Originally created by Gino Levesque of New Brunswick, Canada to break land speed records at Bonneville, the G-Rex eventually became a pure road project. Clearly influenced by the Campagna T-Rex ⇨, it used a small-block Chevrolet V8 engine with 350bhp and a Chrysler Intrepid four-speed automatic transmission. Weighing 658kg (1450lb), a remarkable top speed of over 200mph was claimed.

Grid Beam

USA • 2007-date • 1F2R • No built: n/a

Grid Beam was a building system invented in the 1970s, based on re-usable beams of steel and wood with repeating hole patterns, enabling all sorts of objects to be created without expensive equipment. A community of Grid Beam users wrote books and published online telling builders how to create, among other things, the solar-powered three-wheeled car pictured.

Grilo

BR • 1981-1982 • 1F2R • No built: n/a

This Brazilian car was the brainchild of Marcelo Resende, and was built by a company called Fibron in Belo Horizonte. Measuring 2000mm long, it had a single front seat plus up to two passengers in the rear or, with the rear seats removed, extra cargo. It used a Lambretta 175cc engine and had handlebar steering.

Grinnall Scorpion III

GB • 1992-date • 2F1R • No built: Approx 250 (to 2013)

Utter originality made the Grinnall Scorpion III universally praised in the press and one of the most successful and long-lived sports trikes. It was the brainchild of Mark Grinnall, while its dramatic styling was the work of Steve Harper of MGA Developments.

Grinnall's own square-tube steel chassis made use of Ford front suspension and a BMW motorbike swinging arm suspended on a coil/spring damper unit. The bug-like glassfibre body consisted of an inner tub and outer body section, bonded and riveted to the chassis. Two people could be seated side-by-side in an exposed cockpit with a small wind deflector. As there was no weather protection, the interior materials were water-proof, while an opening rear lid accessed a small luggage tray.

You could choose any BMW K series motorbike engine: initially the choice was between a three-cylinder K75 750cc (75bhp), K100 four-cylinder (90bhp), or K1 16V 1100cc (120bhp). A BMW five-speed sequential gearbox provided

sharp gearchanges and performance was spectacular in a car that weighed a mere 340kg (750lb) – Grinnall claimed 0-60mph in 5 seconds and a top speed of 125mph for the K100 version.

At launch, kits cost £7445 and fully-built cars from £10,250. On the options list were a waterproof cockpit cover, electric reverse gear and a lightweight chassis, the latter being standardised in 1994. A light restyle occurred in 1998, when a BMW K1200 engine option became available, while a BMW K40-powered version arrived in 2010.

Grinnall Trike
GB • 2000-date • 1F2R • No built: Approx 75 (to 2013)

Grinnall's chopper-style Trike could convert a BMW or Triumph motorbike into a three-wheeler. The models that Grinnall contemplated for the conversion were the BMW R850C, R1200C, R1150R and R1200 CL, or the Triumph Rocket and Thunderbird. The conversion procedure took 30 hours to complete, and was fully reversible if you wanted to revert back to two-wheeled motoring. This was one of the more popular bike-to-trike conversions in the UK, and widely regarded as of high quality.

Gryfia
PL • 1963 • 2F1R • No built: 1

In 1963, the motorcycle brand Junak built this prototype. It used mostly Junak components, including the 349cc 15bhp engine and rear suspension. Three passengers could be accommodated side-by-side, but this reportedly unbalanced the car and this was the main reason why the project was abandoned.

THREE WHEELERS A-Z

HHH

Heinkel Trojan 200 ▼

Hagen
N • 1940s • 2F1R • No built: A few

Sverre Hagen ran an engineering company in Hamar, Norway and built a small series of electric three-wheelers during WW2 with enclosed bodywork featuring a roll-back roof.

Hammerhead II
USA • 2012-date • 2F1R • No built: n/a

This DIY plans-built trike's tubular chassis had what was called a "viper's nest" look. Suspension was by unequal-length A-arms with an anti-roll bar up front and a rear swinging arm. Suzuki's TL1000 V-twin engine provided the power, although in-line four-cylinder units were also possible.

Hannigan
USA • 1975-date • 1F2R • No built: n/a

Hannigan kits transformed various motorbikes (including Honda Goldwing, Harley, BMW, Yamaha and Kawasaki) into trikes. The wide-track independent rear end saved weight compared to solid-axle conversions, and benefited from an anti-roll bar and gas dampers. A Ford Thunderbird differential was used, as well as vented disc brakes. Various rear styling treatments were available, including a novel 'whale tail' rear spoiler.

Haoda
CN • 2000s • 1F2R • No built: n/a

Jinan Haoda Motorcycle Co made a variety of crude three-wheelers from the single-seater HD100ZC up to enclosed three-seaters such as the HD125ZK. All were motorbike-based with handlebar steering and engines of between 100cc and 150cc.

Harding De Luxe Model A & B
GB • 1949-1966 • 1F2R • No built: n/a

RA Harding of Bath was founded in 1921 and was the most prolific invalid car maker of its day – and its heyday was undoubtedly between the two world wars. It offered no less than eight different types of vehicle for the disabled in the 1920s. These were either hand-propelled or, from 1926, could be had with petrol engines and electric motors. Early De Luxe Model A and Model B models had 122cc Villiers engines mounted under the single seat, but from 1948 the Model A and B gained a slightly larger 147cc Villiers two-stroke engine. Alternatively, electric power was available. Hand propelled disabled vehicles were built right up until 1973.

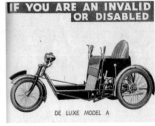

IF YOU ARE AN INVALID OR DISABLED

DE LUXE MODEL A

Harding Consort
GB • 1955-1966 • 1F2R • No built: 12

The Consort was a slightly fuller-bodied invalid carriage, but was still too crude to score any real success. It was offered with a 147cc petrol engine or electric power. Harding continued to make hand-propelled vehicles for the disabled long after it axed motorised production in 1966.

Harley-Davidson Penster
USA • 1998-2006 • 2F1R • No built: 4

One of the greatest names in motorcycling, Harley-Davidson also dabbled in three-wheelers. It made the Servi-Car delivery trike and police patrol vehicle from 1932 to 1973, but could have anticipated the market for performance trikes, had its 1998 prototypes reached production. Under the codename Penster, the trikes were designed for Harley-Davidson by custom car guru John Buttera. Power came from Harley's air-cooled V-Twin, and the machine was designed to tilt into corners. At the time of writing it was possible to see a Penster prototype at the Harley-Davidson museum.

Harley-Davidson Tri Glide & Street Glide
USA • 2009-date • 1F2R • No built: n/a

With the Tri Glide, Harley-Davidson finally recognised the value of the lucrative 'touring trike' market that others had been tapping into for years. Based on the Electra Glide motorcycle, the Harley was converted to a three-wheeler with the help of Lehman Trikes ⇨, which initially built the machines (until 2012, when manufacture was taken in-house by Harley-Davidson). A more basic version was also briefly

offered under the name Street Glide. Powered by a 1690cc V-twin engine with 70bhp, these trikes also incorporated a reverse gear. Perhaps the Tri Glide's greatest moment of fame came when one led the parade at Barack Obama's 2009 inauguration as president of the USA.

Harper Mk1 & Mk4
GB • 1954-1957 • 1F2R • No built: n/a

Harper Engineering of Exeter took over the old Argson ⇨ invalid carriage operation in 1954 but withdrew the existing range, replacing it with a new glassfibre-bodied range. Various body styles were presented, including curvaceous and slab-sided, open and closed, all with a single front headlamp. A rear-mounted Villiers 197cc was the usual engine, but 36V electric versions were also built. The Mk4 of 1956 shared the slab-sided Mk1's bodywork but with a wider windscreen and ridged body lines to improve strength.

Harper Mk6 & Mk7
GB • 1957-1965 • 1F2R • No built: n/a

New Ministry of Health requirements ushered in the Mk6 (pictured) with more generously sized glassfibre bodywork. It retained the option of 36V electric power or a 197cc Villiers engine, the latter also offered with the novelty of Harpermatic continuously variable automatic transmission from 1959. The Mk7 of 1960-1965 had a taller roof and a Villiers Mk11 engine.

Hawaiian Chariot
USA/CN • 2011-date • 1F2R • No built: n/a

This was a wheelchair-accessible trike created by Daniel Ward, a motorbike enthusiast who had lost the use of his legs. A 250cc four-stroke engine and two-speed automatic transmission with reverse were operated by either a hand-control steering wheel or handlebars. The Chariot was actually built in China but offered through Ward's Hawaiian company for $16,000.

Heald
USA • 1970s-1980s • 1F2R • No built: n/a

Heald Inc of Benton Harbor, Michigan produced kit-form trikes using Briggs & Stratton or Kohler lawnmower engines and an automatic gearbox. Intended mainly for off-road use, an optional lighting kit enabled on-road use, while the 'torpedo' glassfibre bodywork option made it more sophisticated than the norm.

Heathfield Slingshot

GB • 1993-1996 • 2F1R • No built: Probably 1

Peter Heath and Michael Fey's Heathfield Slingshot was a Morganesque three-wheeler made in Chesterfield, Derbyshire. It featured a robust round-tube space frame chassis with Ford Cortina front uprights and double wishbone front suspension, with a specially-made rear arm. Steering was by Mk2 Ford Escort. The Slingshot was larger overall than other similar trikes, allowing lots of cockpit space, although its barrel-back bodywork had no luggage space. The bodyshell was glassfibre but there was optional all-alloy bodywork. A Honda CX V-twin motorbike engine (500cc or 650cc) provided good performance as the weight was only 385kg (850lb). Kits were offered at £2650.

Heinkel Kabine

D/AR/IRE/GB • 1956-1965 • 2F1R • No built: Approx 30,000

Ernst Heinkel's credentials for making cars were excellent: he had designed not only Saab's three-cylinder two-stroke engine but also the 1953 Heinkel Tourist scooter, which was highly successful.

The Heinkel Kabine's apparent duplication of the Isetta's shape initially caused a lot of consternation from BMW, but the resemblance was superficial. The egg-shaped steel bodywork and opening front door did indeed look familiar, but the Heinkel did not use a folding steering wheel. The car was also lighter, had more space inside and offered an extra row of children's seats in the rear. Also unlike the Isetta, the Heinkel was far more commonly produced as a three-wheeler (although four-wheelers were also made).

Heinkel used the same single-cylinder four-stroke 174cc unit from Tourist scooter in the Kabine. With 9bhp, it could power the 250kg microcar to a top speed of around 54mph (87km/h). The original Model 150 lasted only a year; by then, the updated Model 153 (three wheels) and 154 (four wheels) had arrived, featuring 204cc engines (later reduced to 198cc for insurance reasons).

Ernst Heinkel died in 1958, just after his little car was withdrawn from production in Germany with around 12,000 built, but production continued for many years in other countries. In Argentina, the local Heinkel was made from 1959 (2962 examples built). In Ireland, the Heinkel-I was made by Dundalk Engineering Company from 1958 to 1961, and some 6486 cars were built here. The Irish firm also developed a full convertible version called the Open Tourer, although this was not productionised.

The Irish licence then transferred to Trojan in Croydon, Surrey, a marque which had not made any cars since 1936. It made three-wheeled cars in both left- and right-hand drive forms, latterly with the name Trojan 200. Trojan also made an Estate Van version towards the end of the model's life (pictured bottom right). The bubble finally burst in 1965, after some 6187 cars had been made by Trojan.

Heli

CN • 1997-date • 1F2R • No built: n/a

Changzhou Wujin Heli Machinery was established in 1997, and offered at least 30 different varieties of rather conventional rickshaw-style electric trikes under the Heli brand. Its two most original designs were the HLT-001 (pictured above left) and the HLT-033 (below left), which had folding concertina side doors. Heli also exported trikes to South America, Africa and Asia.

Hezhong

CN • c2006-date • 1F2R • No built: n/a

This company from Zheijiang, China, offered several three-seaters, including the HY100ZK with a single-cylinder air-cooled 97cc engine with 6.5bhp and the HY125ZK with a 125cc 7bhp unit. These could be ordered with a roof and no doors, or with doors and no roof.

H-M Free-Way

USA • 1979-1985 • 2F1R • No built: Approx 2000

H-M stood for High-Mileage Vehicles, a company based in Burnsville, Minnesota. The Free-Way emerged in 1979 as a simple commuter vehicle. In its original guise, it was launched as an electric-only vehicle with a 6bhp motor, but subsequently it became fossil fuel-powered with a choice of single-cylinder engines of between 340cc and 450cc, or a diesel.

The Free-Way had a very narrow glassfibre hatchback body covering a steel frame and could seat two passengers in tandem (just). Its unusual shape was claimed to maximise aerodynamic efficiency. It was in fact quite long (only five inches shorter than a Mini) and its top speed of 55mph was limited by the car's weight (700lb/318kg). Prices started at a bargain $2495 and large numbers were sold. After the original company foundered in 1982, the project was taken on by a bicycle manufacturer called Pedalpower, while a modified Free-Way was later launched as the D&A Minikin ⇨.

Hoba I & Hoba II

CZ • 1975/1979 • 2F1R • No built: A few

A Skoda employee called František Honc, a resident of Bakov (hence 'Hoba'), designed this coupe rebodying of the Velorex ⇨. Two examples were built by him (one on a Velorex 16/250, the other on a 16/350), but he sold

the moulds on and several more were made. Honc's second design, the Hoba II, was also based on a Velorex, but its design was more sophisticated.

Honda Stream/Gyro

J • 1981-date • 1F2R • No built: Several hundred thousand

British engineer George Wallis patented his tilting trike idea in 1966, and licensed it first to BSA, which made the Ariel 3 ⇨. After that project failed, he sold the licence to Honda, which produced a variety of models using his tilting trike technology. The first was the Stream of 1981. This was powered by a 49cc two-stroke engine mounted in a pod at the rear, driving the rear wheels through a limited slip differential. Two other simpler models – the Joy and Just – joined the Stream in 1983, but all three only lasted until 1984. Another variant was the stripped-down Road Fox of 1984-1985.

The Gyro of 1982 – geared more towards luggage carrying – proved to be the most popular Honda trike of all, and was available in several versions including the Canopy with a rudimentary roof (pictured right). The Gyro switched to four-stroke power in 2008, and remains in production at the time of writing.

Honda XXX

J • 1983 • 2F1R • No built: Probably 1

Appearing at the 1983 Tokyo Motor Show, Honda's curious XXX was an enclosed car whose middle body section hinged sideways to allow access to the single seat. The engine sat in the nose driving the two front wheels.

Honda 3R-C

J • 2010 • 2F1R • No built: n/a

Honda's next single-seater concept car was the 3R-C, which was actually designed by Honda's European R&D operation in Milan. The driver's head stuck out of the top when in motion, while a plastic canopy sealed the car when parked. It used motorbike tyres and handlebars and an electric motor, but clearly had no production future.

Honda E-Canopy
J • 2011 • 1F2R • No built: n/a

This was effectively an electric version of the Honda Gyro Canopy ⇨ with updated bodywork, which debuted in prototype form at the 2011 Tokyo Motor Show. At the time of writing it had not yet entered production.

Hongyan / Hongzhou
CN • 2005-date • 1F2R • No built: n/a

This company started life as the ChangGe Lifan Hongyan Tricycle Co but later became ChangGe HongZhou Vehicle Industry Co. Its annual production capacity was an astonishing 250,000 petrol trikes and 500,000 electric ones. It mainly made three-wheeled delivery vehicles but also rickshaws and an enclosed four-door vehicle called the HZ150QZK (pictured lower right).

Horlacher Ei
CH • 1988-1990 • 2F1R • No built: 32

Max Horlacher founded his enterprise in 1985 with the idea to make a 1F2R solar-powered car (pictured above right). Horlacher went on to make a 2F1R vehicle called the Ei or 'egg', which emerged in 1988 as a tandem two-seater glassfibre-bodied electric coupe. Only 2550mm long, 1310mm wide and weighing 300kg with 11 12V batteries in place, it could do 50mph (80km/h) and up to 75 miles on a charge, thanks to an 8kW Brusa motor. After the Ei, Horlacher concentrated on four-wheeled cars.

Hostaco Bambino Sport
NL • 1957 • 2F1R • No built: n/a

The Fuldamobil ⇨ saloon was sold under the name Hostaco Bambino in the Netherlands, but a novelty unique to the Dutch market was the open-topped Bambino Sport, built by Alweco. This doorless glassfibre roadster was powered by a single-cylinder 200cc Ilo 9.5bhp engine with three forward speeds and reverse, enabling a top speed of 56mph (90km/h). A four-wheeled version was also offered.

Hot Snake
BR • 2001-date • 1F2R • No built: n/a

What could have been just another chopper was made very distinctive by the addition of AC Cobra-inspired glassfibre rear bodywork. A VW 1.4-litre four-cylinder engine provided the power (all 78bhp of it), and the 580kg trike could do a top speed of 109mph (175km/h).

HSVP M3
J • 2008 • 2F1R • No built: 1

HSVP was short for Hamamatsu Smallest Vehicle Project, a Japanese endeavour based in the city of Hamamatsu. The M3 was a very small enclosed single-seater powered by a 49cc two-stroke engine, built under the supervision of Professor Kato of the Hamamatsu Polytechnic College.

HSVP T3
J • 2008 • 2F1R • No built: 1

Professor Takanashi Haneda of Shizuoka University of Art and Culture (SUAC) headed the design and prototyping of the T3, a small open car that looked somewhat like a dodgem car. The plastic bodywork was realised by Takayanagi. The T3 was powered by a 0.6kw electric motor, and HSVP hoped to produce a car based on the T3 in series, apparently without consequence.

Huaxin
CN • 1990s • 1F2R • No built: n/a

Made by the Shandong Gaotang Huaxin Electric Vehicle in the city of Gaotang (Shandong province), Huaxin cars were all electric-powered. An early model was called the QF-002 and had very narrow bodywork made of steel and a single door at the rear. Several other three-wheeled models were made, including one called the XM5.

Hudson Free Spirit & Kindred Spirit
GB • 1989-2003 • 2F1R • No built: Approx 17 / 140

In the 1980s, nearly all trike manufacturers drew on the 1930s Morgan for inspiration. Norwich-based Roy Webb took a different tack with his Free Spirit, which looked original and bucked convention by having just one seat. An extremely

narrow glassfibre body with cycle wings sat atop a twin rail chassis with steel panelling. Almost all the parts derived from the Renault 5, including its engine, gearbox, suspension, steering and brakes. Even the rear trailing arm was a reversed Renault 5 unit. The gear lever was centrally sited and the pedals split either side of the engine housing. As the car weighed under 400kg, a top speed of 130mph was possible.

If the Free Spirit felt anti-social, a second model, the Kindred Spirit (pic below), answered that from 1990: a tandem two-seater version, using a 12in longer wheelbase, with a luggage area too. This proved by far the more popular model. Hudson also mooted a traditional-style three-wheeler in 1994, but this never materialised. The 'Spirits' migrated to Wizard Cars from 1999 until 2003.

Hudson Stinger
USA • 2006-date • 2F1R • No built: n/a

David Hudson of Oakley, Michigan gave his name to the Hudson Stinger. A wide variety of engines could be fitted, from 650cc to 1200cc. A Ford Mustang II front end donated its suspension and steering, with room for a front luggage compartment and side storage. A convertible top and zip-out windows effectively made this an all-weather fun car. The chassis incorporated a tubular roll cage and the bodywork was in glassfibre. Kits were available from $18,500.

Hunt
USA • 1951 • 2F1R • No built: 1

Lloyd Hunt, an engineer at Southern Californian Edison, built a prototype chassis out of the parts of 10 different old cars, including a front-mounted 1925 Buick engine. He hoped to productionise a dramatic dome-topped seven-seater coupe on an enlarged chassis but this came to nought.

Huoyun HY-B2672
CN • 2010 • 2F1R • No built: n/a

Established in 2001, the Shandong Huoyun Electric Car Co built a range of electric cars, golf buggies and lorries. An electric replica of the Smart was one of its more notorious products, but the bizarre HY-B2672 looked like something out of Wacky Races. This three-seater electric car had a claimed top speed of 68mph, but the company seemed not overly confident about it, stating: "We need your suggestions in order to improve it." Apparently not enough encouraging suggestions were received, for nothing more was heard of it.

Husqvarna
S • 1943-1944 • 2F1R • No built: 1

During World War II, Sweden's leading motorbike brand contemplated making a three-wheeler. A streamlined shape was created – possibly – by Sixten Sason, the father of the Saab 92, who was working at Husqvarna at the time. A 20bhp two-cylinder 500cc DKW engine provided the power, with chain drive to the rear wheel. However the project was cancelled and the sole prototype was scrapped in the 1950s.

HyAlfa
IND • 2012-date • 1F2R • No built: 15

The HyAlfa was claimed to be world's first hydrogen-powered three-wheeler, jointly developed by parties as diverse as the United Nations Industrial Development Organisation and Mahindra. An experimental fleet of 15 rickshaws running on compressed natural gas (CNG) was built but high prices and running costs were major challenges to the project.

Hydromobile
USA • 1942 • 1F2R • No built: 1

Built by Joseph Szacaks, a Hungarian living in the USA, the Hydromobile was effectively a boat with wheels. The amphibian's three wheels retracted for use on water. The main body was made of wood, the engine was an 85bhp eight-cylinder Ford 4.7-litre unit and the car could do 75mph (120km/h) on land and 31mph (45km/h) on water. The one and only known example was, at the time of writing, on display in France.

Hyper Division HDX3
I • 2012-date • 1F2R • No built: n/a

Designed for the disabled, the HDX3 added a frame to a Honda scooter to accommodate a wheelchair platform. Engine sizes ranging from 50cc to 300cc could be used, in hybrid with an electric motor, and a reverse gear was included.

THREE WHEELERS A-Z

Isetta BMW-Isetta ▲▼

IndyCycle ▲

▼ Inter

Ian's Custom Cycles
GB • 1977-1979 • 1F2R • No built: Approx 5

This was a traditional chopper-style trike made in the UK.

Ice Bear
J/USA • 2000s-date • 1F2R • No built: n/a

Ice Bear Motor Scooters originated in Japan but from 2006 it also made vehicles in the USA, specialising in trikes and three-wheeled scooters. Its 250cc-300cc range had names that sounded like they came out of an episode of Gladiators: Magnum, Tornado, Zodiac, Compellor and Road Warrior. Its 150cc range comprised the Cyclone, Eagle, Viking and Cruiser, while the 50cc range consisted of the Mojo, Ace, Bullseye, Jupiter and Elf.

Icona E3WM
CN • 2010-date • 2F1R • No built: 1

The Icona design house was based in Shanghai but had strong links with Italy. The E3WM proposal was intended to combine the benefits of motorbikes and cars in one by offering tandem seating for two passengers with a modicum of weather protection. It was electric-powered (E3WM stood for Electric 3 Wheel Mobile) and had a range of 93 miles (150km). Its computer-controlled suspension tilted automatically into corners.

Impuls 77
S • 1977 • 2F1R • No built: n/a

Impuls Innovation was behind this small electric car featuring a single sliding door for entry and a swivelling seat to enable easier disabled access.

Indus-Electrans Nemo
IND • 2007-2008 • 1F2R • No built: n/a

Indus-Electrans, the automotive division of an Ahmedabad-based furnace maker called Electrotherm India (EIL), launched the Yo-byke electric motorbike in 2006. It hoped to follow this up with hybrid CNG/electric three- and four-wheelers. In 2007, it presented the Nemo rickshaw prototype with modern styling by Piyush Sharma. Several full-scale working prototypes were built, but the arrival of the Tata Nano economy car, which undercut the e-autorickshaw on price, effectively killed it.

IndyCycle
USA • 1999-date • 2F1R • No built: n/a

Designed by Jamieson DuRette, who was based in Bel Air, Maryland, the name IndyCycle reflected its concept of being half Indy car, half motorcycle. The bodywork was a mix of glassfibre, laminated wood and aluminium. The powerplant was a Suzuki GSXR 750cc unit, giving it a top speed of 150mph and 0-60mph in 4.2 seconds. At the time of writing, a plans set to build your own IndyCycle cost $75. Despite very strong similarities to the SportCycle ⇨, this project was not related.

Inter
F • 1953-1956 • 2F1R • No built: Approx 300

If the Messerschmitt KR175 was the fighter plane of the German microcar boom, the Inter was its eerily similar equivalent in France. It appeared in the same year (1953) and had more than its profile in common with the 'Schmitt. It was also built by an aircraft factory (SNCAN of Lyon), and its two tandem passengers gained entry by lifting a narrow dome-top sideways (a fully open Torpédo version was also offered). Already narrow at 53in (1350mm) wide, the Inter's party trick was the ability to shrink in size by 'folding' the front wheels inwards

and forwards so that, at just 35.4in (900mm) wide, it occupied no more space than a motorbike for parking. The Inter used

a 175cc Ydral single-cylinder two-stroke engine in the rear, driving the single rear wheel by chain through a three-speed gearbox. With 8.5bhp on tap, it enabled a top speed of 50mph (80kmh).

Internationale
NL • 1942 • 2F1R • No built: n/a

Shortages of fossil fuels during WW2 persuaded this Hague-based company to launch a lightweight electric taxi (dubbed Electrotax) with an enclosed front section; the driver sat exposed to the rear.

Invacar Mk1-Mk6
GB • 1947-1952 • 1F2R • No built: n/a

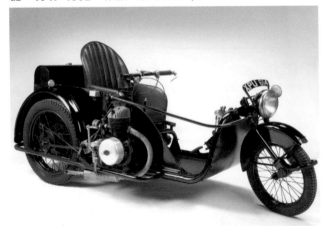

Invacar Ltd of Westcliff-on-Sea, Essex was founded by Bert Greeves and Derry Preston-Cobb, and became Britain's pre-eminent maker of vehicles for the disabled. Early models had tiller steering with a twist-grip throttle and a single seat, while versions were also built that could accommodate a purpose-built wheelchair. Engines were initially 125cc BSA or 122cc Villiers, but a larger 197cc Villiers unit was offered from 1948, always mounted on the offside of the chassis.

Invacar Mk8
GB • 1952-1956 • 1F2R • No built: n/a

The major innovation of the Mk8 was far better weather protection, formed by leathercloth bodywork stretched over a frame, a windscreen and a roof. The same chassis sat underneath it, with power provided by a 197cc Villiers Mk 8E engine. The Mk8A of 1955 gained new rubber-in-torsion rear suspension and a larger roof and rear window.

Invacar Mk10
GB • 1957-1959 • 1F2R • No built: 1003

New Ministry of Health rules for invalid carriages in 1957 forced Invacar to launch the all-new Mk10, which now had a rear-mounted engine (Villiers Mk9E 197cc) and conventional steering. Its pressed steel bodywork and canvas roof felt quite sophisticated for its day, but the car still weighed only 250kg (550lb). The front wheel grew in size from 10 to 12 inches with the Mk10A of 1958.

Invacar Mk12
GB • 1960-1971 • 1F2R • No built: n/a

The Mk12 saw a switch from steel to glassfibre bodywork and a sliding door for entry. Early models kept the 197cc Villiers Mk9E engine, uprated to the 11E in 1962. The Mk12 went through a series of minor evolutions, from the Mk12A to the Mk12E.

Invacar P70
GB • 1972-1977 • 1F2R • No built: n/a

Although built by Invacar, the P70 was in fact identical to the AC Model 70 ⇨, complete with its toilet-blue glassfibre bodywork and Steyr-Puch 493cc flat-twin engine and stepless automatic transmission.

IPAM-Leeds
AR • 1959-1961 • 2F1R • No built: Approx 200

Industrias Platenses Automotrices of La Plata, Buenos Aires was the name of the company that put Guillermo Leeds's intriguing amphibious bubble car into production. The Isetta-inspired bodywork could carry four passengers, who accessed the cabin through both a front door and a side door. Equipped with a 325cc two-stroke Villiers two-cylinder air-cooled engine, the IPAM-Leeds could reach 56mph (90kmh) on land. Water propulsion came from an optional three-bladed propeller, in which case a speed of 8mph (12kmh) could be reached.

Iresa
E • 1950s • 2F1R • No built: n/a

The Spanish motorcycle brand Iresa (Industrias Reunidas Espanolas SA) of Madrid branched out into 1F2R three-wheeled delivery vehicles powered by 200cc engines in 1956. It also made at least one prototype of a passenger vehicle in 2F1R format.

Iron Horse Trikes
USA • 2000s • 1F2R • No built: n/a

This company made custom-built trikes from a base in Lebanon, Ohio. Very much not of the shy and retiring school, they featured Chevy V8 engines.

IRs1000
I • 2004 • 2F1R • No built: n/a

The IRs1000 was one of a flurry of Italian projects that mushroomed on the back of the Piaggio MP3 ⇨, but this

leaning trike was distinctive in not being based on a scooter, but on a 'proper' motorbike. Its 120bhp engine gave strong performance, while the leaning system was reportedly very stable. However a production run was not forthcoming.

iSAVE-SC1
J • 2010-date • 2F1R • No built: Probably 1

Airbags are a modern life-saver, but no car took the idea to such extremes as the iSAVE-SC1. Built by a company called Humanix together with Hiroshima University, this small electric car had airbags all over its exterior. It was therefore claimed to be the "safest electric vehicle in the world." It was a three-seater with inflated airbags front and rear and bodywork covered in tent cloth. A top speed of 31mph (50kmh) was claimed. Humanix planned to offer cars for sale in Japan but as of 2013, this had not happened.

Isetta
I/D/E/BR/GB • 1953-1964 • 2F1R • No built: Approx 200,000

The great bubble car phenomenon was born in Italy when a fridge manufacturer called Renzo Rivolta smashed his brave new egg on to the road. The year was 1953 and the Iso Isetta was a truly remarkable device. For starters, it was tiny: 2290mm (90in) long. Then there was the door: the whole front end hinged outwards, carrying the steering wheel and instruments with it to ease access. Questions were asked about what happened in a crash, so a folding sunroof was provided for emergency exit. A single bench seat provided enough space for two, and possibly a child as well.

The Italians were frankly not ready for the brave metal spheroid, which sold only around 1000 units between 1953 and 1955. However, licences were sold to many other

countries, including Germany (BMW-Isetta, 1955-1962), Spain (Iso Espana, 1954-1958), Brazil (Iso-Romi, 1956-1961) and France (Velam, 1954-1958 ⇨). However, it was the German licensee, BMW, which really cashed in on the charms of the Isetta.

The original Iso always had four wheels, with a very narrow-set rear pair, and German-market cars followed suit, with four wheels and a BMW 247cc motorbike engine. For export markets, however, a 298cc 13bhp engine was fitted from 1956, in which guise the car was known as the BMW-Isetta 300, and this had three wheels. The maximum speed remained the same as before at 53mph (85km/h).

As the engine was slung out to one side, some interesting handling characteristics resulted, especially in unbalanced

right-hand drive cars. In 1957 came a revised version with new 'one-piece' side glass which incorporated a sliding mechanism for ventilation, replacing the three-window fixed glass treatment designed by Iso.

The end of the BMW line came in 1962, by which time a total of 161,728 BMW-Isettas had been built. It is fair to say that BMW's very existence is owed to the success of its three-wheeled bubble cars. In 1957, BMW had sold a licence to the UK, where Isetta of Great Britain manufactured the model at a converted locomotive factory in Brighton. Up until 1964, British Isettas were built in three- and four-wheeled forms, with saloon, convertible and pick-up bodies, at a rate of up to 175 per week. Estimates put the total quantity built in Britain at between 20,000 and 30,000.

ISSI Microbo

I • 1952-1954 • 2F1R • No built: n/a

The ISSI (Istituto Scientifico Sperimentale Industriale) Microbo was an extremely short (2200mm) but relatively tall microcar. The enclosed saloon featured a single door on the right-hand side, integral steel construction and a transparent Plexiglas roof. A rear-mounted 125cc single-cylinder Idroflex 5.5bhp two-stroke engine drove the single rear wheel.

Italindo Helicak

I/RI • Early 1970s • 2F1R • No built: Approx 860

Italindo was the Lambretta scooter concessionaire for Indonesia, based in Jakarta. In 1970, it got the Italian parent company, Innocenti, to make a series of 'Tri Lambrettas' as people transporters. Made in Italy and based on a DL 150 chassis with a 150cc engine, they were shipped to Indonesia where helicopter pods were added by Italindo, complete with conveniences like a sun roof and fully upholstered seats. The front hubs and steering were unique to this model, which was sometimes referred to as the Helitjak. The use of these vehicles was banned in 1987, with Indian-style rickshaws replacing them, and sadly almost all Helicaks made were subsequently destroyed by government decree.

Italindo Super Helicak

RI • Late 1970s • 1F2R • No built: Several thousand

Italindo turned to what was at the time (the mid-1970s) the world's leading three-wheeler expert, Britain's Reliant ⇨ in order to help it build a rather more substantial taxi to follow the Helicak. The Tamworth company developed a Robin-style chassis fitted with coil springs and oil-filled dampers. The resulting Super Helicak was powered by a Lambretta two-cylinder two-stroke engine (6bhp 125cc, or 12bhp 250cc), while four-speed automatic transmission was standard.

Fast the Super Helicak was not, maxing out at 31mph (50kmh), but it was fairly frugal at 42mpg. Inside the all-steel body, there was a single bench seat in the rear for two-to-three passengers, plus either a seat or cargo area beside the driver's seat.

ItalJet Scooop

I • 2001 • 2F1R • No built: Probably 1

Shown at the 2001 Milan Car Show, the Italjet Scooop (yes, it really was spelt with three 'O's) pioneered the idea of a scooter with two front wheels (later popularised by the Piaggio MP3 ⇨). Despite an announcement that Italjet would be launching the Scooop trike in 2002, in fact it stuck with making two-wheelers, allowing Piaggio to make the real 'scoop' in the marketplace.

IVM Vario-8

D • 1998 • 1F2R • No built: Probably 1

The German enterprise IVM Engineering famously formed a partnership with Callaway in the USA to build its Corvette-based supercars, but the IVM enterprise might have taken a very different direction had its Vario-8 three-wheeler prototype taken off. It was shown in 1998 at a show in Beijing, but remained a prototype with no production future.

THREE WHEELERS A-Z

JJJ

JZR ▲

Jurisch Motoplan ▲▼

Jetmobile ▼

JAG
BR • 1961 • 2F1R • No built: 1

Brazilian Joao Augusto Gurgel (hence JAG) built this flying saucer-shaped three-wheeler in 1961. It seated two people side by side and easily its most outstanding feature was that it sported an oversized central fin behind the passenger compartment. Although the JAG three-wheeler came to nothing, Gurgel went on to become probably Brazil's most successful domestic car brand, making all kinds of buggies, city cars and jeeps. Gurgel also developed a range of three-wheeled commercial vehicles under the name TA-01, which remain in production at the time of writing (but not in passenger carrying form).

Japtec Murate
J • 2010-date • 1F2R • No built: n/a

This urban-style scooter-based trike from Japan had the air of something Batman might drive. But instead of jet propulsion or suchlike, it had a mere single-cylinder 249cc four-stroke engine with 10bhp mated to a CVT automatic gearbox. It measured 2490mm long and weighed 190kg, with the front wheel (15in) larger than the rears (13in). It could seat two passengers in tandem and was priced from 888,000 yen (around £6200).

JB
F • 1945-1950 • 2F1R • No built: 3

The JB (or Jamin-Bouffort) was conceived by Victor Bouffort and based on the mechanicals of a Citroën Traction Avant, complete with hydropneumatic suspension. Its extraordinary aerodynamic bodywork featured long enclosed front wings, an elongated tail and gullwing doors. Three prototypes were built in Meaux, while Bouffort ⇨ went on to make several other three-wheeler designs.

JB Minor
AUS • 1949 • 2F1R • No built: Probably 1

Very few 2F1R three-wheelers have a single rear wheel that steers. That's because, dynamically, it's a pretty bad idea. But the Automotive Co of Australia, based in Northgate, Queensland, pursued just such a route for its JB Minor. The

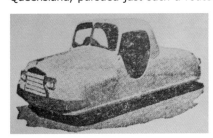

front wheels were driven by a 5bhp two-stroke two-cylinder engine. Designed by Jeffress Brothers, the body was built by the bus builder, Athol Hedges, but a planned production run never transpired.

JBF Boxer
GB • 1991-1992 • 2F1R • No built: 1

John Fernley's ambition with his JBF Boxer was to create a trike which was cheap and easy to build. It used a Citroën 2CV chassis with a single rear wheel connected to only one side of the 2CV's suspension system. The bodywork was made of plywood, glassfibre and aluminium sheet, featuring

a long barrel-back tail ending in the spare wheel. Although Fernley intended to offer kits from his Manchester base at around £2000, in fact only one Boxer was ever built.

JBR
E • 1947 • 2F1R • No built: 1

Josep Boniquet Riera was a Barcelona-based dentist who had made a range of cyclecars in the 1920s. His sole post-war effort was a doorless open trike with a single headlamp and a motorcycle engine; highly unusually, he used papier maché for the bodywork.

Jeluli
AR • 2006-date • 2F1R • No built: n/a

This exacting Morgan replica by Lito Luciani of Buenos Aires even kept the original construction of wood, steel, brass and aluminium. Sliding pillar front suspension was also very authentic, with rear quarter-leaf springs and an optional Hartford damper. The standard engine was a Honda CX but others were possible, plus a two-speed gearbox and optional reverse gear. Body styles included the 1933 'beetle back' or 1929 Super Sports Aero.

Jet
E • 1950s • n/a • No built: n/a

Very little is known about this Madrid-built three-wheeler, which had a 197cc Hispano Villiers single-cylinder two-stroke engine and plastic bodywork.

Jetmobile
USA • 1952 • 1F2R • No built: 1

Richard Harp of Maryland was the man behind the Jetmobile. He ingeniously used three aircraft fuel tanks for the bodywork, mounted over a steel chassis, the whole thing measuring a lengthy 4520mm (178in) and weighing 725kg (1600lb). For motive power, he fitted a Lycoming four-cylinder horizontally-

opposed aircraft engine driving through a Harley-Davidson four-speed transmission to the Willys rear wheels. The single-seater cabin used a mix of Chevrolet and

Grumann aircraft instruments. After a favourable reception at shows, Harp considered making a two-seater Jetmobile for public consumption, but that never happened.

Jiayang
CN • 2000s-date • 1F2R • No built: n/a

The Hangzhou Jiayang Tricycle factory built very basic rickshaw-type three-wheelers such as the JY-002-2 (pictured).

Jinfu
CN • 1996-date • 1F2R • No built: n/a

Produced by Jiangsu Hongzhou Jinfu Vehicle Co, the Jinfu range of tricycles was mostly for cargo. However, the JF150ZK was a typical Chinese enclosed motor tricycle with a 150cc engine, while a range of rickshaw styles was also offered.

Jinma
CN • 2004-date • 1F2R • No built: n/a

Qingzhou Dajinma Motorcycle Co specialised in three-wheelers with Jinma branding, most of which were cargo vehicles, but it also made a broad range of three-wheelers with 150cc, 175cc and 200cc engines, including the JM150ZK pictured.

Jolly 3D
I • 1983-1984 • 1F2R • No built: n/a

This very small saloon resembled a three-wheeled Fiat 126, which is unsurprising as it used Fiat 126 rear side windows and lights in its glassfibre bodywork. It was powered by a

small Ruggerini diesel engine (either 756cc or 856cc), chosen for licensing and tax reasons. Built in Bettona, Perugia, this car is sometimes referred to as the Valjolly.

JPS
E • 1940s • 2F1R • No built: n/a

This Spanish two-seater trike was made in the late 1940s, featuring front-wheel drive, a Tatra-type chassis, Villiers engine and Royal Enfield transmission.

JSA
IND • 1986-date • 1F2R • No built: n/a

JS Auto of Kanpur, Uttar Pradesh made autorickshaws with the names Tiger, Victory, Victory Plus and Victory RE (pictured). CNG was the normal fuel source.

Junior 3R
E • 1955-1956 • 2F1R • No built: n/a

The Barcelona-based company Junior produced the 3R – a dumpy little car with no doors or roof whose plastic body offered just enough space for two. A Villiers 197cc single-cylinder engine sat in the rear, whose 8bhp allowed a top speed of merely 43mph (70km/h). Three distinct series were made but overall production numbers were slight.

Jurisch Motoplan
D • 1957-1959 • 2F1R • No built: 3

Based in Nürnberg, Carl Jurisch built this very small single-seater. It was powered by a rear-mounted 175cc Heinkel scooter engine with 9.3bhp on tap, and had a four-speed gearbox. Despite this low power output, a slender weight of only 173kg (281lb) helped the Motoplan reach a top speed of 62mph (100km/h). The curious open bodywork was formed out of a Steib motorcycle sidecar. Three examples were built, one as a commercial vehicle.

Jurka

E • 1956-1957 • 2F1R • No built: Approx 2

After the creators of the AISA ⇨ realised the name had already been registered, they changed it to Jurka and built at least two three-wheeled prototypes under this name. One looked like a miniature fighter jet and was a single-seater. The other (pictured right) resembled a Brütsch Avolette ⇨ and had plastic bodywork by Carrocerias Capella, the design for which was done by Fermin Antonio Capella Hernandez.

JZR

GB • 1987-98/2000-date • 2F1R • No built: Approx 450 (to 2013)

Machine tool engineer and car restorer John Ziemba's modern reinterpretation of the Morgan entered production at his Darwen, Lancs works under the name JZR (John Ziemba Restoration). This was the first trike to be based on the Honda CX motorbike, using the rear section of the Honda frame complete with its rear wheel and swinging arm, mated to a steel square tube chassis with stressed steel side panels and bulkheads. The bonnet and upper rear bodywork (in either 'Beetleback' or 'Barrelback' styles) were in glassfibre. Basic kits sold for well under £1000, so it was a popular car.

The first-series JZR's CX500 or CX650 V-twin engines (offering 50bhp to 64bhp) drove the single rear wheel via a shaft through a five-speed motorcycle gearbox (electric reverse eventually became optional). Performance was excellent thanks to a weight of 399kg (880lb). The driveshaft dissected the cockpit in a way that limited space for the driver, but a long cockpit version launched in 1992 alleviated some of the problems experienced by taller drivers.

A Moto Guzzi engine option arrived in 1993, with a revised chassis whose wheelbase was extended by 76mm (3in) to accommodate the longer Guzzi rear swinging arm. Up to 95bhp was available with this engine. JZR also offered a version with an 1100cc Honda V4 Pan European engine, with 105bhp on tap. Another engine option was the 65bhp Harley Davidson 1340cc Evolution unit, fitted with a Ford Cortina gearbox with reverse gear. The JZR was also marketed in Spain as the Bandito from 1995.

JZR Daytona

GB • 2003 • 2F1R • No built: 2

JZR essayed this modern, doorless, roofless trike in a style that was reminiscent of the Grinnall Scorpion ⇨. The Daytona used a 128bhp Triumph Daytona motorbike engine, but only two cars were ever built.

THREE WHEELERS A-Z

KKK

Krause Duo ▲

Kobot B ▲

Kurunkov Autoaeromobil ▲

Kirk P-Type ▲

▼ Kroboth

KAL (Kerala)
IND • 1984-date • 1F2R • No built: n/a

KAL stood for Kerala Automobiles Limited, which was based in Aralumoodu in the province of Kerala. This government-backed operation started commercial production of petrol-powered rickshaws in 1984, with the technical collaboration of API ⇨. Diesel engines started being fitted from 1988 (from Greaves, later Elgi). The KAL was also exported to Bangladesh, Sri Lanka, Nepal and Guatemala, and a production rate of up to 15,000 units a year was possible.

KAL (Kranti)
IND • 1995-date • 1F2R • No built: Approx 25,000

The 'other' KAL in India was Kranti Automobiles Limited of New Delhi, which sold its rickshaws under the Nandi name. Various diesel-engined models were offered: the Super (in 325D, 360D and 450D forms) and the Super Shakti 400D. In 2004, CNG and LPG powered models arrived and a new model, the Jai Ho, in 2009.

Kalamazoo
USA • 1960s • 1F2R • No built: n/a

Kalamazoo's main trade was making factory floor runarounds, but it made some three-wheeled personnel carriers that could be classed as passenger vehicles.

Kandi KD-250MB
CN • 2010-date • 2F1R • No built: n/a

Zhejiang Kangdi Vehicles, based in the city of Zhejiang, made all sorts of electric vehicles, ATVs, golf carts and scooters. It also made some of the more striking looking Chinese trikes. The KD-250MB, for example, had an air of the BRP Can-Am ⇨ about it. Measuring 2465mm (97in) long, it was powered by a 250cc single-cylinder four-stroke engine with 13bhp

mated to a single-speed automatic gearbox. In various foreign markets it was sold under different names (such as Cyclone or Prowler), while it also appeared in its home market as badged as the Baoma ⇨.

Kandi KD-250MD
CN • 2010-date • 2F1R • No built: n/a

If the 'MB' looked like a Can-Am, Kandi's 'MD' was inspired by the Campagna T-Rex, although its scooter engine kept its performance credentials well in check. This trike had a roll cage and a roof of sorts, although no doors, and could seat two people side-by-side. It was much bigger at 3500mm (138in) long and weighed some 239kg (528lb). With a 16bhp 250cc single-cylinder engine, it could reach a top speed of around 53mph (85km/h), and was fitted with ABS disc brakes. In some markets it was sold under different names, including Viper, Challenger and Trike-Car.

Kandi KD-200ZK
CN • 2010-date • 1F2R • No built: n/a

Kandi's third trike was a familiar one to Chinese eyes: an enclosed saloon intended mainly as a three-passenger taxi. Its 197cc single-cylinder four-stroke engine powered the 392kg car no faster than 37mph (60km/h).

Kapi

E • 1951-1956 • 1F2R • No built: n/a

Automóviles y Autoscooter Kapi was founded by an ex-army captain in Barcelona, making a variety of microcars. Kapi's first three-wheeler was the 1951 Kapiscooter, offered with either a Villiers 125cc or an AMC 175cc four-stroke engine, or from 1953, a 197cc Villiers. A Platillo Volante version with doors and a roof arrived in 1955; other body styles included an estate and a light delivery van. Like the Gordon ⇨, the engine on some models was placed just in front of one of the rear wheels. The later Kapi Chiqui (Little Kapi) is sometimes erroneously listed as a trike, but was in fact a four-wheeler with close-set rear wheels.

«KAPISCOOTER» 125 F

Kaubamobil

D • 1955-1956 • 2F1R • No built: n/a

Very little is known about the Kaubamobil, a 125cc-engined three-wheeler that resembled a roofless, doorless interpretation of the Messerschmitt KR200 ⇨.

Kaxa

CN • c2010-date • 2F1R • No built: n/a

Founded in 1998 in Zhejiang, China, Kaxa Motos offered a small range of trikes. The KXA-RO8 and KXA-RO9 were two ATV-style trikes with 200cc or 250cc engines, but the KXA-R22 (pictured) was much more interesting. This was a sports-style trike powered by a 249cc Zongshen single-cylinder engine with 16bhp, good enough for a top speed of 75mph (120km/h). A four-speed gearbox with reverse was standard, driving the rear wheel by chain; three disc brakes

were fitted. The KXA-R22 measured only 2650mm long and 750mm tall and weighed 250kg. The doorless, roofless bodywork was very original, with strong aeronautical overtones. The same range was apparently also sold under other brand names such as Bode ⇨, 1it and LeTian, while the KXA-R21 and KXA-R23 models were actually made by Kandi ⇨.

Kayok

CN • 2000s • 1F2R • No built: n/a

This was one of a number of Chinese economy vehicles created by replicating an existing design (in this case the locally made Suzuki Alto), converting it to three wheels and installing a low-

capacity engine. The resulting car was a four-seater weighing only 280kg, whose single-cylinder 174cc engine had a mere 13bhp, enabling a maximum speed of just 34mph (55km/h).

Keinath

D • 1949 • 2F1R • No built: Probably 1

This single-seater cabin scooter from Germany was unusual in that its front bodywork lifted up as one (with steering wheel attached) to allow entry. A complete scooter rear end sat under the curvaceous rear end. It is unlikely that a production run commenced for this unusual microcar.

KeJie KJ-D2X

CN • 2010s • 1F2R • No built: n/a

Sporting a mildly original shape, this product of JiangMen KeJie Electric Vehicle Trade Co measured 2300mm long and weighed 200kg. An 800W DC motor and four 12V batteries

powered the rear wheels by chain, with a top speed of 17mph (27km/h) and a range of 51 miles (82km) being quoted. The basic two-seater bodywork was made of ABS plastic.

Kelsen Electric Sports Rider

USA • 1961-1973 • 1F2R • No built: n/a

One of several electric microcars made in the USA in the 1960s, this was designed by Art Kelsen of Stanton, California. It looked a little different to the standard fare, with its rounded nose and inset headlamps, and was relatively well-equipped (a hardtop, side curtains and chrome bumpers

were standard). A second series was also made, which resembled the Autoette ⇨ quite closely, and was priced at $1295 in 1973.

Kenda Trio

HKC • 1993-date • 1F2R • No built: n/a

Based in Hong Kong, Kenda Technology (International) made a three-wheeler designed in Italy by AD Engineering. While mainly intended for carrying cargo, versions were offered that could carry either seven or eleven passengers.

Power came from a 546cc two-cylinder engine with 25bhp.

Kikos TO40

F • 1980-1983 • 1F2R • No built: n/a

Based in Antibes, Kikos occupied the very bottom rung of the French microcar ladder with a single-seater offered in two guises: an open step-in model and an enclosed version, both with plastic bodywork. The rear-

mounted 50cc air-cooled Motobécane (or 125cc water-cooled Zündapp) engine drove the left rear wheel only through an automatic gearbox, and the steering was by handlebars. This kind of three-wheeled voiturette was, by the 1980s, falling very much out of fashion, so it was short-lived.

King
GB • 1970-1971 • 2F1R • No built: 2

Mike King of Liss, Hampshire, made a Renault 4-based trike of which replicas were offered on an ad-hoc basis, although only two were ever made.

King Hero
PK • 2000s • 1F2R • No built: n/a

As well as making motorbikes, the Pakistani company King Hero Motorcycle Industries also offered a typical three-wheeled passenger rickshaw.

Kington
CN • 2000s • 1F2R • No built: n/a

Chongqing Kington-Liyang mostly made motorcycles but also offered conventional rickshaws with small (150cc and 250cc) engines under the names CK150ZK and CK250ZK.

Kirk P-Type
GB • 2005-2007 • 2F1R • No built: 2

Andrew Kirk of Chorley, Lancashire made two examples of the P-Type (below), a bare-boned doorless, roofless, single-seater roadster with plain metal sides. It boasted a rear-mounted motorcycle engine and handlebar steering, but could hardly be described as the last word in finesse.

KMZ K-1V
RUS • 1947-1951 • 1F2R • No built: n/a

This Ukrainian-built three-wheeler was designed as a vehicle for disabled drivers, of which there was a great need in the aftermath of WW2. A Sachs 98cc engine drove the left rear wheel by chain.

Kobot
J • 2011-date • 2F1R • No built: 2 to date

If the Kobot looked a bit like the robotic wheelchair used by Captain Pike in the 1960s TV show Star Trek, that should not be too surprising; it was the result of a collaboration between medical robot firm Tmsuk and pharmaceutical company Kowa. Debuting at the 2011 Tokyo Motor Show, two three-wheeler prototypes were presented: the single-seater Kobot V (red) and Kobot B (green), as well as a four-wheeled Kobot II. The B and V could fold up: at the tap of a button on a smartphone app, the rear wheel and seat folded into the front of the car. Powered by an electric motor, its cruising speed was 19mph (30km/h). There were plans to market the Kobot, unrealized however by the time of writing.

Koei Kogyo Right Pony
J • 1954-c1960 • 1F2R • No built: n/a

Koei Kogyo started out making basic delivery tricycles with a separate 'tug' unit at the front housing the engine and single front wheel, but from 1954 made the BM and CM models with fuller bodywork and the ability to carry passengers. A 200cc Mitsubishi air-cooled engine drove the front wheel, taking the 200kg trike to a speed of 28mph (45km/h).

Kokuei Romance
J • 1950 • 1F2R • No built: n/a

A company called Kokuei Zoki, based in Osaka, briefly offered the oddly named Romance. This four-passenger car measured 3000mm long, weighed 307kg and was powered by a Meguro air-cooled single-cylinder 346cc engine with 6bhp.

Korff
USA • 1952 • 1F2R • No built: n/a

Walter Korff sold a book of plans for builders to "design your own light car" with illustrations of a three-wheeler of ungainly appearance. Based in Burbank, California, Korff sold the plans for $2. Korff later designed the Mini-K ⇨ and Unisport Duo Delta ⇨.

Krause Piccolo Trumpf
DDR • 1955-1975 • 1F2R • No built: Approx 10,000

Louis Krause of Leipzig started making vehicles for the disabled in the late 1940s, but the Piccolo Trumpf of 1955 was his first major model. This was very basic transport, with a folded sheet metal frame and a Simson SR1 50cc scooter engine sitting under the single seat, driving only the left rear wheel by chain, with no reverse gear. The driver braked by pulling the steering column towards him, and could also boost performance using muscle power. An improved Trumpf / 5 model (1958-1965) benefited from a more powerful Simson SR2 engine mounted to one side of the car, so that the top

speed increased to 19mph (30km/h). The Trumpf / 7 (1966-1975) used the complete front end of a Simson Schwalbe motorbike.

Krause Piccolo Duo / Duo
DDR • 1961-1991 • 1F2R • No built: Approx 20,000

Krause launched the Piccolo Duo in 1961 as a wider two-seater model, based on the Trumpf / 5 but wider by about 200mm and available with basic weather equipment. A slightly larger Duo 2 model replaced it in 1968, followed by a shortlived Duo 3 model in 1970, replaced by a developed model called the Duo 4 with hydraulic dampers. All Duos used a Simson single-cylinder 50cc moped engine with an automatic clutch, so a top speed of barely 37mph (60km/h) was achievable. Production was assumed by VEB FAB from 1973, and a fixed-roof conversion was offered from 1977. The manufacturer became VEB Robur from 1981 and an improved Duo 4/2 was launched at this time. However, the collapse of the East German regime in 1989 hastened

the end of production, also scuppering the launch of a much-developed Duo 5 model (pic right). The Duo is often incorrectly referred to as the Simson Duo because of the proportion of Simson scooter parts it used.

Krauser Domani
D • 1986-date • 1F2R • No built: Approx 100

Most three-wheelers can claim to be half-motorbike, half-car, but few are so literally like this as the Krauser Domani. Although the glassfibre-bodied Domani looked like a motorcycle and sidecar, the latter actually formed an integral part of the structure. A 130bhp BMW K1200 motorcycle engine and five-speed gearbox were installed in a specially developed chassis. Designed by Michael Krauser GmBH, which made its name in motorcycle sidecar racing, the Domani was sold mostly in Japan and Europe. Weighing 390kg, it had a top speed of over 125mph (200km/h).

Krejbich
CZ • 1948-1949 • 2F1R • No built: 72

Vaclav Krejbich built a run of some 72 three-wheelers, of slightly differing designs. Most of them were of an open-topped design that measured 3100mm long and weighed 260kg. These basic but appealingly styled cars could be powered by such contemporary motorbike engines as the Jawa 250cc or 350cc and Ogar 350cc, driving the single rear wheel by chain. Up to 50mph (80km/h) was possible, so it was claimed.

Krishi Auto-Rickshaw
IND • 1970s • 1F2R • No built: n/a

Krishi Engines of Sanathnagar, Hyderabad made a seven-seater rickshaw powered by a single-cylinder, 5bhp diesel engine and four-speed gearbox. Measuring 2750mm long and weighing 600kg, it could reach 27mph (45km/h).

Kroboth
D • 1954-1955 • 1F2R • No built: 55

Gustav Kroboth built scooters before trying his hand at the Allwetter-roller, an open-topped steel-bodied microcar for two people. The chassis was formed of a central tube with leaf springs up front and a longitudinal spring at the rear. The rear-mounted powerplant could be either a 197cc single-cylinder Ilo engine or a 9bhp Sachs 174cc and a top speed of up to 50mph (80km/h) was claimed by the maker.

Kroboth "ALLWETTER"-ROLLER

KS-1
DDR • 1957-1959 • 1F2R • No built: 45

This was a two-passenger vehicle intended for disabled drivers living in East Germany. It was an enclosed car measuring some 2700mm long and 1100mm wide, and weighing 315kg. An MZ 123cc motorbike engine with 5.9bhp was fitted, enabling a claimed top speed of 31mph (50km/h). However, when a government doctor declared in 1959 that the car was unsuitable for disabled passengers – and in the former East Germany this was very much an unarguable point – that was the end of the line for the KS-1.

KTM E3W
A • 2011 • 2F1R • No built: n/a

Austrian motorcycle maker KTM experimented with a three-wheeler in 2011. Created in conjunction with the Kisha design studio, its major innovation was all-plastic construction, keeping weight down to 500kg. A 15kW electric motor was fed by lithium-ion batteries, giving it a range of 62 miles (100km). The side-by-side two-seater boasted Lamborghini-style scissor doors. KTM hoped to build the E3W at the rate of 50,000 per year from 2013 priced at around £7000, but this never happened.

Kumar Parinda
IND • 2005-date • 1F2R • No built: Many thousands

Kumar Motors was founded in 1971 in Pune as a car dealership, but in 2005 launched the three-wheeled Agni truck and a more-stylish-than-normal rickshaw called the Parinda. This had a tubular steel chassis (claimed to be a first in India) with all-round independent suspension. Power came from a 9bhp single-cylinder four-stroke IDI diesel engine, mated to a four-speed transmission. Up to 20,000 three-wheelers per year were built.

Kurier
CZ • 1948 • 2F1R • No built: n/a

Designed by Karel Strejc, the oddly shaped Kurier two-seater was 3300mm long and weighed 200kg. It had a leaf-sprung front end and a coilspring at the rear, where a tiny wheel kept the pointed tail of the aluminium body off the ground. A Jawa single-cylinder 250cc two-stroke engine provided drive to the front wheels, topping out at around 50mph (80km/h).

Kurtis-Thorne Californian
USA • 1941 • 1F2R • No built: 1

Frank Kurtis designed the Californian for millionaire playboy Joel Thorne. Gary Davis bought the car in 1945 and developed it into the Davis Divan ⇨. Kurtis meanwhile went on to make glassfibre sports cars, midget racers and Indy 500 cars.

Kurunkov Autoaeromobil
RUS • 1966 • 1F2R • No built: Probably 1

Few cars can claim the ability to travel in four media, but Kurunkov's remarkable Autoaeromobil was said to be able to fly in the air, float on water, ski on snow and drive on tarmac. Claimed top speeds were 75mph (120km/h) in the air, 50mph (80km/h) on snow and 31mph (50km/h) on water.

K-Way Motus
I • 2010 • 2F1R • No built: 1

The brainchild of Stefano Carabelli of Turin Polytechnic, the K-Way Motus had the distinction of being styled by Fabrizio Giugiaro of Giugiaro Design. One very unusual aspect was the bodywork, which was made of cloth, and so kept the car very light, while there were also transparent panels in the body sides. Electric motors in the front wheel hubs combined with an 850cc petrol engine that drove the rear wheel, and K-Way claimed an average of around 130mpg and a range of up to 25km in electric-only mode. The Motus competed in the 2010 Automotive X-Prize competition.

Kyburz Classic
CH • 1995-date • 1F2R • No built: n/a

Kyburz of Freienstein in Switzerland built a range of electric three-wheeled vehicles (mostly for the mobility market)

under the name Classic. The Classic DX3 version, for example, was powered by a 2.4kW motor and 24V lithium batteries, could reach 27mph (45km/h) and travel for up to 62 miles (100km) on single charge of electricity.

THREE WHEELERS A-Z

LLL

Lomax 223 ▲

Liberty ACE ▲

Lazareth Triazuma ▲

Louis Renard ▲

▼ Lepoix Ding

▼ Lehman Cimarron

Lafbart

NGR • 2010-date • 1F2R • No built: n/a

Lafbart of Nigeria made a variety of three-wheelers, both passenger and commercial. The Basik LF-6 was a six-seater (the driver sitting astride a scooter front end) powered by a 175cc engine, while the Swaaga had seven seats, an engine of 200cc or 250cc and a conventional steering wheel. An ambulance version called the Aidil was also offered.

Laher

USA • 1960s • 1F2R • No built: n/a

The Laher Spring & Electric Car Corp of Oakland, California mostly made light delivery trikes but part of its 25-strong range included passenger versions, both open and closed, for leisure use. All were powered by electric motors.

Lamb-Kar

GB • 1950 • 1F2R • No built: n/a

Strange names are the norm with three-wheelers, but the Lamb-Kar moniker was one of the oddest of all. It was built in Fordham, Cambridgeshire and was clearly inspired by the Bond Minicar ⇨. The body was in stressed aluminium, which was claimed to be so strong that no conventional chassis was needed. A 9bhp 250cc two-stroke twin engine and four-speed gearbox drove the single front wheel by chain. Suspension was by a coil spring up front and rubber-in-torsion at the rear, while the rod-operated brakes worked only on the rear wheels.

Lambretta/Lambro

I • 1949-1972 • 1F2R • No built: n/a

Ferdinando Innocenti founded one of the all-time great scooter manufacturers in Milan, with production of the Lambretta scooter starting in 1947. He also made one of the world's most iconic three-wheelers: starting in 1949, the Lambretta 'F' (Furgone) series of three-wheeled delivery trikes made a big impression in postwar Italy thanks to their cheap prices and low running costs.

A few passenger versions of Lambrettas were built, such as the 1958 Ghia Giardinetta ⇨. Another interesting passenger model was the Tri Lambretta of 1970, made for

foreign markets such as India and Indonesia. This was a three-wheeler based on the Lambretta DL scooter, with two wheels at the front for a passenger-carrying 'box' to be fitted (which was done locally). The spec

was basic: mechanical brakes, no instruments and a seat for the driver. See Italindo ⇨ for the Indonesian version. API ⇨ also made rickshaws based on the Lambretta in India. Innocenti changed the name of its three-wheeled trucks from Lambretta to Lambro in 1963.

Lambro

I • 1952 • 2F1R • No built: n/a

Very little is known about the 'other' Lambro, produced by a Milanese company in 1952. It was a very small three-wheeled two-seater coupe powered by a 125cc two-stroke engine driving the single rear wheel.

Landshark

GB • 2001 • 2F1R • No built: n/a

Speculative designs don't make it into this book, but the Landshark's Lotus connection and the fact that a full-size vehicle might possibly have been built justify its appearance here. Conceived

by David Baker as "the world's fastest amphibious vehicle", it was designed to do 200mph on land and 50mph in water. The three-seater Landshark's single rear wheel acted as a turbine pump in water, with the front end hydroplaning on lowered front mudguards. Engines of between 400cc and 1100cc were planned, with semi-automatic transmission. Despite a quoted price of £10,000-£16,000, and the involvement of Lotus Engineering as consultants, it is believed the project never took to land – or sea.

Langfang Sandi

CN • 1999-date • 1F2R • No built: n/a

The Langfang Sandi Electric Tricycle Co was based in Langfang, in Hebei province. Its main activity was making the Xin Ge and Xin Hang series of rickshaws, pictured above and left. These were electric-powered, with motors boasting outputs from 800W upwards, and of very compact dimensions.

Laruti

NGR • 2009-date • 1F2R • No built: n/a

Laruti was an acronym of Lagos State Rural Transportation Initiative, which launched a tricycle taxi, almost certainly of Chinese origin, that was rather more robust than the regular rickshaws in Nigeria. There were three models, all of which boasted enclosed bodywork with doors, and a capacity to carry either four, eight or ten passengers. The Laruti was restricted to rural areas within Lagos state and was not allowed on major highways.

Las Vegas Trikes

USA • 2002-date • 1F2R • No built: n/a

Las Vegas Trikes was founded in 2002 when Kloehn (bizarrely, a manufacturer of medical equipment) acquired Iron Horse Trikes ⇨. Its machinery was pricey: the least expensive model was the Thunder Trike at $42,000 in 2003, while the Widowmaker cost more than $80,000. Power came from a Chevrolet V8 tuned to deliver up to 525bhp, which gave monstrous performance. Automatic transmission made it easy to drive, however.

Lawil

I • 1984-1986 • 1F2R • No built: n/a

Lawil made a wide variety of four-wheeled microcars from 1967 until 1986, but its only attempt at a three-wheeler was a 1984 model that looked suspiciously similar to the All Cars Charly ⇨.

Lazareth Triazuma

F • 2007-date • 2F1R • No built: n/a

Lazareth Auto-Moto was founded in 1998 by Ludovic Lazareth, who made a name for himself with his Quadrazuma, an extremely high-performance quad-based four-wheeler. It was only logical that he should

make a three-wheeled version called the Triazuma. It was powered by a 180bhp Yamaha R1 engine, and each Triazuma was hand-built to order from around £30,000. A snow-track version of the Triazuma was also made, while a further derivative, the Wazuma, was a four-wheeler with narrow-set rear wheels.

LDF

CN • 2004-date • 1F2R • No built: n/a

LDF Group, based in Jinhua in Zhejiang province, made a range of three-wheeled chopper-style motorcycle-based machinery with engines ranging in size from 125cc to 250cc.

LDV Rixi

GB • 1951-1952 • 1F2R • No built: n/a

The Turner Manufacturing Company of Wolverhampton formed, in the mid-1940s, a new operation called Light Delivery Vehicles (LDV). This made commercial vehicles (the two-wheeled By-Van and the three-wheeled Tri-Van) but also offered the Rixi, a rickshaw targeted at the Far East market. Powered by an enlarged Turner Tiger 168cc two-stroke engine mounted on the front wheel, LDV claimed 80mpg. Two passengers could be carried in the rear, with luggage under the front seat. One Rixi famously travelled from Wolverhampton to John o'Groats and then Land's End, but that didn't seem to help paltry sales.

Leena Kharo

PK • 2000s • 1F2R • No built: n/a

Leena Industries of Peshawar made the Kharo autorickshaw with a 200cc engine.

Lehigh Valley Stealth Tryke

USA • 2008-date • 2F1R • No built: n/a

The very angular aluminium-bodied Stealth Tryke had elements of racing car about it, including Penske push-rod suspension made from chromoly (as was the chassis). Reverse gear was provided through the Quaife gearbox, and the engine was either a GSX-R1000 or Hayabusa. Since it weighed only 444kg (980lb), it was a quick machine. Lehigh Valley Choppers offered to build replicas to almost any spec.

Lehman
CDN/USA • 1984-date • 1F2R • No built: n/a

John Lehman created a real dynasty when he made his first trike in 1984, and over the ensuing years Lehman became one of the best-known names in the trike business worldwide. Things started in Alberta, Canada but Lehman later expanded in 2003 to set up an additional base in South Dakota in the USA. Early trikes were Honda Goldwing conversions, but Lehman moved on to make three-wheeled versions of Harley-Davidson, BMW, Suzuki and Victory motorbikes.

Many different models were offered over the years, with names including the Tour, Sport, GT, Tramp, Raider, Jackal, Storm, Renegade, CrossBow, Pit Boss (pictured above) and Monarch (pictured below). Lehman also had the distinction of being chosen by the motorcycle legend Harley-Davidson ⇨ to supply many of the parts for its own Tri-Glide three-wheeler from 2008.

Leighton
GB • 1997-2009 • 2F1R • No built: Approx 55

This 2CV-engined kit car was conceived by GCS Cars, before passing to BRA ⇨ in 1999, then Leighton Cars in 2002, and finally Aero Cycle Cars ⇨ in 2007. The Morgan-inspired bodywork was in glassfibre over a spaceframe chassis, and the whole car weighed just 350kg.

Le Patron 3
NL • 1998-date • 2F1R • No built: n/a

Based in Ophemert, the Netherlands, Godfrey and Wim van den Bergh started importing the Lomax ⇨ in 1991, then made their own modified version from 1998 as Le Patron. Offered in three- and four-wheeled forms, it was based on a Citroën 2CV chassis and mechanicals, and sold in kit form.

Lepoix Ding
D/F • 1975-1977 • 1F2R • No built: Very few

Louis Lepoix (based in Baden Baden, Germany and Enghien, France) started building electric cars in 1972 with the Urbanix and Shopi (four-wheelers with close-set front wheels and tiller steering). The gloriously named and slightly

unhinged Ding debuted at the 1975 Frankfurt Motor Show. Its most striking feature was an extraordinary external chassis which looped up and around the glassfibre body which sat suspended in the middle of it; the driver stood on a platform behind. The rear wheels were powered by a 1.5kW motor, with the batteries placed under the two front seats, and the top speed was a mere 16mph (25km/h). Alas, the Ding never reached intended production priced at 13,500 francs.

Libelle Allwetter-Autoroller
A • 1952-1955 • 2F1R • No built: Approx 40

Very characterful styling distinguished this three-wheeler microcar, whose name, Libelle, means dragonfly in German. The two passengers sat up front in an open compartment with a single round tube arching up from the nose to the back of the seat, while the rear deck looked like the tail of the dragonfly. A 199cc Rotax 8.5bhp two-stroke single-cylinder engine sat in the tail and had to be kick-started. A version was also made in Italy as the Boselli Libellula ⇨.

Liberator
USA • 2000s-date • 2F1R • No built: n/a

Liberator Trikes of Canby, Minnesota specialised in making modified trikes for paraplegic riders, complete with a swivelling driver's seat.

Liberty ACE
USA • 2005-date • 2F1R • No built: n/a

Pete Larsen was running a Seattle-based sidecar operation called Ace Cycle Car when he had the inspiration to create a reinterpretation of the legendary Morgan Aero three-wheeler – a decision that was to have far-reaching repercussions.

The resulting Liberty Motors ACE (American Cycle-car Endeavor) used a tubular steel chassis, unequal-length wishbone front suspension and a single rear swinging arm with coilovers all round. A Ford Mustang steering rack steered the Harley-Davidson front wheels, while a motorbike-based rear end made use of a wide car tyre.

Harley-Davidson V-Twin engines were chosen, either 88B (1450cc) or 103 (1688cc). Drive was by shaft to the rear wheel through a Mazda MX-5 five-speed gearbox with reverse. Weighing only 431kg (950lb), the ACE's performance was impressive, with a quoted top speed of 120mph in 103ci guise.

Prices were steep, starting at $34,500 complete in 2005, but there was a big market for such a car. Liberty sought a licence from Morgan ⇨ in the UK to make the ACE as "constructed under licence from Morgan," which it duly secured. Indeed, Morgan took such a keen interest in the Liberty that it led to the development of an official 21st century Morgan Three-Wheeler ⇨.

Ligier JS4
F • 1980s • 1F2R • No built: n/a

Racing driver, international rugby player and Formula 1 team founder Guy Ligier also built his own cars, all named 'JS' after his late friend, Jo Schlesser. All had four wheels apart from one: the JS4. This was also usually four-wheeled, with the extraordinary ability to run on three wheels if one fell off, but it was also briefly made with only three wheels. A very square-shaped two-seater microcar, it had all-metal bodywork, a 50cc Motobécane engine, automatic transmission and independent suspension. The Ligier was also sold in the US by Zoë ⇨.

Lithia
USA • 1970s • 1F2R • No built: n/a

Lithia Automotive of Lithia Springs, Georgia made a whole range of VW-engined chopper trikes, the most interesting of which was an unusual glassfibre bodied wedge-shaped three-seater called the Trike Kite (pictured right).

Li Xinhua

CN • 2012-date • 1F2R • No built: n/a

Ex-bricklayer Li Xinhua built this amphibious three-wheeler in Shandong Province. It was capable of 37mph (60km/h) on land and 19mph (30km/h) in water, measured 5000mm long and weighed 1000kg. Li was reported in 2012 to be looking for $100,000 investment to start production.

Lohia Humsafar

IND • 2012-date • 1F2R • No built: n/a

Lohia Auto entered the Indian three-passenger rickshaw market with the Humsafar range. A single-cylinder diesel engine of 436cc, rated at 7.5bhp, provided power, with CNG fuelling also possible.

Lomar Honey

I • 1985-c1988 • 2F1R • No built: n/a

The oddly-named Lomar Honey hailed from Parma in Italy. This two-seater was quite large by three-wheeler standards at 3600mm long, and two versions were offered: a coupe with removable gullwing doors, and a full convertible. A rear-mounted Cagiva 125cc motorcycle engine drove the single rear wheel through a six-speed motorbike gearbox.

Lomax 223 & 423

GB • 1983-2008 • 2F1R • No built: Approx 3500 / 40

Glassfibre specialist Nigel Whall created one of the most ingenious and best-selling kit cars of all time with the Citroën 2CV-based Lomax. It was brilliantly simple: atop an

unmodified 2CV/Dyane floorpan sat a very simple double-scuttle body in a Morganesque style, with no doors or roof. The body was in glassfibre with a bonded-in plywood floor and steel frames to carry the steering column and seat belt mounts. The 602cc engine sat semi-exposed at the front. Whall's first design (the 224) was a four-wheeler, but he created the 223 three-wheeler by the simple expedient of fitting a slightly modified single reversed Citroën rear trailing arm on the rear end.

The 2CV's 602cc engine developed only 31bhp, but in a car weighing just 400kg (880lb), it was an unexpectedly good performer. It handled very tidiliy, too, although body roll could be epic, so Lomax advised the fitment of an anti-roll bar. There was also the option of basing the Lomax on a Citroën Ami Super chassis, with its 55bhp 1015cc flat-four engine and beefed up brakes, in which case a different enclosed front end was fitted. This model was called the 423, and was capable of 100mph (160km/h).

The Lomax was initially built by Falcon ⇨, then Mumford ⇨ before devolving to Nigel Whall's base in Lye, near Birmingham. The basic kit price was a remarkably low £495, helped by the fact that the Citroën floorpan was used (in time, Lomax also offered its own steel tube chassis). Options would eventually include a full windscreen, weather protection, doors and small rear seats. In 1994, Whall sold the Lomax brand to David Low,

who contributed to the total of over 3500 cars sold. The final resting place of the Lomax (from 2003 until 2008) was Cradley Motor Works of St Leonards-on-Sea.

Lomax Supa Vee
GB • 1992 • 2F1R • No built: 1

When an American serviceman showed Lomax a magazine called Super Vee, detailing V-twin engines based on American V8s, Whall was inspired to import such an engine from the USA. The result was the Supa Vee, whose 1543cc V-twin air-cooled engine drove through a Citroën GS gearbox. The new model used aluminium and glassfibre body panels in the same basic style as the 223 but mounted on a lightweight tubular spaceframe chassis with double wishbones and horizontal coil/spring damper units designed by Dick Buckland. Problems with the reliability and cost of the new engine scuppered any chances this model had in the marketplace.

Lomax Lambda 3
GB • 1993-2002 • 2F1R • No built: Approx 50

The Lambda 3's role was as a more up-market Lomax. Although the Lambda could still be built on a 2CV chassis, a new purpose-designed ladder frame was developed for it. This ditched Citroën's connected suspension in favour of adjustable inboard coil/spring damper units. Launched at the 1993 London Motor Show, the Lambda 3's body was designed by Jim Dimbleby, featuring flowing front wings which moved with the suspension, a new bonnet and a revised interior with extra space. The Lambda was costlier than the 223, which explains its relative lack of commercial success.

Longdi
CN • 2002-date • 1F2R • No built: n/a

Unlike the majority of lookalike three-wheelers made in China, the Longdi brand (built by Suqian Chaoyi Ornamental) had some originality. The LDA1, for instance (pic left), featured highly unusual concertina doors

for entry. The LDA2-48V (pic left) had glassfibre bodywork that could seat a driver up front (using handlebars) and up to three passengers behind in a very small (2000mm long) package. All Longdis were electric-powered.

Lonta LT BF1
CN • 1987-date • 1F2R • No built: n/a

Jiangsu Lonta Machinery made the LT BF1, halfway between a mobility scooter and a 'proper' three-wheeler. It was powered by electricity and could seat up to two passengers.

Louis Renard
F • 1940-1942 • 2F1R • No built: n/a

This electric car was built in Lyons during WW2. Power went to the single rear wheel, with a top speed of 25mph (40km/h) and a range of 50 miles (80km) quoted.

Lovel F-20
B/NL • 1991 to date • 2F1R • No built: n/a

The Lovel F-20 was a superbike-engined three-wheeler created by a Belgian engineer called Gerhard ten Vegert. Production cars were made by the Van der Starre brothers of Star Twin Motors in Loenen, the Netherlands. The F-20's chassis consisted of a tubular frame with an alloy-panelled centre section, double-wishbone front suspension and a rear steel swinging

arm. A wide variety of Japanese four-cylinder motorbike engines, such as the Suzuki GSX-R1100 and Yamaha FZR 1000, could be fitted centrally. The open, doorless glassfibre/carbon-fibre bodywork featured twin head fairings, and both complete and kit-form versions were offered.

Lovech
BG • 1960 • n/a • No built: n/a

This three-wheeler, hailing from Lovech in Bulgaria, was powered by a 250cc single-cylinder two-stroke engine. A planned production run apparently did not occur.

Luber Stilet
RUS • 2007-date • 1F2R • No built: n/a

From the workshops of Luber Custom of Moscow in Russia came this dramatic 'Daytona-style' trike. The lone driver sat at the rear end, straddling what was substantial bodywork and operating the single steered front wheel via handlebars. The Stilet used a 5.7-litre V8 engine with 300bhp mated to an automatic gearbox. The company behind the car offered customer examples at prices starting from the equivalent of $50,000.

Lucciola
I • 1948-1949 • 2F1R • No built: n/a

An engineer called Giorgio Pennacchio created the Lucciola ('firefly') coupe, whose short (3000mm) bodywork looked pleasingly modern. A rear-mounted Condor-Guidetti 250cc single-cylinder engine had 8bhp; the brakes and three-speed gearbox were hydraulically operated.

Luego Bike-to-Trike
GB • 2004-2005 • 1F2R • No built: Approx 5

Peterborough-based company Luego Sportscars made this rear-end conversion for a wide variety of motorcycles.

Luka Blaster 200
F • 1998 • 2F1R • No built: 1

Luka Design was founded by Lucas Bignon in Suresnes, France. His Blaster 200 was based on a quad bike, but had only three wheels. Power came from a 35bhp two-stroke engine, and the trike was designed for all sorts of terrain, from tarmac to sand.

THREE WHEELERS
A-Z
MMM

Mercedes-Benz F300 Life Jet ▲

Mink ▲

Morgan F Super ▲

Morgan Three-Wheeler ▲

▼ Messerschmitt KR200

Magic Trikes Gryphon
ZA • 2008-date • 2F1R • No built: n/a

Magic Trikes was a company based in Cape Town, whose creation was the Gryphon supertrike. This was powered by a 197bhp four-cylinder Suzuki Hayabusa motorbike engine and had supercar performance: 0-62mph in 4.5 seconds and a top speed of 186mph (300km/h). Although development of the 3700mm-long Gryphon started in 2008, full production was not due to begin until 2013, priced at 285,000 rand (around £20,000).

Magic Turtle
CH • 2011 • 1F2R • No built: 1

Few cars can claim to be three-wheel drive, but the bizarrely named Magic Turtle was one, kind of: it had electric drive for the rear wheels and pedals for the single front wheel. Roof-mounted solar cells allowed a range of up to 31 miles (50km) per day and the car weighed a mere 118kg. It could seat three people, or the rear seats could be replaced with a cargo deck. Presented at the Geneva Motor Show in 2011, it was the work of a team from Neuchatel.

Mahindra Bijlee
IND • 1999-date • 1F2R • No built: n/a

The Indian jeep manufacturer Mahindra entered the three-wheeled rickshaw market in 1999 with the Bijlee. It planned to persuade the government to use its 10-seater electric cars as a replacement for polluting rickshaws, with owners of recharging stations leasing out batteries to vehicle operators. This didn't happen but it won awards for its 'green' intent. It used a 72V DC motor powered by 12 batteries, allowing a range of 50 miles (80km) at speeds of 22mph (35km/h). In 2000, production was also licensed to Chloride Egypt, while from 2002, CNG and LPG options were added.

Mahindra Champion/Alfa
IND • 2000-date • 1F2R • No built: n/a

The Champion was a three-wheeler of larger than average dimensions (weighing from 685kg) available in estate car, convertible and pick-up guises. It was popular as a rickshaw with 6+1 seats. Power came from a single-cylinder 510cc

engine that could be powered either by diesel (10.2bhp) or bi-fuel petrol/CNG (10.8bhp). The Champion Alfa was launched in 2005 as a smaller version, also offered in passenger guise. In 2009, Mahindra presented the HyAlfa ⇨, claimed to be the world's first hydrogen-propelled three-wheeler.

Malaguti Tricky
I • n/a • 2F1R • No built: n/a

Italian motorbike maker Malaguti presented the Tricky, a hybrid trike with a two-stroke single-cylinder engine plus an Italvel electric motor. It had a top speed of 25mph (40km/h) and a roof that enveloped the passenger compartment.

Malone Skunk
GB • 1996-date • 2F1R • No built: Approx 25 (to 2013)

Devon-based Jon Malone had made a business making go-karts before turning his attention to a three-wheeled road car, the first prototype of which (the S1) was shown in 1996. Production of the Skunk Sport began in 1998, initially with Yamaha 650cc or 750cc engines mounted up front, driving the single rear wheel by shaft and chain. A Super Sport (SS1) model arrived in 1999 with a huge variety of superbike engine options, including Honda 900cc, Yamaha 900/1000/1200cc and Suzuki 1100/1300cc. A Skunk Max model, with 1300cc Suzuki V-Max or Yamaha 1200cc power, was added in 2001, and a Yamaha R1-powered ST/F-1000 model in 2004 (one year after the car was restyled). A spaceframe chassis with an aluminium floor, pushrod front suspension and a single-sided rear swing arm offered serious cornering ability. The very simple doorless open bodywork was in glassfibre strengthened with foam, and a very light weight of just 290kg allowed the Skunk a blistering 0-60mph time of around five seconds. Kits were available, or ready-built cars priced from £13,000.

Malupe Agro

H • 2011-date • 1F2R • No built: n/a

This Hungarian electric trike used lead-acid or nickel cadmium 48V batteries, powering a 3kW hub motor mounted in the front wheel. It boasted air suspension, glassfibre bodywork, seating for three and a price tag of €3500. It was sold in the USA under the name Gypsy Baron EV1 Coach.

Manocar

F • 1952-1953 • 1F2R • No built: 1

This extremely compact (2250mm long) microcar was made by Ets Manom of Saint-Ouen. It was powered by a 4bhp, 125cc single-cylinder engine driving the left-hand rear wheel by chain, and could achieve a top speed of 34mph (55km/h). The doorless convertible bodywork could seat two passengers, but only one car was ever made.

Marketeer

USA • 1954 • 1F2R • No built: n/a

Rather grandly named for such a small car, the Marketeer Towne de Ville was built by the Electric Marketeer Mfg Co of Redlands, California. A very compact open two-seater

electric tricycle with glassfibre bodywork, it was aimed principally at women drivers. The rear wheels were driven by a 2.2kW electric motor fed by 6V batteries, and the range was around 30 miles (50km).

Marketour

USA • 1964 • 1F2R • No built: n/a

Marketour Electric Cars of Long Beach, California offered this tiny electric runabout which featured a removable roof. It was powered by a 36V electric motor and you could expect to get around 50 miles (80km) out of a single charge.

Marold

A • 1951 • 2F1R • No built: 1

Austrian engineer Hans Marold hoped his 1951 prototype would reach production, but it never did. The simple open two-seater aluminium body housed a rear-mounted 300cc Ilo engine (later a 350cc unit).

Marotti

PL • 2009-date • 2F1R • No built: n/a

Markus Rogalski's Marotti was an ambitious and striking sports trike. It used a Honda VFR750 V4 750cc engine with 100bhp driving the single rear wheel by chain via a six-speed sequential gearbox with electric reverse gear. Over the

steel chassis with double wishbone front suspension and a rear swing arm was fitted highly unusual and aerodynamic glassfibre bodywork incorporating a manta ray-like front spoiler, flat underfloor and bizarre rear 'stabilisers' that gave it the air of a Batmobile. It measured 3200mm long and weighed 440kg so performance was strong. Very wide tyres (255mm front and up to 315mm rear) helped the car achieve excellent roadholding. Later the Marotti was scheduled to receive a 200bhp Suzuki 1340cc powerplant, with power options as high as 340bhp being mooted, and estimated prices of 30,000 euros were quoted.

Martin Stationette

USA • 1954 • 2F1R • No built: 1

Captain James Vernon Martin built his first three-wheeler, the Martinette, in 1932, a 2F1R rear-engined machine with a single door at the front (rather like the Isetta). His next car, the Stationette, did not appear until the 1954 World

Motor Sports Show in New York. Its bulbous wooden bodywork had conventional side doors this time. A four-cylinder Hercules water-cooled engine and magnetic fluid drive provided the power. Martin went on to create a quite similar three-wheeled device called the Tri-Car Surburbanette ⇨.

Martino Kamikaze
USA • 2006-date • 2F1R • No built: n/a

Making its debut at the 2006 SEMA Show, the Kamikaze was designed by Marc Martino. Living up to its name, power came from a turbocharged Suzuki Hayabusa 1300 engine with 400bhp, mounted in an aluminium chassis with a Chassis Works front end, and the driver used handlebar controls. If you wanted one, the Martino Motor Co would make you one for $80,000.

Mathis VL 333
F • 1946 • 2F1R • No built: Very few

Strasbourg-based Emile Mathis was one of the pioneers of aerodynamic design in the 1930s and his first project following the war was a wind-cheating three-wheeler which he dubbed the Mathis VL 333. This stood for Voiture Légere followed by the trinity of fuel consumption (3 litres per 100km, or 94mpg), 3 seats and 3 wheels. Mathis certainly succeeded as far as aerodynamics was concerned: the 333 had a Cd of just 0.22, thanks to the design input of Jean Andreau.

A 707cc 15bhp boxer two-cylinder engine was front-mounted, driving the two wheels through a four-speed gearbox. The front of the car was wide at 1740mm (68.5in) and incorporated faired-in lights and grilles. With its aluminium bodywork, the Mathis weighed only 440kg (970lbs). It was displayed at the 1946 Paris Salon and several prototypes were made but, sadly, a production run for this advanced car never materialised.

Matra Side
F • 2012-date • 1F2R • No built: n/a

Matra took its existing e-Mo XP electric scooter, added an extra wheel and an extra seat to the side and – voila! – ended up with the Matra Side. The extra space it freed up allowed

for batteries to be stowed on board, extending the scooter's range four-fold to more than 75 miles (120km). Designed for leisure use, and weighing less than 100kg, Matra announced that the Side would become available to special order.

Mazda 700 PB
J • 1950s • 1F2R • No built: n/a

Mazda would become one of Japan's biggest car giants, but its humble origins lay in three-wheelers, as it made a series of commercial vehicles with three wheels from 1931 onwards. The 700 PB of 1950 was its first attempt at a passenger vehicle, although it was essentially the same underneath. That meant a front-mounted air-cooled single-cylinder engine of 701cc with 15.2bhp, and a four-speed gearbox delivering that power by shaft to the rear axle. It was quite large at 3760mm long and weighed 833kg, and up to five passengers could be accommodated.

Mazda Suitcase Car
J • 1991 • 1F2R • No built: 1

The Suitcase Car was born when one of Mazda's Japanese engineers dreamed of disembarking an aeroplane with suitcase in hand, and then simply driving off in it. He came up with a three-wheeled machine powered by a 40cc two-stroke engine. The fuel tank was big enough for two hours' worth of driving at up to 27mph (45km/h). It was steered by handlebars, and had such 'luxuries' as headlamps, brake lights and indicators. It took just 15 seconds to convert from suitcase to car, but sadly no production run ensued, although the one and only car built still exists in the USA.

MEBEA Bingo
GR • 1972-1978 • 1F2R • No built: 1

MEBEA was a merciful contraction of Messogiakai Epiheiriseis Biomihanias, Emporiou & Antiprosopeion (Mediterranean Enterprises for Industry, Commerce and Representations). It made motorbikes and three-wheeled trucks in Athens over several decades but also made passenger trikes. Its first car was the delightfully named Bingo leisure car, introduced in 1972 and based on its existing motorcycle-derived 50cc light delivery vehicle. Many were exported to Asia, and the Bingo was also assembled in both Indonesia and Pakistan. MEBEA also undertook licensed production of the Reliant TW9 three-wheeled truck (1970-1976) and the Reliant Robin ⇨ from 1974 to 1978.

Megu Mopetta/Student/Boy
A • 1967 • 2F1R • No built: Approx 50

Megu of Vienna, Austria built several alternative versions of Dr Ragnar Mathey's basic three-wheeler. The Mopetta was a tandem two-seater fitted with a 3.5bhp 50cc Puch engine and a three-speed gearbox, which could be fitted with

optional weather gear consisting of wraparound side screens. The Student was a more basic single-seater model with a 2.3bhp Puch 50cc engine and automatic transmission. The Boy was the same as the Student but with a luggage tray on the front. Versions were also sold with a rear pick-up tray and a separate trailer.

Meguru
J • 2010 • 1F2R • No built: n/a

Despite the heavy metal overtones of the builders of the Meguru – metalworking firm Yodogawa and blade maker Kinki Knives Industries – some of the car was actually made from bamboo and paper. The floor was bamboo and the folding fan-style doors were made of washi paper between bamboo batons. The companies involved contemplated manufacturing the Meguru as an £8000 rickshaw, but the lithium ion battery-propelled three-wheeler never in fact made production.

Meihatsu Popular N4
J • 1958 • 2F1R • No built: n/a

In 1954. the first motorcycles were made by Meihatsu, a subsidiary of Kawasaki Aircraft. In 1958, it presented the Popular N4, a 2050mm-long three-wheeled saloon with a 356cc two-cylinder engine of 16bhp which gave it a top speed of 37mph (60km/h). The company soon reverted to motorcycle manufacture under the rather more celebrated name of Kawasaki.

Meister G5N / G6 / Picknick
A • 1969-1979 • 1F2R • No built: Approx 1500

Hans Jörg Meister, based in Thal near Graz in Austria, started making disabled vehicles in 1962. The G5N Mopedkabine

of 1969 was a tandem two-seater with very basic plastic bodywork over a tubular steel frame. Steering was by handlebars and the engine (a 49cc Puch 3.5bhp moped unit), was sufficient for a top speed of just 25mph (40km/h). It drove only one rear wheel and the driver had to kick start it into life. As well as the open-sided G5N, Meister also made a fully enclosed G6 model with doors (pic right), plus a squarer-shaped three-wheeler called the Picknick from 1977.

Meitian MT50QZ
CN • 2000s-date • 1F2R • No built: n/a

Shanghai Meitian Motorcycle made basic three-wheeled mopeds of a non-leaning variety with 50cc engines.

Meiwa
J • 1951-c1956 • 1F2R • No built: n/a

Meiwa Automobile (formerly the Kawanishi Airplane Co) offered many three-wheeled body styles from 1951 onwards, including a seven-seater people carrier. The lone driver sat up front, the enclosed bodywork allowing access for up to six rear passengers. The front-mounted engine was a 744cc, 16bhp single-cylinder air-cooled four-stroke unit, driving the rear wheels via shaft drive and a three-speed gearbox with reverse. It weighed a hefty 800kg and was 3830mm long.

Mercedes-Benz F300 Life Jet
D • 1997 • 2F1R • No built: n/a

Mercedes-Benz debuted this highly unusual three-wheeler at the 1997 Frankfurt Motor Show. It could tilt thanks to a system called Active Tilt Control, a computer-operated hydraulic system that could alter the cornering angle, up to 30 degrees. In construction, it was an alloy spaceframe with double-skinned aluminium body panelling. Overall weight was 800kg. Power came from Mercedes-Benz A160 1.6-litre petrol engine, and a top speed of 130mph and a 0-62mph time of 7.7 seconds were quoted. The interior featured two seats in tandem, with a distinctly jet fighter feel to it. The F300 was never marketed.

Messer KR-50

J • 1985 • 2F1R • No built: Approx 100

In 1985, a company called F1 Create, based in Aichi Prefecture, built probably the world's first Messerschmitt KR201 replica – the Messer KR-50 Kabrio. Its plastic bodywork was fairly accurate but it was scaled down in size and so could only seat one person. Power came from a rear-mounted 50cc moped engine.

Messerschmitt KR175

D • 1953-1955 • 2F1R • No built: 19,668

Willy Messerschmitt had been forbidden from making aeroplanes after WW2, so when he saw the three-wheeled designs of Fritz Fend ⇨ he was enthusiastic enough to enter a partnership. Messerschmitt took the Fend FK150 and developed it into the first Kabinenroller (KR). A larger 174cc Fichtel & Sachs single-cylinder two-stroke engine was chosen and the name changed to Messerschmitt KR175, ready for launch in March 1953.

The KR175 had many striking features, easily the most celebrated of which was the Plexiglass roof, which resembled so closely the canopies of Messerschmitt's aircraft of the second world war – but despite the popular myth, the tops were very definitelty not left-over aircraft items. The whole canopy swang up sideways to allow entry for two passengers, who sat in tandem in the narrow body (a small child could also just be squeezed on to the rear seat).

A pair of bug-like headlamps provided illumination and the front wheels were enclosed in hemi-spherical wings. Even with only 9bhp, the overall weight of 208kg (460lbs) and excellent aerodynamics of the 'Schmitt gave it a top speed of 90km/h (56mph). It was steered by a pair of handlebars which incorporated a twist-grip throttle, while a reverse gear was optional. Early cars were suspended by rubber blocks, with later examples gaining a better swinging arm arrangement. Licensed production took place in Italy under the name Mivalino ⇨.

Messerschmitt KR200 / KR201

D • 1955-1964 • 2F1R • No built: Approx 30,000

The KR175's replacement was the more sophisticated KR200, whose engine grew, as the name suggested, to 191cc and 10bhp. There were now cut-outs in the front wings to allow the front wheels to steer more freely – the KR175 suffered from a very poor turning circle.

A floor-mounted accelerator replaced the old scooter-style twist-grip throttle and the 'Schmitt was also now able to go in reverse as standard, by restarting the engine in the opposite direction, allowing for the possibility of travel in reverse in four gears. There were better interior appointments,

including optional mock-alligator skin upholstery, a radio and ski mounts.

The high-speed streamlined KR 200 Super one-off broke 25 class speed records in 1955, posting a top speed of 87mph. The appeal of the coupe model was significantly extended by the arrival of a soft-top convertible version in 1956, dubbed the KR201.

As a result of court action by Mercedes-Benz (it claimed the 'flying bird' symbol looked too much like its three-pointed star), a new diamond-shaped FMR badge appeared on Messerschmitts from January 1957, standing for Fahrzeug und Maschienenbau GmbH Regensburg.

A four-wheeled Tg500 'Tiger' model kept interest going into the 1960s, but in truth, although production continued until 1964, the Messerschmitt's day in the sunshine really ended when the 1950s drew to a close.

Metamorphicycles
GB • Early 2000s • 1F2R • No built: n/a

This company offered fully built trikes for the UK market which could use either motorbike or car engines, and were offered in two-, three- and four-seat versions. The company had stopped offering trikes by 2004.

Metroquadro
I • 1974 • 1F2R • No built: Probably 1

L/O Design was an obscure Milanese design company run by Roberto Lucci and Paolo Orlandini. Their Metroquadro ('square metre') lived up to its name by occupying very little road space – the car measured just 1100mm long and 900mm wide. A 49cc moped engine was mounted in the rear and could return 140mpg and a top speed of 25mph (40km/h), while an electric version was also mooted. The car's lower bodywork was made of steel, and in wet weather a polyester top section could be fitted using magnetic fixings. A price equivalent to £230 was suggested at the time, but it's believed no production run ever happened.

MEV Tilting Trike
GB • 2005 • 1F2R • No built: 1

Stuart Mills of Mills Extreme Vehicles (MEV) was one of the kit car industry's most prolific designers, and he turned his attention to trikes in 2005 with a patented tilting trike design. This unusually styled open single-seater was never marketed, although the design was sold on to a third party. This commuter trike's whole front end tilted into corners.

MEV Etrike
GB • 2008-2011 • 2F1R • No built: 24

Stuart Mills's next trike project was the Etrike, a tiny single-seater that was not sold as a car, but as a set of plans. The builder had to fabricate the spaceframe chassis and source the glassfibre fairings and aluminium floorpan himself. The whole thing was designed to be made for £1500. The Etrike was powered by 72V electricity, with a single-speed chain drive obviating the need for gears, and was controlled via motorbike handlebars. It measured just 2100mm long by 1400mm wide and weighed 150kg. A four-wheeled version called the Battmobile was also offered, with fuller glassfibre bodywork.

MEV tR1ke

GB • 2009-date • 2F1R • No built: Approx 100 (to 2013)

Having made a four-wheeled single-seater called the Atomic, the tR1ke (pictured bottom of opposite page) was MEV's first two-seater motorbike-engined project, produced as a three-wheeler to keep weight down. This exo-skeletal machine had very minimal glassfibre body panelling and two seats side-by-side. In the rear was mounted a 998cc Yamaha R1 motorbike engine (hence the name tR1ke), which in standard form had 150bhp but could be tuned as high as 200bhp. In a car weighing a mere 325kg (716lb), it made it extremely quick indeed. Power was transmitted to the single rear wheel by chain and sprockets, using the bike's six-speed sequential transmission, with optional electric reverse. The tR1ke was marketed by Road Track Race of New Basford, Nottinghamshire, with kits costing £4799, or fully built cars from £13,995.

Meyra Motorkrankenstuhl 48/50

D • 1948-1951 • 1F2R • No built: Approx 2000

Meyra-Werke was founded by Wilhelm Meyra in Vlotho to make the Motorkrankenstuhl ('vehicle for the disabled') in 1937. After WW2, Meyra's open-topped tandem two-seater cars were in great demand. The first postwar model, dubbed the Type 48, had a 197cc single-cylinder Ilo engine mounted in between the driver's knees, which wasn't terribly convenient for disabled drivers, so the next model (the Type 50) moved the engine to the right-hand side of the car and added a windscreen.

Meyra prototype

D • 1950 • 1F2R • No built: n/a

This 1950 prototype aimed to bring the disabled vehicle into the modern age, with more sophisticated bodywork incorporating a single headlamp, and a windscreen.

Meyra 55

D • 1950-1953 • 1F2R • No built: Approx 430

More enclosed bodywork greeted the new two-seater Meyra 55, which had a pinched-in front end and two headlamps mounted just fore of the windscreen. It weighed only 200kg, so its 7bhp Ilo 197cc engine could take it to 43mph (70km/h) and return 94mpg (3l/100km). Early examples had canvas doors, but later ones switched to metal doors, longer bodywork, and extra weight (260kg), so a switch to a more powerful 246cc Baker & Polling engine with 8.5bhp was welcome.

Meyra Rikscha

D • 1951 • 1F2R • No built: n/a

This 1951 experiment marked a different route for Meyra: a rickshaw with space for two passengers behind the driver, who steered the car by handlebars. The front-mounted 200cc single-cylinder two-stroke engine drove the front wheel.

Meyra 53

D • 1953-1955 • 1F2R • No built: Approx 1000

A slightly more sophisticated disabled vehicle, the 53 had two doors, two seats side-by-side and two headlamps. Its 197cc 7bhp engine allowed it a top speed of 25mph (40km/h).

Meyra 250

D • 1953 • 2F1R • No built: Probably 1

Meyra's first attempt at a 2F1R layout came in 1953 with this 250cc-engined prototype with two rear-hinged doors, a convertible roof and seating for two, but a production run did not ensue.

Meyra 200
D • 1953-1955 • 1F2R • No built: Approx 50

Things were getting big, relatively speaking, for Meyra with the 200, which measured 3500mm long and weighed 350kg. This fully enclosed saloon could seat four passengers, who accessed the car through a single door on the front of the car, which hinged to the side (the rear passengers had to fold the front passenger seat to gain access). It stuck with a 197cc Ilo single-cylinder engine, mounted in the tail, but it now developed 9.5bhp, so the 200 could reach a top speed of 43mph (70km/h).

Meyra 200-2
D • 1955-1956 • 1F2R • No built: Approx 480

Meyra's final fling probably got too big for its own boots, as the 200-2 now weighed 380kg but still made do with a 197cc single-cylinder engine with 9.7bhp (although very late examples switched to 350cc 14bhp engines). In layout it was the same as the original 200, including a rear-mounted engine and single front door, but the styling was quite baroque and was now made of glassfibre (indeed, this was one of the first German cars ever to have plastic bodywork).

Micro-Car
D • 1970 • 2F1R • No built: Probably 1

Jürgen Junginger's Micro-Car looked like a bathtub on wheels. He claimed it was "the world's smallest car" and he might have been right, as it weighed only 28kg. A single joystick controlled the steering, brakes and acceleration (up to 25mph, or 40km/h), while the lever also doubled up as a carrying handle. Despite reports that it stood a good chance of going into production, it's believed that only one prototype was ever made.

MiKitEV
USA • 2009-date • 2F1R • No built: A few

This was a basic chassis package around which builders could create their own electric vehicle. The chassis used donor parts from a motorcycle (such as a Honda Goldwing), and the estimated price for a rolling chassis was around $6000. Initially the MiKitEV was intended to tilt into corners but this proved awkward to engineer, so was not pursued. Either handlebars or car pedals could be used.

Millennium Motorcycles Tracer
AUS • 1996-date • 2F1R • No built: A few

The Millennium MC Tracer had the ability to lean up to 37 degrees around corners, with the balance of the driver tipping it. The Mk1 version used a Honda CX 500 motorcycle as a basis, with the front section removed and connected to a tubular steel chassis. The Mk2 version was restyled. Tech specs included a length of 3150mm, 260kg weight and a top speed of 100mph (160km/h).

Minerva Tri-Scooter
B • 1953 • 2F1R • No built: n/a

A revival of the great pre-war Belgian brand Minerva was attempted in 1953 with not only the production of scooters under licence from MV, but also a three-wheeler called the Tri-Scooter. This was stillborn, however, and the entire Minerva revival had petered out by 1958.

Mini-Cat
F • 1978-1980 • 1F2R • No built: n/a

The bizarre shape of the Mini-Cat was down to designer Serge Aziosmanoff, who had previously been involved with the GRAC racing car. Its rear-mounted 49cc Peugeot GL10 engine was mated to a continuously variable automatic transmission. The steering was by handlebars and the comically tiny rear wheels were suspended by swinging arms.

Mini-K
USA • 1969 • 2F1R • No built: n/a

The Mini-K was designed as a cheap fun car powered by a 250cc Yamaha engine, with motors up to 750cc engines planned. The prototype had plywood bodywork, while production cars (planned to sell for $500) were to have glassfibre panelling, as illustrated below right. That never happened; instead the car's creator, ex-Lockheed engineer Walter Korff, went on to develop the Unisport Duo Delta ⇨ for launch in 1974.

Mini Mouse

GB • 1970-1974 • 2F1R • No built: 7

This doorless Mini-based three-wheeled fun car was created by Ambrose Porter of Lancashire. He made seven examples, one of which featured a sliding glazed hardtop. All cars were sold fully built rather than in kit form.

Mink

GB/BDA • 1968 • 2F1R • No built: 1

Looking more like a flying saucer than a car, the Mink might have become the only car ever made in Bermuda, as the prototype was built by an engineering company in the Midlands of Great Britain for an intended production run in the Caribbean. A 198cc Lambretta scooter engine sat in the tail of the car's backbone steel chassis, and the tiny glassfibre body featured a precipitous front overhang, which engendered by all reports rather unbalanced road behaviour. Stats included a top speed of 55mph, fuel economy of 70mpg and a weight of 240kg (530lb).

Mirda

CZ • 1948 • 2F1R • No built: Probably 1

The Mirda was built by Vaclav Vejvoda in 1948. It featured a 250cc 9bhp Jawa engine and four-speed gearbox, measured 3200mm long, weighed 295kg (650lb) and could do 42mph (70km/h); however it never made production.

Mitsui Humbee Surrey

J • 1947-1962 • 1F2R • No built: n/a

Founded in 1928, Mitsui ventured into vehicle manufacture in 1947 with a range of three-wheeled commercial vehicles. The first passenger model was the Humbee EFII Surrey, a three-wheeler with a motorcycle handlebars and plastic bodywork. Two rear passengers sat behind the single driver's seat,

protected from the elements by a 'Surrey' top. The engine was a 285cc single-cylinder air-cooled 11.5bhp unit mounted in the rear, driving the rear wheels by chain. Mitsui was subsumed by Hino in 1962.

Mitsuoka Bubu Shuttle 50 / Boy

J • 1982-c1985 • 2F1R • No built: n/a

The Mitsuoka Motor Co was founded in Toyama City in 1968 as a body shop, but it turned to car production in 1982 with the launch of a very small single-seater car, or 'cabin scooter' with the curious name of Bubu Shuttle 50. As that name indicated, it used a 49cc moped

engine (from Honda) which allowed the car to be driven on a moped licence. This model was also known as the Bubu Boy.

Mitsuoka Bubu 501

J • 1982-c1985 • 2F1R • No built: Several hundred

The comparatively smoothly styled Bubu 501 also used a Honda 49cc four-stroke moped engine. It measured just 2060mm long and weighed 168kg, and seated a solitary person. An electric reverse mechanism was provided for parking. Both enclosed and convertible versions were made, and the 501 was also marketed in the USA as the Zoe Zipper ⇨. Only a 1985 change in the law regarding the licensing of 50cc vehicles (they could be registered as mopeds up until then) forced the Bubu line out of production, but as many as 300 units per year were made at the peak of production.

BUBU501は **BUBU501**

Mitsuoka Bubu 502

J • 1983-c1985 • 1F2R • No built: n/a

With the 502, Mitsuoka switched back to a single front wheel, but the main talking point was the styling, or lack of it: it would be hard to imagine a more brick-like vehicle. The split-level front screen was oddness personified, and its main use was as a light delivery

vehicle. It measured just 1840mm long and weighed 155kg.

Mitsuoka Bubu 503

J • 1984-c1985 • 1F2R • No built: n/a

Dalek-like styling graced Mitsuoka's next three-wheeler, the Bubu 503. This was another single-seater with enclosed bodywork, which featured a single door on the left-hand side. Measuring 1803mm long and 1203mm wide, it weighed only 128kg. Mitsuoka is thought to have made a fair number of Bubus before turning to four-wheelers.

Mitsuoka Lime
J • 1984–c1985 • 1F2R • No built: n/a

The Lime was the final three-wheeler design from Mitsuoka before it switched to four-wheelers. This was a sleeker effort but it remained a basic single-seater cabin scooter powered by a 49cc engine.

Mitsuyin
CN • 2010s • 1F2R • No built: n/a

The Ningbo Mitsuyin Machinery Co, based in Zhejiang in China, made a variety of ultra-basic budget electric tricycles such as the MY300 (pictured).

Mivalino
I • 1954–1956 • 2F1R • No built: Approx 100

Mi-Val (or Metalmeccanica Italiana Valtrompio for long) made motorbikes from 1950 in Brescia, Italy, before obtaining a licence to make the Messerschmitt KR175 locally. It differed in several respects, however, in particular its engine: a self-made 172cc Motocarrozzetta two-stroke unit with 9bhp.

Mizushima TM
J • 1947–1962 • 1F2R • No built: 91,050

After WW2, the former Mitsubishi aeroplane works at Okayama were turned over to making Mizushima three-wheeled vehicles, which were mostly delivery trucks, although passenger versions were also made – indeed, this might well have been the world's very first rickshaw. The TM series was quite sophisticated for its time, having weather protection for example. Power came from an air-cooled single-cylinder 744cc engine with 15bhp, driving the rear wheels via shaft through a three-speed gearbox.

MK Trike
GB • 2006-date • 1F2R • No built: Approx 100 (to 2013)

MK Sportscars made a range of kit cars, including a conversion to turn a motorcycle into a trike, an operation that was easily reversible.

Mobilek
GB • 1979 • 1F2R • No built: n/a

The Mobilek was the brainchild of Doreen Kennedy-Way of Dudley, West Midlands. Her electric three-wheeler was intended for simple short-journey use, such as shopping trips and commuting. An ultra-basic design, it was set to cost just £1000 when launched to the public, but there were problems with the Ministry of Transport's type classification for the car and so the Mobilek never went into production.

Mobilette

USA • 1950s-c1969 • 1F2R • No built: n/a

Mobilette Sales & Service of Long Beach, California offered a three-wheeler runabout that was remarkably similar in format to the Autoette ⇨. Three on-board 6V batteries provided the necessary power to an electric motor for local community runaround duties.

Moby

GB • 1992 • 1F1M1R • No built: 2

The Moby was a curious British prototype that attempted to turn a Yamaha moped into an enclosed three-wheeler. The moped wheels were retained in-line but the handlebars were offset to meet the covered driver, while a third wheel was placed half-way down the other side of the car, which resulted in not terribly stable behaviour. The costs of developing it scuppered its chances of production.

Modulo

I • 1988-date • 2F1R • No built: 24 (to 2013)

Ex-Alfa Romeo engineer Carlo Lamattina was behind the Modulo, a high-performance three-wheeler built by a company that he set up in Ronco Briantino near Milan, called Italian Car. A tubular steel space frame chassis was dressed in aluminium panelling, with a carbon fibre-strengthened glassfibre body on top; this featured a flip-up back end, a flop-forward front end and pop-up headlamps. There were single-seater and tandem two-seater versions, plus open or closed roofs.

Power came from a mid-mounted motorbike engine: choices included BMW K-75, K-1100 or others such as Moto Guzzi. Rack-and-pinion steering, independent suspension and hydraulic disc brakes all round were all part of a sophisticated package which clearly appealed to Nigel Mansell (pictured below driving the car), who became a famous owner. Pip Car ⇨ continues to offer the Modulo at the time of writing at a price of 25,000 euros.

Moller Skycar

USA • 1983-date • 1F2R • No built: n/a

Paul Moller was one of the most persistent advocates of flying cars and a pioneer of vertical take-off vehicles. His M400 Skycar hardly needed wheels at all, though it had three of them; it was intended to be in flight most of the time. Work began in 1983 but the first car-like prototype didn't emerge until 1997. Four Rotapower Wankel engines, with 180bhp each, provided power to elicit a claimed air speed of 330mph (531km/h). Tests in 2003 showed the car could fly, but only with a tether, and the prototype failed to sell on eBay in 2006 for a reported reserve price of $3.5 million. Several versions of the Skycar were in development: the M400 could seat four, the later M200 seated two, and a six-seater M600 was also planned.

Monark

S • 1958-1965 • 1F2R • No built: n/a

The Monark Senior range of three-wheeled mopeds was designed for ordinary use or, with a swivelling seat, for disabled people.

Monde

CN • 1996-date • 1F2R • No built: n/a

Under the auspices of the extraordinarily named Dongying Monde Golden Horse Motorcycle Co, this company specialised in three-wheelers, selling them under its own Monde brand but also making them for other brands such as Qingqi ⇨. Several different models were sold. The MD150ZK had a 149cc single-cylinder four-stroke engine with 12bhp and a five-speed gearbox, and was offered in many different body styles, including doorless open-topped, three-door and five-door. The MD650ZK used a larger 650cc engine and was available with much more grandly proportioned bodywork intended for taxi use.

Monika

T • 1960s-date • 1F2R • No built: n/a

Monika Motors Limited was second only to the Pholasith/Forwarder ⇨ among Bangkok-based tuk-tuk manufacturers.

In the 1960s it began making the Monika L5, a licensed version of the Daihatsu Midget DA5 three-wheeled truck. Passenger tuk-tuk models included the SPG3, SPG4, SPG6 and SPG8, each number indicating the quantity of passengers that could be carried. Most versions used 175cc, 200cc or 650cc engines, although the SPG8 was also available with an 800cc unit. Bodywork could be in either steel or glassfibre.

Monsta Trike
AUS • 2000s-date • 1F2R • No built: n/a

The Monsta Trike was designed by Gary Butler and manufactured by Butler Motor Vehicles. Power came from a 2.0-litre Subaru engine with automatic transmission.

Moonbeam
USA • 2006-date • 2F1R • No built: n/a

Jory Squibb built this economy car from two old Honda Elite scooters. Power came from a 150cc Honda four-stroke engine mated to a variable-speed transmission, and the car was claimed to average up to 105mpg. While you couldn't buy a Moonbeam, Jory Squibb's website included instructions on how to build your own car from scratch.

Morford Flyer
GB • 1993-1999 • 2F1R • No built: 3

Created by two Morgan enthusiasts, the Morford Flyer was larger than most trikes. The first two examples built by Peter Morley and Pete Crawford had very angular aluminium bodywork glued on to a steel frame, but the Mk2 version of 1995 featured slightly more curvaceous bodywork. The mechanical basis was Renault 5, with double wishbone front suspension and a rear end supported on a Jaguar spring and damper. Replicas could be made for around £2000 by the Morford Motor Company of Whaddon, Cambridgeshire.

MORGAN

Few family-owned enterprises last long in the motoring business, but Morgan has outdone them all. From its inception in 1910 right up until the current day, it has remained in the ownership of successive Morgan family members based in Malvern, Worcestershire.

For its first 25 years, Morgan's mainstay was economy-minded three-wheelers, although it really began to make waves with its sports models such as the Aero and Supersports. By the mid-1930s, Morgan's attention had switched more towards four-wheelers, which remain on sale to this day – and looking remarkably similar to the machinery that was being made 75 years ago.

Three-wheelers continued to exist on Morgan's price lists until 1952, when their day was well and truly over. The world had every right to suppose that was the end of three-wheeling for Morgan, but a remarkable thing happened in 2010: Morgan re-entered the three-wheeler market with a modern evocation of its glorious Supersports. Inspired by companies making recreations of its own designs, Morgan successfully entered the market with its own modern Three-Wheeler, which sold remarkably well.

Morgan Supersports
GB • 1933-1946 • 2F1R • No built: 12 postwar

The cut-off date for this book is 1940, but since a dozen V-twins were made in 1946 (albeit mostly from pre-war parts) and shipped to Australia, this model merits a place here. The Supersports remains the archetypal Morgan three-wheeler, and was the last V-twin engined model standing by the outbreak of WW2. From 1935 it had been built with barrel-back rear end styling incorporating a recessed spare wheel. The 1096cc JAP OHV engine gave a top speed of over 80mph (130km/h). Unlike the two-speed pre-1933 Supersports, these later models had three speeds as standard.

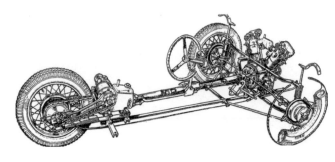

Morgan F4
GB • 1933-1952 • 2F1R • No built: 367 postwar

Prior to 1933, all Morgans had V-twin engines, but the F4 changed all that. Its powerplant came from Ford, in the form of the 933cc Ford Model Y 8HP in-line four-cylinder unit. Rather than the tubular steel chassis of old (pictured on the opposite page), the F-Type used a Z-section pressed steel ladder chassis (as illustrated above), and there was a regular synchromesh gearbox. However, the sliding pillar suspension and chain drive to the rear wheel were typical of all Morgan three-wheelers. The F4 looked more like a conventional car with its upright radiator and long bonnet and sold extremely well before WW2. A larger 1172cc Ford 10HP engine was also offered. Postwar production restarted in 1945, offering four-seater economy motoring at a time when such a thing was sorely needed, but the F4 didn't last very long, with just 367 cars constructed from 1945 up until 1952.

Morgan F Super / Super Sports
GB • 1938-1952 • 2F1R • No built: 265 postwar

A two-seater Morgan F-Type called the F2 had been made from 1935 to 1938, but postwar the only two-seater to be made was the F Super, which was a lightweight sports version of the F-Type. As with the F4, either a Ford 8HP or 10HP engine could be fitted, and you could choose between having a door either on the passenger side only, or two doors.

Morgan Three-Wheeler

GB • 2010-date • 2F1R • No built: Approx 1800 (to 2013)

So impressed was Morgan when the American makers of the Liberty Motors ACE ⇨ approached it seeking a licence to connect it with the Malvern maker that it developed its own Morgan Three-Wheeler from it. Mark Reeves re-engineered the tubular steel spaceframe chassis to accommodate a double-sided rear trailing arm, wishbone front suspension and a Quaife steering rack. Power came from a 1982cc S&S Cycle air-cooled V-twin engine with 80bhp and a healthy 103lb ft of torque. The tough Mazda MX-5 five-speed gearbox was a great match for this engine, driving the rear wheel via its own system of bevel drive and Kevlar belt; it also benefited from a reverse gear. Morgan's designer, Matt Humphries, added his own unique touches to the styling of the aluminium bodywork. Weighing only 525kg, the 21st century Morgan was capable of 0-60mph in 8.0 seconds. Priced from £30,000 fully built, it was an instant hit with the media and public alike, instantly securing itself its place in history as one of the world's definitive three-wheelers.

Morin Aérocar / Triporteur / Taxi-Pousse
F • 1948/1951 • 2F1R • No built: Probably 1 of each

André Morin's first car design was the Aérocar of 1948, a three-wheeled microcar whose open two-seater Duralinox bodywork was supposedly inspired by the contemporary Buick, with a Tatra-esque rear fin too. It had a rear-mounted Ydral 125cc two-stroke engine. In 1951, Morin presented a rickshaw-style device with a semi-enclosed front 'pod' for two passengers, based on the Scootavia scooter that Morin also built in the early 1950s. This was referred to both as the Triporteur and Taxi-Pousse, and was intended for the Indochinese market. Morin also built a four-wheeler in 1957 with very narrow-set rear wheels.

Morton
USA • c1983-c1985 • 1F2R • No built: Approx 40

This unusual car (known variously as the Morton 3 or Morton Fox Star) was produced by the Morton Car Company of San Leandro in California, and was probably a development of the XK-1 ⇨. Over a steel tube chassis was placed a wedgy glassfibre body with removable gullwing doors. A VW Beetle engine normally sat in the tail, but alternatives included Porsche, Mazda and electric units, or indeed a front-wheel drive front-mounted engine. Kits cost from $1500 or fully-built from $7200.

Mosquito
GB • 1971-1977/1984-1987 • 2F1R • No built: Approx 10

Inspired by Owen Greenwood's Mini-based racing trike, Kidlington-based Robert Moss, who ran a glassfibre factory, decided to create the Mosquito. This was one of the earliest Mini-based trikes, and was named after the wartime bomber. A design identical to the prototype was produced as the Trimin ⇨, but Moss went on to offer a modified Mosquito from 1974 until 1977, making six cars, sold by word-of-mouth alone. Then in 1984 a motorcycle shop in Hereford revived the glassfibre moulds and made three more. The design achieved greater success, however, when it was revived in 1992 as the Triad ⇨.

Motalli City Car TR7
P • 1985-c2001 • 1F2R • No built: n/a

Motalli made motorcycles and delivery tricycles for many years, as well as a wheelchair-accessible three-wheeler called the Invacar. In 1985, it launched a microcar, which despite its TR7 moniker shared no traits with Triumph's eponymous sports car. Instead, it was powered by a 50cc Zündapp moped engine and could be bought with three or four wheels.

Moto Guzzi
I • 1928-1980s • 1F2R • No built: n/a

Moto Guzzi is best known to most people for its motorbikes, but it also made three-wheelers from 1928 up until the 1980s. Mostly these were commercial vehicles such as the Motocarri, Trialce, Dingotre and Ercole, but from 1948, passenger rickshaws were also made. A curious three-wheel drive vehicle called the Mulo Meccanico (pictured above) was also made for the Italian military. This was powered by a 704cc V-twin engine with a single steering front wheel and either rubber tyres or half-tracks to the rear. Between 1959 and 1963, some 220 examples were made. A further three-wheeler prototype was the scooter-style Treruote of 1960 (lower pic), which however never made production.

Motorette
USA • 1945-1948 • 1F2R • No built: n/a

This rather basic machine was built in Buffalo, New York, mainly as a factory runaround but it also found favour as a leisure vehicle (Bob Hope was a famous owner). A rear-mounted single-cylinder air-cooled engine drove the left-hand rear wheel only to a top speed of 39mph (63km/h) – either a 4.1bhp Wisconsin unit (Model 20) or a 6bhp Salsbury (Models 20-S and 30-S). The open-topped bodywork (only 90in/2286mm long) was in aluminium, and the steering was by curious ovoid handlebars.

Motor Tech 1000/Vortec
BR • 2008-date • 1F2R • No built: n/a

These Brazilian chopper trikes were fairly typical of the breed, except for the option of a curious hardtop roof and the choice of mechanicals: a VW 1.0-litre turbocharged engine (112bhp) and five-speed gearbox, or a GM Vortec 4.3-litre V6 (180bhp) and four-speed automatic.

Motor Tech Reverso

BR • 2009-date • 2F1R • No built: n/a

Motor Tech's other three-wheeler was a 2F1R supertrike using a mid-mounted Chevrolet Vectra 2.0-litre flex-fuel engine and five-speed manual gearbox, driving the single rear wheel. Double wishbone front suspension with inboard dampers and disc brakes on all three wheels formed part of a fairly sophisticated specification. The glassfibre bodywork could seat two people in tandem, who accessed the car via a hinging Plexiglass canopy.

Motor Trike

USA • 1994-date • 1F2R • No built: n/a

This company offered a whole range of trike conversions for big motorbikes, including Harley-Davidson, Triumph, Yamaha and Honda. A Ford Ranger/Mustang rear axle could be used, or independent rear suspension, or air ride. Motor Trike also developed the Thoroughbred Stallion ⇨.

Möve 101

A • 1953-1954 • 2F1R • No built: Approx 10

The makers of the Felber Autoroller ⇨ supplied rolling chassis to a Viennese coachbuilder called Hofmann & Moldrich, which made its own more grandly proportioned bodywork and sold

the car as the Möve ('Gull') 101. The result was heavier and more expensive than the Felber, and hence it was not as successful. Only one survivor is known.

MSR3

GB • 1992 • 2F1R • No built: 1

Specials builder Alf Richards made a traditional-style three-wheeler that was shown in unfinished form on the Classic Images stand at the Stoneleigh Kit Car Show in 1992. The MSR3 used Renault 5 mechanicals in a cruciform ladder chassis, with a modified Renault 5 trailing arm at the rear. Except for an aluminium bonnet, the boat-tailed bodywork was made entirely of glassfibre. Despite plans to sell the MSR3 for around £5000, nothing more was heard.

MT Maquitrans

E • 1954-1957 • 2F1R • No built: Approx 20

Barcelona-based motorcycle maker Maquinarias y Transportes (or MT for short) presented its first passenger three-wheeler in 1954 – a fully open-topped two-seater. This was followed by a larger two-seater model with enveloping convertible bodywork and doors. Power came from a 125cc or 175cc single-cylinder engine, the latter with 6.9bhp and a top speed of 42mph (67km/h).

Mumford Musketeer

GB • 1973-1978/1983-1999 • 2F1R • No built: Approx 11

The Mumford Musketeer was the brainchild of Brian Mumford of Nailsworth, Gloucestershire. Unusually, it used a Vauxhall Viva engine, gearbox, front hubs and brakes, while the Viva propshaft drove the single rear wheel through a specially-made aluminium final drive with no differential and an axle shaft. The riveted aluminium monocoque chassis used specially designed suspension. The glassfibre bodywork was variously described as "Formula Styled Aerodynamic" and aircraft-inspired: in shape it resembled a large aerofoil with a flat undertray, with a very long nose and a cut-off tail. The headlamps were covered by 'drop-down' panels, and you also got a small boot, but quality was never very high.

Only around four cars were sold between 1973 and 1978 at a cost of £887 apiece, but more examples were made when the Musketeer was revived in 1983 in Series 2 form with minor modifications. Mumford also briefly made the Lomax kit car ⇨.

Musashi Pony 50A
J • 1980s • 2F1R • No built: n/a

The Mitaki Fuji Co of Tokyo made a series of 1F2R three-wheeled trucks with 359cc engines from 1956, but it turned to passenger car manufacture in the 1980s with the Pony 50A, a moped-based enclosed 2F1R three-wheeler.

MyersMotors NmG
USA • 2004-date • 2F1R • No built: Approx 70

Dana S. Myers founded MyersMotors having obtained the remaining stock and parts of the Corbin Sparrow ⇨. The single-seater (pictured at bottom of page) was renamed the NmG (No More Gas) after a number of problems with the original design were ironed out by Robert Q Riley of Quincy-Lynn ⇨ fame. Power came from 13 batteries feeding a DC motor, giving the car a range of up to 40 miles. The top speed was governed at 70mph.

MyersMotors Duo
USA • 2010-date • 2F1R • No built: n/a

In 2010, Myers announced details of the Duo, a new two-seater electric vehicle. Unlike the NmG, it was powered by lithium-ion batteries, giving it a range of up to 60 miles. A price of $24,995 was announced but, as of 2013, the Duo had still to enter production.

Mymsa Rana
E • 1956-1957 • 1F2R • No built: n/a

Mymsa (Motores y Motos SA) was a Barcelona-based company that made motorcycles, but also a range of three-wheeled commercial vehicles from about 1954 under the name Rana 3R. In 1956 it presented a passenger version with four doors, a folding roof and a 175cc engine with 8.8bhp. It could seat four people, or be adapted for wheelchair use. Although the passenger Rana was short-lived, Mymsa continued to make three-wheeler commercial vehicles into the 1960s.

Mystery Designs
USA • 2000-date • 1F2R • No built: n/a

This company offered various trike conversions, mostly for Honda Goldwing and Harley-Davidson. You could choose between a double A-arm independent suspension system or a fixed-axle system. 'Tiltster' tilting suspension was optional, allowing trikes to tilt into corners automatically – claimed to be a world first.

Myzer M-49
USA • 2008 • 2F1R • No built: Approx 3

The Myzer M-49 was not quite an exact replica of one of the world's smallest cars, the Peel P50 ⇨, but it resembled one as closely as possible, given that it was created using only photos of a P50, not an actual example. Originating from Ohio, replica glassfibre shells of the Myzer were offered to the public, and at least three examples were built.

THREE WHEELERS A-Z

N N N

NSU Max-Kabine ▲

NAO Design Aphaenogaster ▲

Nippi ▲

▼ New-Map Solyto

NAO Design Aphaenogaster

USA • 2005-date • 2F1R • No built: 1 (to 2013)

This could just be the smallest roadgoing car ever built, measuring a mere 40in (1016mm) long, 22in (559mm) wide and 20in (508mm) tall, and weighing 20kg (45lb). NAO Design was founded in 2001 in Palo Alto, California by Neal Ormond. His Aphaenogaster (named after an ant) was an exercise in ultra-minimalism. A single 24V battery powered a 350W electric motor, driving the rear wheel at speeds of up to 15mph, with a range of up to 8 miles. The driver sat above the rear wheel, steering with back-and-forth motion of the control stick, with a twist grip for the throttle. It even had lighting. Despite being offered for sale, no-one had actually bought one by the time of writing.

nArrow Streets

GB • 2003-2011 • 2F1R • No built: n/a

Roy Gardiner set up nArrow Vehicles Ltd in 2002 and planned to enter production with his tilting three-wheeler. The prototype was a conversion of a BMW K Series motorbike, featuring an enclosed cabin with a roll cage. The front end (suspended by wishbones and coilovers) was designed to tilt into corners. There was talk of producing the nArrow Streets in Spain but this plan had been scuppered by 2011.

Nelco Solocar

GB • 1947-1967 • 1F2R • No built: Approx 3000

This three-wheeled vehicle was originally launched in 1929 as the Auto-Electric Carriage, but from 1947 was rebranded as the Nelco Solocar and given a light styling refresh. Designed for disabled people, it was one of several such cars powered by electricity – in this case either a 24V or 36V power pack driving the rear wheels. Steering was by tiller to the single front wheel, and rotating the tiller gave a choice of three speeds, while the quoted top speed was just 12mph. Production was assumed by a firm called Reselco in 1952 and was made up until 1967.

Nevco Gizmo

USA • 1996-2005 • 2F1R • No built: 38

Nevco of Eugene, Oregon was founded to make a tiny three-wheeled 'Neighborhood Electric Vehicle' called the Gizmo, powered by a 3bhp DC electric motor turning the single rear wheel. The extremely basic bodywork featured a nose section that lifted up for the lone passenger to get in and out. The accelerator, brake and steering were all operated by levers. Early models had a top speed of 30mph but this was later increased to 45mph. The 154kg (340lb) car cost $12,000 but production was halted in 2005 because of rising costs.

New Asia

PK • 1987-date • 1F2R • No built: n/a

New Asia Automobiles of Lahore, Pakistan, made conventional four-stroke petrol-fuelled rickshaws for the local market. These were clearly inspired by the Bajaj ⇨.

New-Map Solyto

F • 1952-1974 • 1F2R • No built: Approx 4000

The Lyonnais motorcycle company, New-Map, had already had experience building the Rolux microcar when, in 1952, it branched out with the three-wheeled Solyto. This was principally sold as a commercial vehicle, but also as the Break-Camping with a steel rear section and a front cabin with a canvas roof. Powered by a single-cylinder engine of 125cc or 175cc capacity mounted in the tail, its gearbox had three forward speeds but no reverse. Top speed was a mere 25mph (40km/h). The Solyto was also made in Barcelona under the name Delfin.

Nippi
GB • 1984-date • 1F2R • No built: Several thousand

Nippi Cars of Tutbury, Staffordshire, made one of the most popular disabled vehicles of modern times. Designed by Mike Barnes, the unique bodywork was created to cater for the wheelchair user, so a ramp allowed you to enter the car solo; alternatively a motorbike seat could be fitted. The Nippi's bodywork could be made in a variety of widths and was open-topped, but an all-weather hard top canopy was

optional. A welded chassis formed a 'safety cage' and all-independent suspension was fitted. Piaggio scooter engines of 50cc, 80cc or 125cc could be chosen, all with automatic transmission, operated by hand controls with a motorcycle-type throttle. Nippi also marketed the PGO TR3 ⇨ under the name Trippi.

Nissin Sancar
J • Early 1950s • 1F2R • No built: n/a

This was a typical rickshaw-style three-wheeler, produced not by Nissan, but by the Nissin Industrial Co of Kawasaki. It measured 3450mm long, weighed 825kg and could seat five passengers, the driver sitting astride the motorcycle-derived front frame. An air-cooled V-twin engine of 847cc offered 21bhp and drove the rear wheels by shaft through a three-speed gearbox.

Nitta Sangyo Sun
J • 1950 • 2F1R • No built: n/a

Very few electric cars were made in Japan until the Nissan Leaf, but Nitta Sangyo produced the Sun way back in 1950. Its 3150mm long body (weighing 960kg) featured a folding roof to cover the two passengers. A 1.5bhp electric motor drove the rear wheel by chain to a top speed of 24mph (38km/h), up to 80 miles (130km) on a single charge.

Noah
CN • 2009 • 2F1R • No built: n/a

This odd open-topped three-wheeled prototype was shown at the Electric and Clean Auto Show held in Beijing in July 2009, but it's not known if a production run followed.

Nobel 200
GB • 1959-1962 • 2F1R • No built: Approx 1000

The German Fuldamobil was one of the most licensed production cars of all time. The UK manufacturing licence was sold to York-Noble Industries, run by Cyril Lord and operated by Soraya (the ex-Shah of Persia). Manufacture was sub-contracted out: the chassis was made by the aircraft firm Shorts; the glassfibre body by the Bristol Aircraft Company; and assembly was done in Newtownards, Northern Ireland, by shipbuilders Harland & Wolfe.

The Nobel 200 was a Fuldamobil S-7 ⇨ with one major difference: it was also, and more commonly, available with three wheels rather than four. The 191cc Sachs single-cylinder engine with integral four-speed gearbox (plus electric reverse) and plastic-and-plywood bodywork atop a steel tube chassis were basically the same as the Fulda. Drive was to the single rear wheel and a top speed of 55mph and economy of 60mpg were claimed. Cars could be bought either fully-built or in kit form.

Production plans were over-ambitious, as in the event only around 1000 Nobels were ever made. The three-wheeled Nobel was also manufactured abroad in several countries, and there was also an open 'beach car' version, although whether this reached production or not is unclear.

Nobletta
GB • 1961 • 1F2R • No built: n/a

This scooter-style trike was also built by York-Noble Industries. Its two-stroke engine sat over front wheel, turning along with it, and it was capable of a top speed of 40mph; 130mpg was also claimed. The bodywork offered tandem seating for two, while unusually for such a vehicle, a roof and windscreen were also available.

Norimono-ya Sides-Car
J • 1970s • 2F1R • No built: n/a

This very basic machine was based on the Honda Caren moped, and as its name suggested was a sidecar-equipped moped with an enclosed glassfibre body that could seat just one person, who accessed the car via a single door to the side.

Norka
PL • 1992-c1999 • 1F2R • No built: Approx 150

Stanisław Budnik from Chodzieży in Poland made his Norka principally for disabled drivers. The first Norka was made from 1993 but replaced in 1995 by the improved Norka II in four versions (755C, 755-0, 755-B and 755-E Pickup). The car was powered by engines from 50cc (2.2bhp and 40km/h) up to 125cc (5hbp and 60km/h).

Norsjö Partner
S • 1957-1980 • 1F2R • No built: n/a

Norsjö Mekaniska Verkstad was founded in 1951, making delivery vehicles with three wheels. It branched out in 1957 with the Partner, a vehicle intended mainly for the disabled. The handlebar steering and rear-mounted engine were taken from a 50cc moped (initially a 1bhp Husqvarna, later a 1.5bhp Sachs) with a two-speed automatic transmission. Measuring 1980mm long and 990mm wide, it weighed a mere 65kg, and its top speed was 19mph (30km/h).

Norsjö Shopper
S • 1961-1994 • 2F1R • No built: n/a

This was a curious local transport device that consisted of a polyester lower body with a luggage rack on the back and a single seat, protected somewhat from the elements by a canopy that swung sideways for entry. Like the Partner, a 1bhp Husqvarna was used until 1964, when the model was updated and gained a 1.5bhp Sachs engine. Remarkably, it stayed in production until 1994. Norsjö continues to make three-wheeled commercial vehicles to this day.

Norton Shrike
USA • 1984-date • 2F1R • No built: n/a

This was a plans-built trike of simple design with 1+1 seating, created by Dave Norton. First built in 1984, it used Triumph Spitfire front suspension, Porsche steering and a 60bhp 650 Maxim engine. A top speed of 85mph was claimed. An enlarged Shrike II model based on a BMW K1200RS with a 130bhp engine was begun in 2000. The plans set is still available at the time of writing for $70.

Novelty Road King
PK • 2000s-date • 1F2R • No built: n/a

The charmingly named company Novelty Engineers produced the Road King rickshaw for the seemingly insatiable Pakistani taxi market, powered by a 200cc CNG engine, in three- and six-seater forms.

NSU Max-Kabine
D • 1953-1955 • 2F1R • No built: Approx 8 prototypes

The NSU motorcycle factory was doing great business in the early 1950s and was looking to expand by re-entering the car market. In 1953 it made a 1:1 scale model of a proposed new small car with three wheels. The so-called Max-Kabine used an 18bhp 250cc four-stroke engine from the NSU Max motorcycle in the tail, driving the single rear wheel. However, after a failed demonstration of the car to financiers in the Heilbronn forest, the project was developed into a four-wheeler, which would become the NSU Prinz.

THREE WHEELERS
A-Z

Peel Trident ▲

PAL-V One ▲

P.Vallée Chantecler ▼

149.BG.41

Octrun
J • 2011-date • 1F2R • No built: n/a

Built by a sidecar maker based in Chiba, the Octrun was one of a very rare breed of three-wheelers: a motorbike turned into a trike by permanently adding a sidecar. Several models were offered, including the Sport Tourer (pictured) and Gran Turismo, based on superbikes such as the Suzuki GSXR-1000.

Odin Cyclecar
USA • 1982 • 2F1R • No built: n/a

This Morgan-style open-topped sports car used motorbike running gear in its tubular steel chassis, including an exposed front-mounted engine – virtually any unit between 350cc and 600cc could be used. The glassfibre bodywork featured oddly high-mounted cycle front wings and a very short tail. Kits (priced from only $1400) and complete cars were sold from a factory in Cambridge, Indiana.

Okai Jia
CN • 2010-date • 1F2R • No built: n/a

Guangzhou Okai Jia was a subsidiary of motorcycle maker Luoyang Longye, which had plenty of experience in making three-wheeled delivery vehicles before launching the Okai Jia passenger trike range. Petrol models with engines of 150cc, 200cc or 250cc were offered, as well as electric versions, all being rickshaws.

Omega TriStar
USA • 1979-c1985 • 1F2R • No built: n/a

Omega Motors was a California-based car company that specialised in electric vehicles. Its only three-wheeler was the TriStar, which was principally a delivery vehicle, but it had

a detachable rear body section so that it could be converted easily from a pick-up to a van or an estate car. It weighed 381kg (840lb) and travelled up to 40 miles at speeds of up to 30mph (51km/h).

Onyx Bobcat
GB • 1998-2001 • 2F1R • No built: Approx 60

Rally driver David Golightly made a wide range of kit cars from 1990 onwards. His only three-wheeler was the Bobcat – most of which were in fact four-wheelers with a narrow rear track, but a version with a single rear wheel was available. A Mini engine was mounted up front in a spaceframe chassis, which was very visible as the bodywork was minimal, to say the least.

Opus 3WV
CDN • 2005-2006 • 2F1R • No built: n/a

The Campagna T-Rex ⇨ inspired a whole raft of Canadian wannabes, of which the Opus 3WV from Plaisance, Quebec was one of the more obscure. The two-seater could be fitted with one of several motorcycle engines, including 1.3-litre Suzuki and 1.2-litre Yamaha. The 3WV was pricey at $52,000, which might explain why it was so short-lived.

Organic Transit Elf
USA • 2012-date • 2F1R • No built: n/a

The OT Elf was an egg-shaped open-sided commuter car. Its 750W electric motor, driving through a three-speed transmission, could be charged by 30W solar panels as well as by mains, giving it a range of 30 miles (49km). A cargo model with a single front wheel called the Truckit was also offered. Based in Durham, North Carolina, the company offered cars to the public priced from $3900.

OTI Microcar
F • 1957-1959 • 1F2R • No built: Very few

The main claim to fame of OTI (Office Technique International) was that it was based at the old Bugatti factory in Molsheim. That explains why its Microcar became history's least likely recipient of a Bugatti-style horseshoe grille. This applied to the 1959 production-ready model; the original 1957 prototype had been an exercise in pure surrealism – no coincidence, perhaps, as it debuted at the Gala des Artistes (a modern art exhibition). The prototype had a tubular steel chassis and plastic lower bodywork that was protected by Dali-esque rubber bumpers. A hardtop was proposed with a semi-circular roll-over bar anchoring a bizarre bulging Perspex dome. A later body style (lower pic) was far more conventional. OTI Microcars were fitted either with a 125cc Gnome-et-Rhône two-stroke engine or a 250cc unit, in both cases driving the single front wheel.

Ouji Jetgo
CN • 2006-date • 1F2R • No built: n/a

Ouji mostly made monkey bikes but its extraordinarily named Jetgo Apollo Chariot was a chopper-style device with a 110cc 7.5bhp engine that could reach 50mph (80km/h) if pushed.

Pacesetter
USA • 1970s • 1F2R • No built: n/a

Primarily an off-road ATV, the Pacesetter could be adapted to road use with a few optional accessories. Power came from a 9bhp Wisconsin Robin engine.

Padwin
GB • 1951 • 1F2R • No built: n/a

Having built some Invacars ⇨ under contract, Samuel Elliott Ltd of Reading, Berkshire, presented its own invalid car in 1951 under the name Padwin. This was an open-topped single-seater with a rear-mounted 197cc engine and three-speed gearbox. As it never obtained government approval for production, however, it remained a prototype.

Paifu PF
CN • 2010s • 1F2R • No built: n/a

A company called Ningbo Paifu built a very Spartan range of three-wheeled electric rickshaws with open or enclosed bodywork, including the PF004, PF-300 and PF400 (pictured).

Pak Hero
PK • 1996-date • 1F2R • No built: n/a

Pak Hero Industries was founded by Muhammad Javed Iqbal to make rickshaws in Lahore. Two three-seater models were offered (the PH-333 and the PH-335 Tezgam) plus a five-seater, with two-stroke or four-stroke engines.

Palmer Electric Pal
USA • 1960-1980 • 1F2R • No built: n/a

Produced by Palmer Sales & Service Inc of Phoenix, Arizona, the Electric Pal was a vehicle for the disabled. A hydraulic system lowered the ungainly glassfibre-and-metal bodywork (covered by a canopy with side curtains) to allow a wheelchair to be pushed into the car. The electric motor was fed by six 6V golf cart batteries and drove the single front wheel, with two forward speeds and reverse; at full tilt it could do 15mph. Palmer also made a mobility-orientated electric tricycle called the Happy Wanderer.

Palmer
USA • 1973-date • 1F2R • No built: n/a

Palmer Industries of Endicott, New York, mostly made electric power kits for three-wheeled adult tricycles. It also made more substantial electric shopping trikes, including the 3some for three people and the Hybrid (pictured), which used a rear-mounted portable generator to power the batteries.

Palmirani Smile
I • 2000s • 1F2R • No built: n/a

Palmirani was a company based in Bologna that made all sorts of products for disabled people. Its one and only car was the Smile, a tiny trike with semi-enclosed glassfibre bodywork. It used a 49cc moped engine (Morini or Suzuki) driving the rear wheels, with handlebar steering and controls. Production ended during the late 2000s, although the Palmirani company was still operational at the time of writing.

PAL-V One
NL • 2004-date • 1F2R • No built: n/a

As its name – Personal Air and Land Vehicle – suggested, the PAL-V One joined the rarefied ranks of flying cars. Dutch entrepreneur John Bakker was behind the project, aided by Spark Design Engineering. However, much of the PAL-V One's

underpinnings derived from the Carver ⇨.

This was essentially a two-seater gyrocopter crossed with a car and a motorbike. On the ground, it drove like a car in a straight line but could tilt into corners like a motorbike, at angles of up to 30 degrees, thanks to the Carver-derived DVC system. When required, its single autogyro rotor and push-propeller were folded out (a process that took only 10 minutes). The car could take off within a very short distance (165m) from "practically anywhere" with no need for a flight plan, since it was designed to fly under the 4000ft (1500m) floor of commercial air space. However, an autogyro licence was required to fly one.

Powered by a 213bhp rotary engine, it could reach speeds of 112mph (180km/h) and do 0-62mph in under eight seconds. It was a compact car, measuring 4000mm long and 1200mm wide, and weighed just 680kg (1500lb). The PAL-V completed its first test flight in 2012, with production scheduled to begin at an estimated cost of around £200,000 per vehicle.

Pantera SM150
CN • 2000s-date • 1F2R • No built: n/a

Chongqing Pantera made motorbikes and crude three-wheelers, most of which were motorcycle conversions, but there was also the SM150, a fully enclosed model with a 150cc engine.

Para-Cycle
USA • 1970s • 1F2R • No built: n/a

This basic device consisted of a petrol-powered single front wheel mounted in a frame, into which a wheelchair could be attached, the rear wheels of which then doubled up as the rear wheels of the 'car'.

Parhiyar Aerolite
PK • 2000s-date • 1F2R • No built: n/a

Parhiyar Auto Mobile made a range of motorcycles, but also rickshaws under the Aerolite badge, with both open and enclosed body styles. Power came from a single-cylinder four-stroke air-cooled unit of 175cc capacity which could be fuelled by petrol or CNG.

Paris-Rhône
F • 1941-1943 • 1F2R • No built: n/a

As a supplier of automotive electricals, Lyon-based Paris-Rhône was well qualified to join the ranks of electric microcar makers that mushroomed during petrol shortages in wartime France. The first prototype (called the VPR) had simple open bodywork measuring 2500mm long and seating two people. In its tail sat a 2.5bhp electric motor powered by six batteries, powering the two rear wheels to a top speed of 19mph (30km/h), while a range of 40 miles (65km) was claimed. An update in 1942 was the Baby-Rhône with coupé bodywork by the coachbuilder Faurax et Chassende. The last cars built by Paris-Rhône were in 1950.

Pashley Pelican
GB • 1949-1957 • 1F2R • No built: n/a

WR Pashley of Birmingham mostly made bicycles but in 1949 launched a three-wheeled rickshaw called the Pelican – essentially a motorised pedicab. The single front wheel was motorcycle-style and the driver sat astride the vehicle, with doorless rickshaw-type bodywork to the rear. The first examples had an ungainly shape with seating for two passengers in the back, but later ones had two rows of rear seats, which also pioneered the use of glassfibre in cars in Britain; indeed, the novelty of transparent glassfibre was even attempted. The 1949 Pelican was advertised with a 4bhp engine, but by the end of production, a 600cc JAP four-stroke engine was being used.

Pashley
GB • 1953-1957 • 1F2R • No built: n/a

Pashley's other passenger three-wheeler was a conventional machine similar to the Bond Minicar ⇨. This boasted a welded steel chassis and open, doorless bodywork made of metal. The 197cc Villiers two-stroke engine and transmission were attached to the front wheel. Pashley also made three-wheeled delivery trucks and ice cream trikes, but production of motor vehicles ceased in 1957 (although Pashley did carry on making bicycles and tricycles beyond this date).

Pasquali Risciò
I • 1990-c2004 • 2F1R • No built: n/a

Pasquali Macchine Agricole, based near Florence, mostly made agricultural machinery (still in production at the time of writing), but it also offered a small (2190mm long) electric three-wheeler called the Risciò ('rickshaw'). Its 3.8kW electric motor was fed by four 6V batteries. Overall weight was 360kg, and claims included a top speed of 25mph (40km/h) and a range of 31 miles (50km). Two versions were offered: a single-seater needing no driving licence and a two-seater for which a licence was required. Many were used by the Italian postal service, and a hydrogen-powered model was also planned but apparently not realised.

Pasquini Valentine
I • 1976-1980 • 2F1R • No built: n/a

Studio Paolo Pasquini of Bologna made this compact economy car. A steel tube chassis featured a removable front

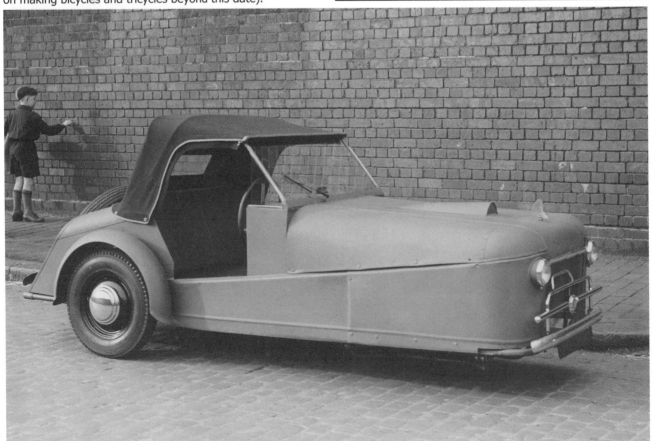

subframe which carried the engine, steering and MacPherson strut suspension. Several engines could be specified: a 251cc 12bhp two-cylinder, a 246cc for export markets and either 48cc or 125cc versions which could be driven by 16-year olds or people without a driving licence. Drive was to the front wheels via a single-speed transmission, while the enclosed two-seater bodywork was plastic. The three-wheeled version was intended for the local market, while a four-wheeled model was also built for export.

Passat Aeolus
D • 1952-1953 • 1F2R • No built: n/a

This space-age-looking machine had smoothly contoured metal bodywork with a Plexiglass upper section. The driver sat centrally, with two passengers behind him. Measuring 3350mm long and weighing 200kg, the Aeolus was powered by a 200cc single-cylinder two-stroke engine in the tail, but its most notable mechanical feature was continuously variable belt-drive transmission, years before DAF launched its own system. One of the partners in the Passat business later produced the Pinguin ⇨.

Patriarca Delfina/Outsider
I • 1993 • 1F2R • No built: n/a

Bruno Patriarca, the son of racing car constructor Rodolfo, was behind this pair of three-wheelers. A Benelli 50cc moped engine provided the power; an electric model was also  proposed. The price tag in 1993 was 1,900,000 lire (£650).

PB
F • 1955-1956 • 2F1R • No built: Very few

Appearing at the 1955 Paris Salon, the PB was one of innumerable microcars of the period. It was a very small three-wheeler with dumpy open doorless bodywork in plastic and a single headlamp.

Its Ydral 175cc engine powered the ultra-light (175kg) car to a top speed of 50mph (80km/h), or a 125cc version was available. The PB would later form the basis of the Decolon ⇨.

PCD
J • 2009-date • 2F1R • No built: n/a

PCD stood for Prominence Commuting Device, which explains the function of this featherweight (125kg/276lb) single-seater electric car from Nagano, Japan. It was based on a recumbent trike chassis made by MR Components of Australia and used a 500W electric motor to power it to a top speed of 47mph (75km/h).

PEEL

Cyril Cannell was a prolific experimenter in the field of microcars. His Isle of Man-based firm, Peel Engineering, looms large in the world of microcar enthusiasts. Despite an output of cars that barely reached treble figures, the extreme compactness, and great charm, of his creations has assured their place in history. Not only was Peel an early pioneer in the field of glassfibre (making motorcycle fairings and boat hulls, for example), it was also one of the earliest European companies to start making glassfibre cars, as much with four-wheeled plastic-bodied cars as three-wheelers.

Perhaps the greatest tribute paid to the Peel was that a P50 sold at auction in 2013 for over £75,000, while replicas of both the P50 and Trident are, at the time of writing, back in production.

Peel Manxman/Manxcar
GBM • 1955 • 2F1R • No built: n/a

The very first Peel model was the Manxman (also referred to as the Manxcar). Its enclosed glassfibre body featured a highly unusual method of entry: the quarter-circular door pivoted at its rear base, swinging upwards and backwards, flush with the bodywork. Two hammock seats were supplemented by a rear compartment which could carry two children or 450 litres of luggage.

The engine (a 350cc Anzani two-stroke two-cylinder or 250cc Anzani unit) was mounted in the rear of a steel tube chassis, driving the single rear wheel by chain. A top speed of 50mph (80km/h) was claimed, as well as fuel consumption of 90mpg. The plan was to sell the 203kg (448lb) Manxcar in kit form for £299 10s, but it seems unlikely that production ever began. Instead, Peel went on to make the P1000 glassfibre bodyshell for Ford Ten chassis.

Peel P50

GBM/GB • 1962-65/2010-date • 1F2R/2F1R • No built: Approx 50

The car for which Peel is unquestionably most famous is the P50. This was undoubtedly the world's smallest passenger car at the time, and continues to hold the Guinness Book of Records title as such to this day.

The prototype P50 (pictured below) measured just 50in (1270mm) long, 33in (840mm) wide and 46in (1170mm) tall. This first P50 had a single front wheel and twin rear wheels, but production models reversed the layout, and were slightly more portly at 53in (1350mm) long and 39in (990mm) wide, but they weighed a mere 60kg (132lb).

In essence, the P50 consisted of a single seat surrounded by a one-piece glassfibre monocoque body/chassis. A DKW 49cc fan-cooled engine sat underneath the driver on the right-hand side, where it chirped away in an extremely noisy fashion, driving the rear

wheel by chain via a three-speed gearbox.

The P50 was hardly a comfortable machine to drive and there were stabilising 'nodules' to the rear of the bodywork on some cars to stop them toppling over on corners, which was all too likely, even at speeds well below its maximum of 30mph (48km/h). Reversing was accomplished by using a handle fitted on the back of the car. At a price of £199 10s in 1963, new P50s were despatched in a wooden box which could double up as a garage.

The P50 exerted a fascination well beyond its time. A 1964 example sold for an incredible £75,000 at auction in 2013. Many unofficial replicas have been built over the years, but a new chapter was written when, in 2010, Gary Hillman Faizal Khan brought the Peel 50 and Peel Trident ⇨ back to life. With the help of financier James Caan of BBC TV's Dragon's Den, cars re-entered production on the mainland.

The main difference of the 21st century P50 (pictured below) was that it was powered by electricity, not fossil fuel. Its 2.2kW (3bhp) electric motor propelled it to the same top speed of 30mph (48km/h) as the old 49cc version, while its claimed range on a single charge was 65 miles (105km). Fully road-legal in the UK, a "strictly limited" run of new P50s was announced by the revived Peel firm, priced from £10,000.

Peel Trident

GBM/GB • 1965-1966/2010-date • 2F1R • No built: 82

Peel's next three-wheeler was the Trident, which was larger than the P50, but only just (measuring 72in/1830mm long). The glassfibre bodywork consisted mostly of a forward-hinging front section with a highly distinctive transparent Perspex dome roof and flat glass windscreen. The umbrella handle-shaped steering column was hinged and rose up with the canopy as it opened for entry.

The Trident could just about seat two people side by side, although some cars were supplied as single-seaters with a shopping basket beside. The engine was initially the same 49cc unit as the P50, but some cars had 100cc Vespa engines, which were kick-started to life using a detachable pedal. With a very tight turning circle of 96in (2440mm), there was really no need for a reverse gear, which is just as well since none was fitted; like the P50, you simply got a

handle on the rear of the car.

Costing £189 19s 6d, the Trident was even cheaper and marginally more practical than the P50. It was advertised as being "almost cheaper than walking", having fuel consumption of about 100mpg. A 125cc Triumph Tina-engined export model was considered but abandoned, while a four-wheeled electric version also appeared in 1966.

After a gap of some 24 years, a revived Peel Engineering installed electric power in a three-wheeled reincarnation of the Trident. Two versions were created: a 30mph model (with a 2.3kW/3.1bhp motor) and a 50mph model (with a 4kW/5.4bhp motor), with a range of 80 miles (130km) and 62 miles (100km) respectively.

Pembleton Super Sport
GB • 1999-date • 2F1R • No built: Approx 350 (to 2013)

Phil Gregori and his brother Roger had previously marketed a mid-engined Ford-based coupe, before Phil formed the Pembleton Motor Company in Leamington Spa, Warwickshire to make the three-wheeled 'Grasshopper' Super Sport (and, from 2002, the Brooklands four-wheeler). This Morgan-inspired trike was powered by a 602cc Citroën 2CV engine, and retained the 2CV's suspension but in a new spaceframe chassis. Aluminium bodywork kept the overall weight down to just 350kg (770lb). Alternative engines, such as BMW and Moto Guzzi, were fitted by owners. The two seats could be folded forwards to access the boot area.

Perscheid Triky
D • 2010-date • 2F1R • No built: n/a

The father-and-son team of Hans and Martin Perscheid built the Triky. Their own chassis was clothed in single-seater glassfibre bodywork and incorporated a Vespa engine and quadbike-based suspension.

Persu
USA • 2007-date • 1F2R • No built: n/a

A Californian company called Venture Vehicles announced plans for the VentureOne in 2007, with three models in  development: the e50 hybrid, the Q100 performance hybrid and the EV electric. In 2008 Venture was renamed Persu Mobility, and development concentrated on the Persu Hybrid. This would be powered by a plug-in electric/petrol system, but a regular internal combustion model called the Persu V3 was also planned for 2014. Described as an "Urban Life Vehicle", the two-passenger Persu very much followed the form of the Carver ⇨, which is not surprising considering it made use of the same DVC (Dynamic Vehicle Control) electro-hydraulic tilting system as the Carver, so it could tilt into corners like a motorcycle.

Petri & Lehr
D • 1940-1950s • 1F2R • No built: n/a

Wilhelm Petri and Adam Wilhelm Lehr made one- and two-seater vehicles for the disabled in Offenbach, with petrol engines of 98cc, 174cc or 197cc, or electric power. The company was bought by Meyra ⇨ in 1964, and was still making disabled conversions for conventional cars at the time of writing.

Peugeot 20Cup
F • 2005 • 2F1R • No built: 2

The French giant Peugeot has a history of three-wheeled designs, having built the Triporteur delivery tricycle after WW2. The 20Cup concept of the 21st century was, however, a very different animal: a motorsport-themed roadster. A one-piece carbon chassis incorporated a separate two-seater cockpit, trimmed in leather. The front-mounted engine was a turbocharged four-cylinder petrol unit developing 168bhp, driving through a sequential six-speed manual gearbox with steering wheel paddles. Double wishbone front suspension was supplemented by a single rear arm. With a length of 3630mm and a height of only 1160mm, overall weight was less than 500kg. Two examples were shown at the 2005 Frankfurt Motor Show, differing only in colour.

Peugeot HYmotion3 / HYbrid3 Evolution / Onyx
F • 2008/2009/2012 • 2F1R • No built: n/a

No doubt inspired by the success of the Piaggio MP3 ⇨, Peugeot embarked on its own three-wheeled scooter project. A series of prototypes appeared at shows. The first was the 2008 HYmotion3 (above), a roofed model with a hybrid engine that worked in three modes (electric only, petrol only, and 'cruising' hybrid).

This was followed by the 2009 Peugeot HYbrid3 Evolution, which swapped the previous 21bhp 125cc supercharged engine for a 41bhp 300cc unit, giving it a total of 49bhp when combined with the two 3kW front-wheel motors (making it three-wheel drive). It could do 0-62mph in 8.0sec.

Then came the 2012 Onyx 'supertrike' (below), whose plug-in electric motor was now combined with a 400cc engine, giving a combined power of 61bhp and a range of up to 500km (310miles). It also featured a two-mode driver position: in Sport mode, the rider was inclined forwards (to the benefit of aerodynamics), while in Urban mode, the feet moved forwards and the head upwards to improve visibility.

Peugeot Metropolis 400i
F • 2013-date • 2F1R • No built: n/a

The three Peugeot prototypes finally culminated in a production model, the Metropolis 400i. First seen as a prototype in 2011, it reached production in 2013. Its 400cc engine developed 35bhp, and it had a leaning mechanism baptised as TTW (Twin Tilting Wheels). Advanced features included an aluminium frame, all-round disc brakes, keyless start system and an electric parking brake.

PGO TR3
RC • 2000s-date • 1F2R • No built: n/a

Taiwanese motorcycle maker PGO's TR3 was based on its T-Rex scooter but had an extra wheel at the rear, plus a rear differential and a reverse gear. The powertrain consisted of a Piaggio-derived 49cc two-stroke air-cooled engine with 5bhp and automatic transmission, and top speed was restricted to 30mph. This model was sold in the UK by the makers of the Nippi ⇨ as the Trippi as a means of disabled transport for those who needed no wheelchair.

Phantom
USA • 1978-1981 • 2F1R • No built: 3

One of the most dramatic three-wheelers ever made was the Turbo Phantom from the Phantom Vehicle Company of Newport Beach, California. The brainchild of ex-GM Corvette design studio man, Ronald J Will, it was utterly exotic but designed to be relatively inexpensive. Measuring only 44in (1118mm) high, its striking plastic/urethane bodywork was accentuated by a width

of nearly 7 feet (over 2.1m). Giant air dams, gill-like ducts and a sharply upswept tail made the Phantom look like a cross between a space capsule and a manta ray. A huge canopy swung forwards, taking the steering wheel and dash with it, to access the two-seater cockpit.

A tubular steel chassis carried widened VW Beetle front suspension with adjustable air dampers. A choice of Japanese superbike engines was offered, including Honda Goldwing engine (turbo or non-turbo, 110bhp and 75bhp respectively), or a Kawasaki six-cylinder 1300cc turbo unit with 180bhp and a top speed of over 140mph.

Two prototypes were built in 1978 and a fully-built price

of $19,500 was announced. From 1981, the Phantom was also available as a set of DIY plans for $20, alongside an abortive second model, the Jet Fighter.

Phiaro P67b Eternity
J • 2005 • 1F2R • No built: 1

The Phiaro Corporation of Saitama, Japan was a design company that celebrated its 50th birthday by displaying the P67b Eternity at 2005 Tokyo Motor Show. If it looked like the Carver ⇨, that was no coincidence: it was indeed based on the Carver, complete with its tilting technology and 659cc Daihatsu engine, and Phiaro merely designed its own exterior and interior. A plan was announced at the time to put the P67b into production by 2007, but this never in fact happened.

Phoenix Trike Roadsters F1 Extreme
USA • 2012-date • 2F1R • No built: n/a

This Arizona-based company was formed in 2009 but by 2012 had still to productionise its trike designs. As its name

hinted, the F1 Extreme single-seater clearly took its design inspiration from Formula 1 racing cars, and was intended to be offered as a full kit to take almost any motorcycle engines from 500cc to 1000cc.

Phoenix Trike Roadsters Roadster
USA • 2012-date • 2F1R • No built: n/a

This unusually styled doorless two-seater used a front-mounted Yamaha 1300cc V4 engine with shaft drive to the rear wheel, in which case a top speed of 95mph was quoted (other motorbike units could also be fitted). The front end was independently suspended and the whole car weighed only 499kg (1100lb). A convertible roof was optional, while another mid-engined model called the Sportster was in planning at the time of writing.

Phoenix Trike Works
USA • 1964-date • 1F2R • No built: n/a

The father-and-son team of Willis and Joseph Wilcken made a whole series of rear-engined custom trikes with very rakish lines. For example, their Touring model used the entire drivetrain and

suspension of a 3.8-litre supercharged V6 Buick Regal.

Pholasith / Forwarder
T • 1987-date • 1F2R • No built: Hundreds of thousands

Bangkok-based Pholasith Tuk-Tuk Motors became the largest manufacturer of motorized three-wheeled rickshaws in Thailand, churning out up to 16,000 a year from its factories in Bangkok. It changed its name to Tuk Tuk Forwarder in 2000. It was one of the pioneers of switching from two-stroke engines to less polluting four-stroke units (550cc engines with 30bhp, able to run on petrol, LPG or CNG), while electric-powered tuk tuks were also developed. The range included models with three seats, six-to-eight seats and pick-ups.

Piaggio Ape Rickshaw
I/IND • 1948-date • 1F2R • No built: Hundreds of thousands

The Piaggio Ape started life just after WW2 as the perfect commercial transport in war-torn Italy. Essentially a Vespa scooter with two rear wheels, it was very cheap both to buy and run. Passenger variants inevitably followed, as taxi operators realised it could be a super-budget mode of metered transport. Various bodywork – open, enclosed, convertible – saw passengers sitting behind the scooter-seated driver.

However it would be India that really took the mantle of the Piaggio

design featured hinged doors, while the rear was adaptable to many shapes, from van to pick-up to estate car. Despite the official involvement of Piaggio, it never reached intended production.

Piaggio P 103
I • 1996 • 1F2R • No built: n/a

The P 103 was an attempt to make a city car prototype with egg-shaped single-seater glassfibre bodywork, two doors and luggage containers front and rear. A Piaggio 50cc scooter engine and automatic transmission with reverse provided the power, with belt transmission and chain drive to the rear wheels. Independent rear suspension combined with a single-arm front fork in a tubular steel chassis. A surprisingly sophisticated spec included a digital dash, airbag and four-point seatbelts. No production run ensued, however.

rickshaw on. Greaves Vehicles – which made the Garuda ⇨ – reached an agreement with Piaggio of Italy to make its Ape model in Baramati, India from 1998, but using all-Indian components; Piaggio would later take 100% control of the enterprise. The Indian-built Ape rickshaw was powered by a choice of engines, including petrol, diesel, CNG and LPG. This was an extremely successful model in India, consistently selling around 50,000 units a year in the 2000s. One interesting variant was the Ape Calessino (pictured above), a luxury four-passenger rickshaw with a 422cc 7.5bhp diesel engine, 999 of which were made in 2007.

Piaggio Spazio 3
I • 1984 • 1F2R • No built: Several prototypes

Piaggio's famous Ape three-wheeled commercial vehicle was one of Italy's most successful delivery wagons. Of the many attempts to create a more sophisticated concept on the same basis, ex-Pininfarina designer Paolo Martin's Spazio 3 was perhaps the most impressive. He envisaged engines ranging from 50cc (two-stroke) to 250cc (four-stroke). The aerodynamic

Piaggio MP3
I • 2006-date • 2F1R • No built: Over 100,000 (to 2013)

There are certain three-wheelers that become instantly iconic, and the Piaggio MP3 (pictured below) is undoubtedly one of them. Piaggio may not have been the first company to make a scooter with two front wheels, but it was certainly the brand that really popularised the idea.

The MP3 (standing for 'Moto Piaggio a 3 ruote') had several benefits over a two-wheeled scooter. It could be brought to a stop and parked like a car, was more stable, and had better weather protection. The front suspension used two arms linked by an alloy parallelogram, which could be locked in place at low speeds or at a halt. Otherwise it would lean into corners like a regular scooter.

Launched with a 250cc engine, eventually 125cc, 278cc, 400cc and 500cc versions became available; the 500cc version was marketed as the Gilera Fuoco ⇨ in Europe. The LT 400 version of 2009 had a front track that was wider by about 50mm, allowing it to be classified as a tricycle rather than a motorcycle in many European countries.

There was also a plug-in hybrid variant in 2009, powered by a 125cc engine and a 2.6kW electric motor. This could do 0–60mph in just 5.0 seconds, despite its 249kg (550lb) weight, compared to 208kg (460lb) for the petrol-only model. An urban version called the Yourban 300cc LT was also launched in 2012 (pictured below), while a protective roof became available in 2007.

Pia Pia
J • 1980s • 1F2R • No built: n/a

This was one of many Japanese 'cabin scooters' built in the 1980s using moped mechanicals clothed in basic glassfibre bodywork.

Picchio
I • 1989 • 2F1R • No built: n/a

The first project of Picchio SpA, which later became famous for its racing cars, was a Morgan-inspired 1930s-style trike. This was powered by a Moto Guzzi motorbike engine.

Pilot
S • 1940s • 2F1R • No built: n/a

Designed by a Swedish Saab engineer called Ulf Cronberg, the Pilot was aircraft-inspired with an aluminium skin, plus steel front wheelarches and doors. It could be made as a velomobile or with a motor (various choices from 175cc upwards) which was placed centrally in front of the rear wheel. Sets of plans were sold to the public.

Pinguin
D • 1953-1955 • 2F1R • No built: Approx 10

Having produced the Passat prototype ⇨, the creators went on to make the Pinguin, produced by Ruhr-Fahrzeugbau of Herne in Germany. This attractive design was first presented as a steel-bodied two-seater coupe, although in 1954 it re-emerged with a refreshed design seating 2+2 in an aluminium shell. A 197cc Sachs single-cylinder engine with 9.5bhp was mounted just in front of the rear wheel, driving it via a three-speed gearbox to a top speed of 53mph (85km/h). However, the Pinguin's projected price was too high and only around 10 prototypes were made.

Pioneer
CN • 2002-date • 1F2R • No built: n/a

As its name suggested, Shandong Pioneer Motorcycle mostly made motorbikes, but it also branched out into the manufacture of passenger trikes. Various body styles were offered. The most basic were scooter-derived tricycles with 70cc (XF70ZK) or 105cc (XF110ZK) engines. Larger four-door and open-topped four-seaters had single-cylinder four-stroke engines: the XF150ZK had a 149cc unit with 12bhp and could do 31mph (50km/h), the XF200ZK a 193cc 10bhp, and the XF250ZK boasted a 229cc 12bhp unit. Pioneer three-wheelers were commonly exported to various countries under the Flybo name.

Pip Car Scooter 050
I • c2005 • 2F1R • No built: Probably 1

Pip Car Engineering, based in San Michele di Ganzaria in Italy, proposed the Scooter 050 as a one- or two-seater commuter car. It was designed to be driven without a license by drivers aged as young as 14 years old. A patented device on the rear wheel allowed it to be parked in a space equal to its own length. Three versions were suggested: a 50cc petrol model with a top speed of 31mph (50km/h); a 4kW electric variant with up to 27mph (45km/h); and a hybrid model. A four-wheeled version called the Scooter 0100-4R was also designed, while Pip Car also made the Modulo ⇨.

Plane-Mobile
USA • 1931-1946 • 2F1R • No built: Probably 1

Daniel Zuck's flying car initially had a three-blade propeller at the rear, later changed to a conventional front prop, and distinctively shaped wings that attached to the top of the saloon-like fuselage. On land, these folded back and stacked one on top of the other. Unlike many such projects, it actually flew but no manufacturer was interested enough to build it.

Planet Ellipse / Japster
GB • 2008-date • 2F1R • No built: 10 (to 2013)

Designed by Alan Pitcairn and Dave Kennell, the Ellipse was made by Planet Engineering of Dinton, Salisbury. Clearly inspired by the Morgan, it had a square-tube steel chassis with unequal-length front wishbones and a double-sided rear swinging arm. It was sold fully built with all-new parts, and power came from a 95bhp S&S 1575cc V-twin engine (which would later power Morgan's new Three-Wheeler). In a car weighing under 385kg (850lb), performance was bright: 0-60mph in 6.5 seconds and a top speed of over 125mph. The bodywork was in glassfibre with removable front and rear sections, and options included a full windscreen, and a roll-over bar.

In 2012, the project passed to a Kent-based company called JA Prestwich, which renamed the car the Japster, as it now used a recreation of the 1920s JAP engine, a 1272cc air-cooled V-twin with 85bhp, with either open or closed rockers. A supercharged version was under development at the time of writing.

Plum Qingqi
PK • 1998-date • 1F2R • No built: n/a

Plum Qingqi Motors was a Lahore-based manufacturer of rickshaws using Chinese-made Qingqi ⇨ mechanicals. The most basic model was the 100cc-engined Millennium but 150cc models were also built

under the names Rickshaw and Shuttle, while CNG fuelling was also possible.

PMC AEV
USA • 1974 • 2F1R • No built: 1

The PMC AEV (Powers Motor Corporation Alternative Energy Vehicle) was a Californian prototype designed to explore different fuel technologies. Four alternative powertrains were proposed: a Daihatsu three-cylinder petrol engine, a Yanmar three-cylinder diesel, a Kawasaki six-cylinder or a Westinghouse electric motor. The polyurethane sandwich bodywork was mounted on a tubular steel chassis, and featured a detachable hardtop. Overall weight was quoted as 680kg (1500lb).

Poinard
F • 1951-1953 • 1F2R • No built: n/a

Poinard was a motorcycle sidecar manufacturer located in Cachan which branched out into three-wheeler production. Several different designs were propagated. There was a rickshaw device that retained motorcycle handlebar steering to the single front wheel and a saddle for the driver, with two passengers sitting on a bench behind. More enclosed body styles were also built. Power came from either a 4bhp Ydral 125cc single-cylinder engine or an AMC 175cc 8bhp unit.

Poirier Monoto
F • 1928-1958 • 1F2R • No built: n/a

Poirier started making disabled vehicles in 1928, but its postwar effort, the Monoto, was in theory available to any driver. This was a very basic open-topped affair with tandem seating for two, measuring 2250mm long and just 790mm wide. Either 98cc Sachs or 125cc Ydral engines were used, the top speed being restricted to 31mph (50km/h), and users could drive the car without a driving licence.

Powerdrive
GB • 1955-1958 • 2F1R • No built: n/a

The Powerdrive was certainly a cut above the average economy three-wheeler of the 1950s, having something of an Austin-Healey air about it. Its capacious open-topped aluminium body was designed by David Gottlieb and could seat three abreast. The Anzani 322cc two-stroke engine was mounted ahead of the single rear wheel and drove through a three-speed Albion gearbox. However, the elevated price tag of £412 meant it never made much impact.

Praga
CZ • 1952 • 2F1R • No built: Probably 1

The famous Czech manufacturer Praga did not restart car production after WW2, but apparently did make a prototype three-wheeler in 1952 with the unusual feature of a diesel engine. This 9bhp unit was mounted up front, driving the rear wheel by chain to a top speed of around 30mph (50km/h). It probably remained a sole prototype.

Prong 3
USA • 2010-date • 2F1R • No built: n/a

Enthusiast Hong Quan liked the BRP Can-Am Spyder ⇨ but wasn't so keen on its tandem seating layout. So he converted it to a side-by-side seating position by the involved method of building a whole new tubular steel chassis (designed by Eric Gauthier of Lotus Engineering). The Prong 3 kept the drivetrain and electronic features of the Can-Am Spyder but added all-new bodywork inspired by the Volkswagen GX3 ⇨. The car sold for $25,000 from California-based Prong Motors.

Protos Ellisse 50
I • 1998 • 1F2R • No built: n/a

Protos Veicoli Innovativi made this tilting three-wheeled scooter concept. It was powered by a 49cc engine, and the 2105mm long Ellisse weighed only 155kg. A sizeable 80-litre boot and tall seat with integrated headrest made it quite practical.

Prozé
P • 1970-1980 • 1F2R • No built: n/a

There was nothing very poetic about the Prozé economy car, which was built by Metalurgia Casal of Aveiro in Portugal. Its steel square-tube chassis housed a 125cc engine driving the rear wheels by chain. Various versions were built, including two- and four-seater passenger models and a light commercial vehicle.

Przybylski P80
PL • 1957 • 2F1R • No built: 1

Polish engineer Josef Przybylski from Katowice in Poland built this doorless open-topped car, which weighed a featherweight 190kg. Initially power came from a WFM unit, but this was later changed to a Jawa 248cc engine, and the top speed

was 46mph (75km/h). It was planned to put the P80 car into production at the WFM factory in Warsaw, but the authorities apparently did not support the move.

Publix
USA • 1947-1948 • 1F2R • No built: n/a

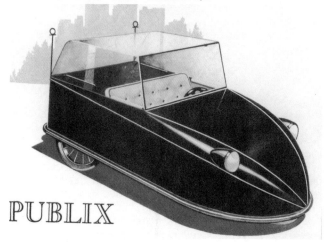

PUBLIX

There were several things that made the ultra-economy Publix stand out. For example: its doorless aluminium body could be stood on end to save space for parking; the steering wheel could be simply pivoted from the left-hand side to the right side; and a transparent Plexiglass hard top could be fitted for weather protection – remarkable considering the year was 1947. Made in Buffalo, New York, the Publix measured only 1829mm long and weighed as little as 68kg. Various engines could be fitted, with outputs ranging from 1.7bhp to 10.4bhp.

Puddle Jumper
USA • 2011-date • 2F1R • No built: n/a

Bob Evans's single-seater microcar was a very basic design for which he sold plans sets for others to build their own at home. The $35 package showed you how to create your own glassfibre bodywork. Measuring only 101in long and weighing 565lb, it had only one door (on the left-hand side) and a removable hard top. The total build cost was estimated at $1262 excluding the donor scooter.

Pulga
E • 1952-1957 • 1F2R • No built: Approx 60

This Spanish three-wheeler had a fake front grille, for the 197cc Hispano-Villiers engine in fact sat in the tail. The open bodywork was inspired by American trends of the time and seated two passengers.

P.Vallée Sport
F • 1952-1954 • 2F1R • No built: Approx 30

Paul Vallée made scooters under the SICRAF brand, and built his first three-wheeler, the Triporteur delivery vehicle, in 1949 (of which around 5000 were made in all). At the 1952 Paris Salon, he presented a very sporty-looking open-topped three-wheeler. This optimistically had seating for three, with a central driving seat and a tiny windscreen, although the screen was later widened and the cabin adjusted to seat two abreast. Using a Triporteur as its basis, an Ydral motorbike engine (125cc or 175cc) and gearbox sat just ahead of the single rear wheel, and the suspension was by rubber in compression.

P.Vallée Chantecler
F • 1956-1957 • 2F1R • No built: Approx 200

Vallée's second model was the Chantecler ('Nightingale') which suffered from very dumpily-styled doorless bodywork (single-piece glassfibre) with a folding soft-top roof. There is some debate as to whether the chassis of Vallée's

delivery trike or a new steel chassis were employed, but the Chanteceler could be powered by either a 125cc or 175cc Ydral engine of between 5bhp and 8bhp, up to a top speed of 47mph (75km/h).

THREE WHEELERS A-Z

Q Q Q

R R R

Reliant Robin ▲

Rollera ▲

Qingqi ▲

▼ Replicar Cursor

Rove Z-Car ▲

▼ Reliant Regal

Qingqi
CN/PK • 1975-2005 • 1F2R • No built: n/a

Jinan Qingqi was established in 1956 and became a major manufacturer of motorcycles, forming links with Suzuki and Peugeot. It was a pioneer of the modern Chinese three-wheeler market, with its first models launched in 1975. From the late 1990s, it made three-wheelers that looked like Suzuki Altos but with only one front wheel, powered by a tiny 125cc motorcycle engine. These were popular with rural taxi drivers, but woefully slow. Another trike design was one with a rear end resembling the Toyota Prius. The company changed its name to Dalong ➪ in 2005. Qingqi-powered rickshaws were also made in Pakistan under the name Plum Qinqi ➪.

Q-Tec Q3R/Q3F
B • 2008-date • 1F2R/2F1R • No built: n/a

Even Belgium has its three-wheeled innovators, and Q-Tec Engineering of Kinrooi was founded by a Harley-Davidson fan called Sandy Poglavec. As well as the Q3R (a traditional chopper trike based on a Harley-Davidson, also available as the Mamuth with a big boot), Q-Tec made the much more interesting Q3F (pictured). This was a reverse trike conversion kit (also available in four-wheeled form) that had a couple of unique features: a patented, independent suspension system and a patented differential. 2510mm long, 370kg, and with a 1584cc Harley engine fitted, it could do 97mph (155km/h). Prices started at the equivalent of around £10,000.

Quadro 3D 350
I/RC • 2011-date • 2F1R • No built: n/a

A design and engineering outfit called Studio Marabese had been working on a three-wheeled scooter from 1999 – in fact, this was an idea that it sold to Piaggio in 2004. Marabese's Quadro reached the market years later as a remarkably similar machine to the Piaggio MP3 ➪, but used different technology to tilt into corners. Its HTS (Hydraulic Tilting System) relied on three hydraulic pistons at the front end to tilt the trike automatically up to 40 degrees. The Quadro used a 313cc engine with 23bhp, mated to a CVT automatic gearbox. The main market was France, where the 3D 350 was priced around the same as a Piaggio MP3. A four-wheeled 4D version followed in 2012. Quadros were actually made in Taiwan by Aeon ➪.

Qui Moto
USA • 1991-c2004 • 2F1R • No built: n/a

Professional British-born car designer Stephen Stringer founded a company called Alternative Automotive Design, based in Westminster, Maryland (later Crockett, Texas). His strikingly styled Qui Moto first appeared as a clay model not intended for production, and was designed to lean into corners. Its intended spec included motorcycle or electric power, Kevlar and carbon-fibre bodywork and an aluminum honeycomb monocoque chassis. After it appeared at a show there was speculation – apparently uninformed – that Myers Motors ➪ might be productionising the car. Stringer himself planned, in around 2004, to launch the car as a kit using a Honda GL1800 as a donor vehicle or with electric power, but this apparently never came to pass.

Quincy-Lynn Urba Trike
USA • 1978-date • 1F2R • No built: n/a

Quincy-Lynn Enterprises of Phoenix, Arizona was founded by Robert Quincy Riley and David Lynn. Both were experimenters in the best sense, creating designs and, rather than setting up a production line, offering plans for enthusiasts to recreate their work. In its prolific life, Quincy-Lynn offered DIY campers, hovercraft and even submarines – as well as several three-wheelers. The first was the Urba Trike, which differed from most chopper trikes by being powered by electricity, so its top speed was a not-very-devilish 55mph (88km/h). As market niches go, the eco-hell's angel is perhaps one of the smallest. Robert Q Riley continued to offer Urba Trike plans at the time of writing at $65 a pop.

Quincy-Lynn Trimuter
USA • 1980-date • 1F2R • No built: n/a

The Trimuter commuter car seated two in a dart-shaped glassfibre/foam body with a clam-shell canopy for entry. The impression of a space capsule was compounded by the fitment of LED digital instruments instead of dials. You could opt for either electric power or a 16bhp Briggs & Stratton two-cylinder engine in the tail, in which case a top speed

of 60mph and fuel consumption of 60mpg were claimed. Since there was a huge 17-gallon fuel tank between the passengers, the potential range was 1020 miles. Sold as a set of plans for $15, the Trimuter instantly became Quincy-Lynn's most successful product, and it even started a magazine devoted to the car, called Trimuter News Line. In less than a year, over 30,000 sets of plans were sold, perhaps helped by a cameo appearance in the film Total Recall. Robert Q. Riley Enterprises continues to sell plans sets at the time of writing.

Quincy-Lynn Tri-Magnum
USA • 1983-date • 2F1R • No built: n/a

Unlike Quicny-Lynn's previous eco-efforts, the Tri-Magnum was a beast built for high performance. Designed by Breck van Kleek, it used a Kawasaki KZ900 motorcycle rear end bolted to a specially-made chassis, and a top speed of 110mph was quoted. The aerodynamic teardrop-shaped body featured a lift-up canopy for entry. You steered via a handlebar-type steering wheel to the twin front wheels, which used VW suspension. Sold as a set of plans for $18.25 from 1983, a finished machine could be on the road for as little as $2000. Later, any motorbike engine from 400cc to 1300cc was declared as capable of being fitted, up to and including the Honda Goldwing, which had the advantage of an electric reverse gear. $95 plans sets remained available at the time of writing from Robert Q. Riley's Phoenix, Arizona base.

Raja
PK • 1990s-date • 1F2R • No built: Many thousands

Raja Autocars started making Vespa scooters in Pakistan in 1948, and much later the Fiat Uno under licence. It also made a range of rickshaws that could be run on LPG or CNG. Production was running at 500 per month in 2002.

Ranger Cub
GB • 1974-1976 • 2F1R • No built: Approx 200

One of the most unusual factories of all time was that of Ranger Automotive: it operated out of a disused cinema in Leigh-on-Sea, Essex. From there, it had built a Moke-style kit car since 1971 before it branched out into three-wheelers in 1974 with the Cub. This used a complete Mini front subframe and engine mounted in a square-tube spaceframe chassis, while the single rear wheel was suspended by half of the original Mini's suspension. The handling was not entirely resolved: one magazine described it as like cornering "a holed pirate's ship."

The pre-coloured glassfibre body was attractively styled by Eric Salmons and Alan White. A rear boot and weather gear were optional, as the standard car had to keep its weight below the 896lb (406kg) limit then in place to qualify for motorcycle classification. Introduced at £199 plus VAT, the Cub sold reasonably well. An electric-powered prototype remained at the prototype stage, while a handful of four-wheeled models were also built.

Rayvolution Evo
F/GB • 2007-date • 2F1R • No built: n/a

The Evo was conceived by Tony Lafaye, who operated Rayvolution Cars from a base near Paris, and also had a branch in Ashford, Kent. A tubular steel chassis housed double wishbone front suspension and a single rear swinging arm with a Suzuki GSX-R damper and rear brake. Originally designed around a Suzuki GSX-R1000 motorcycle drivetrain with chain drive going to the rear wheel, other bikes could be used as a basis as well. The five-piece glassfibre bodywork looked dramatic, and it had space for just a single seat. Complete kits were offered at £10,000, and a four-wheeled version was under development at the time of writing.

Razor

GB • 2011-date • 2F1R • No built: Approx 50 (to 2013)

Razor Cars was founded by John Barlow and David Chapman, who had been running a Lancashire-based kit car company called Imperial for many years. Their Razor unquestionably had some Bond Bug-inspired elements, but it was resolutely a high-performance machine. The bodywork in self-coloured glassfibre was uniquely styled, and most of the cockpit was moulded into the main body, including the seats which could be tailored to individual customers with padded panels. The car could either be open-topped and doorless or you could fit a roof canopy that hinged forwards for entry. The body was bonded to a galvanized steel backbone chassis, and the engine, rear swinging arm, twin adjustable rear coilovers and fuel tank were fitted to a separate subframe. The front suspension was by unequal-length double wishbones with adjustable coilover dampers. Power came from a Suzuki Hayabusa 1300 unit (or other bike engines) and overall weight was below 500kg, so performance was excellent. Kits cost from around £4000.

RCJ Tuk-Tuk

IND • c2004-date • 1F2R • No built: n/a

RCJ Auto Forge made parts for all kinds of Indian-built rickshaws before branching out with its very own Tuk-Tuk. It used either two- or four-stroke engines in a classic Auto Rickshaw format, while cargo three-wheelers were also made.

Recklinghausen

D • 1951 • 2F1R • No built: n/a

This very small single-seater with a convertible roof was powered by an Ilo engine and could attain a top speed of 53mph (85km/h) and fuel economy of 72mpg. It is not known if a production run ever took place.

Red Zone Piiyo

J • 2008-date • 1F2R • No built: n/a

China did not have a monopoly on strange three-wheeled economy cars; Japan got in on the act too. Red Zone exhibited its Piiyo at the 2009 Tokyo Auto Salon. Its 48cc engine and four-speed semi-automatic transmission (with a reverse gear) allowed it a top speed of 40mph (65km/h); a 125cc version was also available. It was tiny at just 2430mm long and 1100mm wide, yet it had a single front and single rear door, allowing access to a single seat up front and two behind; steering was by moped handlebars. There was also

a pick-up truck with a single seat. Prices started at 298,000 yen – around £2000 – at the time of writing.

Red Zone Revo

J • 2011-date • 1F2R • No built: n/a

Red Zone also marketed a range of Chinese-style scooter-based trikes with Revo badging. The Revo-7 had a 125cc engine; the Revo-2 and Revo-6 had 150cc; and the Revo-3 had a 197cc engine. All used CVT transmission.

Reeves Matrix

GB • 1985-1988 • 1F2R • No built: 1

Reeves Developments, based in Newark, Staffs, was an occasional player in the UK kit car scene. Its very first effort was hardly encouraging: the Matrix had the look and feel of an escaped fairground dodgem car.

RELIANT

Ask most people to name a three-wheeler, and chances are it'll be Reliant. That's no surprise, as Reliant was the pre-eminent name in three-wheelers in the post-WW2 era – perhaps as many as 195,000 three-wheelers were made by Reliant over a 65-year period.

Reliant's three-wheeled history stretches right back to 1933, when Nottingham's Raleigh Cycle Co introduced the Safety Seven. In order to liberate the maximum space for passengers, this vehicle used the by-then-unpopular format of a single front wheel on 'girder forks'.

Raleigh's chief designer, Tom Williams, parted company with Raleigh in 1934, and proceeded to set up Reliant Engineering in Tamworth, Staffs in 1935 to make 7cwt delivery vans with three wheels. Production of these commercial vehicles continued after WW2 (not ending until 1955 in fact), but encouraged by owners who had converted their vans to passenger use, Reliant embarked on a mission to bring economy motoring to the masses with a range of new passenger cars that would become iconic not only in Britain but many other parts of the world too.

Through significant models such as the Regal, Robin and Rialto, Reliant tapped into a market that almost every other car maker had abandoned by then. It continued to attract owners who had only motorcycle driving licences in the UK, and could therefore only choose three-wheelers if they wanted a car. But Reliant's appeal stretched beyond this niche as well, offering economy-minded motorists the sort of budget transportation that was lacking among four-wheeled rivals. However, the market for Reliants slowly and inevitably declined; the marque might have continued for longer had Type Approval legislation not intervened to bring to a close three-wheeler production – which against all odds lasted right into the 21st century.

Reliant Regal MkI/II
GB • 1952-1954/1954-1956 • 1F2R • No built: Approx 340/1500

Although a prototype had been shown at the 1951 Motorcycle Show, a full year passed before the much-modified production version of the Regal was presented. This used some elements of Reliant's 'girder fork' vans, most notably the robust and well-liked front-mounted 747cc four-cylinder sidevalve engine, itself derived from the Austin Seven unit. In the Regal, it developed 16bhp, which was enough to power it to a top speed of 65mph (105km/h).

The chassis was a box-section pressed steel affair with torsion bar front springing and semi-elliptic leaf springs for the live rear axle. The rear wheels were driven, via a four-speed gearbox with reverse. The bodywork was, rather archaically, in aluminium over an ash frame, could seat four, and initially was only offered in drophead coupe form.

At £352, it competed directly with the Bond Minicar ⇨ on price but offered much more substantial accommodation, despite the sizeable bulge for the engine/gearbox impinging on passenger space (the engine was accessed from inside the cabin, as indeed was the boot). In May 1954 came the MkII (pic below) with its redesigned grille and rounded-off windscreen corners. A Hardtop model was added in 1955, featuring a glassfibre roof in a contrasting colour. Plastic would eventually be used for the engine cover and rear panels, too. A van version of the MkII also appeared in 1955.

Reliant Regal MkIII/IV
GB • 1956-1958/1958-1959 • 1F2R • No built: 4702/1298 (excluding vans)

November 1956 saw the arrival of the substantially new Regal MkIII. The bodywork – offered in open Coupe and enclosed Hardtop forms – was now entirely in glassfibre (albeit with ash strengthening beams), making the Regal the first mass-produced car in Europe with all-glassfibre bodywork. The body was 5in longer, 6in wider and more rounded, and the doors were also bigger (although still with floppy sidescreens, only later changing to fore-and-aft sliding Perspex). Mechanically the MkIII was almost completely unchanged, except for synchromesh on the upper three gears, plus an updated camshaft for the engine in 1957.

In September 1958 came the MkIV, whose revised chassis allowed the engine to be sited further forwards, an Armstrong front coilspring/damper, smaller 13in wheels, 12V electrics and vertically sliding windows.

Reliant Regal MkV/VI
GB • 1959-1960/1960-1962 • 1F2R • No built: 4772/8478 (excluding vans)

A fractionally longer wheelbase chassis sat under the MkV's newly designed and bigger bodywork, offering more interior space. Unlike its predecessors, the MkV was now only available in saloon form. An opening boot appeared for the first time, as did safety glass. The final development of the original-type Regal was the 1960 MkVI, with altered bodywork providing additional rear headroom and marginally better visibility, while the dashboard was redesigned with a single central dial. The production figures attest to the success of this model in its day.

...the new *Reliant Regal* MK VI

Reliant Regal 3/25, 21E & 3/30
GB • 1962-1973 • 1F2R • No built: 105,824

October 1962 saw the momentous arrival of the Regal 3/25, so called because it had three wheels and a 25bhp engine. This was perhaps the biggest change for the new Regal: a Reliant-designed die-cast aluminium overhead-valve engine based on the original Austin-derived unit but with 598cc – the very first all-aluminium engine built in series in Britain.

Gone was the old wooden internal body frame: the new Regal used glassfibre throughout. The reverse-angle rear window resembled that of the Ford Anglia, only uglier, but at least there was considerably more space inside (saloon only to begin with, with a van version joining it soon after). The chassis was basically carried over from the original Regal, but with slimmer members. At £449, the Regal was significantly cheaper than the Austin/Morris Mini.

A mild styling update front and rear by Ogle Design in 1965 earned the 3/25 the moniker Super Saloon (although the original model, now dubbed Standard, remained on sale into 1966). There was also a minor power upgrade to 26bhp in 1967, and a 'luxury' 21E version the same year.

In 1968 an expanded 701cc engine with 30bhp was launched, available in 3/30 and 21E-700 forms, together with new estate and van body variants. The latter achieved small screen immortality much later as the wheels of choice for Del Trotter in Only Fools and Horses. Despite Reliant broaching the four-wheeler market with the Sabre, Rebel and Scimitar, the Regal was the company's mainstay throughout the 1960s, and production peaked at an impressive 100 units a day. Reliant's TW9 truck (also sold as the Ant) was based on the Regal.

Reliant Robin

GB • 1973-1981 • 1F2R • No built: Approx 56,200 (all Robins & Rialtos)

Could the Reliant Robin be the most famous three-wheeler of all them all? Certainly it was one of the most successful, arriving at a time when Reliant pretty much had the three-wheeler market all to itself.

The chassis was new, a twin-rail perimeter affair, and now had single-leaf rear springs in place of multi-leaf, together with an anti-roll bar. The wheels shrunk in size to 10in diameter. The engine was familiar: the Reliant aluminium four-pot unit, but now bored out to 748cc and boasting 32bhp, good enough for a top speed of 73mph (118km/h) and fuel economy of as much as 70mpg, if Reliant's claims were to be believed. An all-synchromesh gearbox and cable-operated clutch were new refinements for a Reliant three-wheeler.

For the design, Reliant turned to Tom Karen of Ogle Design, who had already styled the Bond Bug ⇨ for Reliant. The shape was pleasing, and even featured a hinging glass hatchback, accessing a big boot and a folding rear

bench seat. An estate version (and van) had a large side-hinged door and extended rear bodywork (all of which was in glassfibre, some of it injection-moulded). The cabin was much more refined than the Regal's, especially if you opted for the luxury-spec Super Robin.

Arriving in October 1973, the Robin was an immediate success. It was joined by a four-wheeled derivative, the Kitten, in 1975, at which time the engine was expanded to 848cc and 40bhp. Also in

1975, the Robin started to be made under licence by Mebea Motors of Greece.

It's true to say that the Robin became a real icon of the motoring scene at the time, offering better fuel economy than almost any other car. As the lone three-wheeler whistling through the 1970s, it was also famously the butt of a thousand jokes. Another Robin claim to fame is that Princess Anne learnt to drive in one.

Reliant Rialto

GB • 1981-1993 • 1F2R • No built: see Reliant Robin

The Rialto was essentially a warmed-over Robin, with fresh styling work by design house IAD. While the centre body section and most of the interior remained unaltered, a new sloping front end featured rectangular headlamps, while at the back there was a squarer look and a new bootlid that hinged downwards. That wasn't particularly practical, though, so the estate version with its side-hinged door arguably made more sense. Underneath it was very much as before, although the 848cc engine now sat in a galvanised chassis.

In 1984 came the Rialto 2. Externally only badging and a new grille identified it, but a revised 'HT-E' engine offered improved torque and fuel economy, and there was a more refined interior. The Reliant Motor Company went bust in 1990 as the results of the recession hit. It was revived in 1991 by Beans Industries, which had been making the engines for the Rialto. The model lasted until 1993, overlapping for some time with the so-called Robin Mk2.

Reliant Robin Mk2/Mk3

GB • 1989-1999/1999-2001 • 1F2R • No built: see Reliant Robin

The enduring fame of the Robin name persuaded Reliant to relaunch the badge in 1989 for a luxury Robin LX version with new frontal styling (featuring Ford Fiesta headlamps). This

became the sole three-wheeler offered by Reliant from 1993, but financial problems beset the parent company, Beans, and receivers were called in again in 1994. The following year, Reliant was acquired by the Avonex Group but its tenure lasted less than 12 months and its addition to the production tally consisted only of completing existing unbuilt cars.

In March 1996, Jonathan Heynes, son of William Heynes of Jaguar fame, emerged as the brand's saviour. Some engine parts were now sourced from San in India, while a pick-up model called the Giant was launched.

After 63 years at Tamworth, production was moved in 1999 to a new purpose-built factory in Burntwood. At this time, a light restyle saw Vauxhall Corsa headlamps and Rover 100 rear lights being incorporated into a newly announced Mk3 model. A batch of 65 examples of a special-edition Robin 65

(to mark 65 years of three-wheeler production) was effectively the last hurrah for the Robin, which had by this time become far too expensive (around £10,000). The Robin finally ducked out of existence in February 2001, by which time over 7000 new-generation Robins had been built. However, there was one final chapter still to write: the Robin BN-1 ⇨, produced by a separate organisation.

Renault Ublo

F • 2001 • 1F2R • No built: Probably 1

In all its history, Renault has really had nothing to do with three-wheeled vehicles, except one: the Ublo 'concept bike' revealed at the 2001 Mondial du Deux Roues in Paris. This was a collaboration between Renault Design in Barcelona, Renault Sport Technologies and Benelli. It had a protective roof with smoked Plexiglas, and a big luggage box to the rear. Renault claimed a world first with its vertical airbag in the centre console. Another unusual feature was a rear-view camera above the top box, to obviate the need for mirrors, which would have widened the car: overall width was just 770mm. Renault said its Ublo could be on the market by 2003, but that never happened.

Replicar Cursor

GB • 1985-1987 • 2F1R • No built: Approx 110

Alan Hatswell formed Replicar Ltd in 1981 to market kit-form replicas of Bugattis, Jaguars and Ferraris. He also experimented with a Bugatti-style trike in 1985 based on moped parts (pictured left). This curious vehicle was known in retrospect as the Pre-Cursor, as it sparked an idea for a "revolutionary micro vehicle" called the Cursor.

This was a single-seater whose main selling-point was that it was classed as a moped and could therefore be driven by 16-year olds. Its extremely odd-looking glassfibre body sat on top of a tubular steel chassis, giving the effect of a fairground dodgem car. Replicar bafflingly described the Cursor as a "GT hatchback convertible", even though it had nothing more sporting than a 49cc Suzuki CS50 moped engine with 2.8bhp in the centre of the car. A top speed of 30mph (48km/h) was offset by fuel consumption of about 90mpg.

Replicar claimed grandly of the Cursor that: "The impact on driving will be much the same as when the Mini was launched in the late 1950s." In fact, drivers hardly gave it a cursory glance. Priced at £1724, some 50 single-seaters were made, whereupon a two-seater version with gullwing doors was launched with a more powerful Suzuki CP50 engine. The final 10 or so of the 57 two-seaters built had 4.2bhp Honda Vision moped engines. Many cars were exported to Austria, while the Cursor project ended up in the hands of a Belgian company, which apparently never restarted production.

Resort Vehicles

GB • c2004 • 1F2R • No built: n/a

Resort Vehicles International was based in Bourne End, Bucks, and created this three-seater three-wheeler intended for use in holiday resorts.

Revolution

GB • 1970s • 1F2R • No built: n/a

Very little is known about this rear-engined trike, other than it was made in Devon in the 1970s.

Revolution Dagne

USA • 2008-date • 2F1R • No built: n/a

The Dagne was designed as a hybrid commuter vehicle that could tilt into corners. All three wheels were driven by electricity, and the steering, acceleration and braking were all controlled through a joystick. The Dagne operated as a pure electric vehicle for the first 100 miles, then switched to hybrid mode to extend the range, with fuel coming from either petrol, diesel or biofuels. Revolution Motors of Goleta, California, intended to sell cars at $25,000, with production planned to start by 2014.

Rewaco

D • 1990-date • 1F2R • No built: n/a

One of Germany's leading trike manufacturers, Rewaco succeeded in building a firm reputation not only in Europe but in America and Asia, too. Its designs were typically long-wheelbase and low-slung, with passengers seated above and behind the driver. The classic HS series usually used a rear-mounted VW Beetle engine (1.6 litres/50bhp or 1.8 litres/64bhp), but other options were available, including Harley-Davidson or RevTech V-twins (FX6) and Ford Zetec (RF1). Rewaco later started making bike conversions, notably for the Suzuki Intruder (C800, C1500 and C1800) and the Triumph Rocket III Touring.

Rex

D • 1948-1950 • 1F2R • No built: n/a

The Rex represented exceedingly basic transportation for disabled people in the aftermath of WW2. A tiny single-cylinder two-stroke engine was fitted just above the front wheel: either 34cc (1.2bhp) or 40cc (1.8bhp). Hand propulsion to the rear wheels was also possible.

Rhino Intruder
GB • 2003-date • 1F2R • No built: Approx 20

Rhino Trikes of Winsham, Somerset offered self-build motorbike conversion kits (from £4295) or turnkey vehicles (from £6945), based on the Suzuki Intruder (VS600, VS800 or VS1400).

Ridley
USA • 2008-date • 1F2R • No built: n/a

The main innovation of Ridley Motorcycles was its automatic transmission for motorbikes, which it extended to three-wheelers with the Auto-Glide Trike in 2008.

Rieju
E • 1955-1956 • 2F1R • No built: n/a

From the Riera & Juanola motorbike works came this Isetta-like car featuring two doors, a curved glass windscreen and seating for 2+2. It appeared at the 1955 Barcelona Motor Show, while three-wheeled 2F1R delivery trikes were also made with Rieju branding.

Rik-Mobile
USA • 1948 • 1F2R • No built: n/a

A very early debutant in the world of rickshaws, the Rik-Mobile was created by the China Engineering Corporation based in San Francisco and, as the company name suggested, it was intended for the Chinese market. A small rear-mounted engine provided the power and handlebars turned the steering wheel.

Riley XR3
USA • 2008-date • 2F1R • No built: n/a

Robert Quincy Riley had already had plenty of experience making three-wheelers (see Quincy-Lynn) before he turned to a car bearing his own name: the Riley XR3. Despite its name, this had no connection with fast Fords but was a

'Personal Transit Vehicle' (PTV) described as a "super-fuel-efficient two-passenger plug-in hybrid." At a time when plug-in hybrids were still in their infancy, this was a major achievement. Power came from a Kubota D902 diesel engine and a DC electric motor, driving through a VW gearbox. It could drive on diesel alone, or work in hybrid form, in which case up to 225mpg was claimed. Weighing 1480lb, a maximum speed of 80mph (130kmh) was possible. Like most of Riley's designs, the XR3 was sold in plans form, with builders required to make their own bodywork from urethane foam with glassfibre on top.

Rinspeed UFO
CH • 1983 • 1F2R • No built: n/a

Despite being described as "futuristic", this chopper-style trike clung to the classic formula of a VW Beetle rear engine and glassfibre bodywork, with rather comical front headlamps. Rinspeed then stuck to what it did best: tuning Porsches and creating show-stopping concept cars.

Roa
E • 1958-1959 • 2F1R • No built: 6

This bubble car, clearly Isetta-inspired but completely unrelated, was presented at the Féria de Muestras in Barcelona in 1958 by a Madrid-based manufacturer of motorbikes and sidecars. Unlike the Isetta, it had doors to the sides, rather than at the front, and its 2870mm-long body could seat two people. Reports are inconclusive about its rear-mounted engine: it was either a 197cc Hispano Villiers or a 249cc unit; a top speed of 59mph (95kmh) was quoted for the 240kg microcar. A rather high price of 45,000 pesetas restricted its popularity.

Roadair
USA • 1959 • 2F1R • No built: 1

One of many flying cars of the 1950s, Herb Trautman's Roadair was said to be capable of 90mph in the air, powered by a 75bhp Continental engine turning a single propeller. Its wings  folded up inside the bodywork, allowing it travel at up to 75mph on land, with drive going to the single rear wheel. Sadly the intended price of $10,000 proved to be pie in the sky, although unlike many such projects the Roadair did actually fly, and the prototype still exists.

Road Prince
PK • 2000s-date • 1F2R • No built: n/a

The Road Prince rickshaw was built by a Lahore-based enterprise called Omega Industries.

Roadstercycle
USA • 1994-date • 2F1R • No built: n/a

The Roadstercycle was made by Fleming Engineering of Torrance, California. It was originally designed for V-Twin power (a Harley Davidson twin cam engine); this became known as the '32' while a second model, the '34', had a four-cylinder Yamaha V-max powerplant. Eventually another version with a 4.3-litre V6 200bhp Chevrolet engine was built, resulting in a trike that reached 60mph (96km/h) in just 4.0 seconds.

Roadsmith
USA • c1980-date • 1F2R • No built: n/a

Roadsmith Trikes was a long-standing manufacturer of glassfibre-bodied trike conversions for bikes such as the Honda Goldwing. The independent rear suspension was manually adjustable by progressive coilover dampers, while options included Accu Ride suspension, an extended boot and a steering rake kit.

Roadster Motors Electron
IND • 2011-date • 1F2R • No built: n/a

Roadster Motors was based in Chennai in India, and offered the battery-operated Electron three-wheeled rickshaw that could seat three passengers in addition to the driver. Its top speed was 28mph (46km/h) and it had a range of up to 87 miles (140km).

Robin BN-1/BN-2
GB • 2001-2002 • 1F2R • No built: 20

By 2001, the Reliant Robin ⇨ had finally bitten the dust. But B&N Plastics of Sudbury, Suffolk successfully negotiated the rights to carry on making the Robin. Reliant continued to build the chassis and engines, and dispatched them to B&N, which made the bodies. The so-called Robin BN-1 had minor upgrades, such as a new dashboard, wider rear seat and better soundproofing. A luxury BN-2 model was also announced, as well as plans to make an electric Robin. However, the cost of modifying the new Robin to comply with the latest regulations had sealed its fate by October 2002, with only 15 BN-1s and five BN-2s made – a quiet end to a proud story.

Robin Hood Bullet
GB • 2008 • 2F1R • No built: 1

One of the world's most prolific makers of Lotus 7-style kit cars turned its hand to a three-wheeler with the Bullet, an oddball of a sheet steel-bodied single-seater open trike, powered by a 125cc scooter engine.

Rogers Rascal
CDN • 1984-c1988 • 1F2R • No built: n/a

Much larger than most other three-wheelers, the Rascal (made by Rogers International Auto of Vancouver, British Columbia) had a single front wheel and a front-mounted Fiat engine. Two body styles were available: a hatchback and a convertible, both featuring faired-in headlamps, an aerodynamic profile and seating for 2+2. The body material was glassfibre, which helped keep weight down to 408kg (900lb) and allowed a top speed of 75mph (120kmh).

Rollera
F • 1958-1959 • 1F2R • No built: n/a

Based on the Brütsch Rollera ⇨ and differing from it only in minor details, this French version (built by Sté Rollera Française of Levallois) was a tiny (2120mm long) open-topped single-seater with glassfibre bodywork. Power came from a Sachs 124cc single-cylinder two-stroke engine with 6bhp mounted on the left-hand side of the vehicle, and it could reach a heady top speed of 50mph (80km/h).

Romanazzi
I • 1953 • 1F2R • No built: n/a

The Romanazzi was built in Bari and started out as a Piaggio Ape delivery trike. Enclosed bodywork was added featuring a bench rear seat for two passengers, with the driver seated up front scooter-style.

Rosenbauer
A • 1950 • 2F1R • No built: n/a

The Konrad Rosenbauer company started out in 1908 making motors for fire-fighting equipment, and also produced the Trio three-wheeled delivery wagon in the 1930s. In 1950 it branched out with a three-wheeled two-seater coupe featuring a single rear wheel, rear-mounted 250cc 10bhp engine and three-speed gearbox. Its ungainly bodywork was in sheet metal over a wooden frame, with a sloping nose and a roll-top roof.

Rove Z-Car

GB • 2005-2008 • 2F1R • No built: Probably 1

Rove Cars, run by art dealer Kenny Schachter, commissioned the celebrated architect Zaha Hadid to design the Z-Car (or Zaha-Car). This was a sleek hydrogen-powered two-seater measuring 3800mm long. It had hinging rear suspension that allowed the car to sit upright for town driving, then shorten itself for parking, or it could drop the passenger pod down at higher speeds to improve aerodynamics. A prototype was shown at the 2006 British International Motor Show in London, and plans were announced for a limited production run. Despite a second, four-wheeled prototype being developed, no production run had commenced by the time of writing.

RSR Side Star

D • 2011-date • 1F2R • No built: n/a

The main activity of RSR GmbH of Wartenberg in Bavaria was making racing motorcycle-and-sidecar combinations, but it also built the roadgoing Side Star. This had a tubular chassis with aluminum sandwich stiffening and two wheels in-line on one side, like a motorbike. Power came from a 185bhp Suzuki Hayabusa 1.3-litre engine, and handlebar steering with a twist throttle was retained. It weighed 540kg so could do 0-62mph in 5 seconds with a top speed of 137mph (220km/h). The bodywork was open-topped and could seat two, but it was a pricey way for two to travel, starting at €47,000 (around £40,000).

RTM Tango

U • 2006-date • 2F1R • No built: n/a

The RTM Tango was a leisure vehicle made in Camino Carrasco in Uruguay. Two versions were built: the Tango 50 with a two-stroke 49cc, 5.6bhp engine and the Tango 200 with a four-stroke 190cc engine with 16.7bhp. Both had CVT automatic transmission and a button-operated reverse gear. The single rear wheel was driven by chain and the steering was by handlebars. The cheeky self-coloured plastic bodywork (mounted over a steel chassis) was designed by Uruguayan

Pablo D'Angelo and measured a compact 2480mm long and weighed 560kg. Half-doors were available. The Tango was sold in some markets as the Sunburst.

Ruko RX 1

D • 2008-date • 2F1R • No built: n/a

This performance trike from German sidecar maker Ruko was an exercise in exoskeletal minimalism. The exposed tubular spaceframe chassis featured double wishbone front suspension with fully adjustable Technoflex dampers. The steering box derived from the old Porsche 914, while the steering column came from the VW Golf MkIII. The single rear wheel was suspended by a tubular swinging arm with twin dampers. Power came from a Honda CBR 1100 XX motorbike or any other suitable in-line four-cylinder engine, with chain drive to the rear wheel. Measuring a generous 3680mm long and 1800mm wide, it nevertheless managed to keep its weight down to 520kg. Top speed with the CBR 1100 XX engine fitted was 130mph (210km/h), and prices started at 55,000 euros (£48,000).

Rupp Centaur

USA • 1974-1975 • 1F2R • No built: Approx 1200

Mick Rupp started making snowmobiles and dirt bikes in Mansfield, Ohio in 1970, and he also made off-road ATVs in three- and four-wheeled form (named the Rat and Go-Jo respectively). His first roadgoing trike was the Rupp Centaur, a unique take on the chopper theme. Several glassfibre body styles were offered with either one or two seats. Originally designed for a VW Beetle rear engine and transaxle, most Centaurs in fact used a Kohler 339cc two-cylinder two-stroke snowmobile engine, which topped out at 55mph and really can't have been much fun.

RW Chopper

GB • 1983-1984 • 1F2R • No built: Approx 5

RW Kit Cars made a wide variety of kit cars in the 1980s, including one three-wheeler design: a classic chopper-style machine powered by a VW Beetle engine.

THREE WHEELERS
A-Z
SSS

Sinclair C5 ▲

Suntera SunRay ▲

Scootacar ▲

▼ Silence PT2

SECMA Fun'Tech ▲

▼ SAM Re-Volt

Sabertooth

USA • 2009-date • 1F2R • No built: n/a

Sabertooth Motorcycles made its name with V8-powered motorbikes but created a new trike division, Cerberus Trikes, to make the Cerberus Inferno and WildCat trikes. A 302ci Ford V8 offered 350bhp, or a 427ci unit had 550bhp. Ford automatic transmission with reverse and fully independent rear suspension were standard. In 2012 came a smaller trike, the BobCat, with a 104bhp Weber 850cc flat-twin engine.

SAC Aerocar

USA • 1946 • 1F2R • No built: 1

The Southern Aircraft Corp (SAC) was the aeronautical division of Portable Products Corp of Texas, which hired Ted Hall to design it a flying car. A 130bhp flat-six Franklin engine powered a front propeller, while the detachable rear boom and wings were covered in fabric. Air speed was 168mph, but this was not regarded as good enough performance for production.

Saccomando

GB • 1985-1992 • 2F1R • No built: 3

Ed Saccomando designed this trike, made in Walkley, Sheffield. Its tubular steel chassis housed a Mini engine up front, while its open 2+2 glassfibre bodywork featured a detachable nose section and front wings.

Saier Trike

D • 1981-1997 • 1F2R • No built: n/a

Automobilbau Saier made a range of classic-style replicas in Germany, but branched out in the 1980s with a conventional VW Beetle-engined chopper trike.

Sakuma

J • 2000s-date • 1F2R & 2F1R • No built: n/a

Sakuma Engineering was the official importer of American-made Champion ⇨ trikes into Japan, but it also offered a large number of its own 1F2R motorbike conversions, including BMW and Kawasaki, but also smaller Japanese bikes, such as the Honda Forza and Suzuki Skywave, and even mini-bikes like the Honda Ape. Other more unusual models included the Maxam (a three-wheeled Yamaha Maguzamu with a wheelchair rack, pictured middle left) and the Tautoraiku (based on the Taiwanese PGO T-Rex). In 2011, it also presented a bullet-nosed 2F1R open-topped trike based on a Honda Fusion (lower left).

Sakuma Omicron III

J • 1990s • 1F2R • No built: n/a

Sakuma had a sidecar business, but the Omicron concept was a radical new form – essentially a halfway house between a sidecar combination and a three-wheeler. It was very much inspired by the Krauser Domani ⇨ but was smaller at 2490mm long by 1290mm wide. It was based on a 244cc Honda Fusion scooter and was claimed to have the world's first fully integrated sidecar body. It was marketed from 1991, but left production soon after, although Sakuma did follow it up with a somewhat more sidecar-like creation called the Kappa, based on a Honda Helix.

SAM Cree / Re-Volt

CH/PL • 2001-date • 2F1R • No built: Approx 100

Switzerland has a long history of making green vehicles, and the SAM Cree aimed high: an electric car designed to be that most difficult synthesis of a car that was at once green, cheap to buy and fun to drive. The designers chose the three-wheeled configuration for light weight and lower costs (the Cree weighed 545kg including batteries).

A patented construction method consisted of an aluminium beam that carried the battery and other electrical components, which was in turn joined to the 15kW electric motor, which drove the rear wheel by belt. The original design used 14 Hawker Genesis lead-acid batteries, giving the Cree a range of 40 miles (70km) and a top speed of 52mph (85km/h). The front suspension was by upper arms and a lower transverse leaf spring, while the rear end was by MacPherson strut. Very narrow 135/70 front tyres were joined by a wider 175/65 rear one.

The design was described as "fancy and stylish" and

certainly the shape and the use of gullwing doors were striking. The body was double-walled and made of thermoplastic, and measured 3162mm long and 1553mm wide. Two passengers sat in tandem in polyethylene seats.

Some 80 vehicles were built in 2001 and driven by members of the Swiss public as a test exercise, with a plan to market the car for the equivalent of around £5000, with batteries leased on top. However, finance did not materialise for a production run and the company laid off its employees in 2004. In 2005, the licencing rights were transferred to fresh investors who re-engineered the car with a new battery pack, and from 2007 a Polish company called Impact Automotive Technologies assisted with development.

The revised model – which was given the name Cree Evolution II – used 36 lithium-ion cells which could be pre-heated to increase battery life and range. Maximum speed was now 56mph (90km/h) and a better range of up to 62miles (100km) was claimed. In 2009 the model was renamed SAM Re-Volt and production began in a factory in Pruszkow, Poland, by which time the price had risen to 18,910 euros (£16,500).

SAMCA Atomo
I • 1947-1951 • 2F1R • No built: n/a

SAMCA stood for Società Applicazioni Meccaniche Costruzioni Automobilistiche, a company based in Parma, which presented the Atomo rolltop coupe at the 1947 Milan Show.

Its tubular chassis contained a 10bhp, 246cc two-stroke twin engine in its tail, mated to a three-speed gearbox. It was only 3070mm long and the whole car weighed only 190kg thanks to aluminium bodywork. A coachbuilder called Bertolini was subsequently asked to improve the design, but if the Atomo ever in fact entered production, very few were built.

Samson Switchblade
USA • 2009-date • 1F2R • No built: n/a

Samson Motor Works had been working on its 'sky wings' idea for a flying vehicle for years before unveiling its Switchblade in 2009. The bullet-shaped two-seater measured 180in (4572mm) long and used a ducted fan propeller to power the car in the air, with retractable wings under the bodywork that swung out (hence the name Switchblade). Engines that were possible to fit ranged from the Lycoming IO-320 to Yamaha

FJR 1300 or Suzuki Hayabusa. A top speed of 90mph on land and 150mph in the air were claimed. The intention was to sell the Switchblade in kit form at $60,000, but this had yet to occur by the time of writing.

Sandi
CN • 2000s-date • 1F2R • No built: n/a

The Jiangsu Sandi Vehicle Manufactory Co (also seen referred to as Taixing Sandi) was situated on the Yangtze River in Jiangsu province, and was quite a big name in motorbikes and trikes. Its passenger trike output consisted of several model lines. There were basic rickshaws with 110cc engines, three-wheeled scooters sold under the ZX badge (with engines of 50cc, 125cc or 150cc), and even 150cc and 250cc chopper trikes. The most car-like model was the SD650ZK, which was sold as a five-seater with a 500cc or 644cc engine, or an implausible eight-seater people carrier measuring 3500mm long, which needed an engine of 644cc or 800cc to keep it moving up to a top speed of 56mph (90km/h). Sandi also built the WF650-C for Wildfire ⇨ of the USA.

Santiago Choppers
USA • 2000s-date • 1F2R • No built: n/a

This Tampa, Florida company claimed to offer kits to convert any chain- or belt-driven motorcycle into a trike.

Sanyo Amorton
J • 1986 • 1F2R • No built: Probably 1

Sanyo of Japan really had very little to do with cars over the years, but to promote its solar panel activity in 1986 it presented the Amorton electric car, a prototype which boasted solar panels,  both on the front end and on a large 'whale-tail'. The similarity to the Sinclair C5 ⇨ was not lost on reporters at the time.

Sazgar
PK • 1991-date • 1F2R • No built: n/a

Sazgar Engineering Works, based in Lahore, Pakistan, built not only the Tempo delivery van, but also two rickshaws: the Deluxe and the grandly named Royal Deluxe (which was described as Sazgar's "flagship auto rickshaw"). The regular version carried three passengers behind the

driver, but Sazgar also made a six-seater model. Power came from a four-stroke CNG-fuelled 200cc engine with 15bhp.

Sbarro Twike.Me
CH • 2000 • 1F2R • No built: 1

Franco Sbarro is a legend of car design, producing some of the world's most outlandish concept cars from the 1960s onwards. It took him until 2000 to design his first three-wheeler, which was based on a fellow Swiss product, the Twike ⇨. He

took the two-seater electric car and gave it a fresh body shape, realised in glassfibre. A joystick took the place of the conventional steering wheel. The curiously named Twike.Me remained a prototype, however.

Sbarro UMA2
CH • 2003 • 2F1R • No built: 1

With the UMA (Unité Motrice Autonome – or independent motor unit) Franco Sbarro did no less than reinvent the wheel. OZ helped him out to create an extremely large wheel which actually incorporated the engine inside it. To illustrate possible applications of this invention, three vehicles were shown at the 2003 Geneva Motor Show, with two, three and four wheels. The three-wheeler was called the UMA2, and resembled a Flash Gordon-style rocket ship with a single-seater fuselage and an enormous rear spoiler. A Yamaha motorbike engine sat inside the wheel rim but it's not known if it actually ran as, like most of Sbarro's designs, it remained a prototype.

Sbarro 3 Wheels Kit
CH • 2011 • 2F1R • No built: n/a

No doubt inspired by the success of the Piaggio MP3 ⇨, Franco Sbarro presented a kit at the 2011 Geneva Motor Show that would convert almost any bike into a three-wheeler. The front fork was modified to accept two wheels, with a hydraulic system allowing the wheels to tilt. The driver could use a lever on the handlebars to lock the front wheels in any desired position. Most of the new parts used were aluminum, so very little extra weight was added. Sbarro even designed a shopping bag with wheels that could be attached to the front suspension. Sbarro said that if the enough interest was shown in his 3 Wheels Kit, he would begin series production – but as of 2013, we were still waiting.

Sceadu SD-1
USA • 2003-date • 2F1R • No built: n/a

The tiny Sceadu (pronounced shay-doo) was the work of aerospace designer David Mounce of Lake Havasu City, Arizona (although he later moved his company, Sceadu Design, to Navarre, Florida). He thought of his two-passenger micro-machine more as a powered recumbent trike than a car, and it was certainly basic, consisting of a steel perimeter chassis with an open glassfibre body, and the whole thing weighed just 159kg (350lb). The

engine could be the customer's choice of either petrol, diesel or electric, and was mated to a CVT automatic gearbox, with a tiller for the steering and other functions. The comoany's plan was to sell both complete cars and kits, the latter costing an estimated $2500.

Schubert
DDR • 1958 • 2F1R • No built: Approx 2

Quite a stir was caused at a microcar rally in Germany when this vehicle showed up. Built in Hainichen in East Germany, it was an appealingly styled steel-bodied car featuring a front door that hinged forwards at its bottom edge. The original engine was an air-cooled IFA BK 350cc two-stroke two-cylinder with 15bhp, but this was changed at some point to a 9.5bhp Heinkel 175cc unit, in which form it could reach 59mph (95km/h). It is thought that two examples were built.

Schwammberger
D • 1950 • 2F1R • No built: n/a

The editor of the German magazine Das Auto designed this odd two-seater three-wheeler. Its single rear wheel steered the car, taking the engine that was slung over it with it (the front wheels were fixed and didn't steer). In this way, the car could be turned in its own length, obviating the need for a reverse gear. It was suggested that a production chassis would cost around 2000 marks, but there's a reason why cars don't normally steer like this. The idea was just daft enough for it never to come close to production.

Scootacar
GB • 1958-1965 • 2F1R • No built: Approx 1000

Isetta, Heinkel and Messerschmitt started the bubble car boom on the continent but the only all-British attempt to produce a true bubble car was the Scootacar. It did look decidedly odd, however, with a disproportionately tall (60in/1524mm) and narrow (52in/1321mm) body. Although it looked like it would

topple over, in fact it worked remarkably well. Steering was by handlebars, which made it very direct, and the handling was helped by the fact that most of the weight sat low down. The driver straddled a narrow seat; a single passenger could sit behind him astride the engine, motorcycle pillion style, or two could just about squeeze in either side of it.

The origins of the Scootacar suppposedly stemmed from the wife of the director of Hunslets, the Leeds-based railway locomotive maker, who wanted something easier to park than her Jaguar. The Scootacar was certainly that, and the whole thing weighed just over 500lb (230kg), thanks to the skimpiness of its glassfibre bodywork

The first Scootacars, made from 1958, came equipped with a Villiers 9E 197cc single-cylinder two-stroke engine with 8bhp, a chain driving the single rear wheel to a top speed of 51mph (82km/h). In 1960 came the MkII De Luxe version which looked rather different, with a more bulbous front and an elongated tail. The seating arrangement was different, too: the driver now had a more comfortable individual seat and the rear passengers got extra room too.

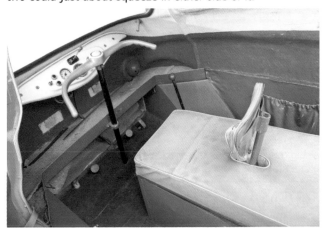

The final Scootacar MkIII De Luxe Twin (pictured above and below) arrived in 1961, powered by a two-cylinder 16bhp 324cc engine and selling for a fairly hefty £50 premium over the MkII version. The MkIII was quick (its top speed was 68mph/110km/h) but only around 20 of the 1000 or so Scootercars built were the MkIII.

Scootcar
IND • 2011-date • 2F1R • No built: n/a

As its name suggested, the Scootcar was a combination of scooter and car, and was intended for local travel, tourists and disabled people. Its sheet metal body, measuring 84in (2134mm) long and 36in (914mm) wide, could seat two people. Power came from a Kinetic Nova 113cc four-stroke engine mated to an automatic transmission, and the total vehicle weight was a mere 200kg (441lb). It was created by Milan Sales but apparently had not entered production by the time of writing.

ScootCoupe
USA • 2004-date • 2F1R • No built: n/a

This was a very small open reverse trike seating two passengers. The first offering, the ScootCoupe P49, became popular with rental companies. A more sophisticated second-generation model had wider front wings, dual wishbone front suspension and ABS disc brakes on all wheels. Two versions of this later model were offered: the P50 (with a 49cc 2bhp engine) and the P150 (with 148cc and 9bhp). In both cases a CVT automatic transmission was used, but it had no reverse gear. The manufacturer was Panther Motors of Lauderdale Lakes, Florida, and at the time of writing, prices started at $6649. The same vehicle was also marketed as the Sunshark.

Scoot-Mobile
USA • 1947 • 2F1R • No built: n/a

If the Scoot-Mobile looked like a car made out of an aircraft fuel tank, that's because it was. Norman Anderson of Corunna, Michigan was behind this project, which he planned to market from $350, although whether he sold any is not known.

Scorpion P6
USA • 2011-date • 2F1R • No built: n/a

This sports trike built by Scorpion Motorsports in Miami, Florida used a Kawasaki ZX6R 600cc engine with 126bhp, mated to a sequential gearbox with a reverse ratio. The chassis was a tubular steel spaceframe with an aluminium semi-monocoque, suspended by adjustable dampers and coil springs all round. The doorless,

roofless bodywork could be ordered in glassfibre or carbon-fibre. Weighing under 330kg (725lb), it could hit 60mph in 3.5 seconds, but Scorpion said its one-off P13 version with a Suzuki Hayabusa 1300 engine could reach a top speed of no less than 202mph (325km/h)!

Sealegs
NZ • 1987-date • 1F2R • No built: Approx 500

Kiwi company Sealegs created a highly original all-terrain vehicle that transformed into a high-speed, ocean-going boat at the push of a button. On land it was powered by a 24bhp four-stroke V-twin air-cooled Honda engine mounted under the centre console, up to a meagre top speed of 6mph (10km/h). In water, an outboard motor of around 150bhp would take it to a top speed of 42mph (68km/h). Hydraulic steering controlled the front wheel on land, while for water use, hydraulics raised all three wheels. This six-seater was a big machine at 7740mm (305in) long and, despite its aluminium hull, tipped the scales at 1980kg (4355lb).

SECMA Scootcar/Fun'Tech
F • 1996-c2006 • 2F1R • No built: n/a

Even by the standards of the microcar class that proliferated in France, the Scootcar by SECMA (Société d'Étude et Construction Mécanique Automobile) was very small and very basic. It was also the only French car of the time with three wheels, although its single rear wheel was supplemented by two stabilising wheels. A Morini 49cc two-stroke single-cylinder engine sat in the tail, driving the rear wheel through an automatic transmission. The front end was by MacPherson strut, with a cantilever-type rear end. SECMA made a four-wheeled version from 1997, and an electric model with very close-set rear wheels. The open-topped version was called the Fun'Tech, while a further variation was the Fun Cab, with full weather protection and doors. In some markets these models were known as the Ma-Goo, while in the UK Noel Edmonds set up a company selling it as the Q-Pod. SECMA still operated at the time writing, but concentrating on four-wheelers. SECMA also made a sports car called the T3 that looked like a trike but in fact had two close-set rear wheels.

Senda
CN • 2000s-date • 1F2R • No built: n/a

Chongqing Senda Industry produced a range of at least eight different three-wheeled models, with engine sizes of 110cc, 150cc, 200cc and 250cc. These ranged from ultra-basic motorbike rickshaw conversions such as the SD110ZK up to fully enclosed taxi-style vehicles like the SD200ZK.

SGS Kleinstauto
D • 1983 • 1F2R • No built: n/a

SGS stood for Styling Garage Schenefeld. Founded in 1979 by Ralph Engel and Christian Hahn near Hamburg, it also stood for some of the crassest and over-the-top Mercedes-Benz conversions of all time. SGS made a radical departure in 1983 with the Kleinstauto, a tiny moped-based single-seater 'cabin scooter'. At least two versions were built, the first with high-set narrow headlamps, the second with lower and more wide-set headlamps.

Shanti Shree
IND • 1994-date • 1F2R • No built: n/a

From a factory in Secunderabad, Shanti Auto built a range of three-wheeled rickshaws powered by engines including a 5.6bhp 325cc, a 6.4bhp 360cc and a 10.2bhp 451cc, with diesel and CNG options available. Various body styles were offered.

Shanyang SY150ZK
CN • 1995-date • 1F2R • No built: n/a

Jiangsu Linzhi Shanyang Group built fairly crude motorcycle-based rickshaws with single-cylinder 150cc engines.

Sheepbridge
GB • c1948-c1953 • 2F1R • No built: n/a

Sheepbridge Engineers of Chesterfield, Derbyshire built a series of very small prototypes, all featuring tubular steel chassis and glassfibre bodywork. Some had three wheels, such as the example pictured, while others had four, but it is believed that none of the prototypes ever reached production.

Shell Valley Apollo
USA • 1980s • 2F1R • No built: n/a

From a base in Platt Center, Nebraska, Shell Valley Motors mostly made Cobra replicas, but also a 2F1R trike called the Apollo with a motorbike rear end and an enclosed cabin.

Shelter
NL • 1947-1958 • 2F1R • No built: 4

One of the most promising microcars ever from the Netherlands was the Shelter. The first prototype was built by an aircraft engineer called Arnold van der Groot in 1947, consisting of two bicycle frames welded together, but a more serious attempt was made in 1954. This very small closed three-wheeler was remarkable for the fact that virtually the whole car, including the drivetrain, was designed by van der Groot. The plan was to fit a specially built 228cc

single-cylinder engine in the tail, although the prototypes were in fact fitted with 200cc Ilo engines, operated via a self-designed three-speed automatic-clutch gearbox. The body was in steel and measured only 75in (1900mm) long. In 1956, the Dutch government gave financial assistance to the project and planned to build 20 cars, the aim being to hire them out to customers. But amid reliability issues, including snapping axles and cars catching fire, the government withdrew its financial assistance (it was by then investing in DAF) and the Shelter was left out in the cold.

Shin Aichi Giant
J • 1950s • 1F2R • No built: n/a

Shin Aichi Kigyo, based in Nagoya, was the former Aichi aeroplane factory. It produced the Giant three-wheeler after the war in commercial and passenger versions. The 1951 six-seater model, for instance, measured 3800mm long, weighed 1000kg and was powered by a water-cooled OHV single-cylinder engine of 636cc capacity and 19bhp. Its three-speed gearbox drove the rear wheels by shaft.

Shine Far Metal Industry
RC • 2005-date • 1F2R • No built: n/a

This Taiwanese company mostly specialised in replacement car parts but it also made a clever universal three-wheeler conversion kit for scooters, which was designed to be ideal for disabled riders.

Shineray
CN • 1997-date • 1F2R • No built: n/a

The Shineray Tricycle Company produced various three-wheel motorcycle-based vehicles at the rate of around 4000 units per month. Its products were mostly rickshaw-style vehicles, with or without weather protection. Powering these rather basic machines were small engines ranging in capacity from 150cc up to 200cc.

Shirouma
J • 2005 • 1F2R • No built: n/a

Japanese bicycle maker Shirouma Science showed a covered pedal-powered vehicle at the 2005 Japan International Cycle Show with an electric motor to supplement leg power. The cost was 800,000 yen (around £6000).

Shuangqing
CN • 2009-date • 1F2R • No built: n/a

Chongqing Shuangqing Motor Tricycle Sales made a variety of uninspiringly typical rickshaw-style and enclosed three-wheelers with a choice of 150cc, 175cc and 200cc engines.

Sidam Xnovo
F • 2007 • 1F2R • No built: n/a

Sidam showed a tilting three-wheeled prototype at the 2007 Mondial Deux Roues, announcing its intention to market a 500cc petrol model, a 200cc hybrid and a purely electric version. Roofed or open versions were planned, intended to sell for around £8,000, but nothing further was heard of the project.

Silence PT2
CDN • 2006-2007 • 2F1R • No built: n/a

Canadian trike maker Campagna ⇨ teamed up with Electric Big Wheel (EBW) to form Silence Inc, with the intention of making an electric version of the Campagna T-Rex. Since EBW had been making the EBW-3 electric three-wheeled go-kart, it was well placed to help. The Silence PT2 used a 100kW

motor and the quoted weight was 408kg (or 900lb) including batteries. A top speed of over 125mph and a range of up to 250 miles were quoted for this $50,000 CDN machine, but the Silence lived up to its name when things went very quiet soon after.

Sinclair C5
GB • 1984-1985 • 1F2R • No built: Approx 9000

Computer magnate Sir Clive Sinclair should surely have known better. His infamous Sinclair C5, financed from his own pocket, was an unmitigated disaster and all but sunk him as an entrepreneur. On paper, the C5 seemed like a good idea: an environmentally friendly vehicle, it cost only £399 and could be driven legally by 14 year-olds.

The trouble was, it was very far from being driver-friendly. The hapless C5 owner sat exposed to the elements, exhaust fumes and juggernauts, with his hands fumbling under his buttocks attempting to steer it. And he had to pedal up hills, as the battery couldn't cope.

Designed with help from Lotus and built at a Hoover plant in Wales, the C5 used a steel chassis and a polypropylene body (a world first). The electric motor was a modified Hoover

washing machine unit and the transmission was by a reduction gearbox with toothed belt drive to the rear axle, which could be supplemented by human-powered pedals and chain. The brakes were cable-operated on the front and on one of the rear wheels, which were made of nylon composite. A top speed of 15mph was quoted, with a range of 20 miles using a single 12V battery (a second battery was optional).

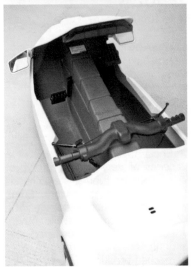

Sinclair aimed to produce no less than 100,000 C5s within the first year. Things got off to a bad start when it snowed heavily on launch day, and the C5 turned into a toboggan. By February 1985, several local authorities had banned

its use amid fears about driver safety. By April, production had halted "due to a gearbox fault", but disastrously poor sales were the real reason, and the receiver was called in in October. That scuppered plans for two larger three-wheelers, the C10 and C15. Sir Clive Sinclair continued researching the possibility of electrically-powered transport, and today, the C5 is something of a collector's piece.

Skip 1000
GB • 1988-1990s • 2F1R • No built: Approx 6

Durham-based Jeffrey Calver originally built the Skip for trialling, although it was equally suited to road use. It was based on the Mini, from which it took its floorpan and mechanicals, to which was added a space frame chassis clad in aluminium sheet, topped off with an open glassfibre body. The single rear wheel was suspended on a Mini arm in a special subframe. Calver came first in the Lands End Trial in 1989, competing in motorcycle classes. Kits cost a modest £750, to special order.

Sky Commuter
USA • 1980s • 1F2R • No built: 3

Boeing engineers based in Arlington, Washington were reportedly behind the Sky Commuter flying car. The bodywork was in carbon-fibre and Kevlar; a Lexan bubble canopy

allowed entry to the cockpit, which had a joystick control and two sets of foot pedals so that it could be controlled from either of the two seats. The engine was mounted in the rear, powering three fans that would provide vertical take-off from land or indeed water (it was designed to float like a boat). Reputedly absorbing over $6m of R&D spend, only one of three examples built remains, which came up for sale on eBay in 2008.

Sky Streak
USA • 1988 • 1F2R • No built: n/a

Charley Holecek of Idaho built the curious Sky Streak, which was concocted out of a Suzuki motorbike and a golf cart, which builders could make themselves using plans and a video. A tall spoiler and winglets covering the rear wheels made it look like a mini aircraft.

SLS1
USA • 2009-date • 2F1R • No built: n/a

Street Legal Sleds of Groton, Massachusetts offered this unusual and ingenious kit which could convert any snowmobile, of which there were many in that part of North America, into a road-going three-wheeler during the summer months. The kit was priced at $6,600. The SLS1 could be converted back to a snowmobile when the weather demanded.

Smite
S • 2009-2013 • 2F1R • No built: n/a

Created in Stockholm by Vehiconomics, the Smite was clearly inspired by the Messerschmitt ⇨, although it was by no means a replica. The Smite was developed in petrol and electric powered guises, weighing 150kg and 190kg respectively, and a top speed of up to 56mph (90km/h) was claimed. The composite chassis/ body could be convertible, fixed-head or speedster, but planned production stalled.

SMZ S1L / S3L
RUS • 1952-1958 • 1F2R • No built: 19,128 / 17,053

Disabled Russian WW2 veterans had to wait seven years after the end of hostilities for motorised transport. The SMZ (Serpukhovskji Motornnyi Zavod) motorcycle works in Serpukhov made a roofless three-wheeled two-seater, the S1L, powered by a 123cc 4bhp engine. This was replaced by a more powerful model, the S3L, in 1956, which despite a 346cc 8bhp engine was still only good for 37mph (60km/h). With the S-3A of 1958, SMZ switched to making four-wheelers.

Snyder ST600C
USA/CN • 2011-date • 1F2R • No built: n/a

After the Wildfire WTF650-C ⇨ was discontinued, effectively the same operation (now called Snyder Vehicles) in America came up with a somewhat similar, but still distinct, model badged the Snyder ST600C. This was a four-door hatchback with economy in mind at every turn. Its power came from a rear-mounted 586cc Hi-Po two-cylinder dual overhead cam engine with 33.5bhp, which was claimed to achieve fuel economy of 70mpg. Like the Wildfire, the Snyder was Chinese-built but targeted at the US market.

SOCO Tri
F • c1950s • 1F2R • No built: n/a

Made in Lyon, this was an open rickshaw-style vehicle with three seats and an engine mounted on the motorcycle-type front forks.

Sona Car
IND • 1970s • 2F1R • No built: n/a

The Sona Car was made by a company called Sona Automobile Industries Ltd in India during the 1970s, and featured boxy four-door saloon bodywork with all-flat glass.

Sonalika Mustang
IND • 2000s • 1F2R • No built: n/a

Sonalika was a major Indian farm equipment brand located in Hoshiarpur, Punjab. It decided, during the 2000s, to branch out and market an autorickshaw called the Mustang. Like most of its contemporaries, this small taxi was produced in petrol, CNG, LPG and electric forms.

Sooraj Sitara

IND • 1988-date • 1F2R • No built: n/a

Sooraj Automobiles specialised in diesel-engined three-wheelers (trucks and autorickshaws) sold under the name Sitara. The 10.2bhp single-cylinder 510cc diesel powerplants were made by Greaves ⇨, and two wheelbase lengths were offered: a six-seater (plus driver) Standard model and a smaller three-seater '3S' version.

Soriano

E • 1950s • 2F1R • No built: n/a

Soriano was a Madrid-based motorcycle maker active between 1941 and 1954, which made cargo tricycles with front luggage boxes that could also be adapted to carry a passenger kangaroo pouch-style.

SP Spi-Tri

USA • 1979-c1983 • 1F2R • No built: n/a

Structural Plastics of Tulsa, Oklahoma created the Spi-Tri, which was clearly based on the Bond Bug, albeit lengthened. The early version was stretched between the cockpit and rear wheels, but later examples were extended both front and rear. A glassfibre monocoque was used in place of the original Bug's separate chassis, and solid doors were specified.

Early versions had Elecxtro battery power, could do 50mph (80km/h) and cost $12,000. Later versions could be ordered with petrol engines, but it is doubtful whether very many people bought one.

Sparta Sportcycle

USA • 1990s • 2F1R • No built: n/a

The Sparta Sportcycle was essentially a two-seater open-topped doorless glassfibre body mounted on a steel frame that could be bolted to the complete rear half of a motorcycle. It is unknown if a production run occurred, although vehicles were certainly offered to the public.

Speedway Motors

USA • 1990s • 2F1R • No built: n/a

Speedway Motors of Lincoln, Nebraska specialised in hot rod and antique kits, but also built a 1920s-style three-wheeler.

Spijkstaal

NL • 1930-date • 1F2R • No built: n/a

From as early as 1930, this Dutch company made electric vehicles in three- and four-wheeled form, principally for commercial use. Some machines were made that can be classified as passenger cars, including people carriers and even motor homes. The electric motor drove the single front wheel up to around 10mph (16km/h).

SpinWurkz TT1

USA • 2007-date • 2F1R • No built: n/a

SpinWurkz of Niagara Falls offered a motorbike conversion kit to transform it into either a three- or four-wheeler. Kits cost from $10,000, or fully built cars started at $30,000. The Suzuki Hayabusa-based version was called the TT-Busa.

Spira

T • 2009-date • 1F2R • No built: n/a

Under the delightful motto "Soft, Safe, Sexy", the Spira was pretty much a unique proposition: bizarrely, a safety-themed three-wheeled foam-bodied car that could float in water. Invented by an American called Lon Ballard but built in Thailand, the Spira was made of a mix of aluminium and glassfibre covered with six-inch thick foam padding that could

be made from renewable sources such as soybeans. The two-seater was powered by a 110cc scooter engine, weighed only 137kg (302lb), could reach 70mph and averaged over 100mpg. As of 2013, it had yet to enter production.

SportCycle

USA • 2000-2012 • 2F1R • No built: n/a

Jim Musser's trike started life as the IndyCycle – unrelated to Jamieson DuRette's identically named IndyCycle ⇨ – but its name soon changed to SportCycle. Through Sport Vehicles of Imlay City, Michigan, a kit sold for $7370, including everything but the donor motorcycle, including a tubular steel chassis and glassfibre bodywork (with an adjustable rear aerofoil over the redundant motorbike seat). Alternatively you could build a SportCycle from plans. The front end was suspended by a single central spring over an adjustable damper, and a car-style steering wheel and pedals were used. Musser used a Kawasaki ZRX 1100 as a basis, but almost any motorcycle would do. Weighing only 380kg, up to 180mph and a 0-60mph time of less than four seconds were claimed. UK sales were handled by Sportcycle Ltd of Corsham, Wiltshire.

Sport Trike

ZA • 1972-date • 1F2R • No built: n/a

This was a classic American-inspired chopper-style trike built by Deon Slabbert in South Africa and offered in kit form or as a set of plans. Its rear-mounted engine came from the Volkswagen Beetle.

Srikandi 200S

RI • c1979 • 1F2R • No built: n/a

Not very much is known about the Srikandi 200S, but it is established that it was an enclosed wedge-shaped three-wheeled economy car made in Indonesia in the late 1970s.

SS Trike

USA • 2010-date • 1F2R • No built: n/a

The most distinctive feature of the trikes built by this Rudolph, Wisconsin operation was their very large front wheel in relation to the rear wheels. Air ride rear suspension was optional.

Stahlco Commando

PK • 2006-date • 1F2R • No built: Approx 100,000 (to 2013)

Stahlco Motors Pvt of Lahore made the Commando four-stroke rickshaw, which was very typical of the breed. Several different body styles were available, including the Econo and Deluxe. Stahlco was one of the larger such enterprises in Pakistan, with a capacity of 20,000 vehicles a year.

Standard Sharp

IND • 2004-date • 1F2R • No built: Approx 20,000 (to 2013)

Standard Tractor of Barnala in the Punjab had made agricultural vehicles since 1975, but in 2004 it also launched the Sharp rickshaw. This had eight seats and could be fitted with Lombardini 422cc or 528cc diesel engines. A smaller four-seater rickshaw with a 150cc engine was also available.

Stimson Scorcher

GB • 1976-1981 • 2F1R • No built: Approx 30

Barry Stimson (pictured below right) was responsible for a whole string of bizarre machines during the 1970s, including the outlandish Scorcher. This used a complete Mini front subframe in a box-section tubular chassis. The glassfibre bodywork resembled a plastic playground horse, with the driver and up to two passengers sitting astride it. The engine sat exposed up front, unless you chose an optional bonnet. The driver operated familiar car controls, with the handbrake and gear lever sited on top of the central tunnel.

With an overall weight of only 254kg (560lb), the Scorcher lived up to its name, reaching 100mph (160km/h) with a 998cc Mini engine fitted. There was some correspondence with the tax authorities over whether to class it as a motorbike or a car; in the end it was treated as a motorcycle-and-sidecar combination, requiring the driver to wear a helmet, but apparently not the passengers. Offered by Stimson's Brighton-based company, Noovoh Developments, a Scorcher kit cost £385. Surviving examples of this utterly unique vehicle are now quite sought after.

Stimson C-Donkey
GB/ZA • 1970s • 1F2R • No built: n/a

Like the Sealegs ⇨, Barry Stimson's C-Donkey (Sea-Donkey) was basically a three-wheeled boat that could be transformed into a buggy for buzzing around on land. There it could reach speeds of up to 30mph. As a boat, the front wheel simply unclipped and the rear wheels swung up, engaging a jet propulsion unit to drive the boat along at up to 10mph. It entered production in South Africa.

Stimson Sting
GB • 2002-2007 • 2F1R • No built: 1

Barry Stimson returned to trikes in 2002 with the Sting. From a base in Portsmouth, Hampshire, he offered kits using all-new parts, rather than a 'donor' second-hand machine. The Sting had two wheels at the front and dramatically swooping roadster bodywork seating two passengers. A conventional car steering wheel was used but the origins of the powertrain were obvious, as the hind-quarters of a 1200cc Suzuki Bandit motorcycle poked out of the Sting's pointed tail. Stimson claimed 0-60mph in under 4.0 seconds.

Stimson Storm
GB • 2002-2007 • 1F2R • No built: 1

The Storm was also based on the Suzuki Bandit but was a more traditional trike using a Bandit front wheel and forks. It differed from most trikes in having all-enveloping glassfibre bodywork that housed four seats. Sadly no-one bought one.

Stinger
GB • 1994-1996 • 1F2R • No built: Probably 1

Stratford-upon-Avon based Tony Bradwell's Stinger was a curious mixture of influences. It was based on a BMW K1100 motorbike but its front end was taken from the Sylva Striker kit car. A spaceframe chassis housed BMW parts in the rear end, plus inboard independent front suspension. The first car had aluminium side panels but an all-glassfibre bodyshell was planned; sadly it's believed no kits were sold at the £1900 asking price.

Story
NL • 1940-1942 • 1F2R • No built: Approx 10

Produced in the Hague, the Story was basic electric-powered transport for two people, with a top speed of barely 15mph (25km/h). About 10 were built during WW2, with construction of the bodies undertaken by the coachbuilder Pennock.

SUB G1
USA • 2005 • 2F1R • No built: 3

Talented designer Niki Smart built a one-off three-wheeled study called the One-Up (pictured below) that had the distinction of being displayed at the Millennium Dome in London. He and two others (Jay Brett and Nick Mynott) then set up an operation called SUB in southern California to develop the car into the G1.

The 'SUB' name came from the inspiration that Smart drew from submarine design. The SUB G1 was a minimal creation, with single-seater open bodywork in glassfibre, with a tubular spaceframe with aluminium and composite bulkheads underneath. In contrast to the One-Up's 600cc Honda CBR engine, the G1 used a Suzuki V-twin 996cc four-stroke engine with 135bhp, sited behind the driver and powering the rear wheel by twin chain and jack shaft. Weighing a mere 330kg, that was enough for very quick performance. A six-speed sequential gearbox made do without a reverse gear.

Perfect 50/50 weight distribution was claimed, so that sharp handling on motorcycle tyres resulted, helped by

double unequal-length wishbone front suspension with Penske dampers and pushrod-activated suspension front and rear. A production run was considered of 25 cars, priced at $80,000 each, but in the event only three were built, one for each of the founders.

Subaru Rabbit RS-3
J • 1965 • 2F1R • No built: 1

This fascinating car was built by an engineer at the Gunma Manufacturing Division of Fuji Heavy Industries (Subaru) and based on a Rabbit scooter. Like the Inter ⇨, its front track could be narrowed (from 1050mm to 670mm) for parking or manoeuvring; impressively for 1965, this was all done electronically, even with the car still running. A planned production run was sadly cancelled.

Subaru X-100 Gyronaut
USA/J • 1970s • 1F2R • No built: 1

This extraordinary streamlined machine was built in California by Subaru of America, along with the Vehicle Research Institute, as an ultra-economical concept car. Legendary stylist Alex Tremulis did the design work on a car that was long at 4877mm (192in) but very lightweight at 311kg (685lb). The single-seater was fitted with a Subaru Rex 544cc two-cylinder engine with 27bhp, enough to power it 60mph in 12 seconds, and in 1980 it averaged fuel economy of 100.2mpg at a steady 55mph. Subaru still owns the X-100.

Suburba-car
USA • 1965 • 2F1R • No built: n/a

The Suburba-car was a project that appeared in Popular Mechanics magazine in 1965. The car itself was designed by students of the Illinois Institute of Technology, and the magazine encouraged readers to build a chassis themselves and then design their own bodywork. A Honda 150cc engine was mounted behind the two passengers driving the single rear wheel by chain.

Succès
B • 1952 • 2F1R • No built: 1

At the January 1952 Brussels Motor Show, Succès showed this two-seater microcar. Built in Borgerhout, near Antwerp, its open bodywork was made of wood with imitation leather  covering, plus steel front wings. It was powered by a rear-mounted two-cylinder two-stroke engine, but a production run did not occur, despite a low price of 30,900 FB.

Sui Tong
RC • 1960s/1981-c1984 • 1F2R • No built: n/a

Sui Tong made rickshaws for the Taiwanese market from the 1960s onwards, but in 1981 it stepped up a rung by forming a collaboration with Convenient Machines Inc in New York, USA, to manufacture the Cub three-wheeler exclusively for the American market. This two-seater looked like a modern bubble car; its rear wheels were enclosed in removable spats and its glassfibre bodywork boasted an opening rear tailgate. A 400cc single-cylinder air-cooled engine could power it to a top speed of 50mph (80km/h). An ambitious production rate of 10,000 units a year was announced but never reached.

Sumo
PE • 2007 • 1F2R • No built: n/a

Rickshaw makers can be found the world over, and Peru's was Sumo Motor. This Lima-based enterprise made enclosed rickshaws with 149cc engines, some of which featured tortured styling work.

Sundown Solution
BR • 2007 • 1F2R • No built: n/a

Brazilian motorbike brand Sundown showed the Solution concept three-wheeler at the 2007 Sao Paulo motorbike show. Bizarrely, its design and concept was honed in the virtual world website, Second Life, before being brought to life in reality. Power came  from a dual-fuel 250cc engine and luxuries included air conditioning, parking sensors and sat nav.

Sunrise Badal
IND • 1975-1981 • 1F2R • No built: n/a

Made in Bangalore by Sunrise Auto Industries, the Badal was a curious vehicle with an odd-shaped glassfibre body whose most unusual feature was that it had two doors on the nearside but only one on the offside (which the manufacturers inexplicably described as "futuristic"). Despite its large size (over 120in/3080mm long), it weighed only 400kg (882lb) thanks to its glassfibre bodywork. This meant that the

Italian-made rear-mounted 198cc single-cylinder 10bhp engine could power the Badal to a top speed of 47mph (75km/h). There was room for four passengers, making it popular as a taxi. Confirming its basic nature, there were brakes on the rear end only. The company changed its name to Sipani Automobiles in 1978, and a fourth wheel was added to the Badal in 1981, after which Sipani stuck to cars with four wheels (including a licensed version of the Reliant Kitten).

Sunrise M3
USA • 1980s • 2F1R • No built: n/a

Sunrise Automobile Corp, run by car restorer Ross Vick in Des Moines, Washington, became a very famous name in the USA for its extravagant neo-classics but it also built a very small Morgan-style trike.

Suntera SunRay
USA • 1994-1997 • 2F1R • No built: 8

Very few cars hail from Hawaii, but Jonathan Tennyson's Suntera was one. Several different prototype glassfibre bodies were built, including the C-Mobile truck and the SunRay two-seater passenger model. All were electric-powered with an enclosed cabin, and at least one example was built for the Hawaiian police with transparent doors that doubled up as riot shields!

Suntrike
U/USA • 2006-2012 • 2F1R • No built: 120

The Suntrike was designed in Uruguay but its target market was the United States, where most were sold. Created by Marcel Correa, Carlos Tabarez and Aldo Delepiane under

the company name Deceleste, the prototype used a 49cc Minarelli engine but production versions also came with 80cc or 125cc options. The bodywork was in glassfibre over a tubular steel chassis, and weight was only 177kg (390lb). Automatic transmission with reverse was fitted, and top speed was limited to 40mph (65km/h).

Super Asia
PK • 2000s-date • 1F2R • No built: n/a

Super Asia Motors (or SAM) followed up its existing business making motorcycles with rickshaws powered by 200cc four-stroke CNG engines and automatic transmission.

Super Kar
USA • 1946 • 1F2R • No built: n/a

Louis Elrad of Cleveland, Ohio built the Super Kar, an open-topped economy three-wheeler with a rear-mounted 18bhp air-cooled engine.

Super Power
PK • 2004-date • 1F2R • No built: n/a

NJ Auto Industry was behind the Super Power rickshaw range, powered by 200cc four-stroke engines with seating for three or six passengers.

Super Sprinter
PK • 2004-date • 1F2R • No built: n/a

The Pacific Motor Company (based in Lahore in Pakistan) made the Super Sprinter rickshaw range, with 175cc CNG/LPG powerplants. The company claimed that it had sourced technological input for its vehicles from Germany and Thailand.

Super Star
PK • 1992-date • 1F2R • No built: n/a

Memon Motor made the Super Star range of rickshaws for the Pakistani market. Several models were offered, with various engine sizes of 100cc, 175cc CNG and 200cc CNG.

SuperTrike
USA • 2000s-date • 1F2R • No built: n/a

Based in Las Cruces, New Mexico, the SuperTrike V8 Trike was offered either fully built or as a rolling chassis. The rear axle was taken from a Ford Mustang with gas dampers and the powerplant was a GM 350ci V8.

Superwin SW-250GK
CN • 1996-date • 1F2R • No built: n/a

Superwin hailed from Zhejiang and offered a very typical enclosed four-seater powered by a single-cylinder 229cc engine enabling a top speed of just 28mph (45km/h). In contrast to many contemporary glassfibre-bodied Chinese cars, it featured metal bodywork.

Surass
J • 1990s • 1F2R • No built: n/a

Very little is known about the Japanese-built Surass, other than that it was an enclosed cabin scooter, typical of the genre, under whose flat rear deck was housed a rear-mounted Suzuki moped engine.

Swallow V-Twin
GB • 2005-2012 • 2F1R • No built: n/a

This was an ambitious project to revive the legendary name of the Swallow Coachbuilding Co – the precursor to the Jaguar luxury car brand – by a Canadian man called Peter Schömer who was then based in Chichester, West Sussex. The Swallow was to be a Morgan-style trike powered by a Harley-Davidson engine driving the rear wheel by shaft. The company hoped to sell the Swallow V-Twin, in both Touring and Speedster versions, through the Harley-Davidson dealer network, but the whole project came up for sale in 2012, and its fate thereafter is not known.

SWAP
RC • 1998-date • 1F2R • No built: n/a

The SWAP electric trike was initially built by Shang Wei EV Tech of Taiwan, although that changed to Ahamani from 2008. A 2.2kW motor allowed a top speed of 25mph and a range of up to 20 miles on a charge. This three-wheeler was sold as the Powabyke in the UK.

Swarovski

A/J • 2008 • 2F1R • No built: 1

This crystal-encrusted car was funded by the Austrian crystalier Swarovski and designed by Alice of Tokyo. The prototype was not powered, but its creators tentatively suggested that the array of crystals on its surface could be used to amplify light to power photovoltaic solar panels. The car ended up being auctioned for charity in London.

Sway

USA • 2012-date • 2F1R • No built: n/a

Joe Wilcox was a designer with a company called IDEO based in Palo Alto, California. He decided to form Sway Motorsports to develop a simple tilting vehicle. It used a patented linkage to lean into corners, and was electric-powered.

Switch

USA • 2011-date • 2F1R • No built: n/a

Switch Vehicles was formed by James McGreen, who had previously been behind ZAP ⇨. The Switch was an exo-

skeletal open car measuring 139in (3530mm) long and weighing 567kg (1250lb), with a central front seat and the option of two further seats behind. Power came from an electric source (between 40bhp and 65bhp), allowing a top speed of between 45mph and 75mph, so it was claimed. Based in Sebastopol, California, the business offered kit-form only vehicles initially, priced at under $15,000.

SYM EX3

RC • 2011-date • 2F1R • No built: n/a

The SYM EX3 Hybrid concept by the Taiwanese firm Sangyang Industry debuted at the 2011 Taipei World Design Expo. Designed by Nova Design, it was a semi-enclosed tandem two-seater that used a 5kW electric motor for a maximum speed of 56mph (90km/h) and a range of 62 miles (100km).

THREE WHEELERS A-Z

TTT

TriSport Scorpion ▲

Toyota i-Road ▲

Taylor-Dunn Trident ▲

TrikeTec X-2 Arrow ▲

▼ Toyota Commuter

Teilhol Messagette ▲

▼ Trautwein Duofront

T3 Motion GT3 / R3
USA • 2009-date • 2F1R • No built: n/a

Is this car a three-wheeler or a four-wheeler? It's a grey area, because the GT3 from T3 Motion had just one rear wheel rim, but two motorcycle tyres fitted to it. This unusual design was claimed to improve traction, stability and handling, while keeping low rolling resistance for good fuel economy. The multi-link dual-damper rear suspension was even claimed to share Formula 1 technology. This open-topped two-passenger was a plug-in electric vehicle whose front wheels were driven by an 18kW lithium battery and front-mounted electric motor. A top speed of 70mph and a range of up to 100 miles were claimed. By 2011 the car was being advertised with an iPad (later a Galaxy Tab) that performed sat-nav, music, video and email tasks, and its name had changed to R3; prices at this time started at $35,000 (£23,500).

T3 Motion T3
USA • 2011-date • 1F2R • No built: n/a

California-based T3 Motion had made around 3000 three-wheeled stand-up electric vehicles called the ESV for the security and site management markets before it launched a 'power sports' consumer model called the T3 in 2011. The 'power' moniker was hard to understand as the swappable lithium battery modules gave it a top speed of just 12mph and a range of 40 miles.

Tachihi TR6
J • 1950 • 1F2R • No built: n/a

Produced by Tokyo-based Tachihi Kogyo out of the former Tachikawa aeroplane works, the TR6 was a fairly primitive open-topped economy car. Measuring 2800mm long and 1200mm wide, it could seat three passengers. The 307kg car was powered by an air-cooled single-cylinder 148cc engine with a meagre 3.1bhp.

Tachó Ballena
E • 1950 • 2F1R • No built: 1

This streamlined car (hence the name Ballena, or 'whale') was designed by Guillem Tachó of Manresa, Spain and built by his brothers Josep and Antoni. It was powered by a rear-mounted 648cc air-cooled two-stroke engine with 18bhp, which was needed as the car was quite big (3900mm long). Only the first prototype had three wheels; a second Ballena was built with four wheels, and another prototype (the Coca) eventually became the PTV, one of Spain's most successful microcars.

Takeoka Abbey
J • 1990s • 2F1R • No built: n/a

The Takeoka Abbey, produced by the Takeoka Auto Craft Co, was a very small (2150mm long) enclosed microcar weighing only 145kg and powered by a 49cc moped engine. Most examples sold were four-wheeled but Takeoka also marketed a three-wheeled version with a single rear wheel, as pictured here.

Talash Iemen
IR • 1999-2005 • 1F2R • No built: n/a

Talash Motive Powers of Teheran, Iran made motorcycles from 1993, but also built this small enclosed car with a single front wheel from 1999. Power came from a Taiwanese engine of either 125cc (12bhp) or 200cc (14bhp). Talash also made a pick-up variant.

Talon / Tanom Invader
USA • 2010-date • 2F1R • No built: n/a

The first product of Viriginia-based Talon Motors was a funky four-wheeler called the Street Quad (2008), but in 2010 it launched a Campagna-inspired trike called the Invader. Power came from a 194bhp, 1340cc Suzuki Hayabusa engine and six-speed sequential transmission (plus reverse gear), good enough to power the 472kg (1040lb) trike to 144mph (220km/h) and 0-60mph in 3.92 seconds. The chassis (incorporating a roll cage) was in tubular steel and featured

fully adjustable suspension, while cross-drilled Wilwood brakes betrayed the serious performance spec of the car.

There was side-by-side seating for two, luggage space in pods on the side of the glassfibre bodywork, and even cupholders in the cabin. Pricing started at $42,900, or more for a special edition of 55 Red Rocker models created in collaboration with ex-Van Halen singer Sammy Hagar. The brand name changed to Tanom Motors in 2011, when a new roadster model was added (the TR-3), whereupon the original coupe version became known as the Invader TC-3.

Taro TT-1
CN • 2000s-date • 2F1R • No built: n/a

The Zhejiang Chuangtai Motorcycle Co designed and built the Taro TT-1, a somewhat BRP Can-Am-inspired machine. It was powered by a 200cc single-cylinder four-stroke engine, had a CVT transmission and weighed only 158kg.

Taylor-Dunn
USA • 1949-1966 • 1F2R • No built: n/a

Taylor-Dunn Manufacturing was formed in Anaheim, California by farmer Davis Taylor and Fred Dunn. Its speciality was small electric vehicles, made in three- and four-wheeled forms, mostly for utility use but also as neighbourhood runabouts. Models included the PG single-seater and later the Trident (pictured).

The latter used a 24V electric motor and reached a top speed of 16mph. With its glassfibre bodywork, it weighed 331kg (730lb). Although its passenger car output halted in 1966, Taylor-Dunn still existed at the time of writing, making electric commercial vehicles.

Teilhol Citadine
F • 1972-1982 • 2F1R • No built: n/a

Teilhol was based in Puy-de-Dôme in France, and made its name building a jeep-style leisure car for Renault called the Rodeo. In 1972, it branched out in a very different direction with an electric three-wheeler called the Citadine. There were strong echoes of the Isetta bubble car in its design. The front-opening door was familiar (although it was hinged

at the top) and the overall shape was something like an angular version of the Isetta. The glassfibre bodywork sat on top of a tubular steel chassis, with a centrally-mounted 48V electric motor driving the single rear wheel by chain, and there were hydromechanical brakes. The top speed was only 31mph (50km/h) and the overall range was 62 miles (100km). Despite its tiny size at 2120mm (84in) long, it was weighed down by its batteries (overall it weighed 500kg). A pick-up version was also marketed as the Citacom.

Teilhol Messagette
F • 1975-1983 • 2F1R • No built: n/a

The Messagette was conceived as a commercial vehicle powered by electricity, sold with a box-type rear end. However, a basic leisure car version was also offered. After 1983, Teilhol concentrated solely on four-wheeled microcars.

Tempo
D/IND • 1933-2000 • 1F2R • No built: n/a

With one of the world's longest continuous production runs of all time, the Tempo lasted over 60 years. Launched in Germany as a commercial vehicle in 1933, production in the fatherland ceased in the early 1970s, while licensed production in India by Firodia (subsequently known as Bajaj ⇨) continued right through the 1990s.

Despite its considerable size, the Tempo was powered by a tiny Ilo 198cc single-cylinder engine developing just 7.5bhp, which powered the single front wheel through a three-speed gearbox, so it ran out of puff at 40mph (65km/h).

A huge variety of body styles were built, mostly commercial vehicles (from delivery vans to pick-ups), but there were also attempts at passenger versions. For example, the Tempo van could be transformed into a sort of `people carrier' by adding seats in the cargo bay and there was also an abortive two-seater coupe called the Tempo Troll in 1951, around 50 of which were built. A third type of passenger Tempo was created by converting the rear deck of the pick-up to carry passengers, forming a rudimentary rickshaw style.

Tercyclo
I • 2011-date • 2F1R • No built: n/a

The Tercyclo was designed by Fuoriserie Design of Milan, which described its look as evoking "the shape of a jet fighter" and built by Tecnotig, based near Monza, Italy. It was designed as a kit to transform scooters into a three-wheeler, and various sizes were envisaged, from 50cc up to 250cc. A canopy and four-point harness protected the lone passenger, who was housed in a steel spaceframe chassis. Kits were advertised at 3500 euros, and options included an electric reverse gear. It was very lightweight at just 180kg (397lb) and measured only 2300mm long.

Terra
J • 2013-date • 1F2R • No built: n/a

Japanese electric bike manufacturer Terra Motors honed in on moves to cut tuk-tuk pollution with its electric three-wheeler, aimed principally at the Philippine market.

Texas Rocket
USA • 1988-c1992 • 2F1R • No built: 1

The Texas Rocket (sometimes referred to as the TX-101) was designed and built by Maurice Bourne, the maker of Aero Sport motorcycle trailers, and who later made the Aero Trike ⇨. The prototype used an 1100cc Honda Goldwing rear end, mated to MGB front suspension, and a sliding canopy enabled entry to the tandem two-seater cockpit. Kits cost from $2995, with turnkey cars costing $10,000, but only one car was ever made.

Tez Raftar
PK • 2000s-date • 1F2R • No built: n/a

This conventional autorickshaw, available in 200cc petrol, diesel and CNG forms, was made at a rate of 3000 per month in Pakistan.

TGV Zeus
F/USA • 2007-date • 1F2R • No built: n/a

If the Trikes Grande Vitesse (TGV) Zeus looked like a motorbike and sidecar, that's no surprise – it was. However, it took a very novel approach to the form by housing the engine in the sidecar; that was a 2.0-litre Peugeot four-cylinder unit. The sidecar section seated two passengers, with another two seated on the motorbike part, with the controls operated from the bike. It  weighed 649kg (1430lb) and featured a two-inch diameter steel tube chassis and composite bodywork. An operation called Sidebike made the vehicles near Grenoble in France but as of 2008 it also announced it would start manufacturing in Woodstock, New York, using Mazda or Mitsubishi engines.

TGV Celtik
F/USA • 2007-date • 1F2R • No built: n/a

TGV's other model was the Celtik, a more traditional style three-passenger trike. It also had an unexpected feature: an enormous boot that was claimed to be larger than that of most cars because it passed through the chassis below the passengers. The chassis also housed a 2.0-litre Peugeot 133bhp engine and four-speed manual gearbox with reverse. Weighing 625kg (1378lb), the Celtik was offered in Roadster spec for €27,200, or €32,232 in plusher Touring form.

Thoroughbred Stallion
USA • 2006-2010/2012-date • 1F2R • No built: Approx 950

The idea behind the Thoroughbred Motorsports Stallion was to make a comfortable trike with automatic transmission, based on expertise from its sister company, Motor Trike ⇨. Unlike most trikes, it used an automotive engine, namely a Ford 2.3-litre four-cylinder unit with 143bhp, mated to a five-speed automatic gearbox. This was a large vehicle, measuring 3810mm (125in) long and weighing 787kg (1736lb). Its tubular/box-section chassis housed a patented air ride rear suspension system, and the glassfibre bodywork was highly

original. Some 800 units were built from 2006 to 2010, with a further 150 planned from 2012 onwards, priced at $33,995.

ThreeWheelFactory T-Bike
D • 2004 • 2F1R • No built: 1

The first project of the ThreeWheelFactory was the 2004 T-Bike, a three-wheeler based on the Kazuma quad. At the rear end, a single swinging arm was fitted with a monodamper. The 223cc air-cooled two-cylinder four-stroke engine delivered 19bhp, which in a vehicle weighing 175kg and measuring only 1880mm long, was good enough for a top speed of 62mph (100km/h). Only one T-Bike was built but the ThreeWheelFactory said it would be possible to convert various quads. This company also collaborated with Luigi Colani to create the Street-Ray, a car that looked like a three-wheeler (and was classified as one in some markets) but in fact had two narrow-set rear wheels.

ThreeWheelFactory T-Rod
D • 2009-date • 2F1R • No built: n/a

This was an original single-seater, designed by Martin Preuss and based on a Suzuki Bandit 650 or 1250. Therefore it had a rear-mounted four-cylinder engine of 656cc or 1255cc, developing either 86bhp or 98bhp; if that wasn't enough, a Suzuki Hayabusa 1340cc or other four-cylinder bike engine could be used. The front suspension was by double wishbones and pushrod dampers, with a single swinging arm to the rear. It weighed a mere 348kg and the top speed was in excess of 125mph (200km/h). The 650cc version was priced from 19,900 euros.

ThreeWheelFactory Terzo
D • 2009-date • 2F1R • No built: n/a

If the T-Rod was original, the Terzo was less so, being clearly inspired by the Campagna T-Rex ⇨. The mid-mounted motor was either a Suzuki Bandit 1250 or Hayabusa 1340, with 98bhp or 197bhp

respectively, while a Honda Fireblade or other units were also possible. The Terzo could seat two passengers, while its lightweight tubular steel chassis and scant bodywork kept weight down to 448kg, enabling top speeds in excess of 170mph (275km/h). Prices started at 29,900 euros.

Thrif-T
USA • 1947-1955 • 1F2R • No built: n/a

The Tri-Wheel Corp of Oxford, North Carolina (and also Springfield, Massachusetts) made the Thrif-T, which was somewhere between a light delivery truck and an economy car with a big boot. Its steel bodywork could seat three people side-by-side, or five people in some versions. Power came from a 10bhp two-cylinder air-cooled Onan engine that could be removed entirely, with the rear axle, for maintenance. Top speed was around 40mph (64km/h).

Thrustcycle
USA • 2011-date • 1F1M1R • No built: n/a

This vehicle could be the oddest of all three-wheelers in this book. American company Thrustcycle Enterprises pursued the idea of gyroscopically stabilised motorcycles, but one of its prototypes (and a fully functioning one at that) featured the strange and unique idea of three wheels aligned one behind the other. The vehicle could remain upright even at zero mph.

Thunderbolt Streamer
CZ • 2005-date • 1F2R • No built: n/a

This Czech chopper trike had, by western standards, an unusual powerplant: a 50bhp 1.3-litre Skoda unit. This gave the 564kg trike a 'recommended' speed of 100km/h (62mph). Prices in 2013 started at 13,000 euros.

Tibicar Bella 125
I • 1978-c1988 • 1F2R • No built: n/a

Originating in Rome, the Tibicar Bella 125 was a very basic three-wheeled microcar powered by a 123cc BCB two-stroke 5.5bhp engine, driving the front wheel via a four-speed gearbox. The all-

independent suspension made use of hydro-pneumatic dampers, and there was a single front disc brake. Removable rear-hinged doors allowed access, and a lift-out targa

roof panel let the air in, while the manufacturer optimistically said the Bella 125 could be used as a hunting car.

Tilbrook
AUS • 1953 • n/a • No built: 1

Rex Tilbrook of Kensington, South Australia, was most famous for making motorbikes and sidecars, but he also displayed a three-wheeler at the 1953 Adelaide Show. A rear-mounted Villiers 197cc engine drove through a four-speed gearbox, while the aluminium bodywork was mounted on a tubular steel chassis. Only one car was ever made.

Tiler
GB • 1999-2000 • 2F1R • No built: 1

Kevin Champion created this trike, which took its engine, front subframe and other mechanicals from the Mini. Its boat-tail rear end evoked the Morgan, but the Tiler Car Company of West Sussex only ever made one car.

Tilli Capton
AUS • 1957 • 2F1R • No built: 4

Reg Tilley's Capton was based on the chassis of an Edith ⇨ but fitted with a more potent (16bhp) British Anzani 350cc two-cylinder engine. Its attractive glassfibre bodywork could be ordered in either open-topped or coupe styles but it found just four buyers.

Tilter
F • 2011-date • 1F2R • No built: n/a

The 2011 Geneva Motor Show saw the debut of this tilting three-wheeler. Created by SynergEthic, this electric urban car

measured 2350mm long and just 900mm wide, and could seat two in tandem, entering the car via a large single door which swung outwards. The power went to the two rear wheels, and a range of 120km and a top speed of 110km/h were claimed. As its name hinted, the Tilter leant into corners, with all three wheels inclining. Production was scheduled to start in 2013 priced at under 10,000 euros.

Tilting Motor Works
USA • 2008-date • 2F1R • No built: n/a

This Marysville, Washington firm, run by Bob Mighell, made two-wheeled tilting front end conversion kits for Harley-Davidson Road Kings, Honda Goldwings and Vmax.

Time Machine
USA • 2005-date • 2F1R • No built: n/a

This was a plans-built two-seater trike designed by Steve Spudic of Jacksonville, Florida, who wanted to make a Quincy-Lynn Tri-Magnum ⇨ but found it "intimidating". The $39.99 build manual showed you how to make your own Time Machine, but it was still involved, requiring you to do your own welding and sheet aluminium bodywork. Any motorcycle rear end could be used, while the front end was sourced from a VW.

Tippen Delta
GB • 1955-1976 • 1F2R • No built: n/a

Frank Tippen & Sons of Coventry started making conventional invalid tricycles in around 1950, powered by a single-cylinder Villiers 147cc engine driving only one of the rear wheels. More unusual was the Delta of 1955, which had uniquely styled glassfibre bodywork (always in blue) with a single door that slid forwards for entry (the first disabled car to have this feature). Power came from a 197cc Villiers engine mated to a four-speed gearbox. Early cars had a single headlamp but from the Delta 3 of 1959, two headlamps were fitted. The Delta 6 of 1966 had 12in wheels, while the Delta 8 of 1968 was restyled with a squarer front end. Petrol-engined production ended in 1970, but electric Deltas were built from 1965 right up until 1976.

Tokyo R&D EC1000 Electrike
J • 1993 • 2F1R • No built: 1

Shown at 1993 Tokyo Motor Show, the EC1000 Electrike was a concept designed by Tokyo R&D. Measuring a compact 2625mm long and 1390mm wide, it was an electric-powered single-seater with a lockable front luggage compartment, but had no production future.

Tomaszo Triker
A • 1980s • 1F2R • No built: n/a

This was a typical chopper-style trike with glassfibre bodywork and a VW Beetle rear engine, whose only real claim to fame was that it was made in Austria.

Tonaro ZHT-4
CN • 2008-date • 1F2R • No built: n/a

The Tonaro brand was perhaps best known for electric bicycles (developed by the China National Aero-Technology Guangzhou Company). The ZHT-4 was a typical Daewoo Matiz-style three-wheeler, measuring 3200mm long and seating four. A 4kW electric motor fed by 48V batteries powered it to a top speed of 37mph (60km/h).

Too Kool Cycles TRT
USA • 2012-date • 2F1R • No built: n/a

Too Kool Cycles of Charleston, South Carolina created the TRT (Tilting Reverse Trike), a leaning trike based on a Harley-Davidson touring bike, whose front wheels could lock vertically at low speed. The cost was from $8975, and you could convert the trike back to a two-wheeler within two hours if desired.

Total Car
F • 2011-2012 • 2F1R • No built: n/a

First seen at the Frankfurt 2011 Show, and then again at the 2012 Paris Show, this concept car came from the French oil giant, Total. It was conceived to showcase a new lightweight bio-polymer material, developed with the help and participation of Queens

University, in Belfast. This was a tandem two-seater, powered by electric motors, but no production run was envisaged by Total or its partners.

Tourette

GB • 1956-1957 • 2F1R • No built: Approx 35

The 1956 Earls Court Motor Show saw the arrival of a new company on to the car scene: the Progress Supreme Co Ltd of Purley, Surrey. Having built some glassfibre-bodied scooters, its first three-wheeler was the egg-shaped Tourette. A Villiers 197cc 7.6bhp engine sat just in front of the single rear wheel. The 2590mm (102in) long glassfibre car weighed only 195kg (430lb) and reached a top speed of 55mph (88km/h). Soft and hard-tops were available to cover the occupants (all three of them, if the manufacturer's optimistic claim was to be believed). A second three-wheeled model, the Car-ette, was stillborn.

Tow-Pac

USA • 2000s-date • 1F2R • No built: n/a

This company made bolt-on 'chopper' trike conversions such as the Insta-Trike (for touring and cruising motorcycles), the Mini Trike and the Micro Mini Trike (for scooters and mini-

scooters). These kits were designed to be removable, so you could revert to two-wheeled motoring in about 10 minutes, which also kept costs down. Reverse gear was also available.

Toyota Commuter

J • 1970 • 1F2R • No built: A few prototypes

Exhibited at the 1970 Tokyo Show was the Commuter from Toyota. Batteries stowed under the seat powered a 2.3kW electric motor that was mounted on the side of the fork holding the single front wheel. A top speed of 16mph (25km/h) and a range of 43 miles (70km) were claimed, but no production future awaited this pure concept car.

Toyota Photic

J • 1991 • 1F2R • No built: 1

This fantasy-realm concept car, presented at the 1991 Greater St Louis Motor Show, used light sensors to read and react to traffic signs and road signals. Two passengers sat in tandem under a Plexiglas dome, which rose for entry and  exit, and the driver grasped a stick to steer.

Toyota i-Swing

J • 2005 • 1F2R • No built: n/a

Toyota pursued a whole raft of 'personal mobility' concepts in the 2000s, the first three-wheeled example of which was the i-Swing. It could be driven like a Segway on two wheels at walking pace, but it could transform itself into a three-wheeler at higher speeds. The driver had a joystick control but could also steer the car by moving his body weight. Unsurprisingly, it only ever appeared at shows.

Toyota i-Real

J • 2007 • 2F1R • No built: n/a

This 'Personal Mobility Concept' appeared at the 2007 Tokyo Motor Show. It was a one-passenger vehicle powered by lithium-ion batteries. Like the i-Swing, it had a 'Low-Speed' mode, with the car being upright, but in High-Speed mode (a bit of a misnomer as its maximum speed was 19mph/30km/h), the car leant back and extended its single rear wheel. It could lean into corners, and was controlled by two joysticks. Despite Toyota declaring that the i-Real might be put on sale by 2010, nothing more was heard of the project.

Toyota i-Road

J • 2013-date • 2F1R • No built: n/a

 The i-Road was something like the Renault Twizy, in that it was a tandem two-seater electric car, but had only three wheels and could tilt into bends using what Toyota called 'active lean' technology. It made its debut at the 2013 Geneva show and was only 850mm wide. A lithium-ion battery provided electricity to two 2kW motors mounted in the front wheels, and a range of up to 31 miles (50km) was claimed. In 2013 Toyota announced that the i-Road would be participating in public road trials in Japan.

TR Hog

USA • 2002 • 2F1R • No built: n/a

With assistance from Dave Norton, who was responsible for the Norton Shrike ⇨, the TR Hog was made by Charles Valentine of Arkansas as a three-wheeled Harley-Davidson for  the disabled (although in fact it used a 750cc Yamaha engine).

Tracetel Whoop

F • 2010-date • 2F1R • No built: n/a

Companies across Europe did not fail to notice the success of the Piaggio MP3 ⇨, one of which, Tracetel, launched a close reinterpretation of the idea with electric power. Going by the bizarre name of Whoop, it was styled by MBD Design and featured a fixed roof. The two front wheels leant into corners, while the electric motor was available in two power levels: 4kW (45km/h top speed) and 6kW (80km/h). Tracetel planned to put the Whoop into production in 2011 but by 2013, this had still not happened.

Tracker

USA • 2012-date • 2F1R • No built: n/a

The Tracker range originated from Anderson, South Carolina. Two versions were offered: the SunTracker (a street-legal model that was approved for use at camp grounds), and the GameTracker (for hunting, complete with camouflage colour schemes). Seating two and able to store luggage on a front basket, Trackers were powered by a 150cc single-cylinder four-stroke engine with automatic transmission, and could reach a top speed of 55mph (89km/h).

Tractavant
F • 1951 • 1F2R • No built: Probably 1

Aviation engineer Henri Lanoy built a prototype called the Trielec in 1948, followed in 1951 by a new car called the Tractavant. The narrow open-topped car featured a tiny single door, and the driver sat centrally up front, with up to two passenger seated behind. The single front wheel was mounted on a motorcycle fork but steered by a wheel rather than handlebars. An Aubier Dunne 125cc or Sachs 150cc engine provided the power by chain.

Trautwein Duofront
D • 1955-1984 • 2F1R • No built: Several prototypes

Over 50 years before the Piaggio MP3 ⇨, a German engineer called Dr Wolfgang Trautwein, based in Meersburg on Lake Konstanz, invented the twin-front-wheeled motorcycle. The front wheels of this pioneering machine were linked by a parallelogram, enabling it to lean into corners. After working at Lockheed on the Lunar Roving Vehicle, he continued to develop his ideas in the 1980s with a prototype based on the Honda CX500 (below left).

He also took two Piaggio Vespa scooters and created a single three-wheeler out of them (below right), and offered Piaggio the rights to build it. However, his ideas were just too far ahead of their time, and Trautwein died in 1988 without seeing any of his brainchildren reach production.

Tremola
CH • 2011-date • 1F2R • No built: n/a

Tremola was based in Bilten in Switzerland, and made a semi-enclosed tilting cabin scooter design, which measured only 2000mm long by 800mm wide. Thanks to a lightweight steel

chassis and glassfibre bodywork, the overall weight was just 220kg. The Tremola's wheel tilt system was patented under the name Multi-TRACKs Curve Tilting Technology (MCTT). Powered by an 11kW (14.5bhp) electric motor, it could reach 56mph (90km/h) and travel up to 62 miles (100km).

TreMoto
USA • 2010-date • 2F1R • No built: n/a

TreMoto of Taylor, Mississippi, built a couple of leaning trike prototypes called the Monstrosity 620 (based on a Ducati Monster 620) and the 3Z1 (on a Kawasaki Z1000). The leaning suspension system used a composite monoleaf spring and Kayaba rotary dampers. Members of the public could commission custom-designed TreMoto motorbike conversions priced from around $10,000.

TREV
AUS • 2007 • 2F1R • No built: n/a

The TREV – or Two-seat Renewable Energy Vehicle – was built by students of the University of South Australia. A tandem two-seater with a canopy top, it used lithium polymer batteries to power it to a top speed of 75mph (120km/h) and 0-60mph in around 10 seconds. It had the distinction of completing a 16,800-mile trip around the world to promote green energy, finishing at the UN's European HQ in Geneva.

Treycycle
USA • 2011-date • 1F2R • No built: n/a

This generously sized trike featured a narrow arrowhead nose section and an expansive tail that housed a Chrysler 300C 3.5-litre V6 engine with 260bhp. Designed by ex-

NASA engineer Ray Ackley and made in Plymouth, Florida, the Treycycle weighed 1200lb and its top speed was limited to 145mph. Models for the disabled, patrol vehicles and even the military were listed.

Triac

USA • 2008-2011 • 2F1R • No built: A few

Triac was essentially the American-market name for the Green Auto SH8500Z ⇨, which a company called Green Vehicles was all set up to sell, and possibly make, in California. This electric car with an 80mph top speed and a 100-mile range was optimistically called "seriously handsome" by the makers. A price of $24,995 was announced but Green Vehicles sold very few cars before it went belly up in 2011. The city of Salinas, California had invested over $500,000 in the company and reportedly filed a lawsuit to regain its funds.

Triad

USA • Mid-1970s • 2F1R • No built: n/a

The Triad was a very odd idea: a Datsun 240Z-style sports car based on a VW Beetle chassis. Not only was a four-wheeled model sold, but also a three-wheeler, powered by either a motorbike or small car engine.

Triad

GB • 1993-1998 • 2F1R • No built: Approx 14

The 'other' Triad was essentially a revival of the Mosquito ⇨, following the acquisition of the body moulds by Ian Browse and Rick Jones. The pair set up in business as Malvern Autocraft, a nod to the fact that Jones was a keen Morgan owner and that the workshops were in Malvern. The Mosquito bodywork was mildly modified but kept the distinctive external exhaust pipes, and was bolted to a newly developed steel tube chassis. Kits cost £1495, with options including weather equipment and a windscreen.

An alternative 'Warrior' version was a lightweight (375kg) Triad designed for hillclimbs, with the passenger's side of the cockpit panelled off and aero screens in place of the windscreen.

Tri-Car Suburbanette

USA • 1955 • 2F1R • No built: Probably 1

Having dabbled with three-wheelers such as the Martin Stationette ⇨ since 1932, James Martin formed the Tri-Car Corporation of America, based in New York, with the intention of marketing his next design, the Tri-Car Suburbanette. This had glassfibre bodywork, created by Clearfield Plastics. Up to three people could be seated side by side, behind whom was a 1.5-litre two-cylinder Lycoming engine, which could power the car to a top speed of 68mph (110km/h). Probably only one working Tri-Car was ever built, despite plans being announced for an open-roofed version and a Kari-van truck model. Martin died in 1956.

Tri-D

USA • 2011-date • 2F1R • No built: n/a

Michigan-based Tri-D Trikes made 2F1R conversions for many kinds of motorbike, such as Harley-Davidson and Honda Goldwing.

Trident

AUS/CN • 2004-date • 1F2R & 2F1R • No built: n/a

Trident Tricars, part of Asian Dragon Enterprise, was an Australian-owned business with manufacturing plants in China. It offered a large variety of three-wheelers, with petrol engines (90cc to 1000cc), electric motors or hybrid power. Model names included T-Pod, Elude, Nifty, Hot Shot and Mantis (pic below). One of its more interesting offerings was the Taser, a 2F1R three-wheeled coupe (above right).

Trifecta

USA • 2007-date • 2F1R • No built: n/a

Trifecta Motors of Lake Jackson, Texas was founded by Kim Freeman, who built something like a cross between a Morgan and a Delahaye, although whether it was "the most elegant

three wheeler available" as claimed is debatable. Steel bodywork made it heavier than most trikes, while power came from a front-mounted V4 water-cooled 110bhp Yamaha V-Max motorcycle engine driving the single rear wheel.

Trifid

GB • 1990-1994 • 2F1R • No built: 5

The Trifid was the brainchild of two Mini fans based in Hopton, near Diss in Norfolk. Initially built as a steel-bodied one-off, requests for replicas persuaded the pair to make glassfibre moulds (by kit car maker Minus Cars) and built four more under the name Brookwell Trifid. The highly distinctive, sharply cut-off body shape was a glassfibre monocoque with plywood strengthening. The front end was dominated by the semi-exposed Mini engine, and as the car only weighed 370kg, it was extremely quick, even with a standard engine.

Trigger 50

NL/CZ • 1999-date • 2F1R • No built: n/a

Dutchman Jeroen Boekhoorn built his first three-wheeler in 1987, a sporty machine with a Yamaha FZR1000 superbike engine (pictured left). Called the Trigger, it could reach 62mph in 5.8 seconds and topped out at 140mph (220km/h). It remained a one-off, and was subsequently renamed Big Trigger, as Boekhoorn's next project lay at the other extreme of trikes: the tiny Trigger 50.

Power came from a 49cc moped engine, mounted in a steel chassis with a rollover bar; driving through an automatic gearbox, it could just about make 31mph (45km/h).

The open polyester bodywork (just 2380mm long) could seat two, the driver controlling the car via handlebars.

Although it was nominally Dutch, the Trigger was actually built in the Czech Republic, from where it was shipped to Dedemsvaart in the Netherlands for worldwide distribution. The Trigger 50 was sold with some success in the USA as well as Europe, particularly as a holiday resort rental car. For instance, in San Francisco, GPS-equipped Triggers were rented out as 'tour guides'.

Trigger Arrow

NL/CZ • 2013-date • 2F1R • No built: n/a

The Arrow was a new model in 2013, very much in the same vein as the Trigger 50. A Vespa 50cc engine mated to CVT automatic transmission gave the 2280mm long two-seater a top speed of 28mph (45km/h), so it could be driven legally by 16-year olds. The steel tube chassis featured unique double wishbone suspension, and like the Trigger 50 it had handlebar steering with hand-operated brakes.

Trihawk
USA • 1983-1987 • 2F1R • No built: Approx 250

The Trihawk was one of the USA's most technically resolved three-wheelers, conceived by CanAm race engineer Bob McKee and designed by ex-GM stylist David Stollery. Its tubular steel perimeter chassis incorporated a roll-over bar and the open glassfibre bodywork was doorless. A Citroën GSA 1299cc engine and 5-speed gearbox was mounted up front, and suspension was by unequal-length double A-arms up front and a single rear trailing arm; coilover dampers were used all round. Road & Track magazine tested a Trihawk and rated it as one of the best two cornering vehicles it had ever driven, partly due to a very low centre of gravity. Harley-Davidson ⇨ was sufficiently impressed by the design to acquire the rights to produce it, but it shelved the project because of fears over product liability and its own precarious financial condition at the time.

Trik
AUS • 2000 • 2F1R • No built: 1

Mike Davies and Michael Taylor of Ballina, NSW created the Trik, whose chassis was in glassfibre and bodywork in ABS plastic. Built around a Kawasaki Z9 engine, the sports trike weighed only 280kg, and unusually, the two seats were arranged diagonally. Despite reported interest from a Korean manufacturer, the Trik never made production.

Trike Design
GB • 2000s-date • 1F2R • No built: n/a

Caerphilly-based Trike Design made a motorbike conversion with a fully independent rear axle, available in kit form from £4050. Some fabrication and welding was required, or fully built trikes were offered. There was also a full-body trike model called the Brooklands (pictured right). A Trike Design vehicle had the distinction of appearing at the 2012 London Paralympics closing ceremony.

Trike Factory Dolphin
J • 2000s-date • 1F2R & 2F1R • No built: n/a

Trike Factory had connections with Japtec ⇨ and offered several scooter-based trike designs under the name Dolphin. Most were 1F2R in layout, plus at least one 2F1R model. All had 200cc engines.

Trike Factory 1it
J/CN • 2010-date • 2F1R • No built: n/a

Trike Factory Japan was also behind the 1it, an excitingly styled 2F1R trike, which was apparently the work of an Italian design professional. It was powered by a Zongshen 249cc engine, and also made production in China as the Kaxa ⇨. It was sold in Japan for 980,000 yen (around £6500) under the seemingly odd name of 1it – this was supposed to suggest the phrase 'Wanit' – or 'want it'.

Trike Japan
J • 2000s-date • 1F2R • No built: n/a

The Tokyo-based company of Trike Japan offered a wide range of three-wheeled motorbike conversions for big bikes

like Harley-Davidsons and the Honda GL 1800, right down to the Suzuki Burgman 650. Independent rear suspension with double wishbones and a differential represented quite sophisticated engineering, while the specially developed bodywork was outlandishly extravagant.

Trikeshop
GB • 1998-date • 1F2R • No built: n/a

Based in Cardiff, Trikeshop was a fairly big player in the UK trike market. It offered its own DIY conversion kit to turn a bike into a trike, requiring welding skills. Prices started at £3200, with rolling chassis kits from £8000. In-house fully bodied trikes with independent suspension were also offered, with most makes of cruiser suitable for conversion.

Trike Shop
USA • 1972-date • 1F2R • No built: n/a

The Trike Shop started off making Volkswagen-powered trike kits in the early 1970s. In the 1980s, tastes evolved and a new Touring Trike model offered a 'cruiser' style, while the 'Ultimate' kit for Hondas had independent rear  suspension and an automotive driveshaft. In 2006, the name of the trike conversion changed to Roadsmith, which evolved into a whole range of styles. An innovation in 2011 was self-levelling suspension called AccuRide.

TrikeTec C2/C3/V2
D • 2001-2010 • 1F2R • No built: n/a

This company, based in Eschbach, Germany, made a variety of chopper-style trikes (such as the one pictured below) including

the V2, C2 and three-seater C3. The choice of engine was unusual: a 698cc Smart three-cylinder unit, available in 61bhp or 82bhp petrol versions or even a 41bhp diesel.

TrikeTec X2-Arrow
D • 2006-2010 • 1F2R • No built: n/a

In 2006 TrikeTec presented something very different among trikes: the X2-Arrow. This tandem two-seater followed the Ariel Atom-style fad for exo-skeletal chassis, but unusually the rear-mounted engine came from the Smart (698cc with either 61bhp or 82bhp). In its most potent guise, it had a top speed of 106mph (172km/h).

Trike-Tek Buckley
GB • 1996-2003 • 1F2R • No built: Approx 35

Trike-Tek was a Brighton-based shop run by Mick Buckley and Tim Nevill, making chopper trikes including the V8-powered Stealth (pictured), plus other models such as the Pinto, Centaur, Genesis and Hornet, the latter Austin Metro-based.

Triking
GB • 1978-date • 2F1R • No built: Approx 190 (to 2013)

When the Triking was launched in 1978, it was the only three-wheeler kit car on sale in the UK (other than the very different Stimson Scorcher ⇨). It was significant in one big way: it was the first of a very long line of cars inspired by the pre-war Morgan. The work of draughtsman Tony Divey of Marlingford, Norfolk, it became the gold standard

of Morgan replicas in terms of quality and integrity.

A strong backbone chassis with a steel spaceframe carried stressed alloy body panels, while the bonnet, rear section and cycle wings were of glassfibre. The whole thing measured just 114in (2895mm) long. The steering was by Triumph rack-and-pinion, and the wishbone coilover front suspension used Lotus Esprit uprights. At the back end, the single rear wheel was suspended on a swinging fork and was driven by shaft. A Moto Guzzi Vee-Twin engine sat exposed up front, either 844cc (68bhp) or 950cc (71bhp), the latter offering 121mph and 0-60mph in 7.8 seconds. There was also the option of a tuned 844cc Moto Guzzi Le Mans (85bhp) and later a 1064cc 90bhp unit. Changing gears was delightful thanks to the five-speed sequential Moto Guzzi gearbox, or automatic transmission with reverse was optional from 1984 (a Toyota five-speed gearbox could also be fitted).

The cost in complete form started at £4500 in 1978, with cheaper kit-form Trikings offered from 1981. Weather gear was also available, albeit very tight-fitting. Without a doubt, the Triking was of the best-handling, best-quality

and best-designed of the modern Morgan-style trikes, which proved very durable in production. It was also very successful in trialling and track racing. Remarkably, at the time of writing, it had been 35 years in production.

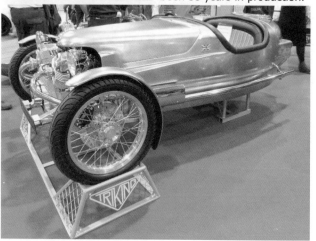

Trilec
GB • 1967 • 2F1R • No built: 1

Electrical engineer David Fox was behind the Trilec shopping car, which ran off two car batteries and could reach a top speed of 20mph (32km/h).

Trilox
GB • 1930s-1959 • 1F2R • No built: n/a

This Trowbridge, Wiltshire company built the Rollsette disabled tricycle (powered by petrol or electric motors) from the 1930s, and the Tricar after WW2. A curious feature was box-

like plywood bodywork, which was unfortunately very heavy.

Trilux
GB • 1986 • 2F1R • No built: 1

This Morgan Supersport Aero-inspired trike cleverly made use of Citroën Ami parts in a self-made chassis. Its fantastic-

looking bodywork was in aluminium sheet over a steel tube frame, with a glassfibre bonnet and boot. Kit-form production was considered but the price deemed too high to succeed.

Trimak
E • 1959-1967 • 1F2R • No built: n/a

An aeronautical engineer of Polish origin based in Spain was behind Trimak. Tricycle cargo trucks and taxis were its staple fare, but at the Barcelona Exhibition of 1963, an extraordinary prototype was presented: a trike that looked like an aircraft, with a big fin behind the driver and small winglets over the rear wheels. Power came from a 250cc two-stroke LEW 250 engine, mated to an in-house gearbox, and the claimed top speed was 84mph (135km/h). However, this was at a time when the Spanish government was required to sanction such projects, and as this was not forthcoming, the Trimak enterprise folded in 1967.

Trimax
USA • 1987 • 1F2R • No built: n/a

MPV Inc of San Antonio, Texas made the Trimax three-wheeler conversion kit that attached a VW front end to a motorbike rear, adding a simple glassfibre nose cone. Two people could sit up front, with the motorbike rear end remaining so that one or two more could sit on the back.

Trimin
GB • c1971-c1972 • 2F1R • No built: 3

Kim Argyle, who helped Robert Moss build the very first Mosquito ⇨, built three more cars just like the prototype under the name Trimin. One of these was a single-seater designed for a speed record attempt.

Tri-Moto Industries Venom
USA • 2008-date • 2F1R • No built: n/a

The Venom, made by Tri-Moto Industries, was one of many performance trikes inspired by Campagna ⇨. In Venom SS guise its power source was a Chevrolet Cobalt SS supercharged unit with up to 300bhp, driving the rear wheel via a patented quadruple chain drive system (Venom R versions used motorbike power). Weight of only 590kg (1300lb) helped it obtain a 0-60mph time of 3.192 seconds. The tubular steel chassis housed adjustable suspension.

Trio
GB • 1993-2000 • 2F1R • No built: Approx 30

The Trio was the brainchild of Ken Hallett of Wareham, Dorset, but was only ever a part-time project. It used a Mini subframe and A-series engine with a cocktail of other parts: Austin 1100 suspension arms and brakes, Austin 1100 rear arm with a Reliant Robin coilspring unit, Metro driveshafts, Allegro steering column, Morris Ital wheels and Renault 5 radiator. The body was extremely basic and made of wood skinned in aluminium and vinyl. The fold-forward bonnet and front cycle wings were glassfibre, which could be supplied by Hallett, who offered DIY sets of plans at £25. The total build cost was quoted at under £1000.

Tripacer
GB • 1994-2001 • 2F1R • No built: Approx 18

Classic Car Panels of Frome, Somerset created the Tripacer, which had the unusual feature of hand-rolled aluminium bodywork, with hundreds of genuine louvres and rivets, over a tubular steel frame. Pleasing touches included shapely front cycle wings and a staggered seating arrangement. A lightly modified Citroën 2CV chassis lay underneath it, with not only three-wheelers offered: you could also opt for a four-wheeler, or a version with close-set twin rear wheels. Customers would have their 2CV converted by the factory into a Tripacer.

Tri-Ped Microcar
USA • 1979-c1981 • 1F2R • No built: n/a

Also known as the American Microcar, this extremely basic two-seater runabout was built in Farmingdale, New York. Little more than a three-wheeled moped with handlebar steering, a roll cage and a windscreen, you could make it more comfortable with optional floppy doors and a roof. Petrol and electric models were offered. The former had a 50cc engine, which would only fire up after the driver had pedalled enough to let the centrifugal clutch turn it over. The

Tri-Ped's rear wheels were driven by chain. The petrol version could average 100mpg, while the electric model boasted a range of 30 miles (48km) and a speed of up to 20mph.

Tri Pod 1
AUS • 2006-date • 2F1R • No built: n/a

Tri Pod Cars was created by Andrew Hutchison of Queensland, Australia, who offered parts, plans and information to build your own Tri Pod 1, as well as selling spaceframe chassis and glassfibre panels in kit form. A Honda VTR1000 engine provided the power.

Tripod
GB • 1985-1987 • 2F1R • No built: Approx 6

The Tripod was the brainchild of Dennis Rowans, managing director of the UK's Suzuki importer, Heron. The idea was to build a weatherproof alternative to a moped that would cost less than £1200, using Suzuki 50cc parts. John Mockett did the design work, employing an aluminium honeycomb chassis with two-seater bodywork in glassfibre. Around six working prototypes were built, and the Tripod was fully tested at MIRA; it also appeared on Top Gear and in the Daily Mail. However, when the car's projected price spiralled above £2000, the project stalled and all six prototypes made were eventually crushed.

Tripolino
CZ • 1950 • 2F1R • No built: Probably 1

This aerodynamic two-seater was designed by Alois Wolf to be a high-speed machine. Even though it only had a 350cc Jawa two-cylinder engine, it still made 71mph (115km/h), helped by weight of just 250kg.

TriRod F3 Adrenaline
USA • 2007-date • 2F1R • No built: n/a

TriRod Motorcycles of San Diego made this three-wheeled straddle-mount motorcycle-derived trike. An advanced specification featured Penske Racing dampers, carbon-fibre bodywork, billet aluminium parts and a 2.0-litre racing engine.

Triscoot
F • 2007 • 2F1R • No built: n/a

Seen at the 2007 Concours Lépine in Paris, the Triscoot added an extra front wheel to a scooter. Intended for disabled riders, it won a prize from the French government but was not heard of again.

TriSport Scorpion
GB • 1990 • 2F1R • No built: 1

The TriSport Scorpion was born in the workshops of Bolton-based Motorsport Components, manufacturers of parts for Formula One and Group C teams. Taking a Yamaha FZR1000, creators Dennis Aldred and George Holt removed its front forks and bolted the unmodified superbike frame to a spaceframe chassis with aluminium cladding. The front suspension was by pushrods using a single damper. Weighing only 270kg (595lb), the top speed of the single-seater was over 145mph (233km/h). It had been intended to offer the Scorpion as a low-cost way into racing, with kits costing £4000, while there

were also plans for a road-going kit with cycle wings and a single headlamp. Sadly, the Scorpion lacked the dynamic stability to make it a feasible racing machine.

Tritan Aero 135
USA • 1984 • 1F2R • No built: 1

Tritan Ventures of Ann Arbor, Michigan, built this extraordinary machine designed by James Amick, an aeronautical engineer. The first prototype, called the Aero 135, was unusual in several respects. It was powered by a Tecumseh lawnmower engine kicking out only 14bhp but it could reach a top speed of 62mph thanks to very aerodynamic glassfibre bodywork (Cd 0.135) with huge rear fins, which also helped fuel consumption (75mpg). Access was via an opening canopy roof.

Tritan A2
USA • 1984-c1987 • 1F2R • No built: 10

When a vice-president of Domino's Pizza took a ride in the Tritan Aero 135, he asked for some to be made for use by the pizza chain. A revised  version was developed, called the A2 (or Aerocar 2). This initially featured a Savkal SP220 rotary engine (440cc/30bhp), reputedly designed for the Israeli military. This drove a rubber belt that turned the rear wheels, acting as a kind of CVT transmission. A later version had an aluminium fuel cell supplied by Voltek coupled with a 4.5kW electric motor, and was good for 55mph (89km/h). Two people could sit in tandem in the glassfibre monocoque (or indeed a pizza box and driver). The 'Amick Arch' at the rear of the car was designed to boost stability in high winds, while the headlights sat in the leading edges of the rear wings.

Tritan A4 Solitair
USA • 1992 • 1F2R • No built: n/a

Another James Amick three-wheeler was the wind-powered Windmobile, designed in 1973. The idea was reprised by his son, Douglas Amick, who developed the idea into the wind/electric hybrid A4 Solitair. Two DC motors powered the rear wheels, while the dramatic rear arch added forward thrust in crosswinds, and featured solar cells on its upper surface. A range of 140 miles at 55mph was claimed. The A4 made its debut at the Epcot Center at Walt Disney World.

Tri-Tech Zetta
GB • 1996-2002 • 2F1R • No built: Approx 17

Tri-Tech Autocraft of Bamber Bridge, Lancashire, specialised in bubble car restorations, so it was a short step for it to offer replicas of classic microcars. The first was the Zetta 300, a copy of the BMW-Isetta on a ladder chassis using Bedford Rascal van front suspension and Mini brakes, plus a bespoke rear swinging arm. A Honda Super Dream 250cc motorcycle engine was standard, or a Kawasaki 500cc optional, with six-speed sequential motorcycle transmission, or automatic. The 250cc version weighed 300kg and was capable of a scary 75mph (120km/h). The unstressed glassfibre bodywork was a pretty accurate replica of the original BMW-Isetta.

Tri-Tech Schmitt KR
GB • 1998-2002 • 2F1R • No built: Approx 31

The second replica from Tri-Tech was the Schmitt KR, a faithful replica of the Messerschmitt KR200. This used separate steel subframes front and rear, with either Honda 250cc or 400cc

motorcycle engines; the latter was claimed to do 0-62mph in 15 seconds and reach a top speed of 95mph (153km/h), helped by an all-up weight of only 270kg. Schmitts were sold either complete or in kit form.

Tritom

NL • 1987 • 2F1R • No built: Probably 1

Dutch trikes are rare beasts; the Tritom was one of the more accomplished. Created by Tom Harmsze (of Donkervoort sports car fame), it had aluminium bodywork over a spaceframe chassis that featured Formula Ford adjustable front suspension. Its engine was a turbocharged Honda CX650 unit with 100bhp. The glassfibre body measured 3350mm long and only 850mm tall (without the rollover bar in place) and the overall weight was a mere 352kg (776lb).

Triton

USA • 1985-date • 2F1R • No built: n/a

Tom Yankaitis of Rockford, Illinois, built his first prototype in 1985, with eight more machines being built four years later, in a design that was developed at race tracks and autocross events. Then in 2007, the Triton Trike was launched. Unusually it was based on the Saturn S, and although most examples were fitted with VW Golf engines, all sorts of power plants could be fitted, including electric and hybrid. In construction, it was a stressed

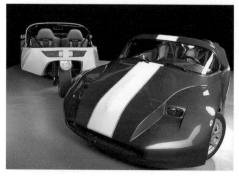

composite tub with a steel rollcage, and an unusual feature was the single-sided rear swinging arm, which could be fitted with electric ride height adjustment.

Tri-Vator

USA • Early 1980s • 1F2R • No built: n/a

If there was something off-the-wall about the Tri-Vator, perhaps it had to do with where it was built: Ruidoso, not far from 'UFO central', Roswell in New Mexico. The rodent-like bodywork consisted of a one-piece glassfibre shell mounted on a steel chassis, while two passengers could enter via a forward-tilting canopy that could be detached for open driving. A VW Beetle engine normally sat in the tail, with Porsche, Corvair, Buick and Mazda rotary options. The maker, Toby Industries, offered both kits and complete cars.

Triver

E • 1957-1963 • 2F1R • No built: n/a

The normal business of Construcciones Acoracadas of Bilbao, which built this all-Spanish bubble car, was the manufacture of heavy-duty strong boxes. This might explain why the Triver's sheet metal bodywork was fully 3mm thick. The car featured two doors, one either side, allowing access to 2+2 passengers. Measuring 2670mm (105in) long, the Triver weighed some 500kg (1100lb). Early cars had a

rear-mounted 339cc Fraso two-stroke two-cylinder engine but later on in the production cycle a Hispano-Villiers 14bhp engine was substituted, raising the top speed by 11mph to 48mph (77km/h).

TriVette
USA • 1974-1978 • 1F2R • No built: 24

The TriVette was developed by physicist Bob Keyes specifically in response to the 1973 Arab oil crisis: this was a fuel-efficient commuter vehicle. On to a tubular steel spaceframe, the narrow glassfibre bodywork had seating for one, with a second occasional seat behind. To get in, you would lift the gullwing door placed on one side; on the other side there was a convertible canopy. One strange feature was the positioning of the headlamps and indicators on the rear wings, because the narrow front end had hardly enough space to fit even the single front wheel.

The TriVette was almost unique among trikes in being based on the Fiat 850. Performance and fuel economy were good from the 517kg (1140lb) car. Road Test magazine tested a TriVette in 1976 and found that it actually outcornered the Corvette of the time. Ford Fiesta powerplants (and others) were tried, but if you really wanted extra performance, the Turbo TriVette had a 220bhp turbocharged engine, and could do 0-60mph in 3.5 seconds. The California Highway Patrol even got interested in the Turbo TriVette, funding a study to build a pursuit vehicle version capable of over 160mph. Built in Ventura, California on a custom-order basis, the TriVette ducked out of production in 1978 but an improved model, the Vigillante ⇨ debuted some 16 years later.

TriVette Two
USA • 2001-2006 • 1F2R • No built: n/a

In 2001, Bob Keyes launched the TriVette Two as a cheaper alternative to his Vigillante ⇨. Kits sold for $12,500 – less than a tenth the cost of a Vigillante. From the rear bulkhead forward, the TriVette Two was very similar to the Vigillante, featuring an aluminium tub structure, but behind was a bolt-on rear subframe carrying a Honda Civic powertrain (other engines could also fit). All the body panels were removable. Sadly the death of Keyes ended production in 2006.

Trivot
GB • 1989 • 2F1R • No built: 1

This Morganesque trike was intended for production, but only one was ever made.

Tri-Wing
CDN • 1992-date • 1F2R • No built: n/a

The Canadian company Tri-Wing Industries made a wide range of fairly conventional trike conversion kits for various motorbikes such as the Honda Goldwing and Yamaha Venture.

Trottolina
I • 1953 • 2F1R • No built: n/a

Very little is known about this bullet-shaped microcar prototype from 1953, which appears to have had some connection with the famous Italian coachbuilder Carrozzeria Castagna.

Tryckle
USA • 2008-date • 2F1R • No built: n/a

Atlas Boat Works of Cape Coral, Florida, offered the Tryckle in kit form at $9500. You had to supply your own donor bike (the prototype was based on a Yamaha FZR), and although the car could be powered by motorbike engines, it was really meant to be electric-powered. In the latter form, a top speed of 50mph (80km/h) was claimed, as well as a range of up to 50 miles (80km). The open bodywork was in glassfibre, and a VW torsion bar front end kept the nose off the ground. Overall weight was 394kg (1000lb).

Tryclops
USA • 2000s • 1F2R • No built: n/a

This was a bizarre – and unique – idea to mate the front end of a motorcycle with the front end of any front-wheel drive car out back, attached via a special adaptor kit. The company even contemplated a Cadillac Northstar engine conversion.

Trylon/Tryon
USA • 1989-c1999 • 1F2R • No built: Approx 300

It should come as little surprise that the Trylon was the brainchild of a Star Trek fanatic. Dale H Fox even called his Arlington, Illinois factory 'Starfleet Headquarters'. Central to the design was the 'clam-shell' canopy which lifted for entry to

the tandem two-seater cockpit. The dashboard featured computer displays and aircraft-style steering controls. Very narrow at the front and very wide at the rear, the Trylon was based on nothing more galactic than VW Beetle components, including the engine, gearbox, rear suspension and steering. A box-section steel chassis was encased in glassfibre bodywork, with two rear hatches allowing access to the engine and boot.

This was a large car by three-wheeler standards, measuring 4675mm (184in) long, but its weight was kept low (just 567kg or 1250lb), so performance was good, especially if the optional Mazda RX-7 Turbo engine was fitted. Two models were offered: the Shuttle and the Viper, the latter including "fender grilles, rear grilles, fin extensions, skirt details and front canard wings" – in other words, a body kit. Kits cost from $6000, with fully-built vehicles starting at $16,000. The model was relaunched in 1997 as the Tryon.

TSH Trikes
USA • c2008-c2012 • 1F2R • No built: n/a

This company made custom-built trikes, including the pictured Honda CRX converted to a three-wheeler in 2009.

Tula Zaika
RUS • 1960s • 2F1R • No built: 1

Tula, or TMZ (Tula Motorzikly Zavod), was a motorcycle brand that began life in 1955 and still exists at the time of writing. In the late 1960s, it made a prototype of a passenger three-wheeler called the Zaika, using a Tula scooter engine, with a top speed of 31mph (50km/h). While this didn't make series production, Tula was still offering a 1F2R commercial delivery trike called the Muravey ('ant') as of 2013.

Tuohe
CN • 1998-date • 1F2R • No built: n/a

The Shanghai-based Tuohe Enterprise Group produced, among other products, a range of very basic rickshaws with internal combustion or electric power, such as the THCL and THCY (pictured).

TvA
AUS • 2009-date • 2F1R • No built: n/a

Tilting Vehicle Australia was a company devoted to developing tilting vehicle technology, called FTC, and it built several three-wheeled prototypes to showcase it. One was called Simple Steer and another was created in partnership with AGIX of Brazil. TvA also built a tilting four-wheeler called the Gazelle.

TVS King
IND • 2008-date • 1F2R • No built: Hundreds of thousands

"Now the common man can travel like a king," said TVS Motor Company of its King rickshaw range. Available in LPG

and petrol versions, it was India's first 200cc two-stroke rickshaw with electric start. Some models had the luxury of double headlamps and some body designs were surprisingly modern. Licensed assembly also took place in Nigeria.

Twheel
CN • 2005-date • 1F2R • No built: n/a

Chongqing Twheel Motors made typical Chinese tuk-tuk rickshaws with petrol- and CNG-fuelled powerplants.

Twike
CH/D • 1995-date • 1F2R • No built: Approx 1000 (to 2013)

The Twike originated in 1986 as a Swiss-designed human-powered vehicle, but was developed for production with electric power supplementing two sets of pedals. An aluminium spaceframe chassis was enclosed with 'Luran' plastic bodywork. With a 5kW power pack, a top speed of 55mph (85km/h) was possible, with a range of up to 50 miles (80km). It was very lightweight at 250kg (550lb) including batteries. After some 200 had been made, a Mk2 version brought improvements to the rear suspension, weather seals, transmission and ventilation. In 1998 production also started in Germany, which became the sole manufacturing location after 2002 when FINE Mobile GmbH took over the rights from SwissLEM AG. At the time of writing, the price for a brand new Twike started at 17,800 euros (around £15,000).

Twike TW4XP
D • 2012-date • 1F2R • No built: n/a

Twike's TW4XP was built to participate in the Automotive X Prize, in which it achieved third place in its class out of 136 participants. Another pedal/electric hybrid with side-be-side seating for two, it could reach 81mph (130km/h) and do 0-60mph in under 12 seconds. Twike said it planned to produce a commercial model based on the TW4XP, but this had yet to materialise by 2013.

Twisted Trikes
USA • 2008-date • 2F1R • No built: 2 (to 2013)

This performance trike, made in Texas, mated what was essentially the front end of a racing car with a Honda 954 CBR rear end. The steel chassis was clothed in carbon/Kevlar bodywork that could seat just one person.

THREE WHEELERS A-Z

Volkswagen Scooter ▲

La Voiture Electronique ▲

Velorex ▲

▼ Volkswagen GX3

ULV

J • 2010-date • 2F1R • No built: n/a

ULV stood for Ultra Lightweight Vehicle, and this single-seater was certainly that, weighing just 72.5kg (160lb) and measuring only 2000mm long. It had motorbike wheels, a 400W electric motor and plastic construction, and boasted a range of 50 miles (80km) and a top speed of 25mph (40km/h). The ULV was developed at Waseda University and went on sale in Japan at the eyebrow-raising price of the equivalent of £30,000, but economies of scale were intended to push the price down to £7000 by 2015.

Unicar Duo Delta

USA • 1974 • 2F1R • No built: n/a

The first product of the Unicar Corp of Anaheim, California was the Duo Delta, designed by Walter Korff. An entire motorcycle rear end was mated to a two-seater glassfibre cabin that featured doors and a sunroof. The 750cc motorcycle engine drove the rear wheel via continuously variable automatic transmission up to a top speed of 98mph, and fuel consumption of 56mpg was claimed. You could buy a Duo Delta in kit form, fully-built, or make your own car from plans.

Unicar Unisport

USA • c1984-c1986 • 2F1R • No built: n/a

Unicar's second project had similarities to the Duo Delta in layout (a motorbike attached to a glassfibre front cabin), but differed in that it leant into corners and its seating layout was two in tandem. A steel tube chassis employed unusual suspension consisting of sliding pillars, while buttons on the

steering wheel allowed the trike to lean into corners. The Unisport was priced at $3000 and in 1985 the company claimed to be making 50 cars per month.

United

PK • 1999-date • 1F2R • No built: n/a

United Auto Industries of Lahore made basic 100cc and 200cc rickshaws, with CNG fuelling possible.

Universal Motor Moby Dick

I • 1960s • 1F2R • No built: n/a

The bizarre-looking Moby Dick was a car with a disproportionately long nose, small doors, bug-eye headlamps and no roof. It was built by an outfit called Universal Motor which was based in Rome, and was powered by an Aquila 175cc motorcycle engine mounted up front.

Urbee

CDN • 2011-date • 2F1R • No built: n/a

Jim Kor's Urbee was the world's first 3D-printed three-wheeler. ABS plastic and Fused Deposition Modeling (FDM) was used to 'print' the bodywork (a process that took 2,500 hours) and the result was said to be stronger than steel. It also had the

distinction of being a hybrid, using a 10bhp diesel engine mated to a 36V electric motor, mounted in a steel chassis. A coefficient of drag of 0.15 and weight of only 544kg (1200lb) enabled a top speed of 68mph for the two-seater. The first prototype was completed in 2013, by which time 14 orders had been secured at $50,000 each.

US Trikes
USA • 2000s-date • 1F2R • No built: n/a

This firm offered various chopper trike models towards the 'heavy metal' end of the spectrum, with names like Reaper, Rebel, Rogue and Pioneer.

V8 Choppers
USA • 2000s-date • 1F2R • No built: n/a

This company, based in Miami, Oklahoma, offered various trike styles (Sport, Hot Rod and Touring). All used V8 engines varying in size from 350ci (5735cc) to 427ci (6997cc).

Vanderhall
USA • 2012-date • 1F2R • No built: n/a

Vanderhall Motor Works was based in Utah. An open-topped single-seater prototype was seen testing in 2012, while a second design featuring a fixed roof (pic above right) was revealed in 2013, alongside a two-seater roadster (above left). Power came from a 1.4-litre turbocharged engine with 200bhp, good for 0-60mph in 4.5 seconds.

Vectrix VX-3
USA/PL • 2007-date • 2F1R • No built: Probably 1

This company specialised in making electric scooters. Although headquartered in America, its vehicles were assembled in Wrocław, Poland. At the 2007 Milan Moto Show, Vectrix presented a concept trike based on its electric two-wheeler, with a top speed of 62mph and a 68-mile range. The VX-3 finally went on sale in 2013 at the elevated price of around £12,500.

Veeco RT
P • 2012-date • 2F1R • No built: n/a

Hailing from Portugal, the Veeco RT was a rare attempt to make an electric-powered sports trike. The electric motor delivered 108bhp and almost 450Nm of torque, enabling claims of 0-100km/h in 8 seconds and a top speed electronically limited to 100mph (160km/h). The Veeco's other main claim to fame was its range: up to 400km (250 miles) with a battery pack of 48kWh, well above average for an electric car.

VEI Pingo 50
I • 1995-1996 • 2F1R • No built: n/a

This tiny car revived the spirit of the Norsjö Shopper ⇨, mating a scooter to a two-wheeled front end and offering a basic weather canopy. It weighed 174kg and measured only 1050mm wide, so the Morini 49cc engine proved sufficient.

Vélam Ecrin
F • 1957 • 2F1R • No built: Approx 50

Production of Iso's Isetta bubble car was licensed to many countries outside Italy, including Vélam in France from 1955. The Vélam's shape differed in several ways from the Italian Isetta, but it kept the close-set rear wheels and rear-mounted Iso 236cc single-cylinder 10bhp engine. While most Vélams were four-wheelers, the final luxury version of 1957 (called the Ecrin) had only three wheels and improved suspension, as well as redesigned bodywork.

Véléance Tri'Ode
F • 2009-date • 2F1R • No built: n/a

This was a single-seater electric tilting trike, with a rear area designed to carry luggage. The patented tilting control system kept the vehicle upright when stopped, but allowed it to lean into corners at speed. It had double wishbones at the front but a very narrow track of only 800mm. The Tri'Ode maxed out at 28mph (45km/h), and its lead-acid batteries gave it a range of 31 miles (50km). First seen in 2009, it finally hit the market in 2011. A four-wheeled version called the Quat'Ode was also presented.

Velorex Oskar
CZ • 1943-1950 • 2F1R • No built: Approx 12

In Czechoslovakia, the Velorex became not only one of the longest-surviving trikes of all, but a real people's car. It lasted from 1943 right up until 1971. The first prototype appeared as early as 1943 from the Stránský brothers, who owned a bicycle repair shop in Česká Třebová – hence the first car

made widespread use of bicycle parts. A batch of cars was built in 1945 with leather cloth bodywork over a steel tube spaceframe, rather like a canoe in construction. These early cars were powered by motorcycle engines such as 150cc CZ, 300cc PAL or 250cc Jawa. Very cheap prices attracted around 12 buyers to these early cars.

Velorex
CZ • 1950-1971 • 2F1R • No built: Approx 15,300

In 1950, the Czech government became involved with the Stránskýs via the Velo co-operative – this outfit was later to be renamed Velorex, although in the early 1950s, the design was generally known as the Oskar. The Stránský brothers' design matured gradually, but the basics remained fundamentally unchanged as the years progressed. The 'classic' Velorex of the 1950s had motorcycle wheels and a 175cc ČZ engine driving the single rear wheel. The canvas panels stretched and fastened over the steel frame, which made life very draughty for the occupants; this could become even more so

if the stud fixings for the panels were unclasped. The bodywork changed to polyurethane in time, while a De Luxe version with all-steel panels was offered for those with misgivings about canvas bodywork.

In 1960, the Velorex was renamed 16/250 and a larger engine was introduced in 1963 with the 16/350 (a two-cylinder 350cc Jawa), which saw the end of the line for the 250cc model. The 16/350 weighed 310kg (682lb) and was capable of 53mph (85km/h). Velorex switched to making four-wheeled cars in 1971, but the plug was pulled on this by 1973. Of the 15,300 or so cars made, around 800 had 175cc engines, 2500 had 250cc and the remainder 350cc. There was a plan to revive the Velorex in India the mid-1980s, but this never materialised. Velorex still existed at the time of writing, making motorcycle sidecars.

Velor-x-trike
CZ • 2009-date • 2F1R • No built: n/a

An enthusiastic owner of an original Velorex called Pavel Brida had the idea to create a modern version called the Velor-x-trike. With help from Motoscoot and Kemling Design, he built an enclosed two-seater trike with scissor doors. Unlike the economy-orientated original Velorex, the new one was all about performance, and it had a Honda 1300cc motorcycle engine driving the rear wheel by chain. In a car measuring 3800mm long and weighing about 500kg, that gave a top speed of over 125mph (200km/h). The prototype was presented at the Motosalon in Brno in March 2010. Brida announced plans to make up to 60 replicas with prices starting from 19,900 euros. Various versions were suggested, up to and including an R (Racing) model with over 200bhp and a weight of 400kg, as well an electric version.

Veloss
CDN • 2007-date • 2F1R • No built: n/a

The Veloss was essentially very similar in appearance and in concept to the Campagna T-Rex ⇨, and it was also made in Canada. As a mechanical basis, you could choose any one of 12 different motorbikes, from Suzuki Hayabusa to Kawasaki ZX12R, and the single rear wheel was suspended by a mono-damper swinging arm. In 2012, a new Veloss CX1 version was added with an enclosed cabin and gullwing doors.

Vernon
GB • 1952-1958 • 1F2R • No built: Approx 1500

Vernon Industries of Bidston, Cheshire, was better known to millions as the operator of the football pools in Britain. Vernon had made the Invacar ⇨ under licence from 1950-1952, but then developed its own vehicle for the disabled. Often called the Vi-Car, it was actually officially called the Vernon Invalid Car. Power came from a 197cc Villiers single-cylinder engine mounted on the offside of the vehicle, driving only one of the rear wheels by chain. Aluminium body panels were attached to a wooden frame, but this soon changed to all-metal with the Mk2. A Mk3 version in 1957 gained the Villiers 9E engine and Dynastart. A 'civilian' version of this crude and uncomfortable car was also developed as the Gordon ⇨.

Vertika Cruiser
CDN • 2008-date • 2F1R • No built: n/a

Vertika Trykes was a division of a Canadian company called Prestige Auto Works, whose main business was modifying other people's trikes, such as the Lehman ⇨ and BRP Can-Am ⇨, but it also made a couple of trikes of its own design. The Cruiser was based on the Honda Goldwing motorbike but had two front wheels sited 66in (1676mm) apart. A kit to convert the Goldwing cost $26,500 in 2008.

Vertika Roadster
CDN • 2008-date • 2F1R • No built: n/a

The Roadster kit converted a Honda VTX 1300cc motorbike

into a three-wheeler with a car-like front end, whose 'bonnet' lifted up to reveal its unique selling point: a huge boot. Kits cost from $23,920.

VH

E • 1961 • 2F1R • No built: 1

Bravely, Pedro Vargas Hernandez decided to build his own engine from scratch for the VH microcar: a 400cc two-cylinder two-stroke unit mounted in the tail driving the single rear wheel. A production run did not follow, however.

Viberti Vi-Vi

I • 1950s • 1F2R • No built: n/a

The Italian bus maker Viberti teamed up with German motorcycle manufacturer Victoria to build the Vi-Vi moped from 1955, which was also offered in three-wheeled form.

Vigilante / Vigillante

USA • 1994-2006 • 1F2R • No built: n/a

Following the Fiat 850-based TriVette ⇨ of the 1970s, Bob Keyes modified the project to become the Vigillante – deriving its name from a 1978 police pursuit vehicle that Keyes made for the California Highway Patrol, based on the TriVette.

Vigilante... the Ultimate Street Machine!

Having lain dormant for 16 years, the project was dusted off and turned into an exotic sports car. Indeed, the Vigillante Corporation of Binghamton, New York claimed it to be no less than "the quickest street legal exotic in the world" with a top speed of over 215mph,

0-60mph in less than 3 seconds and lateral cornering force of 1g. How come? It weighed under 680kg (1500lb), the powerplant was a Chevrolet V8 that was tunable up to 700bhp, and improved aerodynamics from the much longer bodyshell also played their part – and this was an imposing car indeed, at 204in (5182mm) long.

In construction, the 'Vig' was an aluminium/composite honeycomb tub combined with tubular steel subframes front and rear, while the bodywork was a mix of glassfibre, Kevlar and carbon-fibre, with a lift-up canopy for entry which could be removed for open-topped motoring. Prices in the mid-1990s started at $125,000.

Vikram

IND • 1977-1988/1992-date • 1F2R • No built: Many thousands

Scooters India Ltd was formed in 1972 near Lucknow, Uttar Pradesh when it bought the rights to the Lambretta scooter from Innocenti. In 1977 it started making three-wheeled Lambretta-based rickshaws and cars under the Vikram name.

It abandoned three-wheelers in 1988, only to restart in 1992, finally concentrating solely on trikes from 1997. Although mostly petrol or diesel powered, Vikrams were also offered with electric motors from 1998. At the time of writing, the range consisted of the Vikram 450D (395cc diesel), 410G and 600G (both 198cc petrol), 750D (510cc diesel) and EV (electric-powered). A wide variety of rickshaw bodywork and seating configurations was offered.

Vimp

GB • 1954 • 2F1R • No built: 1

Tom Karen – who would later design the Bond Bug ⇨ and Reliant Robin ⇨ with Ogle Design – was behind the Vimp, along with Andrew Waddicor. There was just space for two people in the tiny bodywork, with entry gained by folding the windscreen forwards. A 197cc Villiers engine nestled just ahead of the single rear wheel. A planned production run came to nothing.

Vincent

GB • 1954-1955 • 2F1R • No built: n/a

Phil Vincent's motorcycle company has long been a legendary brand among two-wheeler fanatics, but three-wheeled Vincents were also made from 1932 when the Bantam delivery tricycle arrived. Then in 1954, as motorcycle sales began to look shaky, Vincent built a new three-wheeler. Power initially came from a rear-mounted Vincent Rapide 998cc V-twin engine, together with motorcycle transmission, chain drive and monodamper rear suspension.

Over a tubular steel chassis, the elegant open two-seater bodywork was made of aluminium, the rear end of which was hinged to allow access to the rear wheel and engine. A distinctive nose opening channelled cooling air to the engine, with extra vents at the side helping too.

In 1955 the Rapide engine was replaced by a Vincent Black Lightning unit, in which form the prototype reached a remarkable 117mph. Indeed, several prototypes were built and a price of £500 was announced in 1955 – but that was too pricey for the time, especially as the Vincent had no weather gear, electric starter or reverse gear. No customer cars were built, and Vincent went bust in 1956.

Vintage Reproductions Gamma

USA • 1980-c1988 • 2F1R • No built: n/a

The main business of Florida-based Vintage Reproductions was making replicas of turn-of-the-century horseless carriages, but the Gamma Roadster was an interesting aside. It used a complete motorcycle rear end (Honda 750 or 1000), ensconced under a lift-up tail section. The chassis was in steel tubes and the bodywork glassfibre, and standard was a roof and sidescreens. The VW Beetle donated its steering, brakes and front suspension.

VIPO

E • 1980s • 2F1R • No built: 28

The VIPO microcar was made in Coruña, Galicia by Cortiplas. The standard bodywork was enclosed, made of glassfibre and

weighed 360kg, but other body styles were essayed. Either 50cc or 125cc engines could be fitted, with a top speed of up to 35mph (56km/h) possible. Of the 28 units built, most were exported to Uruguay.

Vitrex Riboud

F • 1974-1980 • 1F2R • No built: Approx 3000

Vitrex Industries of Paris was a prolific developer of microcars. It began its activities with the Riboud, a very basic runabout designed by architect Jacques Riboud. It was built by a French buggy manufacturer, Marland (indeed the earliest cars were sold as the MR1, or Marland-Riboud 1). The Riboud used a 47cc 2.4bhp Sachs engine in a rather plain two-seater open body. It was offered in both three- and four-wheeled forms, the former slotting in as the cheapest car on sale in France (at 6430F in 1979).

Vitrex Addax

F • 1974-1980 • 1F2R • No built: n/a

The Addax was actually developed and built by SECAM of Chambly but absorbed by Vitrex. This was was even more Spartan than the Riboud. The two-seater used either a 47cc or 50cc engine with automatic or three-speed manual gearboxes

respectively. There were also Bord de Mer and 4.5bhp Sport versions, as well as a four-wheeled model called the Gildax. Even by the standards of rural old age pensioners, the Addax was simply too crude to last.

VMAG
BR • 2008-date • 1F2R • No built: n/a

VMAG Vehicles was set up in Rio Grande do Sul in Brazil to produce electric two- and three-wheelers. As well as a 600W V-Trike (pictured above right), a four-door saloon was offered (pic below right) whose design apparently originated in China.

Voiture Electronique
F • 1968-1976 • 1F2R • No built: Approx 170

'La Voiture Electronique' is a simple name, but this French machine, conceived by the Jarrett brothers, was one of the simplest cars ever built. It was little more than a 66in (1680mm) long plastic triangle with built-in seats, between which sat a single joystick. This controlled acceleration, braking and steering, so the car could be driven from either seat. Two electric motors drove the rear wheels. The car weighed only 200kg (440lb), could reach a top speed of 15mph (25km/h) and could travel to 40 miles (60km).

A 1972 'leisure' model called the Porquerolles had such luxuries as bumpers, indicators and wing mirrors, while a Cab version boasted a hardtop. A licensed version of the Voiture Electronique was also made in Spain by Montesa.

Volante
USA • 1983-date • 1F2R • No built: n/a

Fighter pilot Colonel KP Rice designed the Volante flying car as a three-wheeler whose wings could be carried behind on a trailer. He hoped to put it into production in kit form but by the time of writing this had not happened.

Volkswagen Scooter
D • 1986 • 2F1R • No built: 1

Even Volkswagen dabbled in three-wheelers. The Scooter of 1986 was really nothing more than a design exercise for VW's junior designers, but the result was credible. Up front sat a VW Polo engine which, in this light frame, enabled a top speed of 125mph. Gullwing doors gave access to a very car-like interior with space for two people sitting side-by-side.

Volkswagen GX3
D • 2006 • 2F1R • No built: n/a

When Volkswagen unveiled its GX3 concept car at the 2006 Los Angeles Auto Show, most people saw it as another flight of fancy, but the GX3 came surprisingly close to production as a regular VW model. It was designed by Volkswagen's California design office, and VW described it as a "crossover between sports car and motorcycle". The spaceframe chassis (developed with help from Lotus) was clothed in open, screenless glassfibre bodywork that seated two people in a minimalistic cabin. A 1.6-litre engine from the Lupo GTI powered it, and since weight was just 570kg, the GX3 could do 0-60mph in 5.7 seconds and reach 125mph (200km/h). VW fuelled speculation by suggestion a production future for the car depended on public reaction, and it even quoted a projected retail price of $17,000. Tragically, qualms about potential litigation in America put the kibosh on plans to produce the GX3 in series.

Vortex VX1
CDN • 1988 • 1F2R • No built: n/a

This was a two-passenger vehicle powered by a 650cc Honda motorbike engine, which could lean into corners. A second model, the VX2000, was to have active hydraulic lean control, but this apparently did not materialise.

Voyager
USA • 2008-date • 1F2R • No built: n/a

The Voyager trike conversion was made by Motorcycle Tour Conversion Inc to suit most tourer and cruiser bikes. The conversion could be removed in around 10 minutes, and put back on in 15 minutes.

Vulture
USA • 2000s • 2F1R • No built: n/a

The ultra-swoopy 1930s-style Vulture was designed by Ron Russell, who offered plans sets to build replicas. The prototype used a VW Beetle engine and VW Golf suspension, but Russell envisaged that all sorts of powerplants – electric, motorcycle or other car engines – could be fitted by builders.

THREE WHEELERS
A-Z

W W W
X X X
Y Y Y
Z Z Z

Wanhoo WH150ZK ▲

Yakey Salamandra Scorpion ▲

XK-1 ▲

▼ ZAP Xebra

Wildfire WF650 ▼

Waggonbau Bautzen
DDR • 1950s • 2F1R • No built: n/a

Waggonbau Bautzen was an East German railway carriage builder which turned its hand to making a microcar in the late 1950s. A 350cc Jawa engine was used, mounted in the rear, but a planned production run never took place. Bautzen continued to make caravans into the 1980s.

Wanhoo
CN • 2000s-date • 1F2R • No built: n/a

Based in Chongqing, Wanhoo (sometimes spelt Wanhu) offered two enclosed passenger three-wheelers: the WH110ZK with a 110cc engine (pictured above) and the slightly larger WH150ZK with a 150cc unit. There was also an Indian-style rickshaw model called the WH175ZK.

Wanlong CY150ZK
CN • 1995-date • 1F2R • No built: n/a

Shandong Shouguang Wanlong built this odd little egg-shaped three-seater only 2550mm long, powered by a 149cc front-mounted engine. Its top speed was a mere 31mph (50km/h).

Wasp
AUS • 1983-1984 • 2F1R • No built: n/a

Produced by Autocycle Engineering, the Wasp was first displayed at the Sydney Motor Show. It was a glassfibre-bodied targa-roofed coupe that combined

a car front end and steering system with a motorcycle rear end. Various drivetrains were offered up to 150bhp, but the Wasp was simply too expensive to make much of a mark.

Waterman Aerobile
USA • 1947-1957 • 1F2R • No built: 1

Waldo Waterman worked in the aeronautical industry for many years before conceiving his own flying car, the Arrowbile, in 1935. This was a road-going three-wheeler with wings that could be attached to fly, and can be claimed to be the world's first true flying car, taking to the air in 1937. Studebaker became involved and five prototypes were built, with an intended on-sale price of $3000. Production never started, but work on a developed version called the Aerobile began in 1947, using a Tucker six-cylinder engine. However, by the time it was completed in 1957, the fad for flying cars had long since passed.

Wayfarer
USA • 1975 • 2F1R • No built: n/a

Bob Way built the Wayfarer as a car that could be marketed for less than $1000. Boasting fewer than 90 parts in all, its bodywork was in Dacron over plywood frames, bolted to a steel frame. A 293cc single-cylinder engine fed its power through an automatic gearbox, for a top speed of 70mph. Sadly he found nobody interested in productionising it.

Westcoaster Super 36
USA • 1960s-1970s • 1F2R • No built: n/a

Westcoast Machinery of Stockton, California produced this electric golf cart-style three-wheeler. It was a glassfibre two-seater with a removable roof but no doors, and was powered by a General Electric 36V electric motor driving the rear wheels.

Wildcat

GB • 2000s-date • 1F2R • No built: n/a

The Wildcat was made by Chris Spalding Engineering of Grantham, Lincolnshire, and was unusual in using the running gear of a Rover 114 automatic, including its Hydragas rear suspension. Glassfibre bodywork was mounted on a steel chassis, and the whole thing weighed 440kg; prices started at £9100 fully built in 2013.

Wildfire WF650-C

CN/USA • 2008-2012 • 1F2R • No built: n/a

Like the ZAP Xebra ⇨, the Wildfire was a three-wheeled vehicle made in China and sold in the USA with its own branding. Wildfire Motors of Steubenville, Ohio marketed the WF650-C three-wheeled hatchback saloon (a WF650-T truck version was also offered). Power came from a 26bhp Hi-Po 650cc water-cooled four-stroke two-cylinder engine, claimed to average 60mpg and cruise at 65mph. The WF650 range was manufactured in China by Taixing Sandi (see under Sandi) and sold at the very cheap price of $7064. However, a

range of technical issues beleaguered the cars, forcing them to be recalled for fixes and ultimately withdrawn from sale. The follow-up model was the somewhat similar Snyder ⇨.

Wildfire WF250-C

PK/USA • 2007-2012 • 1F2R • No built: n/a

While the WF650 was made in China, the smaller WF250 was manufactured by the Ammar Motor Company ⇨ in Karachi, Pakistan for the US market. The WF250-C was a hatchback, and the WF250-T a flatbed truck. Both were powered by a 17bhp Hi-Po 248cc water-cooled engine, so performance was meagre: a top speed of 50mph but an average of 72mpg. The $5495 asking price was very low but there was no escaping the crudity of the car.

Winn

GB • 1966 • 1F2R • No built: n/a

A designer called Russell Winn was behind this tiny British electric car dating from 1966. It was an enclosed single-seater which was constructed by Telearchics Ltd of Lechdale, Gloucestershire.

Witkar

NL • 1972-1974 • 2F1R • No built: 35

The Witkar ('white car') followed on from the 'white bicycles' experiment in Amsterdam, where white-painted bikes were freely available to use as transport. Founder Luud Schimmelpenninck's electrically-powered Witkar was a little less anarchic: individuals joined a system and were provided with a magnetic key to operate a Witkar at one of several electric charging stations. The car itself was a curiously-styled telephone-kiosk shaped two-seater with a transparent passenger cell and a single rear wheel. A company called Cock ⇨, based in Assen (which built the Little Tyrant three-wheeled truck from 1958 until 1974) constructed the first 10 Witkars, with the remaining 25 being built by Spijkstaal ⇨. Although production ended in 1974, the Witkarplan system was still in operation as late as 1986.

WK
D • 1996-date • 1F2R • No built: n/a

From Aubstadt in Bavaria, WK Trikes offered a range of VW-powered classic-style trikes, including the Chopper, Family, Highway and Rebell. In 2007 came a much more original machine, the Strike, whose main claim to fame was that it had (or so said the makers) the biggest boot of any production trike. It used VW Golf parts, including engines of 1.6 litres (102bhp) or 2.0 litres (150-270bhp) and the novel option of diesel power. Either automatic transmission or VW's DSG automated manual were offered.

WMC Bond Bug
GB • 1990-1995 • 1F2R • No built: Approx 4 three-wheelers

Mike Webster and his brother Gary came across some original Bond Bug ⇨ moulds and, under the banner of the Webster Motor Company, relaunched the car as the WMC Bug. The Websters turned the Bug into a four-wheeler, but some potential customers preferred the idea of three wheels, so WMC also resurrected the three-wheeled model, the revival actually being sold as the 'Bond Bug'. WMC's ladder chassis was designed to accept Reliant Robin/Rialto parts, so either the 748cc or later 850cc engine could be used, and a top speed of 100mph was claimed with the larger engine.

Newly designed five-link rear suspension incorporated a Panhard rod, and there was a choice of 10in, 12in or 13in wheels in place of the original Bond's 10-inchers. Many parts were reproduced to mimic the original Bond, including the black graphic package, or you could modernise your Bug with things like circular dials and folding glassfibre side screens which hinged like doors, so that you could get in without having to lift the canopy every time. A curious 'Sport' option was basically a Bug with a cut-down canopy and aero screens for pure summer use. WMC's new Bug sold in kit form for around the £2000 mark.

World Champion
RC • 2005-date • 1F2R • No built: n/a

World Champion International mostly made trailers but also dabbled in three-wheelers. Its enclosed three-seater was offered in electric form (HLDZK03) or with a 125cc engine (HG125ZK).

Xingyue
CN • c2007-date • 1F2R • No built: n/a

This Honda Stream ⇨ inspired scooter trike was a tilter: the rear section (wheels, engine and transmission) remained upright in corners, while the front half tilted like a scooter. Although a fully open model was listed, full weather protection was more common. A four-stroke 150cc engine with 7.5bhp powered the 160kg trike to about 50mph (80km/h). The Xingyue obtained significant popularity in many export markets including the UK, where it was sold as the Zing Vogue. Other export names included Automoto, MotoMojo, Orbitor, Manhattan, Palmo and Tri-Fecta.

Xin Ya
CN • 2000s-date • 1F2R • No built: n/a

Langfang Xin Ya was a company based in Langfang in Hebei province, making motorbikes and rickshaw-style trikes of very basic construction. All its models were prefixed by the XYZ designation, and some bore the cryptic description 'Climbing King'. Xin Ya made both petrol-powered and electric models.

XK-1

USA • 1981-c1983 • 1F2R • No built: n/a

Following in the footsteps of the Trimuter from Quincy-Lynn ⇨, the XK-1 from Western Front of Texas was co-developed with Quincy-Lynn. It had elements of Bond Bug about it, with eye-like headlamps and a swing-up canopy allowing access to the two seats, although the rear end tapered in a coupe style. The windscreen came from the Honda Civic, the steering column from the Toyota Celica and the rear suspension from a Datsun. The engine choice ranged from a 16bhp Briggs & Stratton industrial motor up to a VW Beetle, mounted in the rear and driving through a Salisbury torque converter. You could buy a chassis from either Western Front or Quincy-Lynn, or build your own to a set of plans. A complete kit, including the glassfibre body, came in at $1695. The subsequent Morton ⇨ was apparently a modified version of the XK-1.

THE FUTURE IS NOW WITH THE **XK-1**
The Practical Three Wheeler

Xotic X1F Endeavor

USA • 1986 • 1F2R • No built: 1

Lionheart Creations, a company better associated with aircraft, built what it called "the ultimate three-wheel high performance sports car." It was intended to be powered by

either electric power or a jet turbine engine (!) but it ended up with an air-cooled Porsche unit. The ladder-chassised prototype was disassembled to make glassfibre moulds for replicas, but no further cars were ever made.

Xzilarator

USA • 2006-date • 2F1R • No built: n/a

The Xzilarator was designed by Bob Kinney and used a 1500cc Honda Goldwing motorbike as a donor, so it had the benefit of a standard reverse gear. The skeletal frame had a skimpy body 'skin' as a later addition. The two-seater weighed 556kg (1225lb), so performance was good (130mph/210km/h top speed). Offered as a complete build-it-yourself machine, Kinney sold plans sets at $89 each.

Yakey Salamandra Tri0

PA/CO • 2010-date • 2F1R • No built: n/a

Yakey Corp was a firm set up in Panama in 2007 which decided to launch a design competition for a new vehicle. The winner was an Argentinean 25-year-old called Ariel Marioni, whose design Yakey put into production in neighbouring Colombia in 2010. The Salamandra Tri0 was a 2F1R trike, powered by a 20kW electric motor with a top speed of up to 75mph (120km/h), or a 1200cc petrol unit. One version had Audi R8-style side body accents, while a Sport variant had more conventional bodywork with a glassed-in rear end, and could be powered by a 225cc single-cylinder engine with 15bhp or an 870cc diesel.

Yakey Salamandra Scorpion

PA/CO • 2011-date • 2F1R • No built: n/a

This sportier-looking model from the Panamanian/Colombian Yakey organisation was longer than the Tri0 (at 3250mm) but also lighter (weighing 220kg). Like the Tri0, it could be powered by a 225cc single-cylinder engine but a hybrid version was also developed, as was a fully electric model. An additional Yakey model, the Ultra Salamander, was in preparation at the time of writing, but this was set to be a four-wheeler with two narrow-set rear wheels.

Yamaha Powerhorse 302

J • 2005 • 1F2R • No built: n/a

The organisers of the 2005 Tokyo World Expo forbade taxis to be used between pavillions, so Yamaha inventively created this swoopily modern take on the rickshaw to do the job. It had pedals but also a hybrid electric assist system. The cabin made of use of flax fibres.

Yamaha EC-Miu

J • 2011 • 1F2R • No built: n/a

Yamaha's EC-Miu 'Electric Concept' trike, presented at the 2011 Tokyo Motor Show, was designed specifically for women. Powered by electricity, it had the novelty of wifi capability.

Yamasaki

CN/J • 2011-date • 1F2R • No built: n/a

Changzhou Yamasaki was a joint Japanese/Chinese enterprise making motorbikes and tricycles. The most basic was the

YM50QZK with a 50cc engine (also made with electric power as the YM602), while three-seater open rickshaws with engines of 110cc, 125cc and 150cc were also offered.

Yatri

IND • 2012-date • 1F2R • No built: n/a

The Yatri e-rickshaw was very basic transport powered by four 12V batteries, feeding a 650W electric motor.

Yaxi Prince

CN • 2011-date • 2F1R • No built: n/a

The Wuxi Yaxi Electric Vehicle Co, based in Wuxi in Jiangsu Province, was responsible for one of the oddest-looking three-wheelers from China, which is certainly saying something. Yaxi started making a distinctively

styled four-wheeler called the Princess in 2010, and the following year launched a three-wheeled version badged Prince. Power came from a 4kW electric motor fed by 48V batteries, giving it a range of

75 miles (120km) and a top speed of 28mph (45km/h). In its narrow bodywork, two people could sit in tandem. Prices started at the equivalent of £600.

YDS WCV S-01

J • 2010-date • 1F2R • No built: n/a

The WCV (Wheel Chair Vehicle) lived up to its name: you simply rode your wheelchair on to an aluminium platform. An in-wheel electric motor at the front provided motive power, with a range of 50km (31 miles) and a top speed of 30km/h (19mph). The price in 2013 was 700,000 yen (around £4700).

Yingang YG250ZK

CN • 2000s-date • 1F2R • No built: n/a

This faintly original-looking open-topped four-door vehicle, made by Chongqing Yinang Sci & Tech, used a 250cc engine to power the 398kg three-wheeler to a top speed of 34mph (55km/h).

Yogomo MA3

CN • 2009-date • 1F2R • No built: n/a

The Hebei Yogomo Motorcycle Co was set up in 2009 specifically to mass-produce three-wheelers with "car-class performance with motorbike price." Yogomo's specialisation was electric trikes, and by 2012, had taken international orders for 6300 of them; but it also made petrol-powered models. The Yogomo resembled a Peugeot 107 with just one front wheel. Unusually, it was made of steel, not glassfibre, and its five-door four-seater body measured a generous 3045mm long. The MA3G model's tiny rear-mounted engine (either Lifan 200cc or Longxin 250cc) could just about muster a top speed of 37mph (60km/h). The MA3E electric version used a 4kW motor and ran out of juice at 31mph (50km/h).

Yongkang Olympu
CN • 2001-date • 1F2R • No built: n/a

The four-door saloon made by this company could be bought in electric- or petrol-powered forms. The former came with a 5kW 48V motor and topped out at 45km/h (28mph); the latter had a 150cc water-cooled unit and could reach 60km/h (37mph). Both models were relative featherweights, coming in at less than 400kg.

Yuejin YJ110ZK
CN • 2000s-date • 1F2R • No built: n/a

Jiangsu Yuejin Motoycle Manufacturing made a typical low-cost, low-quality open rickshaw powered by a 110cc engine, which could also be used by the disabled.

Yue Loong Rickshaw
RC • 1970s-1990s • 1F2R • No built: n/a

Yue Loong (or YLN) is best known for making Nissans under licence in Taiwan, but it also made rickshaws of the typical type, with the driver sitting on a motorcycle saddle and passengers seated under basic weather protection behind.

Zanella Zity
AR/CN • 2011-date • 1F2R • No built: n/a

The Argentinean company of Zanella, based in Caseros near Buenos Aires, produced motorcycles, as well as the Z-Carga three-wheeled cargo truck from the 1970s. In 2011, it announced that it would be making the Zity passenger car: essentially a licence-built version of the Chinese Yogomo ➪, a five-door glassfibre-bodied hatchback powered by a 200cc single-cylinder engine of 15bhp.

ZAP Xebra
USA/CN • 2006-2009 • 1F2R • No built: A few hundred

ZAP (Zero Air Pollution) was founded in 1994 in California with the intention of making a big impact on the electric vehicle market – and indeed it claimed it had succeeded in a spectacular way. It said it was one of the world's most prolific electric vehicle suppliers, delivering over 117,000 electric vehicles from 1994 onwards, including scooters, trucks, vans and three-wheelers. There was plenty of controversy about the firm but it did market one of the best-known electric cars in America: the ZAP Xebra. Launched in May 2006 in the USA, it was actually made by the Shandong

Jindalu Vehicle Company in China (see Fulu ➪) and was probably the first Chinese car sold in the USA in numbers.

The Xebra was offered in four-door saloon form as the SD and as a pick-up (PK); there was also an SD Xero model with roof-mounted solar panelling. The Xebra was powered by a rear-mounted 5kW (6.7bhp) DC motor fed by six 12V lead-acid batteries and had a 110V charger on board (optionally 240V). Its top speed was 40mph (64km/h), with a range of about 25 miles (40 km), or 40 miles (64km) with optional extended-range batteries – although owners reported its speed and range didn't match these claims. With a length of 2900mm, the Xebra weighed 815kg and could carry four people. It was priced low at $11,200 but problems with reliability, poor-quality glassfibre bodywork and waterproofing issues forced the Xebra to be withdrawn in 2009 with only a few hundred sold.

ZAP Alias
USA/CN • 2008-date • 2F1R • No built: n/a

ZAP's second three-wheeled passenger car was a complete departure from the unromantic Xebra: the Alias was an out-and-out performance trike. For this project, it partnered up with Jonway (a car and motorbike maker based in Zhejiang, China) and hired Lotus Engineering to help develop it. A fairly sophisticated specification included rack-and-pinion power steering, a composite structure incorporating a steel roll cage and solar panels.

The main power, however, came from two electric motors, one mounted on each of the front wheels and powered by lithium batteries. The initial prototype had combnined peak power of 322bhp (240kW) and was claimed to go 156mph (251km/h) and do 0-60mph in 5.7 seconds. The revised 'production' specification brought those figures down to 85mph (140km/h) and 7.8 seconds, but the claimed range on each charge of up to 100 miles (160km) remained the same.

The Alias was one of eight designs to make the 2010 finals of the Automotive X-Prize competition, driven by Al Unser Jr. However, as of 2013, production had yet to begin at a projected price of $38,500.

Zeal
IND • 1995-date • 1F2R • No built: n/a

Zeal rickshaws were made by the Mithani Group of Mumbai, and offered with petrol, CNG and LPG engines.

Zedis
I/D/GB • 1998 • 1F2R • No built: 1

Zedis stood for Zero Emission Downsized Improved Safety Urban Vehicle, and was a tilting electric vehicle project developed by a collaborative partnership across three countries (Italy, Britain and Germany), involving Piaggio, Fiat, Hydro Raufoss, Breed, the University of Bath and the Technical University of Berlin. The single-seater was a research prototype only, despite talk of production possibilities within three years of the completion of the project.

Zero Move Zero Q
J • 2012-date • 1F2R • No built: n/a

The Zero Q was an egg-like enclosed tandem-two-seater scooter-trike. It measured only 2000mm long and 900mm wide and weighed 130kg. A 500W DC electric motor was fed by 48V batteries to a top speed of 25mph (40km/h). The price in Japan in 2012 was 880,000 yen (the equivalent of £5500).

ZEV Virgola
I • 1996-1997 • 1F2R • No built: n/a

ZEV was a company based in Vicenza in Italy which was set up to make the Virgola 'zero emissions' vehicle. At a time when most such cars being presented were four-wheelers, ZEV's choice of only three was unusual.

The Virgola (pictured below) was a two-passenger car with enclosed bodywork measuring some 2130mm (84in) long. Power came from two electric motors mounted in the rear of the car, with a total output between them of 6kW. The claimed top speed was 43mph (70km/h) and the overall range was 68 miles (110km).

Both basic and 'luxury' versions were catalogued, priced from 15 million lire in 1996 (which worked out at around £5000 at the time). The ZEV project was short-lived, however, and it is unknown how many Virgolas were actually made.

ZhongYu
CN • 2010s • 1F2R • No built: 1

Jiangmen ZhongYu Motor mostly made scooters and motorbikes, but also three-wheelers with scooter front ends and a variety of rear bodywork, including the ZY150ZH-3 tuk tuk-style trike (pictured). This was a lightweight (228kg) machine powered by a single-cylinder, air-cooled, four-stroke engine of 149cc and 12bhp.

Znug Design Ouroboros
J • 2009 • 2F1R • No built: 1

Ex-Toyota designer Kota Nezu established Znug Design in Tokyo in 2005. His first (and only) three-wheeler was the good-looking Ouroboros, which took its name from the Greek mythical snake that ate its own tail. And in the tail of this trike sat 140bhp worth of Yamaha FZR 1000 superbike engine which, in a vehicle weighing 390kg and measuring 2950mm long, provided excellent performance. The single rear swinging arm sat in tubular steel rear frame, while double wishbones suspended the front end. The flip-up front bodywork hid a 118-litre luggage space.

Zoë Zipper
J/USA • 1983-c1986 • 2F1R • No built: Approx 50

Zoë Products Inc of Los Angeles, California was an ambitious company that acquired the rights to sell the Japanese-made Mitsuoka Bubu 501 ⇨ in the USA, which is did under the name Zoë Zipper. This was a very small one-seater vehicle with a single rear wheel and glassfibre bodywork. It was offered either as a single-door coupe or a convertible with 'step-in' sides. Its rear-mounted Honda Lead 50cc moped engine propelled it to a claimed top speed of 45mph (72km/h) and Zoë said it could average 112mpg. Despite a very low price tag of just $3500 in 1983, the Zipper never did find much favour in the American market and it had vanished by about 1986.

Zoë Z/3000 & Z/5000
GB/USA • 1984-c1986 • 1F2R • No built: n/a

Zoë also imported the British-made Reliant Rialto ⇨ to the USA, where it sold it as the Zoë Z/5000. In addition, Zoë made some US-specific modifications such as very broad wheelarches to cover a wider rear axle and extended bumpers; this version (pictured below) was marketed as the Z/3000. At $5595, the American version of the Rialto was claimed to be the cheapest car on sale in the USA in 1985. Zoë also imported Ligier ⇨ microcars, including a three-wheeled version which it called the Zoëtrans.

Zongshen
CN • 2000s-date • 1F2R • No built: n/a

Zongshen was a major motorcycle brand in China, which also produced various three-wheelers. Four-seater models included the ZS150ZK (150cc) and ZS175ZK (175cc), the latter available in both fully enclosed and open-sided forms, while the ZS110ZH was a basic open rickshaw.

Zorplan Shopper
GB • 1977 • 1F2R • No built: n/a

This British idea for a local shopping vehicle was essentially a three-wheeler conversion of a Puch Maxi moped with a large enclosed boot added to the rear end.

ZW2-C
USA • 2008-date • 2F1R • No built: n/a

ZW2-C stood for 'Z Wheelz 2-seat Custom' and had overtones of hot rod about it. Based in San Antonio, Texas, the first prototype was built by electrical engineer Gary Krysztopik in 2008. The chassis was essentially a long battery box containing 24 lead-acid batteries. An AC electric motor drove the rear wheel via an automatic gearbox and belt. It had a maximum range of 100 miles (160km) and could reach 60mph (96km/h). A Honda Fit (Jazz) windscreen was used. As of 2013, Krysztopik was preparing to release the car as the EZ-EV in several forms: open-source plans, DIY kits and complete vehicles.

Zzipper Triton
USA • Late 1980s • 2F1R • No built: n/a

"By hook or by crook, I'll be last in this book," Jim Tervort must have thought when he named the Zzipper. Founded out of the ashes of Commuter Vehicles (an electric four-wheeler), the Zzipper was an ABS plastic-bodied two-seater with a single driven rear wheel. It was designed to be towed behind a motorhome, the rear wheel being hydraulically retractable for towing, the front wheels remaining on the ground. A 12bhp GE DC motor provided the power, and a top speed of 55mph (89km/h) and a range of 35 miles were quoted.

THREE WHEELERS INDEX FROM A-Z

AB1

Bond Bug

Carver

David

Epic Torq

Fuji Cabin

General Motors XP-511

Isetta

JZR

Kandi KD-250MD

Lamb-Kar

Meyra Rikscha

Morgan Three-Wheeler

Nippi 125

Phantom

Piaggio Ape Calessino

Reliant Regal 3/25

Sabertooth Cerberus

SportCycle

Stimson Scorcher

ThreeWheelFactory T-Rod

Tripod

Tryon

Veeco RT

Quiller Print